Taylor's Guide to Fruits and Berries

Copyright © 1996 by Houghton Mifflin Company
Drawings copyright © 1996 by Steve Buchanan

For information about permission to reproduce selections from
this book, write to Permissions, Houghton Mifflin Company,
215 Park Avenue South, New York, New York 10003.

For information about this and other Houghton Mifflin trade
and reference books and multimedia products, visit The
Bookstore at Houghton Mifflin on the World Wide Web at
http://www.hmco.com/trade/.

Taylor's Guide is a registered trademark
of Houghton Mifflin Company.

Library of Congress Cataloging-in-Publication Data
Taylor's guide to fruits and berries / Roger Holmes.
        p. cm — (Taylor's guides to gardening)
    Includes index.
    ISBN 0-395-71086-3
    1. Fruit–culture. 2. Berries. I. Holmes, Roger. II. Series.
SB355.T25 1996   95-36861
634 — dc20   CIP

Printed in Hong Kong

DNP 10 9 8 7 6 5 4 3 2 1

Cover photograph © by Rosalind Creasy

Contents

Preface

Growing fruits and berries at home can be a lot of fun. The harvest is, of course, the most obvious reward. There's nothing quite like eating an apple, peach, or plum that you've just plucked from your own tree. Blueberry jams, cherry pies, a topping of fresh strawberries or raspberries on a bowl of ice cream. You can try exotic fruit — kiwis from New Zealand; plums, pears, and apricots from the Orient; grapes from France. Or you might explore native fruits your grandparents might have grown — persimmons, pawpaws, and jujubes. As you contemplate this delectable bounty, don't forget that many fruit trees and bushes are handsome plants as well and can hold their own with other ornamentals in your landscape. No matter how small your garden, you've got room for fruit — even a simple pot of strawberries can be a treat.

Our goal in this Taylor's Guide is to introduce you to some of the best fruits and berries for home growing. In 12 chapters we present individual or closely related fruits — apples, pears, cherries, plums, peaches and nectarines, apricots, citrus, strawberries, raspberries and blackberries, blueberries, gooseberries and currants, and grapes. Two additional chapters introduce a number of less common hardy and tender fruits.

We have tried to make the chapters as self-contained as possible, so you don't have to jump back and forth in the book. Each chapter provides a portrait of the fruit and the plant on which it grows, including a selection of color photos. We discuss the criteria you can use to choose types of fruit and appropriate cultivars for your climate and conditions, as well as for your eating and landscaping needs. We discuss common pests and diseases and their controls. Lists of recommended cultivars round out each chapter.

Because many of the basics of planting, training, pruning, and ongoing care are similar for most fruit trees and bushes, we've devoted chapters specifically to those issues, including drawings to make the techniques easier to understand. There is additional information on those topics specific to individual fruits in each chapter.

Local nurseries usually carry a small number of fruits and berries, and some offer broader selections. Knowledgeable staff at local nurseries, along with your local extension agent or extension fruit specialist, can be good sources of information about the kinds of fruit and specific cultivars that do best where you live, as well as about the pest and disease problems you'll encounter and how to cope with them. These people may also be able to suggest experienced local fruit growers who can provide valuable advice; this can be especially helpful if you're trying to grow fruits organically. It's hard to beat the counsel of a local expert.

You'll find the widest choice of fruits and cultivars, however, in specialist mail-order nurseries, and we've included a listing of these suppliers at the back of the book. The staff at these nurseries are often excellent advisers. They're regularly in touch with growers all over the country and are likely to know what varieties do well and what problems to expect in a number of areas.

Contributors

Nancy Beaubaire wrote the chapter on strawberries and consulted on the pest and disease discussion in the chapter "Ongoing Care." She is editor of *Country Living Gardener* and frequently talks to groups about gardening. She has grown fruits and vegetables organically for many years.

Roger Holmes edited this book. He was co-editor (with Rita Buchanan) of *Taylor's Master Guide to Gardening* and several other titles in the Taylor's Guide series. He lives in Lincoln, Nebraska.

Mark Kane wrote the chapter "Growing Fruits and Berries at Home," and he also contributed to the chapter on planting. He is executive garden editor for *Better Homes and Gardens* magazine. He has grown fruits and berries at home for 20 years and lives in Des Moines, Iowa.

Paul Otten wrote the chapters on raspberries and blackberries and gooseberries and currants. He is editor and publisher of *Northland Berry News,* past president of the North American Bramble Growers Association, and program chairman of the International Ribes Association. He lives in St. Paul, Minnesota.

Sally Roth wrote the chapters on apples, plums, peaches, apricots, blueberries, grapes, other hardy fruit, and other tender fruit, planting, pruning, and ongoing care. She has written extensively on gardening in books and magazine articles. With her husband, Rick Mark, she publishes a nature journal, *A Letter from the Country.* She has grown fruits and berries in Pennsylvania, Oregon, and at her current home in New Harmony, Indiana.

Jack Ruttle wrote the chapters on pears and cherries. He is senior editor of *National Gardening* magazine and a former editor of *Organic Gardening* magazine, where he initiated the apple production research project. He has reported extensively on all aspects of fruit culture, traveling to the major

Taylor's Guides to Gardening

fruit-growing regions in North America and England in the process. A long-time member of the North American Fruit Explorers (NAFEX), he edits its journal, *Pomona*. In his own eastern Pennsylvania garden he specializes in espaliered apples, pears, and cherries.

Lance Walheim wrote the chapter on citrus. He is a horticultural consultant and author of numerous gardening books. He lives on a 17-acre citrus ranch in Exeter, California, where he grows unusual citrus.

Consultants

Mary Lu Arpaia consulted on citrus. She is extension subtropical horticulturist at the University of California, Riverside.

Hector Black consulted on the chapter "Other Hardy Fruits." He is owner of Hidden Springs Nursery in Cookeville, Tennessee, which propagates low-care and disease-resistant varieties of common and uncommon fruits, berries, and nuts. He is also a consultant on fruit growing.

Jerry Black consulted on hardy fruits. He is the owner of Oregon Exotics Rare Fruit Nursery in Grants Pass, Oregon.

Rita Buchanan was an editorial consultant for this book. She was co-editor of *Taylor's Master Guide to Gardening* and several other titles in the Taylor's Guide series. She lives in Winsted, Connecticut.

John R. Clark consulted on cultivar recommendations for muscadine grapes. He is associate professor of horticulture at the University of Arkansas in Fayetteville.

Jack Cruttendon and **Walter Logan** consulted on apples. Both work for Stark Bro's Nurseries and Orchards, in Louisiana, Missouri. Jack is commercial sales manager, Walter is mail-order manager.

Anna Flory consulted on plums and apricots. She works at Newark Nurseries in Hartford, Michigan, which propagates nearly two million fruit trees each year for sale around the world.

Dan Finch consulted on blueberries. He is owner of Finch Blueberry Nursery, Bailey, North Carolina, which specializes in northern highbush, southern highbush, and rabbiteye cultivars.

Timothy Gibb consulted on the pest and disease section of "Ongoing Care." He is extension IPM specialist/entomology at the Plant and Pest Diagnostic Laboratory of Purdue University in West Lafayette, Indiana.

Theo Grootendorst consulted on grapes. He is owner of Southmeadow Fruit Gardens in Lakeside, Michigan, which offers a wide selection of fruit trees, grapes, and berries, including many antique varieties.

Carolyn Harrison consulted on apples. She is co-owner of Sonoma Antique Apple Nursery in Healdsburg, California, which specializes in organically grown heirloom apples, pears, plums, and peaches and also offers figs, persimmons, and other fruits.

Ian Merwin consulted on pruning. He is assistant professor of fruit and vegetable science in the College of Agriculture and Life Sciences at Cornell University in Ithaca, New York.

William Nelson consulted on tender fruits. He is the owner of Pacific Tree Farms in Chula Vista, California, which offers a wide selection of fruit, nut, and ornamental trees, including many California natives.

Robert Pool consulted on the list of recommended grapes. He is professor of viticulture at Cornell University.

Julian W. Sauls consulted on citrus. He is extension horticulturist at the Texas Agricultural Extension Service in Weslaco, Texas.

David Tucker consulted on citrus. He is a citrus specialist at the Citrus Research Center in Lake Alfred, Florida.

Pete van Well consulted on peaches. He is co-owner of Van Well Nursery, Wenatchee, Washington, a 50-year-old nursery specializing in fruit trees for home gardeners and commercial growers.

Growing Fruits and Berries at Home

'Honeoye' strawberries

A bowl of fresh strawberries, an apple ripened to perfection, still warm with sun — these are the rewards of growing berries and fruits yourself. You plant a sprig of blackberry or a spindly, young pear tree, then you mulch and water and prune, and a year later, or two or three, you harvest the first crop and taste the unforgettable flavor of homegrown fruit — a blend of ripe sweetness and your own pride.

In much of North America, gardeners can grow a huge range of fruits and berries. Except at its hottest and coldest, the climate suits all the major tree fruits — apples, European pears, Oriental pears, plums, peaches, nectarines, and sweet and sour cherries. Grapes and kiwis, the major vining fruits,

Winter Chill

All temperate zone deciduous trees need to spend a certain amount of time every year at cool temperatures in order to successfully break dormancy. If they get too little chill, flowering may be sporadic or sparse, and the plant itself may languish and fail to grow vigorously.

It was once thought that a tree satisfied its chilling requirement by accumulating a certain number of hours (varying by type of tree and cultivar) below 45°F. Recent research has revealed more complexity than that. First, the temperature range is narrower and higher — only time between 32° and 55°F counts. Second, the amount of chill accumulated (chill units) varies with the temperature. Optimal chill occurs at 45°F. As temperatures drop, so do the chill units accumulated per hour, down to none at 32°F and below. As temperatures rise above 55°F, plants actually lose chill units from their accumulated store. (From this, it is clear that chill units are not, strictly speaking, equal to accumulated hours between 32° and 55°F, but chill "hours" is still the term in common use.)

have an even broader range; nearly anyone can grow the brambles — blackberries, raspberries, and their hybrids. And gardeners from Alaska to Florida can grow strawberries, the only backyard fruit that bears a crop the same year it's planted. To round out the family, there are the less-often-grown but equally rewarding fruits, among them blueberries, pawpaws, quinces, figs, jujubes, bananas, serviceberries, currants, gooseberries, and many more.

While every North American gardener can grow fruits and berries, it's important to select the right ones. Fruits have preferences that suit certain conditions but not others. Many need to spend a certain amount of time during their dormant period at temperatures between 32° and 55°F. This "winter chill" requirement can vary from less than 100 hours to over 1,500 hours. In Southern California, where winter low temperatures rarely drop below 45°F, a 'Delicious' apple tree does not get enough cold to bear well. (See the box above for more on winter chill.)

On the other hand, too much cold harms fruit and berry bushes, just as it does the annuals and perennials in your garden. In Minnesota and upstate New York, where winter lows can fall to -30°F, no peach variety is reliably hardy. The su-

Trees begin accumulating chill units as soon as they lose their leaves in the autumn. In most areas of North America, there is plenty of time from November to December and from February to March to accumulate the necessary amount of chill. In New York State during a typical year, for example, most fruit trees are fully chilled by the first of January.

In mild-winter climates, chill requirements can limit the range of fruits and cultivars that can be grown. Gardeners in the southwestern deserts, southern California, southern Florida, and other places with mild winters should check with suppliers or their extension agent to make sure they're selecting fruits that will be satisfied by the amount of winter chill available.

Odd as it seems, gardeners in extreme northern areas may also have trouble with chill requirements. Temperatures there may become too cold too fast to accumulate large numbers of chill hours, and trees that have large chill requirements may not thrive.

permarket kiwi will not tolerate temperatures near 0°F. Oriental pears are equally tender. Like perennials, many fruit trees and berry bushes have been rated by zones according to the lowest temperatures the plant can reliably withstand. Where appropriate (and available), we have provided hardiness ratings or minimum temperatures in the text and cultivar lists. You'll find a hardiness zone map on page 432.

Some fruits can't bear heat and humidity. In Louisiana and Mississippi, where summers are long, hot, and humid, the 'Concord' grape, which provides the grape jelly on our breakfast tables, succumbs to leaf diseases, fails to thrive, and does not bear reliable crops.

One of the missions of this book is to help you choose wisely. Southern gardeners cannot grow 'Concord', but they happily grow the muscadine grape, a native species with a distinctive flavor. Pears fare poorly in Florida, but tropical and subtropical fruits thrive. On the northern plains, where temperatures can drop to -40°F and lower, the native sand cherry shrugs off the cold and bears heavy crops of small, tart fruits. The 'Anna' apple, discovered in Bermuda, needs barely 100 hours of cold weather; in Los Angeles, too warm for most apples, gardeners harvest good crops.

Tried-and-True to New-and-Improved

The fruits that North American gardeners grow and the way they grow them have both changed dramatically over the last 100 years. Apples were once the main dooryard fruit. Full-size trees, up to 40 feet tall and at least as wide, produced small, tart fruits, many wormy and blemished, fit mainly for cider. Even gardeners with acreage might have room for only a few of these big trees. Hundreds of varieties were grown, but most of them were local. Gardeners in Virginia ate apples unknown to gardeners in Massachusetts. Few nurseries existed and those tended to serve only their region. The trade in trees by mail arose only after the railroads spread far and wide. The state extension services were just beginning, and no one had yet collected and compared fruit varieties, let alone begun to breed them for better taste and bigger yields.

From the 1880s onward, the search for better varieties gave rise to fruit breeding programs at all the state universities. Plant breeders collected desirable fruits, crossed them with each other, and then grew thousands of seedlings, watching for the rare plant that outperformed its parents. The results were remarkable. New apple varieties appeared by the dozen. The fruits were larger, sweeter, and tastier, the trees stronger and more productive. Breeders wrought equally dramatic changes for pears, cherries, peaches, and plums. Fruit sizes often doubled, and yields grew manyfold.

At the same time, fruits that had never been domesticated were brought into cultivation and improved. The strawberry changed from a tiny, semiwild fruit into a backyard staple when an early breeder crossed species from two continents, combining the best qualities of each. The blueberry remained a wild plant until the 1940s, when 20 years of quiet work by one plant breeder produced new varieties with fruit four times larger than wild berries. Since then, two generations of breeders have transformed blueberries into a commercial fruit, and backyard growers have come to take it for granted that blueberries belong in the garden.

Small is bountiful

While some breeders were increasing the size and yield of the fruit, others were discovering how to make trees grow one-fourth their usual size and still yield full-size fruits and bountiful crops. For reasons that are still not understood today, grafting a conventional apple or pear variety onto certain rootstocks has the happy effect of making the conventional variety — the top of the tree — grow far smaller than it would if it were growing on its own roots. At the same time, the grafted tree reaches maturity and begins to bear fruits years earlier than the conventional variety does.

At first, breeders focused on dwarfing rootstocks for just apples, but over the years dwarfing rootstocks have been found for all the tree fruits. Today, apples are grafted on any of a dozen or so widely available rootstocks, each with its own degree of dwarfing and resistance to pests and diseases. (Rootstocks do not, however, pass resistances on to the grafted variety.) The most severe dwarfing rootstocks for apples produce trees that bear fruit the year after grafting and may grow no taller than 7 feet at maturity, while other rootstocks produce fruit in two or three years on 10- or 12-foot trees. While the other fruits are grafted on fewer kinds of rootstocks, the trees offer a similar range of sizes.

The innovations have continued. Strawberries, once a late-spring crop, have acquired the ability to flower and bear fruit more or less continuously from spring through fall. Some raspberries now bear the usual crop in spring and another crop in fall. Some blackberries have lost their thorns while their fruits have quadrupled in size. The rabbiteye blueberry of the South, until 30 years ago a wild species, now yields berries as big as quarters. Another formerly wild native, the muscadine grape graces trellises in southern gardens. The kiwi, once an obscure Chinese vine, bears fuzzy brown fruits the size of plums.

Finally, plant breeders have begun to fashion new varieties that resist the most common and troublesome fruit diseases. Apple scab, a fungus disease that withers leaves and weakens or even kills trees, has no effect at all on a new generation of apple varieties. They are immune, thanks to genes introduced from wild apples. On the horizon are new varieties that will also resist common pests. Concern about the personal and environmental effects of synthetic pest and disease controls has given additional impetus to identifying resistant strains and natural controls. Some serious fruit problems still lack natural controls; nevertheless, growers have found ways to minimize their use and harvest worthwhile, if not blemish-free crops. (See the chapter "Ongoing Care" for a discussion of pest and disease control.)

Amid the flood of new fruits and improved varieties, gardeners have a wonderful range of choices. All the familiar varieties of the supermarket can be bought from local or specialty nurseries. Hundreds of varieties unsuited to the mass market solely because they have unfamiliar shapes or colors, because they don't store or travel well, or (amazingly) because they have too much flavor are available through specialty mail-order suppliers. Recent interest in "heirloom" varieties has led to the recovery of fruits that once were the pride of a particular region, town, or even family, fallen from favor and now available to a new generation of aficionados. Today, your choices include apples known to Thomas Jefferson to modern strawberries bred to produce throughout the season. The bounty of fruit gardening has never been greater.

Fruits and Berries in Your Landscape

Many people, when they think of growing fruits and berries, imagine an orchard or rows of bushes, marching with military precision across a garden as large as a parade ground, and just as separate from everything else on the property.

Two developments have changed the way we grow fruits

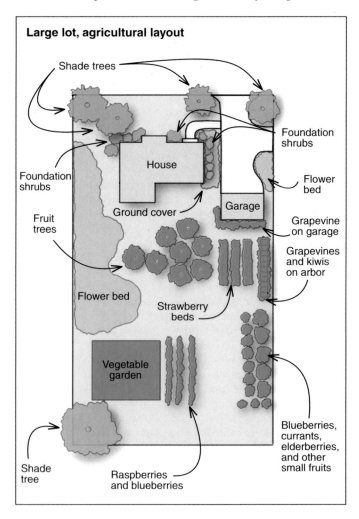

Large lot, agricultural layout

Shade trees

Foundation shrubs

Foundation shrubs

House

Flower bed

Ground cover

Garage

Fruit trees

Grapevine on garage

Grapevines and kiwis on arbor

Flower bed

Strawberry beds

Vegetable garden

Blueberries, currants, elderberries, and other small fruits

Shade tree

Raspberries and blueberries

and berries at home. First, dwarfing rootstocks have compressed the space required for fruit trees — where four standard-size trees once grew, more than 40 dwarfs can be planted. Second, gardeners have come to appreciate the ornamental value of many fruits and berries. These developments are put to use in both of the styles in use today for placing fruits and berries in the yard.

The first style is agricultural. Placed in rows, on a grid, or in a block, the plants stand apart from the rest of the landscape. With dwarf varieties, you don't need an acreage to harvest a considerable range of fruit. In the other style, fruit and berry plants join the landscape, set in places that would otherwise be given to ornamental plants. This style is particularly good for those trying to make the most of a cramped lot.

The agricultural style

The advantage of this style is convenience. If you grow more than five or six fruit trees, placing them in a block makes care easier, or at least more efficient. You can spread lime around the trees without accidentally raising the soil pH too high for neighboring plants. You can spray for curculios or apple scab without trampling through a flower bed or sending overspray onto neighboring plants. You can check the health of your plants or pick part of the harvest with one visit instead of a tour of the yard.

The agricultural style may be crucial if your yard suffers badly from four-legged pests. If rabbits browse your tulips, deer chew your arborvitae, and raccoons pull down your sweet corn, you may have to group your fruit crops together so you can fence them. While there are alternatives to fencing — for example, many gardeners report that hanging bars of soap in fruit trees repels deer — no other deterrent is as reliable as a fence.

The main disadvantage of the agricultural style is style itself. If you feel that two rows of blackberries, supported by wire strung on posts and surrounded by lawn, call too much attention to themselves and disrupt the harmony of the landscape, then you may want to try the alternative.

The edible landscape

Placing fruit crops with other plants in the landscape has two attractions. First, it conserves the landscape. Instead of interrupting the design by calling attention to themselves, the fruit crops blend in. Second, it saves space. In a small yard, you may not have room to plant an ornamental crab apple by the patio and a 'Golden Delicious' in a separate orchard. Why not omit the crab apple and plant the 'Golden Delicious' in its place? As ornamentals, both trees cover themselves with white flowers in spring and then give way to green canopies. But in fall, the crab apple yields small, sour fruits while the 'Golden Delicious' yields apples for fresh eating, baking, and storage.

Growing fruits in the landscape is sometimes called edible landscaping. Though the term is appealing, no landscape should be composed entirely, or even mainly, of fruits and berries. It's true that some fruit crops are highly ornamental. A blueberry in fall color blazes with the same red as a maple; a pear in bloom makes a cloud of flowers as soft as a Japanese cherry. No fruit crop, however, can match the best ornamentals for long-lasting appeal. A cut-leaf maple is beautiful year-round. By contrast, an apple or a cherry blooms for one week and then looks barely tidy until the leaves color briefly in fall. A row of raspberries, pruned and lined up neatly, has less ornamental value than the slats in a picket fence. The flowers are negligible, the stems and leaves are undistinctive. If the row sprawls a bit, it's a mess.

So, place fruit crops in the landscape with restraint. As a rule of thumb, fewer than half of all the shrubs and trees in your yard should bear fruit crops. The same proportions hold for vines and ground covers. Also, make sure fruit plants blend with landscape. For example, group a blueberry or two with a rhododendron. Both species make medium-size shrubs and both need acid soil, so they make good companions. They also offer a succession of ornamental interest. The rhododendron provides a big show of color in spring, the blueberries turn vivid red in fall, and the coarse branches and evergreen leaves of the rhododendron offer a bit of interest in winter, when the blueberries have no leaves.

Fruit trees have many uses in the landscape. Mingle three dwarf apple trees and a small ornamental tree such as a redbud, dogwood, or Japanese maple. Put them in a sunny back corner and underplant them with a tidy, shade-loving ground cover such as vinca so the combination looks well groomed after the apple flowers fall. Grow a row of dwarf fruit trees along the south-facing side of a fence. Space them evenly so they have a formal look year-round, and train clematis along the top of the fence to hang a stage curtain behind the trees. If you're a fearless pruner, espalier the trees or a row of grapevines to make a decorative screen.

Vines are versatile, too. Train a grapevine or a kiwi along the eave of your garage, over the arch of a gate, up a trellis, atop a fence, or over an arbor. Let a flowering vine such as clematis or morning glory mingle with the fruiting vine to provide color for part of the growing season. Set spring and summer bulbs below the vines to grace their ankles.

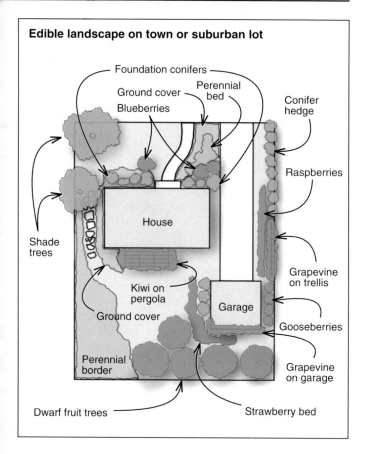

Edible landscape on town or suburban lot

Foundation conifers

Ground cover

Blueberries

Perennial bed

Conifer hedge

Raspberries

House

Shade trees

Raspberries

Grapevine on trellis

Kiwi on pergola

Ground cover

Garage

Gooseberries

Perennial border

Grapevine on garage

Dwarf fruit trees

Strawberry bed

Finally, consider strawberries as a ground cover. Place them carefully. Seen close-up, they lack the uniformity and tidiness of ornamental ground covers such as pachysandra, vinca, ivy, and ajuga, so avoid placing them in a prominent spot. Instead, set them at a distance. Grow them at the front of a perennial bed or border. Or set them where the bed gives way to lawn in a foundation planting that's most often seen from the street. And remember to keep them out of traffic, or the harvest will get squashed.

Once you start thinking about it, there are all sorts of ways to include fruit trees and berry bushes on your property. To get you started, we've provided two sample designs, one an integrated, edible landscape on a typical town or suburban lot, the other a more "agricultural" arrangement on a larger lot. Though the situations may not match your yard, we hope you'll find ideas that you can put to use directly or adapt to suit your conditions.

Apples

Apples come in a wide range of shapes, sizes, and colors, and can be grown in most of North America.

For variety, versatility, and sheer eating pleasure, apples are hard to beat. More than 7,500 varieties are grown worldwide, in all climates and conditions except tropical and arctic, and in so many shapes, colors, and tastes as to defy classification. Harvest stretches from midsummer well into December; after they're picked, some exceptional keepers are edible right through winter into May. Delicious eaten fresh, apples can be put to as many uses as your imagination will allow — baked in their skins, or in pies, cakes, and breads; preserved as applesauce and jam; pressed into juice, and fermented into cider, wine, and brandy.

Apples are big trees, with the standards reaching 25 feet or more. Fine if you have an acreage, but too much for most folks who live in town. Fortunately, you can grow most varieties as dwarf and semidwarf trees. The smaller trees take up less space, are easier to care for, and don't call for an extension ladder to harvest the crop. Genetic dwarf trees grow 6 to 10 feet tall and produce reduced crops of normal-size fruit. A number of dwarfing rootstocks produce a range of tree sizes. In general, dwarf trees reach about 8 to 12 feet tall, begin to bear two to four years after planting, and yield about 1 to 5 bushels of fruit. Semidwarf trees reach from 12 to 20 feet tall, bear fruit in about three to five years, and yield about 5 to 10 bushels of apples.

Fruit isn't an apple's only appeal. A dwarf tree is just the right size to accent a mixed border or to underplant with a drift of daffodils or grape hyacinths. In spring, pink buds cluster along newly leafed branches, opening to a snowy haze of fragrant five-petaled white flowers that buzz with bees and other insects. During spring migration, blossoming apple trees are a favorite haunt of wood warblers, orioles, and other songbirds that are drawn to the feast of insects.

Unfortunately, apple trees and their fruit are just as appealing to pests and diseases as they are to the rest of us, making them more demanding than many other fruits in the home garden. To get picture-perfect apples, commercial orchards spray their trees with toxic chemicals seven or eight times a season. The same prospect in the backyard has frightened off some would-be apple growers. It shouldn't. With careful selection of new disease-resistant varieties, regular observation and quick action when problems arise, and humbler expectations than the blemish-free crop sought by commercial growers, apples can be grown in the home garden with far less intervention.

Some Apple Background

People have been cultivating apples for thousands of years, so long that its early history is all but obliterated. Taxonomists agree that apples belong to the genus *Malus*, but some trace them back to a native of southwestern Asia, *Malus pumila*. Others say it was *M. sylvestris*, a European species. Still others believe modern apples developed from a hybrid of the two. Regardless of parentage, apples are grown today in temperate areas around the globe.

Ancestors of the apples we now grow in North America arrived with the first Europeans (there were no native apples), who started orchards as soon as they cleared a patch of land. As the settlements spread, so did the apples. Every schoolchild knows the story of Johnny Appleseed, who from around 1800 until his death 40 years later helped to turn large parts of the frontier along the Ohio River valley into orchards.

Apples populate and reflect our history, and some growers seem to take as much pleasure in apple lore as in the fruit. Apples interested the tireless Thomas Jefferson; his favorite, 'Esopus Spitzenburg', an orangish fruit with a spicy, juicy bite, recently marked its 200th birthday. Henry David Thoreau wrote fondly of discovering delectable old varieties in abandoned orchards. 'Woolman's Long Pippin' carries the name and sprightly character of the well-known Quaker preacher and abolitionist of the 19th century. The ubiquitous 'Delicious' apple first appeared in the 1870s as an uninvited seedling in the Iowa orchard of Jesse Hiatt, who twice sliced it to the ground to get rid of it. Impressed with its vigorous regrowth, Hiatt kept it, tasted the fruit, and an empire was born. And there really was a Granny Smith. About 100 years ago, Margaret Smith of New South Wales, Australia, brought home some apples from Tasmania and threw the rotten ones out into her garden. One of those discards sprouted a seedling that became 'Granny Smith'.

Apples for the Home Garden

Choosing which apples to grow in your garden can be daunting, given the wide adaptability of most varieties and the range of possibilities in everything from taste and appearance to productivity and uses. With so many varieties to choose from, beginners may be tempted to start with the apple they most like to eat, the sprightly 'McIntosh' or the sweet and crisp 'Delicious'. But first, be practical, consider hardiness, disease resistance, tree size, pollination, and winter chill. Once these criteria are met you can turn to taste, appearance, productivity, and uses, with confidence that your choice will have the best chance of a long, healthy life with a minimum of maintenance. As for other fruits, expert local advice is invaluable. Your extension agent or a knowledgeable staff at a local or mail-order nursery can help you make good decisions. (The list of recommended varieties in this chapter provides information to help you make choices.)

Hardiness

Gardeners throughout most of North America are able to grow most of the apples available today. Local and mail-order suppliers can be depended on to provide suitably hardy plants that will do well on all but the worst soils. Only in tropical and low desert climates (zone 10 and parts of zone 9), where apples don't get the winter chill they need, and in the frigid northern climates (the colder parts of zone 2 and beyond), where the growing season is too short to ripen fruit, are apples out of their range. Within the temperate zones, choices may be limited by extremely cold winters or winters with little cold, extremely heavy and wet soils, or soils that are very light and dry.

Hardiness depends on the cold tolerance of tree, rootstock, and buds. In general, apple trees are hardy to zone 5. They will tolerate brief spells of cold as low as -31°F. Lower temperatures will damage dormant fruit buds and may kill twigs and branches. Continued cold at that level can kill the tree. Varieties that are marginal for your zone may do fine for years, if winters are on the mild side. But when the cold sinks to extremes, all those years of nurturing an apple can be lost. Older trees are better able to withstand cold than young ones, but there is still fruit bud hardiness to consider.

Finally, remember that trees on dwarfing rootstocks may be less cold-hardy in zone 4 or colder. The reduced roots support less vigorous growth, which in turn makes the tree susceptible to cold damage. Buds and flowers are also closer to the ground, where cold air settles.

Disease resistance

Long before modern pest and disease controls were available, gardeners grew apples successfully. To be sure, they used whatever controls were available — they picked off bugs, pruned away diseased wood and used home or "patent" remedies with varying degrees of success. At harvest time, they sorted the less-than-perfect crops into eating, cooking, and cider grades depending on the number of blemishes, and they trimmed away bad spots before eating or cooking the fruit.

Today, gardeners who wish to minimize or avoid the use of chemical controls are turning to old practices. They also have the considerable advantage of access to nontoxic innovations unknown to their forbears. High on this list are many new disease-resistant cultivars. Developed at universities and agricultural experiment stations by selection, breeding, and new genetic techniques, these cultivars offer resistance to one or more of the traditional apple scourges — fire blight, cedar-apple rust, apple scab, and powdery mildew. The list of recommended varieties notes disease resistance. One astonishing variety, 'Liberty', developed by the New York Agricultural Station, is highly resistant to scab, rust, and fire blight and holds its own against mildew in many climates.

Tree size

Apple growing is easier than ever now that dwarf and semidwarf trees are available at nurseries everywhere. The smaller trees take up less space in the garden and are easier to prune, thin for larger fruit, monitor for pests and diseases,

The most disease-resistant variety available, 'Liberty' is a fine eating, cooking, canning, and baking apple.

and harvest. Unless you have a lot of space and don't mind ladders, choose a dwarf or semidwarf tree.

Except for trees dwarfed by their genes, trees smaller than "natural" are created by grafting to a dwarfing rootstock. A number of rootstocks are used for apples, depending on the size and other characteristics desired. (See the sidebar Apple Rootstocks on page 16.) Fortunately, trees sold at garden centers and through many mail-order catalogs can usually be counted on to be grafted to widely adapted rootstocks that will thrive in most areas. All you need to know is how large the tree will grow, not which rootstock is grafted to it.

Dwarf rootstocks have one drawback. The smaller root systems anchor dwarf trees less solidly than those of larger trees, and many dwarfs require staking, so that the weight and wind-catching mass of leaves, branches, and fruit don't pull

Apple Rootstocks

All apples trees are sold grafted to rootstocks that affect cold hardiness, size, the tree's performance in different soils, susceptibility to disease, and even the age at which the tree first bears fruit. Most gardeners will be able to rely on their local nursery or a reputable mail-order supplier to provide rootstocks appropriate for their climate, conditions, and size requirements.

If your growing conditions pose problems out of the ordinary, it is helpful to know a bit more about rootstocks. It is possible your nursery or mail-order supplier may be able to supply a specified rootstock. The following list provides a summary of the qualities of some of the most common rootstocks. The "M" or "Malling" indicates that the rootstock was developed by the Malling Research Station in England. (You may see them listed as "EM" for East Malling, or "MM" for Malling Merton.)

Malling 7 (M-7) Good in most soils; resistant to fire blight; needs snow cover for cold-winter protection; semidwarf (60–75% of standard size). May lean; prone to suckering.

Malling 26 (M-26) Not good for light or shallow soils or wet soils; tree will need staking; very susceptible to fire blight; good cold hardiness; semidwarf (55–65% of standard size).

Malling 9 (M-9) Best in moist, well-drained soil and in clay; tree will need staking; moderately susceptible to fireblight; moderate cold hardiness; tree fruits at a young age. Tree is dwarf (40–50% of standard size), fruit is generally larger.

MM-106 and MM-111 The semidwarf rootstock MM-106 and the semistandard rootstock MM-111 are useful because of their resistance to the wooly apple them over during a storm. If you object to staking and don't want to risk leaving a dwarf tree unstaked, you might look for trees grafted to "Mark," a rootstock introduced by Michigan State University, which grows deep enough to provide a good anchor. (The graft union is brittle when young, so it's best to stake the tree for the first four years.)

aphid — a problem for roots in warm-weather climates, often stunting growth. Only the 100 series of Malling stocks are resistant to the pest. They were developed for Australian growers who have this problem.

Mark Good in all but light, dry soils; moderately susceptible to fire blight; excellent cold hardiness; tree fruits at young age; dwarf (40–50% of standard size). Because of the brittle bud union, you should stake the tree for the first 4 years; then you can often remove the stake unless fruit set is heavier on one side of the tree than the other and it needs support. From Michigan State University.

Budagovski 9 (Bud 9) All soils; tree needs staking; moderately susceptible to fire blight; outstanding cold hardiness from this Polish rootstock; tree bears fruit at very young age; dwarf (40–50% of standard size).

In northern areas, the most widely used dwarf rootstocks may present problems. A dwarf rootstock produces fewer roots than a standard rootstock, thereby dwarfing the tree's growth. Some growers feel that trees grafted to dwarfing rootstocks have less vigor in northern climates and are more susceptible to winterkill and disease problems. If you garden where winters are long and extremely cold you may want to consider planting a standard-size tree, since the restrictions of your short growing season and long cold winter will have a natural dwarfing effect on the tree. (Standard trees begin to bear 5 to 7 years after planting.) Orchardists in the far north often use seedling 'Red Delicious' for rootstocks, and sometimes hardy crab apple stock. The Polish rootstock Bud 9 shows better cold hardiness than most, and there are a number of extra-hardy dwarfing rootstocks new to the market that may prove successful. If you are unsure about the suitability of dwarfing rootstocks for your climate, call your county extension agent for advice.

'Golden Delicious' is excellent for fresh eating; unlike its red namesake it is also superb for cooking and baking.

Pollination and fruiting

'Golden Delicious' is one of the few self-pollinating apples. Although nearby apple or crab apple trees may cross-pollinate your tree, it's best to plant two varieties for a good harvest. Apples can be pollinated by almost any other apple that blooms at the same time. Fortunately bloom times overlap, so early and midseason cultivars will pollinate each other, and mid- and late-season varieties will work together.

Some apples can be fertilized by another tree but cannot fertilize in return. To grow "sterile-pollen" varieties such as 'Gravenstein', you'll need to plant at least two other non-sterile varieties to ensure pollination of all three trees. Nursery tags and catalogs will usually advise you on the kinds and numbers of pollinators to plant.

Winter chill

Like other hardy fruit trees, apples require a dormant period of temperatures between 32° and 55°F or growth will be weak and they'll produce no fruit. Known as chill hours, the number required varies widely among apple varieties, from low chill (300 to 400 hours) to high chill (700 to 1,000 hours). Translated roughly, 400 hours of chilling is about 17 days at temperatures below 45°F, 800 hours is a little more than a month. (See "Growing Fruits and Berries at Home" for more on winter chill.)

Gardeners in zones 3 through 7 should be able to grow most apple varieties, and nurseries and garden centers usually stock the right plants for regional climates. Your county extension agent can tell you the length of the winter-chill period in your area and suggest suitable cultivars to grow. If you buy from a nursery catalog, don't rely only on the designation "low chill" or "moderate chill." Growers sometimes differ on what they mean by those terms, so read the fine print to find the number of hours required.

Depending on where you live, you may have to pay special attention to winter-chill requirements. Gardeners in warm-winter areas (zones 8 and 9) have fewer varieties from which to choose and might have to consult a specialty nursery to find something suitable. (We've included low-chill apples in the list.) If you live in or near mountains, where nurseries serve gardeners who live at varying elevations, remember that higher elevations are colder. Be careful to get varieties suitable for the winter chill at your elevation—a variety that does well higher up may not work for you.

Because low-chill apples tend to bud out at the first hint of warmth, they're not a good idea in those parts of zones 6 and 7 where spring arrives in fits and starts and late frosts are possible. If a week of springlike weather arrives in February or March, your apple may respond with swelling buds that will be at the mercy of any later cold snaps. Look for a late-blooming cultivar, such as the disease-resistant 'Enterprise'.

Likewise, if you garden in the deep freeze, it's a good idea to choose a high-chill cultivar that will remain safely dormant until spring really arrives, avoiding the threat of damage to buds, blossoms, or young fruits. Varieties such as 'Rome' and 'Northern Spy' are so slow to leaf out in spring that you may begin to wonder whether your new fruit tree is still alive.

Beyond Practicality

Having considered those factors that affect the tree's general health and fruitfulness, now come the choices that make apple growing so much fun.

Timing the harvest
If you have enough room in your garden, you can enjoy fresh-picked apples from summer through late fall by planting varieties for different seasons. Though most of us associate crisp apples with crisp fall weather, the apple season actually begins in July, with the very early 'Lodi'. August brings

'Pristine' and a handful of other early cultivars. Apples peak in September ('McIntosh', 'Cortland', and many other favorites) and October ('Northern Spy', 'Rome', and many others). A few very late varieties round out the year in November, including the old-fashioned 'Calville Blanc d'Hiver'.

Flavor and looks

Apples come in all sizes, shapes, colors, and flavors. Tastes range from sour to sweet and textures from tender to crunchy. There are apples that taste like grapes and bananas, apples with smooth tender flesh, and those that produce a solid crunch. If you like the lively bite of tart apples, the green 'Granny Smith' and other sprightly apples like 'Freedom', 'Gordon', or 'Haralson' are excellent choices. For a smooth sweet dessert apple, there's 'Calville Blanc d'Hiver', the tender, flavorful apple enjoyed by Louis XIII almost 400 years ago. For good taste and a striking contrast in the fruit basket, plant a pale green dessert apple like the spicy sweet 'Calville Blanc d'Hiver' along with 'Arkansas Black', a ruby-black gem with aromatic golden flesh. (You'll need to plant a third variety to ensure pollination of 'Calville Blanc d'Hiver', because 'Arkansas Black' has sterile pollen. 'Roxbury Russet', a wonderfully sweet apple with yellowish brown russet covering its greenish skin, would be a good third for this trio.)

Apples look as different as they taste. Some are long, conical fruits, others are short and squat or even flattened. There are green apples, yellow apples, brown apples, almost-purple, and nearly black apples. The skin may be all one color, or it may have a blush of red or be streaked, blotched, or speckled with various colors. The fruit may dangle on long stems or be held tight to the branch. And on the inside, you can find snowy white, green-tinged, golden, and even bright pink flesh ('Pink Pearl').

Heritage apples

It can be great fun to pluck from your backyard an apple that earned the praise of Louis XIII, Thomas Jefferson, or your great grandmother. Many antique apples have wonderful flavor and grow vigorously. To play it safe, ask about varieties of old apples that are resistant to diseases and pests prevalent in your area.

Many of the old-timers really look like antiques. The skin may be blotched, heavily streaked, or "russeted" with a rough brown webbing. 'Cornish Gilliflower', for example, is an old variety with a rather unappealing exterior but a wonderful fragrance (like cloves, some say) and firm yellow flesh with good flavor. 'Northern Spy', one of the more widely known old apples, dates from about 1800. Its fruit is round and often flattened, the greenish yellow skin striped with pinkish red blushes and, sometimes, russet patches. The French 'Fameuse', on the other hand, has beautiful red skin and tender, snowy white flesh, sometimes shading to crimson near the skin. It's as fine-flavored as it is pretty, though it can be prone to scab and has an alternate-year bearing cycle. Other antique apples may be golden-orange, deep red, or the palest green.

Apples for all uses

Deciding what you want to do with your crop will narrow your choices considerably. Some apple varieties, including the redoubtable 'Cox Orange Pippin', are all-rounders, with flavor fine enough for fresh eating and texture that holds up in cooking and baking. But many are best suited to one use. 'Delicious', for example, is just that when you eat it fresh, but cooked it turns insipid. The thin-skinned, fine-grained 'Gravenstein', on the other hand, has been unexcelled in cooking since its origin in Italy in the 1600s. (It's also a crisp, juicy, and flavorful fresh-eating apple.) For cider-making you'll want an apple like 'Grimes Golden' that bears heavily and has enough tang to liven up the the juice. 'Dollars and Cents', an old Virginia variety, is famed for cider-making.

If you want to stretch the apple season out as long as possible, you'll want to consider apples that are "good keepers." All apples will keep for at least a few weeks at room temperature. Placed in cooler surroundings, some varieties will stay fresh right through winter. 'Lodi' is on the short side of the scale, losing quality in a few weeks. 'Newtown Pippin' ripens in October and will keep until March in cool, dry storage. 'Red Delicious' will keep for six months at temperatures below 50°F, but its firm flesh will turn mealy in a matter of days if you keep it at room temperature.

Planting and Care

Most of the information you'll need to plant, train, prune, and care for apples is covered in the last three chapters. We'll summarize here and note particularly important points.

Apples are sold as one-year-old whips or as two- or three-year-old young branched trees, either bare-root, balled-and-burlapped, or in containers. They can be planted in spring, summer (container-grown only), or fall (mild-winter areas). Apples need full sun and well-drained soil of average fertility. Choose a site that is protected from late spring frosts and in very cold climates from freezing or drying winter winds. Avoid planting at the bottom of a hill or other "frost traps," where cold air settles, unless you are trying to boost the number of chill hours provided for a marginal cultivar in a mild climate. Plant trees at least as far apart as their expected height at maturity (6 to 12 feet for dwarf plants, 12 to 20 feet for semidwarf varieties) and no more than 50 feet apart for good cross-pollination. The limited root systems of dwarf trees need more frequent watering than those of larger trees.

Training

Apples stay healthiest and bear best if they are trained to produce a branching structure that can support the weight of the crop and that allows plenty of sun and air to reach all parts of the tree. Apples naturally produce a strong central leader, and in general central-leader or modified-central-leader training best suits them. Some apples, such as 'Red Delicious' and 'Northern Spy', produce strongly upright branches, and these should be spread to strengthen them and open up the tree to light and air. Others, such as 'Haralson', 'Cortland', and 'McIntosh', have more naturally horizontal branches and are easier to train. Apples also do well as espaliers, allowing gardeners to grow a number of varieties in a small space.

Pruning

It may take a few tries to get the knack of pruning, but fruit trees are forgiving. A yearly once-over with the pruning shears should keep the tree open to light and air and renew fruiting wood. Apples bear flowers and fruit on short, stubby twigs called spurs. Spurs grow from wood that is two to three years old or older, and they may produce for as long as 20 years. You'll usually see your tree's first spurs in three to five years after planting. See "Pruning for Fruits and Berries" for tips on pruning spur-producing trees.

Most apples are heavy bearers, and some have a tendency to bear heavily one year and lightly the next. You trick these trees into more regular habits by thinning about two weeks after pollination, when the fruits are the size of a pea. (This is before buds for next year are completely developed.) This can look like a daunting task — each cluster may hold a half-dozen tiny green apples. Make it simple by using pruning shears to snip off whole clusters at a time. The danger in early thinning is that a heavy June drop (a natural self-thinning that occurs later) may leave you with a scanty harvest. You can also thin after June drop to increase the size of the apples. One apple per cluster is plenty. Choose the best apple of each cluster and remove the others with a snip of the pruning shears. Be careful not to injure the spur or the selected fruit when you are removing the unwanted apples. Organic growers continue thinning right up to harvest time, removing any apple that shows signs of insect infestation.

You can grow a lot of different varieties in a small space by espaliering dwarf trees. Be sure to coordinate bloom times to ensure cross-pollination.

Trees that bear too heavily for their own good benefit from thinning when the fruit is about thumbnail size.

Some apples, including popular cultivars such as 'Starkspur McIntosh', have been selected for their extra-heavy production of fruiting spurs. Called "spur-type" or "spur" apples, these varieties produce spurs earlier and in greater numbers than other apples. Because of the extra fruiting capacity, these trees require more thinning. They are a good choice for commercial orchards, where thinning is often done chemically. For the home garden, a spur-type apple may be less practical.

Consider how big a crop you want to harvest and how much time you're willing to invest in thinning fruit before you buy a spur apple.

Harvest

Let your apples ripen on the tree to develop full flavor. Apples ripen over a period of two to three weeks, a leisurely pace for the harvest. Some late-season varieties ripen almost all at once.

You can tell your apples are ripening when their skin takes on color, but you won't know for sure until you bite into one. Ripe apples have full flavor; unripe fruit is starchy and ultra-hard. Some varieties will drop their fruit when it is ripe. But insect damage can also cause apples to drop. Watch for the first dropped apple and sample one that is still hanging on the tree to find out for sure. Pick carefully to avoid damaging spurs, which will bear for years. Hold the apple in your palm and twist the stem. If it's ripe, it'll separate easily from the spur.

Many people enjoy the taste of "green apples," eaten when the fruit has reached full size but before it's colored. Green apples have a sour, tangy bite that many find delicious. They're good to nibble, but just as mothers used to warn, they can give you a bellyache if you eat too many.

Unless you spray heavily, chances are your harvest will be less than perfect. Sort your crop into grades as in the old days, choosing the pick of the crop for eating fresh or for winter storage and saving the blemished fruit for cooking and baking or for cider.

It's also a good idea to think about storage space before it's actually time to store that bumper crop. If you have only one or two young trees, you'll probably be able to fit your fresh-eating apples into the refrigerator. But as your trees mature, you may find yourself with more fruit on your hands than you can accommodate. A cool basement or garage will work, as long as temperatures stay below 50°F and above 32°F. Many gardeners invest in a second refrigerator. Check stored apples once a week, and use or discard any that are showing signs of rot. One bad apple really will ruin the whole bunch. You can also "store" apples in prepared form, as sauce, jams, and jellies. If you like to bake, you can store apples by preparing and freezing apple pies.

Pests and Diseases

Apples, as we mentioned earlier, are prone to more than their fair share of pests and diseases. How many will cause your trees problems depends to some extent on where you live and on changing conditions from year to year. Before you decide to grow apples or make variety selections, it is a good idea to contact your county extension service about the type and extent of pest and disease problems in your area.

Think about the level of intervention you're willing to take to control problems. (See the chapter "Ongoing Care" for more on the choices you have.) If you are a committed organic gardener, ask the agent to suggest experienced local organic apple growers and find out what varieties they grow and how they deal with problems.

Timing is very important in controlling pests and diseases, particularly in applying sprays to counter fungal diseases. Your extension agent can provide information on timing sprays (whether organic or chemical). Choose disease-resistant varieties, regularly monitor your trees, practice good housekeeping (promptly clean up leaf litter and dropped fruit), remove damaged and diseased fruit and branches, and you'll go a long way toward minimizing pest and disease problems. In some areas gardeners can get by with a single application of a dormant oil spray just as the first green shows in the buds. The oil smothers a variety of insects and the spores of diseases that overwinter in bark or in ground-litter.

For the best fruit, both chemical and organic gardeners follow a regular schedule of spraying through the season. Dormant oil starts the routine, in spring when buds are just beginning to show green. Then a mixture of insecticide and fungicide is sprayed at three points during the season: when leaf buds begin to open; when flower buds are ready to bloom; and when petals fall. For further control, you can continue using the all-purpose insecticide-fungicide spray during the summer, spacing the applications about a week and a half apart.

Apple scab

Prevalent throughout the country, this fungal disease produces rough brown spots that look just like scabs on the apple skin. The fruit is still edible but is cosmetically blemished and won't keep as long in storage. Scab can also cause premature fruit drop and leaf drop that will eventually weaken the tree and reduce harvests.

In commercial orchards, the disease is controlled by intensive chemical spraying with such toxic chemicals as captan, benomyl, dodine, and carbamate. Organic controls are ineffective. In the home garden you can avoid the problem by planting resistant varieties; unfortunately many desirable apples are not resistant.

Cedar-apple rust

This fungal disease is shared by apples and eastern red cedars *(Juniperus virginiana)* growing less than two miles apart. The disease is limited to the eastern half of the country, where eastern red cedars are a common wild plant of hedgerows and fields. Small brown galls sprout from infected cedars in spring, developing orange tentacle-like horns that distribute spores on the wind. When the spores land on susceptible apple trees, they produce yellowish to black dots within a reddish circle on the leaves. Infected leaves drop early, weakening the tree and reducing the crop.

In the old days, apple growers simply sawed down every cedar for at least two miles around an orchard. There are no other effective organic controls. Modern gardeners can choose resistant varieties instead. If your trees become infected, the chemical polyram is an effective control.

Fire blight

Less a problem of apples than pears, fire blight attacks the tips of growing branches, causing them to look suddenly withered, and then brown or blackened and curled, as if burnt by fire.

Fire blight is heaviest in the South, but it can happen anywhere there's a warm and rainy spring. Lush new growth produced by severe pruning and unnecessary fertilizing can fall prey to the disease. Prune regularly, at least once a year, to minimize "blitz" pruning, and avoid fertilizing apples. Make sure to choose resistant varieties if fire blight is a particular problem in your area.

To control fire blight before it gets out of hand, remove infected branches as soon as you notice them. Cut the twig off at least 12 inches below the visible signs of infection, so that you are cutting into healthy wood. To avoid spreading the disease, dip your pruners into a sterilizing solution of 10 percent bleach between each cut, and clean the shears of the corrosive bleach when the pruning is complete. Destroy or discard the infected branches immediately.

In resistant varieties, the tree can wall off the infection and stop it. A visible canker will form that can spread the disease. Prune cankers off during the dormant season, following the same procedure outlined above, then burn them.

Powdery mildew

This fungal disease coats the leaves and sometimes the blossoms with a whitish powder. It distorts the growth at the tips of branches and may cause a tan netting on fruit. As growth is interrupted, the tree may lose its vigor.

If powdery mildew is prevalent in your area, plant resistant cultivars. Prune off and destroy infected shoots as soon as you see them. The fungus can also be controlled with sulfur sprays.

Apple maggot

This tiny pest lays its eggs under the skin of developing apples. The larvae burrow in, leaving brown tunnels through the fruit. Apple maggot is well established in many northern areas, especially in New England and the Great Lakes states.

Organic growers have some success spraying with rotenone and trapping adult flies on sticky red spheres (sold at garden centers for this purpose) hung 4 to 6 feet apart in the trees. The chemical Imidan is highly effective, and the chemicals Diazinon and Carbaryl also offer some protection.

Codling moth

This imported pest gets its name from the word for immature green apples (codlings). It can be a problem in all areas. The larva of the codling moth is a tiny white fellow with a brown head. Moths lay eggs on leaves, twigs, and fruit in June and July. Larvae tunnel their way into apples, leaving telltale "sawdust" around entry holes. Besides damaging the flesh, the infestation may also cause fruit to drop.

In summer, the caterpillars emerge, usually leaving an exit hole near the calyx of the fruit. They overwinter under loose bark. To help control them, you can rub the trunk and branches with a loose ball of chicken wire in July. Wrap burlap or corrugated cardboard around the trunk and branches after rubbing; remove the coverings in November to kill any remaining caterpillars. Imidan and Carbaryl offer protection, applied every two weeks after petals fall, following label directions.

Oriental fruit moth

Wilted leaves at the tips of twigs are often the first sign of infestation, marking the place where the half-inch adult moth laid eggs. The larvae tunnel into the twig tip, killing the twig. When adult, this first generation lays their eggs on fruit, where subsequent generations of larvae (three or four are common) burrow into the flesh. Widespread pests, they can be a problem in all areas except Texas and the south-central states, the Pacific Northwest, and the Midwest.

To help control, remove affected twig tips, cutting back to healthy wood. Ryania, an organic control, and the chemicals Imidan and Carbaryl are effective. They are best applied from mid-July through mid-August.

Plum curculio

The larvae of plum curculio resemble little worms, which infest the fruit soon after bloom. This small snout-nosed gray or brown beetle makes small crescent-shaped scars on the young fruit where it lays its eggs. Begin control as soon as you spot the first scars. Once the eggs are laid, the damage to fruit is irreparable.

No organic sprays are effective. The chemical Imidan is effective; consult with your extension agent about timing.

■ RECOMMENDED VARIETIES OF APPLES

We can, of course, give only a small sampling of the 7,500 varieties of apples. We have tried to provide a good selection for beginning growers in all parts of North America.

- *All listed varieties are available grafted to rootstocks that will produce semidwarf or dwarf trees.*

- *Varieties described as "long" keepers may stay fresh in cold storage for 12 to 30 weeks (depending on variety); "good" keepers generally last at least 8 weeks in storage; "fair" keepers should be eaten in 4 to 6 weeks.*

- *So-called "heritage" apples are mixed among the others, their age or date of introduction noted under "Comments."*

- *Unless otherwise noted, listed varieties should do well in zones 5 through 8. Those listed as being hardy in zones 4 and colder may be less cold-hardy when grafted on dwarfing rootstocks. Gardeners in warm climates should consult the section "Low Chill Apples" starting on page 39.*

- *If no special disease resistance or susceptibility is noted, variety is average in those respects.*

Hardy Apples

Arkansas Black

Fruit: Waxy, round, dark purplish red to purplish black fruit with very firm yellow flesh. Ripens in late October to November.

Disease resistance/susceptibility: Resistant to cedar-apple rust.

Uses: Aromatic, good for fresh eating, cooking, cider. Excellent keeper.

Comments: Infertile pollen. Pollinate with 'Yellow Delicious'. Originated in 1870 in Arkansas.

'Arkansas Black'

Calville Blanc d'Hiver (White Winter Calville)
Fruit: Round, somewhat flattened, pale green apple with pale red dots on side toward sun. Excellent spicy-sweet yellowish white flesh. Late October to December.
Disease resistance/susceptibility: Resists scab; susceptible to cedar-apple rust.
Uses: Fresh eating, cooking, sauce.
Comments: French variety introduced in 1598.

Cortland
Fruit: 'McIntosh' type with dark red skin, some striping, and crisp white tangy flesh. Mid-September to early October.
Uses: Fresh eating, cooking, cider.
Comments: Hardy to zone 4. Introduced in 1898 in New York.

Court-Pendu Plat (Wise Apple)
Fruit: Very flat yellow or orange fruit with rose blush and fawn marbling. Firm yellow flesh with full flavor. November to December.
Disease resistance/susceptibility: Resistant to scab.
Uses: Fresh eating. Good keeper.
Comments: Blooms very late, so is good in areas with late spring frosts but long growing season.

'*Cox Orange Pippin*'

Cox Orange Pippin
Fruit: Conical red-striped over orange fruit with mellow, aromatic yellow flesh. Mid-September to mid-October.
Disease resistance/susceptibility: Susceptible to scab and fire blight.
Uses: Fresh eating, cooking, cider, excellent in pies.
Comments: Late bloomer, good for areas with late spring frosts. An 1830 variety from England.

Dayton
Fruit: Mostly red fruit, with some yellow. Tasty, tart-sweet, pale yellow flesh. September.
Disease resistance/susceptibility: Scab-immune. Moderate resistance to fire blight and powdery mildew. Moderately susceptible to cedar-apple rust.
Uses: Fresh eating. Short storage life, up to one month.
Comments: Vigorous tree.

'Red Delicious'

Delicious (Red Delicious)
Fruit: Tapered red fruit with crisp, mild white flesh. Late September to mid-October.
Disease resistance/susceptibility: Resists fire blight and cedar-apple rust.
Uses: Fresh eating. Long keeper.
Comments: Most widely grown apple in U.S.

Empire
Fruit: Round dark red fruit similar to 'McIntosh'. White juicy flesh. September to October.
Uses: Fresh eating, cider. Fair keeper.
Comments: Hardy to zone 4. Upright, early-bearing tree.

Enterprise
Fruit: Large, round red fruit with crisp mildly tart flesh. October.

Disease resistance/susceptibility: Extremely resistant to scab, rust, fire blight; moderate resistance to powdery mildew.

Uses: Fresh eating. Excellent keeper.

Comments: One of the new disease-resistant cultivars. Good trouble-free selection for the home garden.

Esopus Spitzenberg (Spitzenberg)

Fruit: Famed for rich, aromatic flavor of its yellowish flesh. Tough orangish skin with russet dots and slight striping. Ripens in October, holds ripe fruit for weeks on tree.

Disease resistance/susceptibility: Susceptible to fire blight and scab.

Uses: Outstanding fresh-eating apple. Long keeper.

Comments: Hardy to zone 4. Slender, willowy growth with drooping limbs. Often bears biennially. Very cold-hardy. Originated in Esopus, New York, in 1790.

Freedom

Fruit: Bright red fruit with crisp, lively flavored flesh. Late September to early October.

Disease resistance/susceptibility: Scab-immune. Resistant to fire blight, mildew, cedar-apple rust.

Uses: Fresh eating, cooking, cider. Good keeper.

Comments: Introduced in 1983. Developed by Cornell University. Cold-hardy to -45°F.

Golden Delicious (Yellow Delicious)

Fruit: Large, conical golden fruit with aromatic white flesh. Mid-September to mid-October.

Disease resistance/susceptibility: Resists cedar-apple rust.

Uses: Excellent fresh-eating apple, and unlike 'Red Delicious', also superb in cooking and baking. Good keeper.

Comments: Zones 5–9. Not a yellow version of 'Red Delicious', though the shape is similar, but a fine apple in its own right. Self-pollinating. Generally healthy tree.

GoldRush

Fruit: Like a pale yellow 'Golden Delicious', with spicy, tart flesh. October.

Disease resistance/susceptibility: Scab-immune. Resistant to powdery mildew. Susceptible to cedar-apple rust.

Uses: Superb for fresh eating. Extra-long keeper. Flavor improves with storage.

Comments: An excellent late variety for the home garden. Late bloomer.

Gravenstein

Fruit: Round to flattish orangish yellow fruit with red stripes and crisp ivory flesh. August.

Uses: Excellent fresh and for cooking, sauces, cider, and especially baking. Fair keeper.

Comments: Sterile pollen. Tends to bear biennially; thinning may help. Italian variety from the 1600s, introduced in U.S. in 1790.

Grimes Golden

Fruit: Golden fruit with spicy-sweet yellow flesh. September to October.

Disease resistance/susceptibility: Moderate resistance to cedar-apple rust and fire blight. Susceptible to collar rot.

Uses: Superb for fresh eating, cooking, cider; not for baking.

Comments: Self-pollinating. An American variety from the mountains of West Virginia (1804). May be a parent of 'Yellow Delicious'.

Haralson

Fruit: Striped or all-red fruit with mild, sweet-tart white flesh. September to October.

Disease resistance/susceptibility: Moderately resistant to fire blight and cedar-apple rust.

Uses: Good for fresh eating and cider. Excellent for baking. Extra-long keeper.

Comments: Very cold-hardy; to zone 3. Tends to bear biennially; thinning may help. Bears early.

Jonafree

Fruit: Mostly red fruit, some green, with flavorful, crisp, light yellow flesh. Mid-September to October.

Disease resistance/susceptibility: Resistant to scab, fire blight, cedar-apple rust. Some susceptibility to mildew.

Uses: Very good for fresh eating, also good in cooking.

Comments: A disease-resistant version of Jonathan; fruit quality similar but not quite as good.

Jonathan (Philip Rick, Ulster Seedling)

Fruit: Round, red fruit (striped in cooler regions) with lively flavor. Tough but thin skin. Mid-September to mid-October.

Disease resistance/susceptibility: Resistant to scab. Susceptible to fire blight and cedar-apple rust.

Uses: Good for eating fresh and cooking. Average keeper.

Comments: Bears young and prolifically.

Liberty

Fruit: 'McIntosh' type; mostly red fruit with tart pale yellow flesh. Early October.

'Newtown Pippin'

Disease resistance/susceptibility: Best disease resistance: immune to scab, good resistance to fire blight, mildew, and cedar-apple rust.

Uses: Excellent for fresh eating, cooking, canning, baking. Extra-long keeper.

Comments: Hardy to zone 4. Excellent apple for the home garden. No spraying needed to control diseases.

Lodi (Improved Yellow Transparent)
Fruit: Large green fruit with sweet-tart white flesh. July.
Disease resistance/susceptibility: Resistant to scab.
Uses: Cooking. Poor keeper.
Comments: Hardy to zone 4. Extra-early apple. Pick when partly yellow for fresh eating.

McIntosh
Fruit: Tender-skinned red fruit, richly aromatic, with sweet-tart white flesh. September.
Disease resistance/susceptibility: Resistant to cedar-apple rust.
Uses: Superb for fresh eating, excellent in cooking. Good keeper.
Comments: Hardy to zone 4. Bears prolifically.

Newtown Pippin (Yellow Newtown, Yellow Pippin)
Fruit: Flattened, yellow-green fruit, russeting at stem end. Aromatic, spicy, pale yellow flesh with a hint of resinousness. October.
Disease resistance/susceptibility: Susceptible to scab.

'Northern Spy'

Uses: Old favorite for cider, also delectable fresh eating though not a beauty. Unbelievable keeper, gets sweeter in storage.
Comments: An early-1700s variety from Newtown, Long Island.

Northern Spy (Red Spy)

Fruit: Round, flattened greenish yellow with red stripes, may be russeted. Tart, aromatic pale yellow flesh. Late October.
Uses: Excellent for fresh eating, cooking, and baking. Very long keeper.
Comments: May be slow to bear. Tends to bear biennially; thinning may help. A New York variety of about 1800.

Novamac

Fruit: Similar to 'McIntosh' in flavor and looks, with a bit more sweetness. September.
Disease resistance/susceptibility: Scab-immune. Resistant to cedar-apple rust, moderately resistant to powdery mildew.
Uses: Fresh eating, cooking, baking. Good keeper.
Comments: A good choice for trouble-free fruit growing.

Pink Pearmain

Fruit: Unusual upside-down shape, broad at bottom, tapering at top. Red-striped skin with deep pink, tart-sweet flesh (color can vary, depending on climate). Late September.

Uses: Good for fresh eating.
Comments: Found in an old orchard in California.

Prima

Fruit: Round bright yellow fruit with red blush, mild white flesh. Late August to September.
Disease resistance/susceptibility: Immune to scab. Moderately resistant to fire blight and mildew. Susceptible to cedar-apple rust.
Uses: Excellent fresh eating. Fair storage.
Comments: One of the new disease-resistant cultivars. Good trouble-free selection for the home garden.

Priscilla

Fruit: Slightly conical fruit is almost all red with a touch of yellow, crisp white to greenish flesh. Mid-September.
Disease resistance/susceptibility: Immune to scab. Resistant to fire blight, powdery mildew, and cedar-apple rust.
Uses: Good fresh-eating apple. Good keeper.
Comments: Another new disease-resistant variety. A trouble-free choice for home gardens.

Pristine

Fruit: Clear yellow fruit with slight red blush, crisp sweet-tart flesh. August.
Disease resistance/susceptibility: Scab-immune. Moderately resistant to cedar-apple rust and powdery mildew.
Uses: Excellent fresh eating. Fair keeper.
Comments: New variety. Superior apple for the home garden.

Redfree

Fruit: Yellow-green background with red. Mild, slightly tart flavor. August.
Disease resistance/susceptibility: Scab-immune. Resistant to cedar-apple rust, moderately resistant to powdery mildew.
Uses: Good for fresh eating. Fair keeper.
Comments: Prolific bearer, must be thinned.

Rome (Rome Beauty)

Fruit: Very large round red fruit with medium-firm greenish white flesh. Late September through October.
Uses: Best for baking and drying. Good keeper.
Comments: Late bloomer. Old and popular baking apple — "two apples makes a pie." An 1848 variety from Ohio.

Roxbury Russet

Fruit: Green, bronze-tinged skin with yellowish brown russet. Very sweet white flesh. Mid-October.
Disease resistance/susceptibility: Resists scab and mildew.

Apple blossoms are a lovely added bonus for the home grower.

Uses: Fresh eating, cooking, cider. Long keeper.
Comments: Hardy to zone 4. Blooms late. Good in late-spring frost areas.

Sierra Beauty
Fruit: Large yellow fruit with red stripes. Firm flesh, sweet-tart sprightly flavor. September to October.
Uses: Fresh eating, cooking. Good keeper.
Comments: Self-fruitful. Old California variety. Still commercially grown in Mendocino County.

Sir Prize
Fruit: Large, elongated yellow fruit with red blush, aromatic and spicy-sweet. October.

Disease resistance/susceptibility: Scab-immune. Resistant to powdery mildew; moderate resistance to cedar-apple rust.
Uses: Good for fresh eating. Very long keeper. Flavor improves with storage.
Comments: Good disease-resistant apple, but very tender to bruising.

Spartan
Fruit: Medium-size red fruit with pure white flesh. Aromatic, fine sweet-tart flavor. Mid-October.
Disease resistance/susceptibility: Resistant to scab, mildew, fire blight.
Uses: Fresh eating. Long keeper.
Comments: Good choice for Midwest. Hardy to -45°F.

Stayman (Stayman Winesap)
Fruit: Medium to large red-green apple with tender juicy yellowish flesh. Tart, winy flavor. October.
Disease resistance/susceptibility: Resistant to fire blight.
Uses: Fresh eating, cooking, baking, cider. Good keeper.
Comments: Sterile pollen — will not pollinate other apples.

Wealthy
Fruit: Medium-size light yellow fruit striped with red (turns all red in storage). Very juicy white flesh with pink veins. September to October.
Disease resistance/susceptibility: Resists scab, fire blight, cedar-apple rust.
Uses: Fresh eating when ripe; pies, cooking, preserves when not fully ripe.
Comments: Hardy to zone 2. Compact tree. Bears young. Prolific.

Williams Pride
Fruit: Bright red with some green or yellow and firm, crisp flesh with mild, slightly tart flavor. August.
Disease resistance/susceptibility: Scab-immune. Very resistant to cedar-apple rust, moderately resistant to powdery mildew.
Uses: Good for fresh eating. Fair keeper.
Comments: New variety for trouble-free home fruit growing.

Winesap
Fruit: Medium-size dark red fruit. Highly flavored sweet-tart flesh. Winy taste and aroma. October.
Uses: Fresh eating, cooking, cider. Good keeper.
Comments: Excellent multipurpose apple. Heavy producer. Pollen sterile — will not pollinate other apples.

Low-Chill Apples
Less than 600 hours below 45° satisfies dormancy. Will flourish in areas as warm as zone 9.

Anna
Fruit: Green fruit with red blush. Good flavor, crisp. Mid-June to July.
Uses: Fresh eating or cooking. Short keeper.
Comments: For Deep South and desert Southwest. 100–300 chill hours. Zone 5.

Beverly Hills
Fruit: Medium to large greenish yellow fruit with red blush and dots. Slightly tart. August.
Uses: Fresh eating or cooking.
Comments: Self-fruitful. Good in warm climates. 300–500 chill hours. Zone 7.

Braeburn
Fruit: Yellow background with orange-red blush; crisp, sprightly flavor. Late October.
Disease resistance/susceptibility: Susceptible to scab, mildew, fire blight.
Uses: Fresh eating. Long keeper.
Comments: Early bearing. Prolific; requires thinning. Popular new introduction from New Zealand. Zone 6.

Dorsett Gold
Fruit: Medium-size fruit with sweet crisp flesh. June to July.
Uses: Fresh eating, cooking, canning. Long keeper.
Comments: Self-fruitful. Upright tree. Excellent in South, desert, and coastal areas. Less than 100 chill hours. May produce fruit in tropical climates. Zone 8.

Ein Shemer
Fruit: Large yellow fruit with tinge of red. Sweet-tart flavor. Early to late June.
Uses: Fresh eating. Poor keeper.
Comments: Israeli cultivar. Good for hot areas and South. 100–400 chill hours. Zone 8.

Fameuse (Snow Apple, Chimney Apple)
Fruit: Beautiful red fruit with snowy flesh, often stained with crimson near skin. Distinctive spicy flavor. September.
Disease resistance/susceptibility: Susceptible to scab in wet summers.
Uses: Fresh eating, cooking, cider. Fair keeper.

Comments: Tends to bear fruit biennially; thinning may help. A parent of 'McIntosh'. Needs 600 chill hours. Zone 4.

Fuji

Fruit: Yellow-green skin with orangish red blush and stripes. September to October. Crisp. Juicy, sweet white flesh.
Uses: Long keeper.
Comments: Only for areas with long growing seasons; needs 200 days to mature. Somewhat bushy tree needs strict pruning. 100–200 chill hours.

Gala

Fruit: Heavy red stripes on gold skin gives it an appealing pink-orange color. Crisp flesh is aromatic and mild with a touch of tartness. September.
Disease resistance/susceptibility: Susceptible to scab.
Uses: Fresh eating. Excellent keeper.
Comments: New Zealand selection that has become very popular in supermarkets. Needs 600 chill hours. Zone 5.

Gordon

Fruit: Round green fruit with red stripes or blush and crisp, sweet-tangy white flesh. August to October.
Uses: Excellent fresh eating and cooking apple. Good keeper.
Comments: Excellent choice for milder areas. Needs only 250–400 hours winter chill. Popular in southern California. Zone 5.

Granny Smith

Fruit: Grass-green, waxy fruit with snappy white flesh.
Uses: Excellent fresh eating and cooking; superb in baking. Good keeper.
Comments: Prolific, annual bearer. For areas with long growing season — fruit needs up to 190 days after bloom to ripen. 1868 variety from Australia. Zone 6.

Lady Williams

Fruit: Medium to large red fruit. Crisp, full flavor. October.
Uses: Fresh eating. Long keeper.
Comments: Good only in zones 7–8. Vigorous tree.

Mutsu (Crispin)

Fruit: Large yellow fruit with crisp, juicy flesh. Delicate, spicy flavor. October.
Disease resistance/susceptibility: Resists powdery mildew. Susceptible to scab.
Uses: Fresh eating, cooking, cider. Long keeper.

Comments: Hardy to zone 4, but also good in mild areas. 400–500 chill hours. Spreading habit makes good shade tree.

Pink Pearl
Fruit: Cream and green skin with sweet, bright pink flesh. September.
Disease resistance/susceptibility: Susceptible to scab.
Uses: Excellent fresh eating, good for cooking. Good keeper.
Comments: Blooms early with deep rose-pink blossoms. Needs 600 hours winter chill. Zone 7.

White Winter Pearmain
Fruit: Round to oval, green-to-yellow fruit with tender, aromatic flesh. Late October.
Uses: Excellent for fresh eating, cooking, baking. Long keeper.
Comments: Dating to about 1200, this is the oldest known English apple. Healthy, productive tree, widely adaptable. 100–200 chill hours. Zone 5.

Winter Banana
Fruit: Large yellow fruit with pink blush. Tangy, crisp flesh with aroma like bananas. October to November.
Uses: Fresh eating.
Comments: Old variety from Indiana. 100–400 chill hours. Zone 5.

'Winter Banana'

Pears

'Clapp's Favorite'

As easy to grow as they are delicious to eat, pears should probably be your first choice in fruit trees. If you start with fire blight–resistant varieties, you'll find pears to be the least demanding of the tree fruits. Pears require less pruning than other tree fruits once they settle into fruit production and they are better adapted to heavy clay soil (as long as it's well drained). Spraying is minimal no matter where you live and unnecessary in many places.

You can choose between two kinds of pear, European and Asian, each with distinctive qualities (which we'll discuss below). Despite deriving from different species, Asian and European pears have nearly identical cultural needs and can even cross-pollinate if they flower at the same time. Both thrive where apples grow, generally zones 5 to 8, although

Asian pears will grow slightly farther south into zone 9 and
European pears slightly farther north — a few tough customers can make it even in zone 3. They have similar training and pruning requirements and suffer from the same pests.
Both bear flowers and fruit on long-lived spurs, and on the
tips of some branches. They bloom for a week, starting about
a week before apples. The buds are hardy, and because the
clusters of bloom open gradually according to the temperature, a frost will rarely kill an entire pear crop.

Pears ripen over a long season. Planting only three trees,
an early, midseason, and late variety, you can harvest pears
for a long time. (You'll want to plant at least two trees to ensure good crops through cross-pollination.) Because some varieties keep for up to four months when refrigerated, you can
extend "pear season" to almost seven months. European
pears require some patience, as they don't usually begin fruiting until the fifth year after planting and aren't in full production until about the tenth year. Dwarf Asian pears begin
bearing younger, often in their third season.

Pears can be attractive additions to the home landscape.
Like their ornamental pear relatives, they bear snowy white
flowers in spring, and the large pendant fruit are handsome
to look at summer and autumn. Standard trees can reach 30
feet tall, but most home growers will plant dwarfs because of
limited space, ease of harvest, and disease control. Because of
their susceptibility to fire blight, and the possibility of having
to lop off infected branches, you might think twice about
using them in prominent ornamental positions. On the other
hand, pears are wonderful espalier subjects and can be
trained in many attractive patterns.

European Pears

The shape, fragrance, and buttery smooth sweetness that
most of us associate with pears is exemplified in the European variety, 'Bartlett', easily the most popular pear in the
world. Less well known, but equally desirable are a number
of its European kin, 'Anjou', 'Comice', 'Bosc', and 'Seckel.'
('Comice' has become famous in North America under the
trademark name 'Royal Riviera' given it by the Harry and
David company, which sells boxes of the fruit mail-order; a
good way to taste the fruit if you can't find it locally.) All are
excellent for dessert, whether eaten fresh and unadorned, in
a fruit salad, or lightly poached in wine or syrup. European
pears range in color from green through yellow to brown and
in size, they're usually from 1 to 3 inches in diameter. The
tender skin encloses flesh that softens rapidly from the inside
out as it ripens.

European pears *(Pyrus communis)* have been grown for centuries on their home continent, and for more than 300 years in North America. Today there are a few dozen varieties available from specialty nurseries. Hardy to -20°F, most European pears grow well from the warmer parts of zone 4 south through zone 8. These zones generally provide the 600 to 1,400 winter-chill hours (depending on cultivar) needed by the tree to break dormancy. A handful of varieties, including 'Gourmet' and 'Luscious', have been developed for zones 3 and 4 by crossing European pears with the Asian species *P. ussuriensis*. When grafted to *P. ussuriensis* roots, these varieties may be hardy to -40°F.

European varieties ripen from midsummer to autumn. 'Bartlett' is the earliest among the old favorites. The newer and slightly smaller 'Harvest Queen' ripens a week earlier. Early pears typically keep in cold storage for only a few weeks, but some of the best ones also make very good canned or dried pears, giving you options other than overeating to deal with their productivity. Most midseason pears will keep, about a month. Late-season pears, which ripen right up to frost, tend to be excellent keepers. 'Magness' is a late-ripener with exceptional keeping powers.

Asian Pears

Asian pears are relative newcomers to North America, most having been introduced within the last 100 years from Japan and China. Deriving from *Pyrus pyrifolia, P. ussuriensis,* and their hybrids, they are usually round and look much like apples, with skin that varies from pale green to yellow-brown, often with a rough russeting. Inside, the flesh is crisp and juicy, the taste sweet and mild. Properly grown, the fruits will weigh in at a hefty half-pound apiece. Because the skins are coarse and there are many gritty "stone cells" near the core, Asian pears are often peeled and cut into slices rather than eaten out-of-hand. Some Asian varieties popular in China have a more familiar pear shape, smooth green skin, and aromatic flavor. (While there are no pear-shaped Japanese pears, there are some round Chinese varieties.)

Asian pears will grow and fruit from zones 5 to 9. Lower chill requirements extend their range farther south than European pears. Japanese cultivars require between 400 and 900 hours, and the Chinese types even less, from 300 to 450. Low-chill varieties bloom earlier and are therefore more susceptible to damage from late frosts. You're unlikely to find Asian pears in catalogs listed as Japanese or Chinese varieties, so you'll need to look for (or ask about) their chill requirements. Like European pears, Asian varieties can be chosen that ripen early, mid- and late-season. Many Asian pears are good keepers.

Pears for the Home Garden

When choosing a pear, you need to consider disease resistance, size, and bloom time (to ensure cross-pollination). Of these, by far the most important is resistance to fire blight.

Blight resistance

Because of the popularity of 'Anjou', 'Bartlett', and 'Comice' in stores and roadside orchards, beginners often want to plant them at home. Don't. At least not first. These old European favorites are very susceptible to fire blight, which can kill a mature tree in one season and a young one in a week or two. Though fire blight pressure is generally heavier in the South than in the North, it can occur almost anywhere there's a warm and rainy spring. No matter where you live, it is prudent to start with blight-resistant pears. (Because of their fire blight problems, we haven't listed 'Bartlett' and 'Anjou' on the list of recommended varieties.)

Fortunately, there is a good selection of blight-resistant varieties to choose from, and many taste as good as or better than the classic pears. 'Harvest Queen', for example, is indistinguishable in flavor from 'Bartlett' but is extremely resistant to blight. You can stretch the season by planting a blight-resistant midseason variety such as 'Harrow Sweet' and late-ripening ones, such as 'Magness'. (An excellent keeper, 'Magness' combines high blight resistance with the flavor and texture of two superb parents, 'Seckel' and 'Comice'.) There are fewer blight-resistant Asian varieties at this time.

Blight-resistant varieties are not blight-free. Once infected, however, they wall off the infection, forming a canker that keeps the disease from spreading. If, over a period of years, your blight-resistant trees haven't developed any of the telltale cankers, your site may be blessedly free of the disease. If so, you can then consider growing some of the many blight-susceptible European classics or Asian varieties. But remember, no site is absolutely blight-free.

Tree size

Because of fire blight, size is a doubly important consideration for pears. Standard European and Asian pears grow to 30 feet tall, which makes monitoring and caring for fire blight very difficult. Home fruit growers, particularly beginners, should start with dwarf trees grown on the blight-resistant OHxF rootstock. (The abbreviation stands for "Old Home by Farmingdale.") Hardy from zone 9 into the warmer parts

The "classic" European pear, 'Bartlett' is very susceptible to fire blight.

of zone 4, the rootstock is compatible with both European and Asian varieties and produces well-rooted, half-size trees, about 10 to 15 feet tall at maturity. Quince, the traditional dwarfing rootstock for pears, produces a very small tree (about 8 to 10 feet tall), but it is susceptible to fire blight, hardy only to zone 6, needs to be staked, and is incompatible with Asian varieties. (Remember that a blight-resistant rootstock does not impart blight resistance to the variety grafted on top.)

Northerners outside the range of the OHxF rootstock should consult with their extension agent or a knowledgeable person at a local nursery or northern mail-order supplier. These folks will know which rootstocks (as well as which varieties) are proven performers in their area.

Pollination
Most Asian and some European varieties are partially self-fruitful, but without cross-pollination, they will too often yield small, misshapen, and poor quality fruit. For good crops, plant two or more trees of different varieties, and make sure they flower at the same time. Though Asian pears begin to bloom a few days earlier than European pears, the bloom period is usually long enough for the two kinds to cross-pollinate. To be safe, however, plant two different cultivars for early-blooming varieties. A few varieties, such as 'Seckel' and 'Bartlett', won't cross-pollinate; check compatibility before you buy. If your garden space is extremely limited, look for trees grafted with multiple varieties. Some specialty nurseries will even graft trees with varieties of your choice.

Bumblebees are the best pollinators for pears. Honeybees will visit pear blossoms, but they prefer other flowers when

---

Multiple-leader training

First summer: After planting and heading back (to a bud 30–32 in. above the ground) a whip will form new shoots. In early summer, select from these an extension for the central leader (growing from the top bud) and 3 side leaders. Remove other shoots.

Second year: If leaders haven't produced a lot of secondary branches, head them back as shown to promote secondary growth.

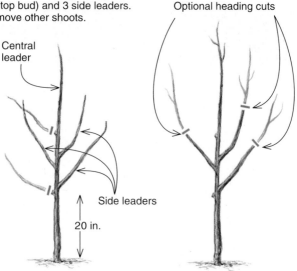

Central leader

Optional heading cuts

Side leaders

20 in.

they have a choice. A cold, wet spring can deter bees from their appointed rounds; you can fill in for them by hand pollinating if you're hardy and dedicated enough.

Training and Care

Other than being somewhat more adapted to heavy soils, pears require a full ration of sun, well-drained soil, and adequate moisture and nutrition, just like other tree fruits. Plant trees on dwarf rootstocks 12 to 15 feet apart; space those on standard rootstocks 20 feet apart. (See the chapters "Planting Fruit Trees and Bushes" and "Ongoing Care" for details.)

Training

Pears have a stronger tendency than other fruit trees to grow straight up. (Asian varieties even more so than European.) To keep the tree performing at its best, you will need to train it from an early age, spreading the branches to enable them to support the weight of later crops. After training, you'll need to prune it minimally to maintain the form,

Third year: Remove central leader just above uppermost side leader, unless you need it to replace a side leader lost to fire blight. Head back other leaders and secondary branches if necessary to promote further branching.

Subsequent years: Continue to select and train secondary branches at wide angles. Thin branches to keep center open, promote fruiting growth, and control tree size. Prune as little as possible to reduce chances of fire blight. The remaining leaders will revert to vertical growth; try to keep their secondary branches at wider angles.

provide easy access to the fruit, prevent overproduction, and protect against blight.

The upright habit of pears makes them natural candidates for central-leader training. Because of their susceptibility to fire blight, they are often trained with multiple leaders. If blight strikes one, you have several to fall back on. The basic steps in central-leader training are outlined in the chapter "Pruning for Fruits and Berries." We'll outline here how to create a tree with multiple leaders. (See drawing pages 48–49.)

If you plant a branchless whip, head it back to a bud about 30 to 32 inches above the ground. In early summer, when the heading back has stimulated new growth, select three shoots to become side leaders. ("Side leader" isn't an orchardist's term but will serve us to distinguish these shoots from the original central leader, now extended from the top bud.) The first should be about 20 inches above the ground and the other two spaced 4 to 6 inches apart up the trunk above the first. The three should be more or less evenly spaced around the circumference. Pinch out other side shoots. If you buy a branched tree, look it over to see if any of the existing branches can provide the scaffolds you need to create the structure just described. If you need more, head back the central leader to stimulate new shoots below it.

During the first and second seasons, allow the central leader to grow straight up. The shade from this leader will encourage the side leaders to grow less upright. Select secondary branches on the central and side leaders to form scaffold branches (as you would if each were a single central leader). To keep the center of the tree from becoming crowded, be sparing in your selection of secondary branches that head into the center.

Upright branches tend to bear less fruit and are more likely to break under weight of the heavy fruit than branches at a greater angle to the trunk. Branches at wider angles also tend to extend less, keeping the tree in bounds. So, as secondary shoots develop along the multiple leaders, train them to grow at an angle of at least 45° to the vertical. See "Pruning for Fruits and Berries" for a variety of ways to do this — with clothespins, spreaders, and weights.

During the tree's first several years, if the secondary branches are not themselves producing many branches, head back the secondary branches to a bud about 24 inches from the branch's point of origin. Heading back branches encourages development of strong side shoots along their length and reduces sections of limb without fruiting buds. In general, however, keep pruning to a minimum. Dormant pruning tends to stimulate lots of growth, which is prone to fire blight.

In the third season, the center of the tree will be getting

too crowded. In late winter when the tree is dormant, remove the central leader just above its juncture with the uppermost side leader. (You could wait until after the fire blight infection period is over, about a month after the tree leafs out.) Exposed to additional light, and lacking competition from the central leader, the side leaders will begin to grow more upright. Continue to train their scaffolds and secondary branches to wide angles. When the basic scaffold system is complete, with about three to five scaffold branches on each leader, prune minimally to remove weak or poorly positioned shoots, and to keep the center of the tree open to light.

If fire blight strikes a secondary branch, scaffold branch, or leader, you'll have to remove it. Having multiple leaders to choose from, you may well be able to select and train branches or shoots to replace the blighted wood.

Ongoing care

Like other fruit trees, healthy pears ought to grow a certain amount each season. In the first few seasons, dwarfed pear trees should grow about 20 to 30 inches a year depending on variety, soil, and moisture. If the tree is growing too slowly, look for pest or disease problems, water or nutrient deficiency, and so on. (You may need expert help to determine a cause.)

To maintain water levels, supplement rainfall if it falls below an inch per week. A generous mulch will retard evaporation. If your soil is average to begin with, an application of 5 to 10 pounds of composted manure in early summer should provide all the nutrients a young pear needs.

Once the tree settles into fruit production (after about five years for European pears; three years for Asians), a well-nourished dwarf tree should put on about 12 inches of new growth a year, and a standard should grow 18 to 20 inches per year. If your trees are vigorous growers, you can slow them down by allowing grass to grow under the canopy and compete for nutrients and moisture. Keep the grass mowed and clean up dropped fruit and foliage regularly to prevent pest build-up.

Thinning fruit

Both Asian and European pears have a tendency to set far too many fruit. Too many fruit competing for light and nutrients mean each fruit will be smaller. Too many fruit can also divert energy from making new fruit buds for the next season, resulting in biennial bearing — a good crop just every other year.

Asian pears require ruthless thinning to ensure a harvest of the large fruit (about half a pound apiece) the trees are capable of producing. About a month after the petals drop, thin the fruit to no more than one per blossom cluster and spaced at least 6 inches apart. Don't skimp on thinning. You can thin as late as 30 days before harvest and still see a benefit. Be careful not to break off the brittle spurs as you thin. Thin European pears to one or two fruits per flower cluster three to six weeks after bloom is finished.

In addition to fruit thinning, remember to thin branches as necessary to allow light to reach the leaves on most spurs. Ample light keeps spurs productive and producing sweet fruit. Fruit size can decline on spurs older than five or six seasons. Remove the old spurs and prune to create new ones. (See "Pruning for Fruits and Berries" for details on renewal pruning.)

Espalier training

Pears on dwarfing rootstocks are excellent subjects for espaliers. You can train them in about any shape you want by tying them loosely to a framework of wire, bamboo, or similar material. A classic shape is the vertical cordon, a single stem, like a rope or cord, with the only branches being spurs, which bear all leaves and fruit buds. Others include variations on the U-shape, and angled cordons, either parallel or crossing in a diagonal grid. (See "Pruning for Fruits and Berries" for details on creating a basic espalier.)

Harvest

European pears usually begin fruiting as five-year-olds, reaching peak production of one or two bushels a season as fully mature 10-year-old dwarf trees. Dwarf Asian pears bear a few years earlier and also yield one to two bushels as mature trees.

Probably the trickiest part of growing European pears is picking them at the right time. Unlike most tree fruit, they ripen from the inside out. So if left on the tree until the outside of the fruit appears ripe, the inside will be mushy. To avoid this, you must pick European pears before they ripen. The fruit should be full-size with the green skin showing a slight lightening toward yellow. Look for a color change in the lenticels, small dark flecks on the skin. When the lenticels turn from white to brown the fruit is ready to pick, though not to eat. Lift the fruit and give a little twist and it should break cleanly from the spur.

Promptly put the fruit in a plastic bag and store it in the refrigerator for a week or two. Then pull out a half dozen or so and let them ripen for several days at room temperature. The fruit is completely ripe when the flesh near the stem gives under pressure from your fingers. Early pears ripen more

This espaliered pear provides a lovely springtime accent on the way to a tasty harvest later in the year. Pears have a long history in North America; this one grows in Colonial Williamsburg.

quickly in cold storage than later varieties, the best of which can keep as long as four months in refrigeration.

Asian pears are best when ripened on the tree. Watch for the color to change from green to yellow-green or light brown. Taste them at different stages to determine the degree of ripeness you prefer. Ripe Asian pears will keep in good condition for a couple of weeks at room temperature and at least two months in refrigerated storage. Many varieties will last from four to five months when refrigerated.

Pests and Diseases

As mentioned above, the major problem facing pear growers is the bacterial disease fire blight. The common insect problems are pear psylla and codling moth.

Fire blight

The best way to deal with fire blight is to plant cultivars resistant to the disease. Fire blight is caused by a bacterium, *Erwinia amylovora*, which is native to North America. Telltale signs of disease are branch tips and leaves that look as if they've been scorched by a flame. Leaves blacken and shrivel and the tips curl into a crook.

The organism enters through an opening into fresh living

tissue, in pears typically though the blossoms. After the tree finishes blossoming, the disease can enter only through breaks in the leaves, stems, or bark, such as damage from hail, wind, insects, birds, or pruning shears can produce. Once inside the tree, the blight spreads in the conductive tissue just under the bark. It produces an infectious ooze that can be spread by gravity, rain, and insects.

Fire blight needs certain conditions to thrive. It is active when the temperature is between 65° and 90°F and the relative humidity is above 70 percent, and those conditions need to persist for about 48 hours. With a cool or dry spring, fire blight is unlikely to gain a foothold for the season. If it's warm and rainy, check your trees daily if possible.

At the first signs of blight in a tree, prune all infected wood, cutting about a foot below the visible damage. To avoid spreading the disease during pruning, clean your shears with alcohol or a 10 percent chlorine bleach solution between each cut, and be sure to wash the highly corrosive chlorine off of your shears promptly when the job is finished. Immediately burn all prunings.

In resistant pear varieties, the tree can wall off the infection and stop it. A visible canker will form that can spread the disease. Prune them off during the dormant season, following the same procedure outlined above, then burn them.

Pear psylla

The most serious insect problem, pear psylla are small sucking insects, like aphids. Their feeding weakens pear trees and their "honeydew" wastes become black with fungus. The honeydew easily washes off the fruit, but you'll need to control the psylla with dormant oil sprays, which also take care of scale and aphids.

Codling moth

Many insects that bother apples are occasionally found on pears. The only one that regularly does damage is the codling moth, but it is rarely serious because infected fruit is still edible. When thinning your fruit to prevent overbearing, make sure the fruits don't touch each other, and you'll discourage the moth from laying eggs.

There are no effective organic controls for codling moth except the removal of affected twig tips, cutting back to healthy wood. Use pheromone traps (the hormone attracts insects) to determine when numbers warrant intervention. A week after the moths are on the rise, apply Imidan. Repeat 10 days later.

■ RECOMMENDED VARIETIES OF PEARS

European Pears
All these do well in zones 5–8.

Clapp's Favorite
Season: Early.
Fruit quality: Good.
Fire blight resistance: Poor.
Keeps in storage: 2 weeks.
Comments: Good for Northwest. Flavor similar to 'Bartlett'.

Comice
Season: Late.
Fruit quality: Best.
Fire blight resistance: Poor.
Keeps in storage: 20 weeks.
Comments: Buttery flavor and rich texture improve in storage.

Gourmet
Season: Midseason.
Fruit quality: Good.
Fire blight resistance: Fair.
Keeps in storage: 4–8 weeks.
Comments: Good in far north.

Harrow Delight
Season: Early.
Fruit quality: Very good.
Fire blight resistance: Excellent.

'Harrow Delight'

Keeps in storage: 2–3 weeks.
Comments: Best early pear for both flavor and blight resistance.

Harrow Sweet
Season: Midseason.
Fruit quality: Best.
Fire blight resistance: Excellent.
Keeps in storage: 8 weeks.
Comments: Superb flavor, slightly tough skin.

Harvest Queen
Season: Early.
Fruit quality: Best.
Fire blight resistance: Excellent.
Keeps in storage: 4–8 weeks.
Comments: Flavor nearly identical to 'Bartlett'.

Luscious
Season: Late.
Fruit quality: Very good.
Fire blight resistance: Fair.
Keeps in storage: 4–8 weeks.
Comments: Good in far north. Similar to 'Bartlett' but stronger flavor.

Magness
Season: Midseason.
Fruit quality: Best.
Fire blight resistance: Excellent.
Keeps in storage: 12 weeks.
Comments: Smooth, fragrant, fresh taste. Pollen is sterile.

Seckel
Season: Midseason.
Fruit quality: Best.
Fire blight resistance: Excellent.
Keeps in storage: 8 weeks.
Comments: Small fruit (2 in.), but excellent aromatic flavor and tender skin.

Starking Delicious
Season: Midseason.
Fruit quality: Good.
Fire blight resistance: Good.
Keeps in storage: 2–3 weeks.
Comments: Similar to 'Bartlett'; can be eaten when flesh slightly crisp. Also called 'Maxine'.

'Seckel'

Stark Honeysweet
Season: Midseason.
Fruit quality: Best.
Fire blight resistance: Excellent.
Keeps in storage: 4 weeks.
Comments: Similar flavor and texture to 'Seckel', but fruit twice as big.

Asian Pears: Japanese Types
All these do well in zones 5–9.

Chojuro
Season: Midseason.
Fruit quality: Good.
Fire blight resistance: Poor.
Keeps in storage: 20 weeks.
Comments: Strong aroma, tough skin.

Hosui

Season: Early.
Fruit quality: Best.
Fire blight resistance: Poor.
Keeps in storage: 8–12 weeks.
Comments: Juicy, tender, very sweet. Some resistance to psylla.

Kikusui

Season: Midseason.
Fruit quality: Very good.
Fire blight resistance: Poor.
Keeps in storage: 24 weeks.
Comments: Nice combination of sweet and tart. Bitter skin.

'Hosui'

Nijiseike

Season: Midseason.
Fruit quality: Best.
Fire blight resistance: Poor.
Keeps in storage: 20 weeks.
Comments: Also combines sweet and tart flavors. Tender skin. Also known as '20th Century'.

Shinko

Season: Late.
Fruit quality: Very good.
Fire blight resistance: Good.
Keeps in storage: 12 weeks.
Comments: Excellent flavor and tender flesh. Only Japanese type with good blight resistance.

Shinsui

Season: Early.
Fruit quality: Very good.
Fire blight resistance: Poor.
Keeps in storage: 4 weeks.
Comments: Very juicy and sweet. Top-selling pear in Japan.

Asian Pears: Chinese Types

All these do well in zones 5–9.

Tsu Li

Season: Late.
Fruit quality: Good.
Fire blight resistance: Good.
Keeps in storage: 32 weeks.
Comments: Classic pear shape. Flavor improves in storage. Good in the South. Plant with 'Ya Li' for good pollination.

Ya Li

Season: Late.
Fruit quality: Good.
Fire blight resistance: Good.
Keeps in storage: 24 weeks.
Comments: Classic pear shape. Sweet, juicy, fragrant. Good in the South. Plant with 'Tsu Li' for good pollination.

Cherries

*'Meteor' features sour cherries on a
naturally dwarf tree.*

Eating a well-ripened cherry is an ambrosial experience. Unfortunately, it's an experience you're unlikely to have unless you grow your own. Ripe cherries are perhaps the most ephemeral of fruits, which makes them a nightmare for commercial growers. The longer cherries stay on the tree, the sweeter they get. But they also become soft and perishable, and once picked, their sweetness declines. Really good cherries are almost impossible to find in stores and are increasingly rare at farmsteads and orchards.

Two kinds of cherry — sweet and tart — are commonly grown as fruit trees. The deep-red cherries you find in the produce section of supermarkets are sweet cherries, cultivars of *Prunus avium*. Sweet cherries have soft yet meaty flesh and flavors as powerful as red wine. 'Bing' is the classic variety in this group, but gardeners have other interesting choices. (See the list of recommended cultivars.) Sweet cherries, usually those with yellowish fruit, are also used for canned fruit cocktails or maraschinos. The subtle flavors of sweet cherries don't stand up to cooking, so they are best eaten fresh.

Tart cherries are a different species entirely, *P. cerasus,* and are almost never seen fresh in the marketplace. They have a distinctly different flavor — the cherry taste you encounter in tarts, pies, jams, and cherry confections. (They are sometimes called pie or sour cherries.) They are superb for cooking, but allowed to ripen fully, they can be delicious fresh from the tree. 'Montmorency' is by far the most popular variety, largely because the tree is very productive. There are a few crosses between the sweet and tart species of cherry, and these hybrids are often called Duke cherries, after the name of the best-known hybrid cultivar.

Cherry trees are lovely additions to a home landscape as well as the home larder. In the spring they bear attractive clusters of white flowers, just like their cousins the flowering cherries, which have been bred for that purpose (though from different species).

Sweet and tart cherries are similar in many ways. Both ripen early in the season, sweet cherries beginning with the earliest raspberries (mid-June around the Great Lakes), and tart cherries about two weeks later. They have similar cultural, training, and pruning requirements, and both are troubled by the same pests.

Choosing a Cherry

Gardeners in the northern two-thirds of North America will find both sweet and tart cherries fairly easy to grow. Farther south than zone 7, however, high humidity and summer temperatures encourage diseases that make growing cherries difficult. For the beginning fruit grower, the tart cherries are considerably easier to grow than sweet cherries. The trees are smaller and slightly more tolerant of heat and cold. They bloom later, making them less susceptible to damage from late frost. And, unlike most sweet cherries, they are self-pollinating, so you don't need to plant two kinds.

The mature size of any plant is an important consideration for home gardeners, who frequently want to grow far more plants than they have space for. Small trees are often the only choice for a residential landscape. Small cherry trees have an additional advantage. Birds are a serious threat to ripe cherries in any part of the country, and smaller trees are easier to protect with netting. Smallest and easiest to protect, though most labor intensive to establish and maintain, are cherries

'Montmorency' is the most popular tart cherry.

trained as espaliers, a popular form in Europe, where fan-training is a favorite.

Like many fruit trees, cherries are grafted onto rootstocks to give them qualities, such as increased hardiness or reduced size, that they wouldn't have if grown on their own roots. Unfortunately, the two rootstocks most commonly used for cherries, Mahaleb and Mazzard, have little effect on size. Sweet cherries get big quickly, reaching 40 feet if left un-pruned. They can overwhelm a small property. Tart cherries grown on these rootstocks are smaller. 'Montmorency' at 15 to 20 feet is one of the largest; 'North Star' reaches only 8 to 10 feet, making it an excellent choice for home gardeners.

Newly introduced rootstocks (the GM series and the Gisela

series) promise to reduce the height of both tart and sweet cherry trees by about half. A few suppliers have begun to offer 'Montmorency' on GM rootstocks, producing a tree that can, with training, be kept at 10 feet or less. If your extension agent isn't familiar with cherries, mail-order nurseries specializing in fruit trees are the best sources of information about the rootstocks (as well as the type of cherry and cultivars) that will do best for your area.

Tart Cherries

Only a handful of tart cherry varieties are offered in North America. All are extremely soft and very juicy, and flavor differences among them are slight. The main distinction is whether the juice is deep red or clear. Tart cherries with red juice and red flesh are called Morello cherries, named after a prominent cultivar of the type. Morellos are popular in Europe for their appealing juice. Amarelle types, which include 'Montmorency', have clear juice and yellow flesh. (Processors frequently add red coloring when they cook 'Montmorency' to give a deeper "cherry" color to tarts and pies.)

Tart cherries grow from zones 4 to 6 and south into parts of zone 7. Temperatures below about -20°F will kill the tree. Tart cherries require approximately 1,000 chill hours. (See the chapter "Growing Fruits and Berries at Home" for more on winter chill.) After the chill hours have been accumulated, the flower buds can become damaged at progressively higher temperatures.

Tart cherries need very well drained soil. If you have heavier soil, a tree on Mazzard roots will do better than one on Mahaleb, though it will grow marginally larger. Tart cherries on Mahaleb roots are somewhat more tolerant of both cold and dry soils. (Mahaleb roots may also be less appealing to gophers.) Full sun is crucial for sweet cherries and high quality tart cherries. Trees grown in the shade produce fewer cherries that are less sweet.

Training and care

Tart cherries require no special attention at planting (see "Planting Fruit Trees and Bushes"). But they will perform best if you train them to restrict their height and spread. In summer a well-trained tart cherry for the home garden will look more like a bush than a short shade tree. It will present a dome of foliage about 10 feet wide and 8 to 10 feet tall that nearly touches the ground, providing the most fruit-bearing surface under the smallest bird-discouraging net. To achieve this form, you should prune tart cherries to the basic modified-central-leader shape (see "Pruning for Fruits and

Berries"), but with a few modifications. Train big cherries, such as 'Montmorency', as well as smaller ones, such as 'North Star' and those on dwarfing rootstocks, the same way — their height will vary slightly.

At planting, trim off all the side branches, but don't shorten the leader. The next season, choose a branch about 30 inches above ground level for the first scaffold branch, then choose two to three more scaffolds spaced about 6 inches apart up the trunk. Prune off all other side branches. Finally, cut the leader back to a bud that is near the position of the next logical choice for a scaffold branch. Continue modified central-leader training as described in "Pruning for Fruits and Berries." As the years pass, the lower branches will grow out and down in response to shading from the upper branches.

Flower buds of tart cherries are borne on either one-year-old branch tips or on short-lived spurs. Older wood becomes unfruitful after three to five years and should be pruned out so the tree can replace it. You can either prune off individual unfruitful spurs or entire branches that consist largely of unfruitful spurs. To make the tree smaller and the cherries you harvest bigger, you can also cut back new growth (which won't bear fruit this season) during the two weeks prior to ripening. You can do as little as pinch the tips or as much as cutting off two-thirds of a branch's length.

Monitor your tree's health by checking its rate of growth. A healthy 'Montmorency' tree should grow about 12 inches a year, a 'North Star' about half that, and trees on dwarfing rootstocks the same or somewhat less than a 'North Star'. Trees that don't grow vigorously enough sometimes produce only fruit buds on new growth. Next year's crop will be heavy, but no vegetative buds means no renewal growth, and subsequent crops suffer. To encourage healthy growth, make sure the tree is getting enough water (about 1 inch per week) and nutrients. An organic mulch extending out to the drip line will remove competition from lawn grass, help conserve water, and if your soil is reasonably good, provide ample nutrients as it breaks down.

Harvest

Tart cherry trees begin bearing in their third or fourth season. A seven-year-old tree can produce 25 to 35 pounds of fruit, though yields vary depending on variety, size, and training. The first tart cherries begin to ripen about 60 days after bloom, just as the sweet cherries are finishing and about two weeks before apples. Harvest from one variety will last about a week. Taste is the best measure of ripeness. Cherries are perishable and will keep only about a week in the refrigerator.

Sweet Cherries

Sweet cherries are connoisseur fruits, with a range of flavors and textures. 'Bing' is popular with commercial growers in part because its flavor is relatively mild, so people can eat a lot of them. Some of the most intensely flavored kinds are so rich that they can cause a kind of "flavor fatigue" on the tongue.

Sweet cherries fall into two groups according to whether their flesh is crisp or soft. Most people prize the crisp-fleshed cherries, but they are harder to grow. Cherries can absorb water directly through their skin, and as they approach full ripeness, they can swell enough to split. The crisper the cherry, the more easily it will split, and split cherries are highly vulnerable to brown rot. Very susceptible varieties will crack in a mist or light rain and are therefore usually grown in arid parts of the Far West. (Crack resistance is noted on the list of recommended varieties, beginning on page 71.) 'Bing' is very susceptible to cracking, which is one reason it isn't included on the list. It is also so commonly available in grocery stores that there's little point in growing it when you can choose better varieties.

Sweet cherries grow a little farther south than tart cherries, from zone 4 through 7. When fully dormant, their bud hardiness is similar, to -20°F and occasionally lower. But they have a lower chill requirement, between 600 and 700 hours, so they awaken to bloom earlier and are therefore more susceptible to damage from late frosts.

The biggest problem sweet cherries pose for home gardeners is size. Even a trained tree on the Mazzard rootstock will reach 20 feet, which is still too large to net easily. (Some sweet cherries are incompatible with Mahaleb rootstock.) The Gisela and GM dwarfing rootstocks promise to make sweet cherry growing, and especially bird protection, easier, producing mature trees (15 to 20 years old) reaching only about 10 feet tall.

Pollination

Most sweet cherries require a pollinator. Unfortunately, annoying pollen incompatibilities make it essential to get the match right — advice from a knowledgeable supplier is invaluable. Breeders have recently introduced several self-fertile varieties, so gardeners with limited space can now plant just a single sweet cherry. In addition, all the self-fertile varieties developed so far are good pollinators for other sweet cherries. 'Stark Gold', while not self-fertile, is a universally compatible pollinator and the hardiest sweet cherry, reportedly good to -30°F. It also has the considerable advantage of being bird-resistant. Birds strongly prefer the color red and will

These yellow sweet 'Stark Gold' cherries are the most bird-proof. The variety is a universal pollinator for sweet cherries.

often leave the yellow 'Stark Gold' cherries untouched. Tart cherries are capable of pollinating sweet, but sweet cherries have usually finished blooming by the time the tarts start.

If the sweet cherry bug bites and you want to try a range of varieties but have limited space, grafting provides a way around the pollination problem. If you can't do it yourself, check with your supplier to see if they offer the service. (It will be at least a year and more likely two before delivery.) Graft other varieties to a universal pollinator — one of the self-fertile cultivars or 'Stark Gold'.

Training and care

Like their tart cousins, sweet cherries require no special attention at planting. They also do best trained to a modified central-leader shape, as described in "Pruning for Fruits and Berries." The goal is to keep the bearing surface low and within easy reach. The first scaffold branch should be about 30 inches above the ground. Sweet cherry trees are more vigorous and larger than tart, so leave slightly more space between the four or five scaffold branches you choose — 12 inches on Mazzard and 8 inches on the dwarf rootstocks. Some varieties tend to produce clusters of branches at the same height around the trunk. Prune these to leave no more than two or three at any height.

The branches of some varieties are inclined to grow sharply upward, forming a narrow angle where they meet the trunk. Spread those young scaffold branches as soon as possible to an angle of 45° or more with the trunk. A wooden wedge or a weight on the branch will do the trick. Increasing branch angles not only avoids disease problems that split crotches can cause but encourages the tree to set fruit buds and produce fruit earlier in its life, thereby diverting some of the tree's vigorous growth.

Most fruit is borne on long-lived spurs. Look for fruit buds at the base of one-year-old wood; some of the buds immediately above them (farther out on the branch) will become spurs the following season. To restrict growth and encourage fruiting, in late summer remove branches that are becoming less fruitful or shoots that shade promising renewal growth. Where late frosts are a regular threat, however, delay pruning until after bloom the following spring, when you can see how heavy the crop load will be. Starting right after fruit set, you can lighten a heavy crop load by pruning two- and three-year-old branches; you can also thin excess new growth at the same time.

Sometimes one branch will grow more vigorously than others, shading out its neighbors and giving the tree an awkward form. Look for branches exhibiting thicker growth and big, strong buds with longer spaces between them, and discourage them by cutting back the tip in spring, or bending down the whole branch with a weight in summer. You may need to take a branch like this out completely, back to a junction on the main limb. (Don't try to bend older, inflexible branches.)

Some gardeners try to limit the growth of sweet cherries by growing the tree in mown lawn. But competition from grasses can retard growth too much. If new growth on a fruit-bearing tree is less than 12 to 18 inches a season, suppress the grass with an organic mulch. If growth still lags, check that the tree is getting enough water and nutrients.

Harvest

Sweet cherry trees begin bearing heavily around their fifth season, ultimately producing between 50 and 100 pounds of fruit per tree, depending on how it is trained. Sweet cherries bloom early and thus are susceptible to frost damage. But they also tend to overproduce, and the fruit are difficult to thin. Even if only 40 percent of the blossoms survive, the tree will produce a full crop, as measured by weight. And the larger cherries will be easier to pick and have better flavor and sweetness.

With just two trees — an early and a late variety — the sweet cherry harvest can last three to five weeks. Again, taste is the measure of ripeness, and the fruit will keep only about a week if refrigerated promptly.

Pests and Diseases

Sweet and tart cherries suffer from most of the same problems, which may be treated in the same way. Cherry-loving birds are everywhere, but insect and disease problems vary widely by geography and from year to year. Sanitation is important in controlling all pests. Gather problem fruit, leaves, and prunings promptly and destroy them in a hot compost pile or by burning to kill insect larvae and disease spores. We can provide only general information about common problems here. Specific advice from someone knowledgeable about the pests and diseases in your area is indispensable.

Birds

Birds can decimate a home gardener's cherry crop. The closer you can place a cherry tree to sites of frequent activity by people, cats, and dogs, the less trouble you'll have with birds. Netting is the main control. Construct a lightweight frame to hold plastic garden netting above tree branches, or throw the net over the tree and fasten it at the bottom with weights or ties. Trees next to a fence or wall are easier to net; espaliered trees are easiest of all.

Plum curculio

The larvae of plum curculio resemble little worms, which infest the fruit soon after bloom. This small snout-nosed gray or brown beetle makes small crescent-shaped scars on the young fruit where it lays its eggs. When you spot the first scars, begin control immediately. Once the eggs are laid, the damage to fruit is irreparable.

No organic sprays are effective. The chemical Imidan is effective if applied during and after the petals fall, generally in mid-May. Consult with your extension agent about timing.

Cherry fruit fly

Like its close relative, the apple maggot fly, this insect lays its eggs beneath the skin of the fruit, which soon crawls with the resultant larvae. A heavy infestation will ruin the crop; a few cherry maggots are tolerable to most people and can be picked out as you clean the fruit.

Control by trapping the flies on sticky red spheres or yellow cards (both available from nurseries) hung from the branches. Where infestations are severe, use the cards to determine the arrival of the flies and begin to spray. If the organic control rotenone is not effective, Imidan will do a better job. Heavily infested fruit will drop prematurely; clean it up daily and destroy it to prevent the insect from completing its life cycle in the ground.

Brown rot

This fungus is very weather-dependent, thriving when it is warm and wet; it can wipe out the crop in a bad year. The problem first appears as a small brown spot, which can spread over the entire cherry in a few hours during warm weather. You may be able to salvage a crop of infected tart cherries by picking somewhat prematurely and cooking with extra sugar.

To control brown rot, use fungicides or sulfur. Cleaning up dropped fruit, especially those that are mummified, helps stop the spread of brown rot from crop to crop and year to year.

Cherry leafspot

Another fungus, cherry leafspot can defoliate trees in some years. The tree will be able to grow new leaves and survive, but leaf loss will seriously reduce fruit quality and the ability of the tree to make strong fruit buds for following seasons.

Purplish spots first appear on the upper surface of the leaves. The centers of the spots may eventually drop out and the leaves eventually yellow and fall off. The fungus that causes this disease winters on the fallen leaves. Right after the cherries finish blooming and new leaves begin to appear, spores are released from the leaves on the ground. The disease is worst during damp weather with temperatures between 60° and 70°F.

'North Star'

It is essential to clean up and destroy leaves soon after they drop. If the problem is severe, use a fungicide labeled for this problem, at petal fall. The variety 'North Star' is somewhat resistant to cherry leafspot.

Bacterial canker

Oozing lesions on branches are a sign of this problem, which can also affect leaves and fruit and may kill whole branches. It can usually be controlled by careful pruning and destruction of the diseased wood.

■ RECOMMENDED VARIETIES OF CHERRIES

Tart Cherries

All are self-pollinating, with very soft, juicy fruit. All will do well in zones 4 through the northern parts of zone 7.

Meteor

Season: Late.
Juice color: Clear.
Comments: Naturally dwarf tree, to 10 ft. tall. Fruit very similar to 'Montmorency' but larger, ripening 1 week later.

Montmorency

Season: Midseason.
Juice color: Clear.
Comments: Most popular tart cherry. Large tree, to 20 ft., and very productive.

Morello

Season: Late.
Juice color: Red.
Comments: Naturally dwarf tree, to 10 ft. Very tart fruit. Ripens a week after 'Montmorency'.

North Star

Season: Late.
Juice color: Red.
Comments: Very dwarf tree, to 8 ft. Ripens a week after 'Montmorency'. Somewhat resistant to both leaf spot and brown rot.

Sweet Cherries

All these will do well in zones 4–7. All require a pollinator, except where noted in Comments. You can plant those that don't self-pollinate with 'Stark Gold', 'Stella', or 'Lapins', or ask a nursery for other recommendations.

Emperor
Season: Midseason.
Fruit color and texture: Yellow, soft.
Crack tolerance: Good.
Frost tolerance: Fair.
Comments: Somewhat bird-resistant, though it blushes red at maturity.

Kristin
Season: Midseason.
Fruit color and texture: Dark red, firm.
Crack tolerance: Good.
Frost tolerance: Good.
Comments: Excellent flavor and large size.

Lambert
Season: Late.
Fruit color and texture: Black, crisp.
Crack tolerance: Poor.
Frost tolerance: Fair.
Comments: Superb flavor.

Lapins (Starkrimson)
Season: Late.
Fruit color and texture: Black, crisp.
Crack tolerance: Fair.
Frost tolerance: Fair.
Comments: Self-pollinates. High quality fruit and a good pollinator for all others.

Napolean (Royal Ann)
Season: Midseason.
Fruit color and texture: Yellow, firm.
Crack tolerance: Poor.
Frost tolerance: Fair.
Comments: Somewhat bird-resistant, though blushed with red at maturity.

Sam
Season: Midseason.
Fruit color and texture: Black, soft.
Crack tolerance: Good.
Frost tolerance: Good.
Comments: Trees are very cold-resistant.

Stark Gold
Season: Midseason.
Fruit color and texture: Yellow, soft.
Crack tolerance: Good.
Frost tolerance: Good.

'Napolean'

Comments: Pure yellow when ripe, so the most bird-proof. Trees are very cold-hardy. Good pollinator for all other sweet cherries.

Stella
Season: Midseason.
Fruit color and texture: Black, firm.
Crack tolerance: Fair.
Frost tolerance: Poor.
Comments: Self-pollinates. The fruit is large and attractive.

Summit
Season: Midseason.
Fruit color and texture: Red, soft.
Crack tolerance: Good.
Frost tolerance: Good.
Comments: Flavor is sweet and very good.

Van
Season: Midseason.
Fruit color and texture: Black, firm.
Crack tolerance: Fair.
Frost tolerance: Good.
Comments: The fruit is very attractive and with excellent flavor.

Plums

An American native that thrives in sandy soil, beach plums make tasty preserves.

You wouldn't know it from a visit to the supermarket, but there are more than 2,000 varieties of plums available today. This marvelous palette of fruit sizes, textures, colors, and flavors includes time-tested favorites such as 'Reine Claude', an 18th-century European plum with sweet, amber flesh, as well as the small but full-flavored American plums that Jacques Cartier saw in native canoes as he traveled up the St. Lawrence River in 1534. More recent additions include hardy, disease-resistant Japanese-American hybrids such as 'La Crescent', a cultivar hardy to -50°F, whose small, melt-in-your-mouth yellow fruit is so aromatic that its sweetness can be smelled throughout a room.

Many plums bear fruit as soon as three years after planting, when you can begin to enjoy the harvest in a variety of forms — eaten fresh, juiced, fermented as a liqueur, preserved in jams and jellies, or dried as prunes. But even if plum trees never produced a single fruit, their delicate, sweet-scented clouds of spring flowers and often bright-colored fall foliage would earn a place in the landscape. Reaching at most about 20 feet tall, plums are ideal for anchoring the end of a perennial border or for drawing the eye to a curve in a path. In the small garden, a single self-pollinating cultivar grown on a dwarfing rootstock can fit into a corner or a container. A hedge of native plums bordering your property will appeal to wildlife and small children seeking a snack.

Plum trees are an excellent choice for a low-maintenance gardener. Vigorous and hardy, they are suited to almost all except the tropical garden. Unfortunately, plums are susceptible to troublesome diseases and insect attacks. Choosing varieties resistant to diseases in your area and suitable to your climate is essential if you hope to have plums to pick. Luckily, of the numerous plum cultivars, there are likely to be many that suit the requirements of your garden as well as those of your palate.

A Plum Primer

Plums for the home garden come from three distinct backgrounds: Japanese, European, and American. All are members of the genus *Prunus,* as are apricots, cherries, and peaches. Japanese plums are the kind most often found on produce shelves across the country. European plums include the common late-season prune plums and the Gage types, small mostly greenish plums esteemed for their delicate sweetness. The fruit of native American plums, including beach plum, Canada plum, and others, is sometimes sold at local fruit stands. Their small, tasty plums are a treat eaten fresh and superb as preserves, jellies, wines, and liqueurs.

Commercial growers separate plums into canning, drying, and fresh-market types, depending on the taste, color, and keeping qualities of the fruit. (Home growers have the advantage of being able to eat their plums fresh and can select cultivars without regard to keeping qualities.) Japanese plums are usually clingstone, with the flesh adhering to the pit. Separating meat from stone can make canning difficult. Europeans, on the other hand, are generally freestone. The thick, sweet flesh slips away easily from the pit when the fruit is bitten or split in half. If you're planning to can or dry your harvest of European or Japanese plums, selecting a freestone cultivar will make processing easier and faster.

But even the European "prune plums," whose name implies a long, shriveled life, are really perfect for eating fresh.

'Green Gage' is a famed European dessert plum with sweet juicy golden flesh.

Because these sweet, meaty plums aren't as juicy as Japanese types, they are less messy, which makes them ideal to tuck in your lunch bag for a healthy snack.

In general, plums are fast-growing and relatively young when they begin bearing, usually at three to five years old. A standard tree bears well for at least 15 years, and often as long as 25 years. Although the fruit yield may decrease with age, venerable specimens are still valuable as ornamentals. (Native plums may be shorter-lived, but they often renew themselves from suckers.) Fruits vary in size, depending on the type or cultivar, thinning practices, and growing conditions. Japanese plums bear the largest fruits, about 2½ to 3 inches across. European types are usually medium-size, about 2 inches, and American plums are small, about 1 to 2 inches.

Japanese plums

Best eaten fresh, Japanese plums are round fruits whose red, yellow, gold, or black-purple skin protects very juicy red or yellow flesh. The taste is sweet, although there is often a surprising tartness near the pit.

Japanese plums *(Prunus salicina)* are really Chinese natives. Introduced to America in the 1800s, their leaves are smooth with a sharp-pointed tip, and the bark is rough. The trees grow best where peaches thrive, generally in zones 6 through 9. They tolerate heat and need only a short period of winter dormancy, making them ideal for mild-winter areas. Japanese plums bloom early, often at the first breath of warm weather, so they are susceptible to damage from late spring frosts. Most trees require a Japanese or American pollinator, but if your garden space is limited, look for a self-fruitful cultivar, such as 'Catalina', a vigorous, productive tree that bears large black plums.

European plums

The only European plums well known in America are the oval-shaped blue or purple prune plums that appear on produce counters in September. Mild and sweet, prune plums are tasty eaten fresh, with freestone pits that separate easily from the flesh. They are also ideal for drying, hence the designation "prune plum." The meaty pulp dries sweet, and the pits can be left in place. In Europe, Gage types, a delicacy when eaten fresh, are more prized than prune plums. (Gages are named for Sir William Gage, who brought the 'Reine Claude' plum to England from France.)

European plums *(Prunus domestica)* are descended from species native to Eurasia. Unlike the Japanese plum, they have toothed leaves and smooth bark. They are also hardier, thriving in zones 4 through 9, depending on the cultivar. Most European plums are partly self-fruitful; many will bear if only a single tree is planted, but the crop is multiplied and more consistent with a pollinator. Some cultivars, such as 'Mount Royal' and 'Stanley', are self-pollinating. Europeans bloom later than Japanese plums, making them a good choice for gardeners where late-spring frosts may pose a danger to flower buds or blossoms. The fruit also ripens late — from September through October — so if your growing season is short, European plums are not the best choice.

American plums

Americans are most likely to know these native plants from trips to the beach or to the countryside. Included among native species are the Canada plum *(Prunus nigra)*; the American plum *(P. americana)*; the Sierra or Klamath plum *(P. sub-cordata)*; and the beach plum *(P. maritima)*. Most of these American natives are very cold-hardy and tolerate drought and hot summers.

Once thought to have great potential for commercialization, American plums failed to attract sufficient interest among breeders. Today, only a small number of cultivars offer consistency in taste and habit. Some offer other useful traits, however. 'Bounty', a dark red-fruited cultivar of *P. nigra* introduced in 1936, is remarkably hardy and can be grown in zone 1. Some local nurseries may carry native plums; otherwise you'll need to order from a specialty mail-order source.

At its best, the fruit of these shrubs or small trees is sweet and delicious, but the small plums vary widely in quality from one seedling plant to another. Native plums are a perfect addition to an informal garden or hedgerow, where the fruit can be nibbled as it ripens, or collected for preserves and liqueurs. Many sucker naturally from the roots, creating an appealing thicket that is beautiful in spring bloom. The plants grow vigorously, but the flowers have such a heady fragrance that you won't mind clipping a few branches for a vase. Small insects drawn to the abundant flowers soon attract birds. During their spring migration, tiny wood warblers are lured down from perches on high tree tops to glean insects from wild plum blossoms. A planting on a gentle slope allows the best view of the blossoms in spring and the rich and vivid hues of red, purple, and yellow leaves in the fall.

Japanese-American hybrids

The hardy, disease-resistant Japanese-American hybrids are well suited to gardens in zones 4 through 8. Many combine the best of both parents, retaining large fruit of the Japanese plum, along with the cold hardiness and disease resistance of the American. 'Ember' is a large golden yellow plum with a beautiful orange-red blush and sweet, solid flesh. 'Superior', a super-fast grower and early bearer, produces beautiful big, pink plums that redden when fully ripe and peel as easily as a peach.

Unfortunately, the Japanese parent also passes along the legacy of early bloom. Avoid these hybrids in regions with unsettled spring weather, where a late frost might damage buds or bloom. A Japanese or American cultivar is needed for pollination.

Sizing Up a Plum Tree

The temptation is strong to begin the search for plums with the fruit — do you want plums for fresh eating, for preserves, or for drying — or with the tree's looks. Because of their susceptibility to insect predation and disease, however, it's best to begin with a call to your county extension agent or a nursery specializing in fruit. If you live in a southeastern state, for example, you'll learn from the agent or nursery staff about brown rot, a fungal disease that thrives in warm, damp conditions and causes fruit to turn to brown mush. To avoid the disease, you'll likely receive a recommendation to grow resistant Japanese cultivars such as 'Redheart' or European plums, which are less susceptible to brown rot than Japanese.

Hardiness and size are the next important considerations. Except for American plums (often called "bush plums" in catalogs), most plums are grafted to a rootstock in order to affect the tree's hardiness and growth rate, the resistance of its roots to pests and disease, its tolerance of certain soils, and its ease of maintenance and harvest. Experienced home fruit growers sometimes like to graft their own combinations of rootstock and top cultivar. But you can confidently accept the combinations offered by reputable local nurseries. It is useful to learn about rootstocks even if you leave the selection to others.

The most popular rootstock for European types is 'Myrobalan'. Long-lived and hardy, it produces a tree about 20 feet tall. Selections of this rootstock are resistant to canker and nematodes and have a good tolerance of heavy soil, making them a good choice for clay soil. 'Marianna 2624' offers resistance to oak root fungus, a problem in western states, and tomato ring spot virus, troublesome in New England and the Great Lakes region.

Rootstocks with a dwarfing effect are commonly used to control the size of larger-growing European and Japanese cultivars. Smaller trees require less space in the garden, and picking and pruning a shorter tree is easier than caring for a standard. The St. Julian series provides selections of rootstocks with a number of useful traits. 'St. Julian' has a slightly dwarfing effect on grafted plums. 'St. Julian A' ('St. Julian A EMLA') is a semidwarf rootstock that produces a tree 10 to 15 feet tall. 'St. Julian GF-655-2' is a clonal selection of 'St. Julian' that produces semidwarf trees with good root anchoring, disease and bacterial canker resistance, and a low suckering tendency. 'Pixy', a selection of the 'St. Julian' series, produces a dwarf tree about 8 to 10 feet tall; however, because the roots don't range widely, it is susceptible to drought. The species *Prunus cistena* is sometimes used as a rootstock to produce dwarf plum trees.

American native plum species are often used as rootstocks for plums suited to cold-winter areas. *P. americana* is often the rootstock for American-Japanese hybrid trees. American plum as a rootstock has weak anchorage and is not compatible with European or Japanese cultivars.

Pollination

Most plum cultivars of all types need cross-pollination to produce a good crop, but many will bear, although on a reduced scale, if grown alone. Some cultivars, such as the Japanese 'Methley', are self-fruitful. Most nursery tags or catalogs will suggest a pollinator by name if one is needed. Remember that trees paired for cross-pollination must bloom at the same time.

Planting Plums

Plums are usually sold as one-year-old trees, about 3 to 6 feet tall, and can be planted in spring, or in fall in mild-winter areas. (See the chapter "Planting Fruit Trees and Bushes" for more on planting.)

A sunny site is best, out of the bite of winter winds that can dry out or freeze the buds. If you garden in an area with uncertain spring weather and late frosts, choose a north-facing slope if possible, which will delay flowering by an often critical week or two. Because many plum rootstocks tend to sucker, it is best not to plant the trees directly in the middle of a flower bed. A site at the end of a border or behind a bed will let you enjoy the spring beauty of the blossoms while keeping suckers where they are easy to mow or snip off. Within the drip line of the tree (equal to its mature height) you can plant spring bulbs.

All plums do well in average garden soil and in heavier clays. Although plums thrive in moisture-retentive soils, they will drown in waterlogged ones. If water pools after a rain, the site isn't suited to plum trees. Plums are vulnerable to verticillium wilt, a widespread disease common to garden plants like tomatoes, potatoes, peppers, strawberries, and raspberries. Do not plant your plum trees near your vegetable garden, or in soil where these plants have been grown in the last several years.

Plant trees intended to cross-pollinate close together, not on opposite sides of the garden. Allow as much space between them as their expected mature height: plant standards 20 feet apart; semidwarfs, about 15 feet apart; dwarfs, about 8 feet apart.

Native plums are undemanding plants. They do well in average garden soils, on light or scanty soils, in full sun or light shade. Because of their suckering habit, they look best in a naturalized "thicket," which they will quickly fill. Plant on a slope near a window or other vantage point to enjoy a wave of white blossoms in spring.

Training and Pruning

All plums will bear well with no more pruning than removing dead, damaged, and diseased wood. But you can keep the fruit accessible and strengthen the structure of the tree by training and selective pruning. European plums tend to grow in a strongly upright direction and are well suited to central-leader training. Japanese types are generally spreading (although they can vary in habit depending on the cultivar) and do well trained to an open-center style. (See the chapter "Pruning for Fruits and Berries" for more on training and pruning fruit trees.)

Plums are formed on long-lived fruiting spurs. These short, stubby branchlets produce fruit for years, and new spurs are constantly forming from lateral buds on last year's growth. European plums bear on spurs in the interior of the tree and sometimes need more sunlight than the leaves allow. A judicious thinning of foliage and twiggy branches will allow better ripening. Japanese plums bear on year-old wood as well as older spurs, which remain fruitful for years.

All plum trees, especially those in areas with steamy summers, can benefit from selective thinning to allow good air circulation. Prune just after flowering, when the still-leafless branches allow a good view. Pruning before flowering, in winter or early spring, may encourage the trees to break into early bloom.

Plum trees yield generously. An established standard cultivar can bear 50 pounds or more of plums. But too much heavy fruit can weaken the tree, leaving it vulnerable to disease and winter damage, and a very heavy crop one year may mean a scanty one the next, as the tree directs energy into regaining its strength rather than producing fruit. An overburdened branch will droop; Japanese cultivars are notorious for heavy bearing. To avoid these problems or to encourage larger plums, thin out the fruits. Just after "fruit drop" (a natural thinning that occurs in early- to midsummer when fruits are about 1/2 inch in diameter), remove all but the single best plum per cluster or spur; try to leave 4 to 6 inches between fruits.

Shrubby American plums are often low-growing plants. They usually need no pruning for better fruit production, but if they are densely twiggy or somewhat thorny, some thinning will make the harvest more accessible.

Ongoing Care

Plums don't require much care. The trees flourish in the heat of summer, and hardy cultivars hold their closed buds safely throughout the coldest winters. You'll need to prune only occasionally to shape the tree and ensure a steady supply of fruit. Many disease and insect problems can be avoided by carefully selecting cultivars and by practicing good housekeeping. (See the chapter "Ongoing Care" for a detailed discussion of care; we'll summarize important points here.)

Plum rootstocks are generally shallow rooted but fairly drought-resistant. Established trees are more drought-tolerant than young; all trees do best with periodical deep watering in summer. Mulching out to the drip line will conserve moisture and avoid competition with grass.

Plums grow well in soil of average fertility, but the need for nutrients varies with type and cultivar, age, and soil conditions. Keeping tabs on the growth of your trees is the best way to monitor their nutrient needs. European plums should grow at about the rate of 12 inches per year, measured on a young shoot. Japanese cultivars should be even more vigorous, growing 15 to 20 inches a year. A layer of compost spread about 2 inches thick in early spring from the trunk out about 2 or 3 feet, or as far as the drip line, is usually sufficient to support growth in average soil. (Pull back the mulch and spread the compost under it.)

Fertilizing whether a tree needs it or not can lead to weak growth that is vulnerable to disease and injury. If your tree is growing significantly slower than the usual rate, test a soil sample to determine nutrient deficiency or other soil problems. If supplemental fertilizing is called for, apply it in early spring so that new growth has plenty of time to harden before winter.

Plums for the Picking

Plum season begins in midsummer and continues into fall, depending on the type and cultivar. Most of the fruit on individual trees ripens over a week or two. Japanese plums are the first to ripen. Late-ripening Japanese varieties overlap with the season for European plums, which generally begins in September, after McIntosh apples. American plums ripen in late summer.

Ripe plums will fall into your hand with a gentle twist. If you have to tug, the fruit isn't ready. A taste test is another sure indicator of ripeness. A ripe plum will be sweet, not mouth-puckeringly tart. Japanese plums can be picked before they are fully ripe; they will continue softening and sweetening off the tree. European plums should ripen fully on the tree, but keep a close eye on them so they don't get overripe and mushy. Pick American plums when they are soft and ripe. If you're picking for fresh eating, leave the stem attached to the fruit to avoid tearing the skin — the fruit will keep longer. Handle all plum types as gently as possible. Plums don't "keep" on the tree. If you don't eat or process them right away, plums can be stored for a couple of weeks in the refrigerator. Europeans plums can be sun-dried without removing the pit; their high sugar content allows them to dry without fermenting.

Pests and Diseases

In most areas, black knot, brown rot, perennial canker, and bacterial leaf spot cause the worst plum problems — serious infestations can kill the tree. Plums are also susceptible to the plum curculio, an insect that damages the fruit but doesn't harm the tree. Apple maggots, mites, and oriental fruit moths can also be pesky. Verticillium wilt can also kill the tree.

As we mentioned earlier, check with your county extension agent to find out what pests and diseases are prevalent in your area. Some can be avoided by planting resistant stock; look for cultivars beginning with 'Au', which were developed for disease resistance at Auburn University. Insect and disease problems can be reduced by practicing preventive care. Remove fallen fruit and dropped leaves to dispose of overwintering spores and insects, and promptly snip out any diseased twigs or afflicted fruits. The most common problems and their treatments are identified below; for further information on pest control strategies, see the chapter "Ongoing Care."

Plum curculio

Common throughout eastern North America, these snout-nosed, 1/3-inch-long gray or brown beetles cut the skins of plums and other tree fruits to lay their eggs inside. The cuts create crescent-shaped scars on the plum's skin, and the developing larvae — tiny white grubs — tunnel into the flesh of the fruit, which often drop prematurely.

Remove and destroy infested fruit. No organic controls are effective. The chemical Imidan is effective if applied during and after the petals fall, generally in mid-May.

Oriental fruit moth

Oriental fruit moths are widespread, causing problems in all areas except Texas and the the south-central states, the Pacific Northwest, and the Midwest. Wilted leaves at the tips of twigs are often the first sign of infestation, marking the place where the half-inch adult moth has laid eggs. The larvae tunnel into the twig tip, killing the twig. The first generation adults lay their eggs on fruit, where subsequent generations of larvae (three or four are common) burrow into the flesh around the pit.

Remove affected twig tips, cutting back to healthy wood. Ryania, an organic control, and the chemicals Imidan and Carbaryl are effective. They are best applied from mid-July through mid-August.

Black knot

All plums, but especially Europeans, are susceptible to the ravages of black knot, a severe disease that produces large black growths that girdle twigs and branches, cutting off nutrients to the areas beyond the tumors and killing the branches. The knots produce spores that quickly spread the infection to healthy wood.

The most effective control is vigilance. If you see any black knobby growths beginning, immediately prune off the branch at least 4 inches below the knot. Collect and destroy all pruned-off twigs. Dip pruning shears into a disinfectant solution after each cut to avoid spreading the disease. If the growth is on the trunk, dig out the knot, cutting back to healthy tissue an inch on all sides of it. Coat the wound with a lime-sulfur/white latex paint mixture. Unfortunately, removing affected branches may not halt the disease, because the black knot may have already released its spores. It may be necessary to remove the entire tree. Wild trees within 600 feet may spread the disease, so keep an eye out for infected ones and cut them down.

Resistant cultivars, such as 'Au Roadside' are available, and a sulphur spray, applied in winter when trees are dormant, may help prevent problems.

Brown rot

This fungal disease is especially troublesome in the South, Southeast, and other areas with hot, humid summers. The afflicted fruits rot to brown mush inside, then shrivel and drop. White and brown fungus may grow on the outside of the fruit.

If brown rot is a problem in your area, plant resistant cultivars such as 'Seneca'. Keep the fruits well thinned so that no two touch, and remove leaves to allow air to flow freely through the branches. To lessen the chance of future outbreaks, collect and destroy all fruit, including dropped plums, after harvest.

Wettable suphur, applied every week and a half if weather is wet, is an effective organic treatment that should be applied from full-bud stage of flowers through early September. Make the last application no later than two weeks before harvest.

Verticillium wilt

Sudden wilting of a plum tree may indicate infection by this fungal disease. A widespread disease, verticillium wilt cannot be cured. Be sure your planting site is well drained; the fungus flourishes in wet soils. The disease also affects tomatoes, eggplants, peppers, potatoes, raspberries, and strawberries, and the disease-causing spores can survive in the soil for years. Avoid planting plums for about 3 years where other susceptible plants have grown.

Perennial canker

Found in all parts of the country except the West, perennial canker is caused by two different organisms that produce sunken, oozing sores (cankers) on branches, twigs, or the trunks of plum and other fruit trees. The cankers may be oozing with sap or appear gummy with collected sap. Eventually, the branches will wilt and die.

Plant resistant cultivars such as 'Red Heart' and 'Au Amber'. At the first sign of the disease, immediately prune off affected branches, as for black knot. Mechanical injury, such as damage caused by a weed whacker, is a common entry point for perennial canker. Coat any wounds with a mix of lime-sulfur and white latex paint to make entry difficult for the organisms.

Bacterial spot

This disease is most common in the East. Spread by bacteria, it infects both leaves and fruit of plums and other fruit trees. The first symptom is a water-soaked black or brown spot on the underside of a leaf. The spot may fall out of the leaf, leaving a hole outlined in red. Severely infected leaves drop, weakening the tree and possibly reducing the size of the fruit as photosynthesis is restricted. When bacterial spot infects the fruit, the flesh appears sunken in spots or the skin may crack.

There is no sure cure. Maintain good hygiene, remove any affected leaves or fruit immediately, and plant resistant varieties such as 'Red Heart', 'Au Amber', and 'Green Gage' if bacterial spot is prevalent in your area. Native plums are also resistant to bacterial spot. The disease is spread by water, so pruning to allow air and light penetration will help.

'Italian', a European prune plum, is well suited for drying.

■ **RECOMMENDED VARIETIES OF EUROPEAN PLUMS**
Less hardy than American or Japanese; best for zones 5–9 unless otherwise stated.

Prune Plums
Freestone except where noted. Ideal for drying; eaten fresh they have a mild sweet taste.

Bluefree (Bluefre)
Fruit: Large blue fruit, yellow flesh.
Comments: Partially self-fruitful. Vigorous, early-bearing tree.

Earliblue
Fruit: Purplish blue with yellow flesh. Soft.
Comments: Late-blooming, good for areas with late spring frosts. Ripens in July. To zone 8.

Early Italian
Fruit: Large purple fruit, yellow-green flesh.
Comments: Self-fertile. Ripens late summer.

Early Laxton
Fruit: Pink-orange fruit with purple dots. Juicy.
Comments: Partially self-fertile. Old European variety. Unusually heavy bearer; must be thinned.

Fellenburg
Fruit: Large purple fruit, yellow flesh. Smooth texture.
Comments: Self-fertile. Hardy tree. Fruits hang for as long as two weeks after ripening.

French Petite
Fruit: Small to medium violet fruit, green-yellow flesh. Sugary sweet.
Comments: Very old variety, one of the best for drying.

'Stanley'

Imperial Epineuse
Fruit: Mottled red-purple skin, green-yellow flesh. Sweet, intense flavor. Clingstone.
Comments: Ripens mid-September. Old variety.

Italian (Italian Prune)
Fruit: Medium to large black-purple fruit, yellow-green flesh.
Comments: Self-fruitful. Cold-hardy, vigorous tree. Fruit may need thinning. To zone 4.

Mount Royal
Fruit: Medium to large, bluish black. Tender.
Comments: Good pollinator for wild plums and other European cultivars. To zone 4.

President
Fruit: Large, blue-black fruit with yellow flesh. Fine-textured.
Comments: Resistant to perennial canker and black knot.

Seneca
Fruit: Large, reddish blue fruit with yellow flesh. Very sweet, firm.
Comments: Vigorous tree, resistant to brown rot.

Stanley
Fruit: Medium to large, dark blue fruit with yellow-green flesh. Firm, smooth.
Comments: Self-fertile. Heavy bearer, may need thinning. To zone 4.

Victoria
Fruit: Large, pink to rose fruit with a blue bloom, gold flesh.
Comments: Superb for canning. Old variety, introduced in 1840.

Gage (Reine Claude) Plums
All are clingstone and will do well in zones 5–9.

Bryanston Gage
Fruit: Small to medium, greenish yellow, dotted with red. Firm, intensely plummy flavor.
Comments: Ripens mid-September.

Count Althan's (Count Althan's Gage)
Fruit: Small to medium, dark crimson with golden flesh. Sweet, juicy.
Comments: Old variety from Bohemia, selected by the gardener of Count Althan.

Green Gage (Reine Claude)

Fruit: Small to medium, yellow-green with golden flesh. Sweet, juicy.

Comments: Self-fertile. Famed European dessert plum. Susceptible to brown rot. Resistant to bacterial leaf spot.

Imperial Gage (Reine Claude Imperiale)

Fruit: Small, green fruit with transparent green flesh. Sweet, refreshing, rich fragrance.

Comments: Very old variety, introduced in 1790.

Pearl

Fruit: Small to medium, golden fruit with red speckles. Sweet, tender, superb flavor.

Comments: Luther Burbank cross, believed to be progeny of a French prune type and Reine Claude type.

■ RECOMMENDED VARIETIES OF JAPANESE PLUMS

Bloom earlier than European or American plums; susceptible to frost damage. Best in same areas where peaches are a success, zones 6–9, unless otherwise stated.

Au Amber

Fruit: Medium-size red-purple fruit with golden flesh. Fine flavor.

Comments: Resistant to perennial canker and bacterial leaf spot. "Au" in cultivar name denotes introduction of Auburn University.

Au Producer

Fruit: Medium-size fruit with juicy red flesh. Good flavor.

Comments: Resistant to perennial canker, black knot, bacterial leaf spot.

Au Roadside

Fruit: Very large magenta fruit with red flesh. Good flavor.

Comments: Resistant to perennial canker, black knot, bacterial leaf spot. Slight resistance to brown rot.

Au Rosa

Fruit: Red fruit with yellow flesh. Good flavor.

Comments: Resistant to perennial canker, black knot, bacterial leaf spot.

Black Amber

Fruit: Large, dark purple fruit with amber flesh. Freestone.

Excellent flavor.
Comments: Fast-growing, early-bearing. May need thinning of fruit.

Burbank
Fruit: Large, purple-red fruit with golden flesh. Sweet, meaty.
Comments: Bears early and prolifically, may need thinning of fruit.

Catalina
Fruit: Large, black fruit.
Comments: Self-fruitful. Vigorous tree with abundant fruit.

Crimson
Fruit: Medium to large crimson-red skin and flesh. Fine flavor.
Comments: Heavy bearer. Resistant to perennial canker, black knot, bacterial leaf spot.

Duarte
Fruit: Large, deep red fruit. Sweet red flesh.
Comments: Partially self-fruitful. Vigorous tree. Hardy. Good pollinator for other Japanese cultivars.

Elephant Heart (Burbank Elephant Heart)
Fruit: Large bronze-green to reddish purple fruit with red flesh. Sweet, juicy. Freestone.
Comments: Self-fruitful. Vigorous and hardy. A popular dwarf cultivar.

General Hand
Fruit: Very large, golden fruit. Solid, good flavor.
Comments: From the home of General Hand in Lancaster, Pennsylvania.

Homeside
Fruit: Large fruit with light red skin and amber flesh.
Comments: Resistant to perennial canker, black knot, bacterial leaf spot.

Mariposa
Fruit: Large green fruit with pink-purple mottling. Maroon, nearly freestone flesh. Excellent flavor.
Comments: Upright, hardy tree.

Methley
Fruit: Medium to large purple-red fruit. Fine flavor.
Comments: Self-fruitful.

Morris
Fruit: Medium to large, red-purple fruit with red flesh. Excellent flavor.
Comments: Some resistance to brown rot; good resistance to other major plum diseases.

Ozark Premier
Fruit: Large bright red fruit with yellow flesh. Refreshing mild tartness.
Comments: Resistant to perennial canker, black knot, bacterial leaf spot. Ripens over a long period in late summer.

Purple Heart
Fruit: Small dark purple fruit, only 1 to $1^{1}/_{2}$ in. Sweet flavor.
Comments: Hardy to -25°F.

Red Heart (Redheart)
Fruit: Medium to large dark red fruit with red flesh. Juicy. Partly freestone.
Comments: Resistant to brown rot, perennial canker, bacterial leaf spot. One of the best pollinators for other Japanese cultivars.

Santa Rosa (also available are the related cultivars Santa Rosa Late, Santa Rosa Weeping)
Fruit: Very large, red-purple fruit with purple and yellow flesh. Excellent flavor.
Comments: Resistant to black knot. Partially self-fertile.

'Santa Rosa'

Satsuma (Blood Plum)

Fruit: Medium to large dark red fruit with red flesh. Juicy, sweet, excellent flavor.

Comments: Partially self-fertile. Upright-growing tree.

Shiro

Fruit: Medium to large yellow fruit with pink blush and translucent yellow flesh. Mild, sweet, fine flavor.

Comments: Resistant to black knot. May need thinning. Good pollinator for other Japanese cultivars.

Starking Delicious

Fruit: Very large fruit with very good flavor.

Comments: Disease-resistant. Fruit needs thinning to achieve largest size.

Wickson

Fruit: Large, greenish yellow fruit with translucent flesh. Very sweet, firm, excellent flavor.

Comments: Self-fruitful.

■ RECOMMENDED VARIETIES OF AMERICAN PLUMS

Very hardy, disease-resistant, but small fruit (1 in.), variable in flavor. Can be very tart. Good for preserves.

American Plum (*Prunus americana,* aka Native Plum, Wild Plum)

Fruit: Abundant red and yellow fruit.

Comments: Small, well-branched tree with excellent fall color. Hardy to zone 3. Cultivar 'Red Diamond' has red-purple, meaty fruit.

Beach Plum (*Prunus maritima*)

Fruit: Purple, red, or yellow fruits famed for preserves. Also good fresh.

Comments: Spreading shrub with stiff, prickly branches. Reaches to 10 ft. tall and 6 ft. wide. Thrives in poor soil and sand. Hardy to zone 4.

Cherry Plum (*Prunus cerasifera,* aka Thundercloud, Myrobalan Plum, Newport Plum, Purpleleaf Plum)

Fruit: Small red fruit. (Photo on page 95.)

Comments: Upright tree to 20 ft. Dark red-purple foliage, pink flowers. Good for wildlife planting. 'All Red' is a cultivar with purple fruit with red flesh; freestone. Self-fertile, it reaches 12 feet.

Klamath Plum (*Prunus subcordata,* aka Sierra Plum)
Fruit: Yellow and red fruit, excellent in preserves.
Comments: Can grow as medium-size to large shrub or small
   tree. Orange-red fall color. Hardy to zone 5.

■ RECOMMENDED VARIETIES OF JAPANESE-AMERICAN
HYBRIDS
*Good choice for cold areas where Japanese cultivars are a
gamble. Disease-resistant.*

Alderman
Fruit: Large burgundy fruit with yellow flesh. Clingstone.
   Sweet-tart, soft, fine flavor.
Comments: Hardy to zone 3.

Ember
Fruit: Large gold fruit. Sweet, solid flesh.
Comments: Hardy to zone 4. Reliable bearer.

LaCrescent (La Cresent)
Fruit: Small yellow fruit with yellow flesh. Excellent sweet
   flavor. Freestone.
Comments: Vigorous, fast-growing. Hardy to zone 3.

Pipestone
Fruit: Large red fruit with golden flesh. Skin peels easily. Fine
   flavor, sweet, juicy.
Comments: Hardy to zone 3.

South Dakota
Fruit: Medium-size yellow fruit with red blush and yellow
   flesh. Sweet, fine flavor.
Comments: Productive tree. Hardy to zone 4.

Superior
Fruit: Large gold fruit with pink-red blush. Skin peels easily.
   Sweet, firm, fine-textured.
Comments: Bears at an early age. Hardy to zone 4.

Tecumseh
Fruit: Medium-size dark red fruit with yellow flesh. Sweet,
   juicy, firm.
Comments: An old cultivar from a breeding program in South
   Dakota. Hardy to zone 4.

'Opata', *a named cultivar of the native American cherry plum* Prunus cerasifera

Underwood
Fruit: Large dark red fruit with amber flesh. Sweet, mild flavor.
Comments: Bears at an early age. Ripens over an extended period. Hardy to zone 3.

Waneta
Fruit: Large yellow-red fruit with deep yellow flesh. Juicy, good flavor.
Comments: Heavy bearer. Bears at a young age. Hardy to zone 3.

Peaches and Nectarines

'Redhaven' is the standard for early-season peaches.

Few pleasures of the palate compare with the taste of a fresh, tree-ripened peach, its juice escaping down your chin after the first big bite. Peaches also make mouth-watering desserts, from crisps and cobblers to pies. They are superb sliced and sugared, then served over pound cake or ice cream. To prolong the pleasure of peaches, you can freeze or dry them, can them, or make them into preserves.

Peaches and nectarines are the same species, *Prunus persica*, differing by only a single gene. Peaches have the gene and are fuzzy; nectarines lack it and are smooth skinned. Nectarines appear naturally on peach trees, and occasionally a nectarine tree will produce "mutant" fuzzy fruit. You care for nectarines just as you would care for peaches.

Both peaches and nectarines were first cultivated by the

Chinese more than 2,000 years ago, valued initially for their lovely flowers and attractive branches. Selection improved the fruit, and the trees were introduced in other lands. In Europe they were known as "Persian apples." Spaniards brought peaches to Mexico some 400 years ago, and by the time William Penn got to Pennsylvania, he noted that "not an Indian plantation [wa]s without them."

Like the early Chinese, modern gardeners can make good use of these attractive trees in the home landscape. With delicate pink flowers in early spring and long, pointed glossy leaves through the growing season, dwarf peaches and nectarines are at home in a mixed bed or border, or planted as a backdrop for a small metal garden table and chair. Dwarf cultivars are small enough to adapt to life in a large patio tub.

Most varieties are self-pollinating, so you'll only need a single tree to get fruit. But the short-lived trees last only about 12 years. Plant a new tree or two to take the place of one that will be retiring. It takes two to three years for a newly planted tree to bear fruit.

Choose Wisely

Peaches and nectarines are prima donnas among fruit trees, demanding tolerable winter cold, warm and dry spring weather, and long, hot summers. The trees are early bloomers, their buds swelling at the first sign of spring, so they are extra-sensitive to the cold touch of a late frost. If your area is prone to unpredictable spring weather that swings between balmy and brrr, you can boost your chances of success by choosing a late-flowering variety, such as 'Harbrite', to minimize spring frost damage. You could also plant on a north- or northeast-facing slope, where the tree will be slower to bloom.

Peaches and nectarines can't take extreme winter cold, and they do best in warmer areas, such as Georgia, South Carolina, and California, where half of the commercial crop is grown. Like apples, they require a certain period of cold in order to maintain vigor, but with a number of low-chill varieties available, only in tropical south Florida do peaches and nectarines fail to thrive because of lack of winter chill. The fruits also do well in the temperate Great Lakes area and elsewhere throughout zones 6 through 9. If you live in zones 4 and 5, plant cold-hardy peaches, such as 'Reliance', though severe cold or late spring frosts may deny you a crop every now and then.

Peaches are susceptible to a slew of insects and diseases, and nectarines may be even worse. Regular preventive care is absolutely necessary. In a bad year, when wet weather encourages the spread of fungal disease or pests build to explosive populations, you may not harvest much of a crop unless you turn to chemical pesticides. On the other hand, a bad year doesn't come every season. In most years, careful monitoring and organic measures will keep your crop and your trees reasonably healthy.

There are a great many peaches and quite a few nectarines from which to choose. Consult your extension agent or a knowledgeable local or mail-order nursery person for advice on which varieties do well in local conditions (pests and diseases, in particular, can vary from place to place). Once you've narrowed the field, you can choose according to time of harvest, taste, use, and other personally appealing qualities. By planting several cultivars that ripen at different times, you can harvest peaches from mid-summer to fall.

Peaches range from from old heritage varieties like the hundred-year-old 'Belle of Georgia', a creamy white peach with superb flavor, to classic favorites like 'Redhaven', a 1940 introduction that is the standard for early peaches, and the excellent 'Elberta', the most popular peach in America. Nectarines may be lustrous red, like 'Mericrest', or an appealing red and gold, like 'Durbin'. Flavor varies from one cultivar to the next, just as with any fruit. The flesh of most peaches and nectarines is yellow, but a few are white, which aficionados consider the best for eating fresh from the tree. Some peaches and nectarines, called "freestone," relinquish their large "pit" or "stone" easily. Others, called "clingstone," put up a struggle. Still others fall between these two. Clingstone peaches are generally more desirable for cooking; their flesh is firmer and holds up better.

Tree Sizes

Grown on their own roots, peaches and nectarines will reach 8 to 20 feet in height. Most are grafted to other rootstocks to increase cold hardiness or pest and disease resistance or to control size. You can generally accept the nursery's selection of rootstock, but if your conditions tend towards the extreme, be sure to read the catalog or hangtag description of the conditions in which the rootstock thrives. 'Siberian C' rootstock may give your tree a better chance of survival in cold climates, for example. In the South, where root knot nematodes can cause serious problems, the nematode-resistant rootstock 'Nemaguard' is a popular choice.

As for most tree fruits, smaller trees are the best bet for home gardens. They are easier to care for, and problems are easier to spot before they get out of hand. Dwarfing rootstocks are used to restrict grafted trees to about 6 to 10 feet tall. Some peaches and nectarines are natural dwarfs, and these are grown on their own roots. The dwarf nectarine 'Garden Beauty' is a genetic dwarf that reaches only 4 to 6 feet tall; 'Compact Redhaven' and 'Compact Elberta' are genetic dwarf peaches that will stay pint-size.

Planting, Pruning, and Care

Much of the information you'll need on these topics is in the last three chapters; we'll provide a brief overview here. Since peaches and nectarines are treated exactly the same, we'll refer only to peaches for convenience.

The trees need a sunny site. They do best in soils that are light and loose in the topsoil layer and heavier beneath, such as loam or sandy soils, so that the crown stays dry to prevent disease problems. The soil should be moist and well drained, not excessively dry. The trees thrive at a pH level of 6.0 to about 6.5.

If your spring weather is slow and steady, without devastating late spring frosts, plant trees about halfway up a southern slope, if possible, or on the south side of your house or garden. If late spring frost is a threat, plant on the north side, to slow down buds in spring.

If you're planting more than one tree, allow as much space between the trees as their expected mature height. Plant dwarfs about 6 to 10 feet apart; standards, 8 to 20 feet apart.

Training and pruning

Peaches and nectarines are always open-center trained to make sure sunlight reaches well into the tree. Training takes two or three years, at which time the trees should be ready to bear their first crop. Peaches bear fruit only on one-year-old wood, so an established tree must be pruned every year to remove unproductive older wood and encourage a fresh flush of vegetative growth for the following season's crop.

In general, prune in late winter or early spring, when trees are dormant. If winterkill is a problem, you might prune later, when swelling buds or flowering make the extent of the damage easier to see. Choose a stretch of dry weather to prune, to avoid problems with canker. Make heading cuts (to a bud along the length of a branch) to encourage side shoots, and thinning cuts (at the base of a branch) to keep the center of the tree open.

Don't worry too much about cutting away part of your crop: peaches are generous overbearers. Even with the tree's normal self-thinning "June drop," you may need to hand-thin further to keep the burden of the crop within the limits the tree can bear. Peaches bear fruit from buds along the

The early-spring blossoms of peaches and nectarines beguiled the Chinese 2,000 years ago.

A dwarf peach tree fits nicely in the home landscape.

branches. After blooming, branches produce a new crop of fruit buds that stay dormant until the following spring. A mild fall followed by an unusually cold winter can devastate these buds. If most buds survive, the tree will bear a big crop of small fruit. If the natural June drop leaves fruits clustered or closer than 6 inches apart, thinning them provides room for development and reduces the ratio of fruit to the leaves that feed them, producing bigger fruit. How much to thin depends on the age, size, and vigor of the tree — a fruit every 6 inches is an old rule of thumb. If brown rot is a problem in your area, you'll want to thin so no two fruits touch.

Ongoing care

Peaches need regular, deep moisture, especially when the fruit is filling out. Water deeply every week if natural rainfall is scarce, and mulch heavily to conserve moisture. Peaches grow well in soil of average fertility, but the need for nutrients varies with type and cultivar, age, and conditions. Fertilizing whether a tree needs it or not can lead to soft, succulent new growth that will be killed off quickly by winter cold or attacked by aphids and other pests during the growing season. A healthy peach tree should grow about 12 to 18 inches a year. A yearly application of about 2 inches of compost around the tree should keep it growing well. If growth is significantly slower, or if you notice a yellow-green or reddish purple tint to the foliage, test your soil for nutrient deficiencies. Add fertilizer, if indicated, in early spring, so that new growth has plenty of time to harden before winter.

Harvest

Peaches and nectarines ripen in midsummer to fall, depending on the cultivar. Individual trees ripen over about a week or two; it's best to pick every three days. Harvest when the fruit is highly colored, with all green gone (unless you are growing a green-skinned fruit, such as the delectable 'Stump-the-World' peach). Ripe fruit will easily leave the branch when you give it a gentle twist. Place the fruit into the picking basket with gentle care, to avoid bruising (particularly the white-fleshed varieties). Ripe peaches and nectarines will keep for about a week in the fruit drawer of your refrigerator.

Pests and Diseases

Growing peaches and nectarines can be frustrating because of the army of pests and diseases that always seem to be on the attack. But even with so many enemies, backyard peaches still manage to produce a good crop for many home gardeners.

The trick is vigilance. A few insects are tolerable, but be alert for building populations that can cause trouble. Clip off sick foliage as soon as you see it, and always practice good house-keeping, neatening up under and around your peach tree and disposing of any fallen leaves or fruit. We've listed the most common and most troublesome of the pests and diseases below; others may be mentioned in the list of recommended cultivars if they affect a particular variety. Not all pests and diseases pose the same problem everywhere. Again, advice from experienced local experts or knowledgeable staff at a mail order supplier on what to expect and what to do about it is invaluable.

Peach leaf curl

Puckered, thickened, often reddish leaves are the first sign of this fungal disease, the major headache to peach growers in the West. Infected leaves turn yellow and fall, and fruits may have a rough surface. The disease weakens the tree by defoliating it, which cuts down on future crops.

To control peach leaf curl, apply copper or lime sulphur either in late fall, after the leaves have dropped, or in early spring, while the tree is still dormant. Plant resistant varieties, such as 'Dixired' and 'Indian Free'.

Oriental fruit moth

These insects are a problem in all areas except Texas and the the south-central states, the Pacific Northwest, and the Midwest. Wilted leaves at the tips of twigs are often the first sign of infestation, marking the place where the half-inch adult moth laid eggs. The larvae tunnel into the twig tip, killing the twig. When adult, this first generation lays their eggs on fruit, where subsequent generations of larvae (three or four in a season are common) burrow into the flesh around the pit.

To control, remove and destroy affected twig tips, cutting back to healthy wood. Ryania, an organic control, and the chemicals Imidan and Carbaryl are effective. They are best applied from mid-July through mid-August.

Peachtree borer

Also called twig borer, it is troublesome in New England, the mid-Atlantic states, and in the Pacific Northwest. Adult inch-long, clear-winged moths lay eggs near the base of the tree, and larvae climb and burrow into the trunks of apricot and other fruit trees, weakening the tree and making an en-trance for other diseases and pests. If you see sawdust or sap oozing from a hole, insert a straightened paper clip and kill the borer with a jab or two.

Plum curculio

Common throughout eastern North America, these snout-nosed, 1/3-inch-long gray or brown beetles cut the skins of peaches, plums, and other tree fruits to lay their eggs inside. The cuts create crescent-shaped scars on the peach's skin. The tiny white larvae tunnel into the flesh of the fruit.

Fruits attacked by curculios often drop prematurely; be sure to remove and destroy them as soon as possible. No organic controls are effective. The chemical Imidan is effective, applied during and after the petals fall, generally mid-May.

Brown rot

This fungal disease is especially troublesome in the South, Southeast, and other areas with hot, humid summers. The afflicted fruits rot to brown mush inside, then shrivel and drop. White and brown fungus may grow on the outside of fruit. In one of the few differences between the fruits, nectarines are even more susceptible than peaches.

If brown rot is a problem in your area, keep the fruits well thinned, so that no two touch, and remove leaves so that air can circulate freely throughout the branches. To lessen the chance of future outbreaks, collect and remove all fruit, including dropped peaches, after harvest.

Wettable suphur, applied every week and a half if weather is wet, is an effective organic treatment from full-bud stage of flowers through early September. Make the last application no later than two weeks before harvest.

Perennial canker

Found in all parts of the country except the West, perennial canker is caused by two different organisms. Both produce sunken, oozing sores (cankers) on the branches, twigs, or trunk of peaches, nectarines, and other fruit trees. The cankers may be oozing with sap or appear gummy with collected sap. Eventually, the branches will wilt and die.

The first line of defense is to plant resistant cultivars. Mechanical injury is a common entry point for the diseases. Take care when pruning and when mowing or weed whacking near the trunk. Coat any wounds with a mix of lime-sulfur and white latex paint to minimize disease vulnerability. Immediately prune off branches with any sign of disease.

Bacterial leaf spot

Common in the East, this bacteria-spread disease infects both the leaves and fruit of peaches and other fruit trees. The first symptom is water-soaked black or brown spots on the undersides of the leaves. The spot may fall out of the leaf, leaving a hole outlined in red. Severely infected leaves drop, weakening the tree and possibly reducing the size of the fruit as photosynthesis is restricted. When bacterial spot infects the fruit, the flesh appears sunken in spots or the skin may crack.

There is no sure cure. Maintain good hygiene, remove any affected leaves or fruit immediately, and plant resistant varieties if bacterial spot is prevalent in your area. Apply copper or lime sulphur in late autumn after leaf fall or in early spring before buds break. Lime sulfur also controls leaf curl and fungal diseases.

■ Recommended Varieties of Peaches
Best in zones 6–8 unless stated otherwise.

Very Early

Desert Gold
Fruit, appearance: Medium-size, yellow fruit.
Fruit, flesh: Firm, yellow. Semifreestone.
Comments: Best in zones 8 and 9. Good for desert areas. Low chill: 200–300 hrs.

Earligrande
Fruit, appearance: Large, yellow fruit with red blush.
Fruit, flesh: Medium-firm, yellow. Semiclingstone.
Comments: Vigorous tree. Good for southern Texas. Low chill: 200–275 hrs.

Early Redhaven
Fruit, appearance: Medium-size, beautiful bright red.
Fruit, flesh: Firm, yellow. Semiclingstone.
Comments: Early 'Redhaven' type. Excellent choice for areas with 950 chill hours. Resists bacterial leaf spot.

Golden Monarch
Fruit, appearance: Medium-size red fruit.
Fruit, flesh: Firm yellow flesh. Semiclingstone (freestone when fully ripe). Flesh resists browning when cut.
Comments: Good for canning and freezing.

Springold
Fruit, appearance: Yellow with red striping and blush.
Fruit, flesh: Fairly firm, yellow. Clingstone.
Comments: Very hardy, through zone 5.

Early

Fairhaven
Fruit, appearance: Large golden fruit with red blush, light fuzz.
Fruit, flesh: Firm, yellow with red at pit. Freestone.
Comments: Hardy to zone 5. Productive.

Florida King (Flordaking)
Fruit, appearance: Large yellow fruit with red blush.
Fruit, flesh: Firm, yellow. Clingstone.
Comments: Excellent fruit. Vigorous tree. Outstanding for Deep South (only 150 chill hrs.). Hardy in zones 8 and 9.

Florida Prince (Flordaprince)
Fruit, appearance: Medium-large yellow fruit, striped and blushes with red.
Fruit, flesh: Firm, yellow. Clingstone or semiclingstone.
Comments: Vigorous, productive tree. Excellent for desert, Deep South. Only 150 chill hrs.

Garnet Beauty
Fruit, appearance: Medium to large lovely red fruit, almost fuzzless.
Fruit, flesh: Firm, yellow streaked with red. Semifreestone.
Comments: Fruit will be good size and color even if pruning is neglected. Good for north, hardy to zone 5. Resists split pits. Susceptible to bacterial leaf spot.

Golden Jubilee
Fruit, appearance: Medium to large with mottled red skin.
Fruit, flesh: Tender, yellow. Freestone.
Comments: Old favorite. Excellent flavor, good for all uses. Widely adapted and cold-hardy in zone 5. Self-thinning.

Hale Haven
Fruit, appearance: Large orangish yellow fruit with red blush.
Fruit, flesh: Sweet, juicy yellow flesh. Freestone.
Comments: Dependable, high-yielding tree.

Harbelle
Fruit, appearance: Golden fruit with red blush.
Fruit, flesh: Yellow. Semifreestone. Resists browning when cut.
Comments: Good quality fruit. Good in areas with late spring frosts.

Harbrite
Fruit, appearance: Medium-size red fruit.
Fruit, flesh: Yellow. Freestone.
Comments: Vigorous, very productive tree. Good in areas with late spring frosts.

Harken
Fruit, appearance: Medium-size red fruit, almost fuzzless.
Fruit, flesh: Yellow. Freestone.
Comments: Good for areas with late spring frosts.

Newhaven
Fruit, appearance: Medium-size, red.
Fruit, flesh: Firm, yellow. Freestone.
Comments: Strong, productive tree.

Redhaven (Red Haven)
Fruit, appearance: Medium-size, beautiful red.
Fruit, flesh: Firm, yellow. Freestone.
Comments: Benchmark for early-season cultivars. Vigorous tree, outstanding fruit. Bears at a young age. Thinning essential.

Redhaven Compact (Com-Pact Redhaven)
Fruit, appearance: Medium to large fruit, almost fuzzless.
Fruit, flesh: Firm, yellow. Freestone.
Comments: Naturally small, genetic dwarf tree. Hardy in zones 5–8.

Reliance
Fruit, appearance: Medium-size yellow fruit with red blush.
Fruit, flesh: Medium-soft, yellow. Freestone.
Comments: Extraordinarily hardy, to -25°F. Bears young. Fast-growing.

Sunhaven (Sun Haven)
Fruit, appearance: Large bright red fruit with short fuzz.
Fruit, flesh: Firm, yellow. Freestone. Fruit resists browning when cut.
Comments: Vigorous, reliable crops. Good in all areas with 950 chill hours.

Ventura
Fruit, appearance: Medium-size yellow fruit with red blush.
Fruit, flesh: Firm, yellow. Freestone.
Comments: Good for southern California and coastal areas.

Veteran
Fruit, appearance: Medium to large yellow fruit with slight blush, medium fuzz. Easy to peel.
Fruit, flesh: Soft, yellow. Freestone.
Comments: One of the most cold-hardy (zone 5). Excellent in cool, wet climates. Good for Pacific Northwest.

Midseason

Belle of Georgia (Georgia Belle)
Fruit, appearance: Medium-size, creamy white fruit with red blush.
Fruit, flesh: Firm, white. Clingstone.
Comments: Superb flavor. Vigorous, very hardy tree. Does well in zones 5–8. Old cultivar from Georgia, circa 1870. Susceptible to brown rot.

Brighton
Fruit, appearance: Medium-size, red fruit.
Fruit, flesh: Medium-firm, yellow. Semifreestone.
Comments: Vigorous tree. Resistant to canker.

Candor
Fruit, appearance: Small to medium-size red fruit with some yellow.
Fruit, flesh: Medium-firm, yellow. Semifreestone. Resists browning when cut.
Comments: Productive tree. 350–900 chill hrs. Resistant to bacterial spot.

Champion
Fruit, appearance: Large, red fruit.
Fruit, flesh: Tender, white. Freestone.
Comments: Hardy, vigorous tree. Best in zones 5–8. Top white peach for commercial use; excellent in home gardens.

Dixired
Fruit, appearance: Round, deep red fruit.
Fruit, flesh: Juicy, yellow. Clingstone.
Comments: Productive, bears well when young. Resistant to peach-leaf curl.

Early Elberta (Improved Early Elberta, Kim Early Elberta)
Fruit, appearance: Large yellow fruit with red blush.

Fruit, flesh: Yellow. Freestone.

Comments: Wonderful flavor. Vigorous tree hardy to zone 5; does well through cooler areas of zone 9. 500–750 chill hrs.

Hale

Fruit, appearance: Jumbo fruit, deep red, almost fuzzless.

Fruit, flesh: Firm, yellow. Freestone.

Comments: Delicious fruit, good for all uses. Widely adapted, very hardy; good in zones 5–8. Needs pollinator. Susceptible to leaf curl, brown rot, oriental fruit moth, peach twig borer.

Nectar

Fruit, appearance: Medium to large creamy-colored fruit with red blush.

Fruit, flesh: Tender, white. Freestone.

Comments: Very vigorous tree. Susceptible to leaf curl, oriental fruit moth, brown rot, peach twig borer.

Ranger

Fruit, appearance: Medium to large fruit with red blush.

Fruit, flesh: Medium-firm, yellow. Freestone.

Comments: Vigorous, prolific tree. Good choice in areas with late spring frosts.

Raritan Rose

Fruit, appearance: Large, bright red fruit.

Fruit, flesh: Tender, white. Freestone.

Comments: Exceptional fruit. Vigorous, bud-hardy tree. Resistant to canker and bacterial leaf spot.

Late

Angelus

Fruit, appearance: Large yellow and red fruit.

Fruit, flesh: Firm yellow flesh. Freestone.

Comments: Vigorous tree.

Elberta

Fruit, appearance: Large, golden fruit with red blush.

Fruit, flesh: Yellow. Freestone.

Comments: The standard for late-season peaches. Hardy through zone 5; grows well through zone 9. Resistant to brown rot.

'Elberta', America's most popular peach, is harvested late season.

Fay Elberta (Gold Medal)
Fruit, appearance: Large, golden fruit with red blush.
Fruit, flesh: Yellow. Freestone.
Comments: May need thinning. Popular all-purpose freestone peach in California.

Indian Free
Fruit, appearance: Large, dark red fruit.
Fruit, flesh: Dark crimson flesh. Clingstone.
Comments: High yields. Hardy to zone 5. Resistant to peach-leaf curl. Susceptible to brown rot, peach twig borer, oriental fruit moth.

Redskin
Fruit, appearance: Large red fruit.
Fruit, flesh: Firm, yellow. Freestone. Resists browning when cut.
Comments: Superb fruit for all uses. Extra-vigorous tree must be kept well pruned. Prolific. Moderate resistance to bacterial leaf spot.

Stump-the-World
Fruit, appearance: Pale green with red blush.
Fruit, flesh: Tender, white. Freestone.
Comments: Very old variety (New Jersey, 1876). Unappealing skin color, but delicious.

Sunapee
Fruit, appearance: Yellow, medium to large fruit.
Fruit, flesh: Yellow. Freestone.
Comments: Hardy to zone 5.

■ RECOMMENDED VARIETIES OF NECTARINES
More susceptible to pests and diseases than peaches. Best in zone 6–8 unless stated otherwise.

Durbin
Fruit, appearance: Large red and gold fruit.
Fruit, flesh: Yellow. Semifreestone.
Comments: Hardy in zones 5–9. Midseason. Better disease resistance than most cultivars.

Fantasia
Fruit, appearance: Large, red with yellow fruit.
Fruit, flesh: Yellow. Freestone.
Comments: Smaller tree. Vigorous, productive. 500–600 chill hrs. Mid- to late season. Susceptible to leaf curl, brown rot, oriental fruit moth, bacterial leaf spot.

Flavortop
Fruit, appearance: Medium to large mostly red fruit.
Fruit, flesh: Yellow. Freestone.
Comments: Hardy only in zones 8–9. Vigorous, prolific. Early season. Susceptible to bacterial leaf spot.

Garden Beauty
Fruit, appearance: Yellow, medium-size fruit.
Fruit, flesh: Yellow. Clingstone.
Comments: Genetic dwarf; reaches 4–6 ft. 500–600 chill hrs. Late season. Susceptible to leaf curl.

Garden Delight

Fruit, appearance: Large, yellow fruit blushed red.
Fruit, flesh: Yellow. Freestone.
Comments: Genetic dwarf reaches 4–6 ft. 500–600 chill hrs. Prolific. Midseason. Hardy to zone 5, but thrives through zone 9.

Goldmine

Fruit, appearance: Small to medium-size red fruit.
Fruit, flesh: White. Freestone.
Comments: Vigorous, prolific. 400–500 chill hrs. Midseason. Good in California and western Oregon.

Hardired

Fruit, appearance: Medium-size red fruit.
Fruit, flesh: Yellow. Freestone.
Comments: Overabundant fruit must be thinned. Midseason. Extremely hardy, to almost -30°F (zone 5). Grows well to zone 8. Resistant to brown rot and bacterial leaf spot.

June Glo

Fruit, appearance: Medium to large red fruit.
Fruit, flesh: Yellow. Clingstone to semiclingstone.
Comments: Superb fruit. Early season. Good for late-frost areas. Moderately resistant to bacterial leaf spot. Susceptible to leaf curl, brown rot, oriental fruit moth.

Mericrest

Fruit, appearance: Medium-size dark red fruit.
Fruit, flesh: Yellow. Freestone.
Comments: The hardiest cultivar, to -20°F (zone 5), through zone 8. Mid- to late season. Resistant to brown rot and bacterial leaf spot.

Pocahontas

Fruit, appearance: Medium to large red fruit.
Fruit, flesh: Yellow. Freestone.
Comments: Vigorous, productive. Very early season. Resistant to brown rot.

Red Chief

Fruit, appearance: Large, red fruit.
Fruit, flesh: White. Freestone.
Comments: Late season. Resistant to brown rot.

'Red Chief', a white-fleshed nectarine, is harvested late season.

Red Gold

Fruit, appearance: Large to very large, red fruit.

Fruit, flesh: Yellow. Freestone.

Comments: Vigorous, prolific. Late season. Hardy to zone 5; thrives through zone 8. Crack-resistant. Susceptible to mildew.

Sunglo

Fruit, appearance: Large, red with yellow fruit.

Fruit, flesh: Yellow. Semiclingstone.

Comments: Good in zones 5–8. Midseason. "Sun" prefix indicates cultivar developed by the University of Florida.

Sunred (Sun Red)

Fruit, appearance: Medium-size red and yellow.

Fruit, flesh: Red and yellow. Semifreestone.

Comments: Best in warm-winter areas. Good choice for the Deep South. Good in Florida. 150–500 chill hrs. Early season.

Apricots

Planted near the street on a suburban lot, the apricot 'Flora Gold' is fruitful, useful, and ornamental.

Apricots are sensuous fruits, velvety soft, heavy in the hand, their golden cheeks suffused with red. The firm flesh yields easily from the stony pit, making a mouthful of delicious sweetness. Almost any garden has room for an apricot tree. Asking only a few hours of care a year, that single tree can give you enough fruit for a winter's worth of cobblers and preserves. "Seeds of the sun," the Persians named the apricot, and every jar of translucent preserves seems to hold the secret of summer.

Gardeners should take advantage of the apricot's ornamental qualities as well as its fruit. The delicate, sweet-scented flowers have long inspired artists and poets. The small, round-headed trees throw a pool of shade and are easy to maintain. Shelter a garden bench beneath a pair of apricot trees, slip a young tree into a bed of chionodoxa and other early spring bulbs, or train a fan-shaped espalier against a wall.

Apricots are a good choice for planting in cities and other areas where smog is a problem, because they are less affected than other plants by two common pollutants, ozone and peroxyacetyl (PAN), produced by sun on smog. These pollutants cause discolored foliage and early leaf drop in many woody plants, and they can also retard growth.

Climate Caveats

The delights of apricots come at a price. First of the fruit trees to bloom, apricots are truly precocious. Their buds swell at the earliest breath of warm air, and before you know it, the bare branches are studded with pink or white blossoms. Unfortunately, in much of North America, spring is capricious, teasing with a week of gentle warmth, then retreating before another blast of frigid air.

Late frosts are cruel to the eager-to-bloom apricot. Swelling buds or blossoms are devastated by frost and cold, and no flowers means no fruit. If the trees have had an even bigger headstart and have already set fruit, a sudden cold snap can drop the crop overnight. (Frost isn't the only danger. Unseasonably damp or chilly weather can ground honeybees and other flying pollinators attracted to the early blossoms, leading to a reduced harvest.)

In mild areas such as California, where most of the commercial crop is raised, apricots are in no danger. Many cultivars require only a short period of winter dormancy with little chilling, perfect for areas with long growing seasons and mild winters. Likewise favored are cold regions where winter holds a firm grip until late in the season. There, hardy apricot varieties stay safely dormant, waiting for the slow, measured arrival of spring before they bloom. Climate-right cultivars for cold regions can take temperatures as low as -30°F.

It's in the in-between areas, where the only predictable thing about spring weather is its unpredictability, that harvesting a crop can be a gamble. If your spring weather is fickle, think about growing an apricot tree for its considerable ornamental appeal, and count any fruit a bonus. Most years, you'll get to enjoy at least a sampling of the frothy pink or white blossoms; some years you'll be rewarded with fruit.

From Spain to California, Siberia to Minnesota

Native to Asia and cultivated there for at least 4,000 years, apricots *(Prunus armeniaca)* were long ago brought to the sun-baked warmth of the Mediterranean, where European plant breeders tinkered with the species to produce the familiar large, orange-fleshed fruits we enjoy today. Spanish priests heading for California in the 16th and 17th centuries tucked the pits of some of those selected varieties into their belongings and before long European apricot trees were sprouting around the adobe missions, where they thrived in the mild winters and long, warm summers.

Nearly all of the apricots grown in America today are European apricots *(P. armeniaca* var. *armeniaca),* but that statistic is heavily weighted by the dominance of the California apricot industry, which depends on Europeans. A count of backyard trees, especially in cold-winter areas, might reveal a more even balance between the familiar European and their small, tough, cold-hardy Siberian and Manchurian relatives more recently introduced in North America.

European apricots

Small trees, reaching up to 30 feet tall at maturity, European apricots have a neat, round-headed silhouette. They do well wherever peaches grow, generally from zone 6 through zone 9. Selected cultivars vary in their tolerance for cold — and for heat. The warmth and wetness of a humid summer can take as heavy a toll as a hard winter. Fungal diseases, such as brown rot, proliferate in humid climates, making disease resistance a top priority for gardeners in those areas.

Seedlings on their own roots are sometimes available, but they vary widely in quality. Most gardeners buy grafted nursery stock. A variety of rootstocks, including apricot (both European and the hardier Manchurian), peach, and plum are used as a base for grafted apricot trees. Rootstocks affect growth rate and survival, as well as the ease of maintenance and harvest. A plum rootstock, for example, has a greater tolerance of heavy soil than apricot roots and is a good choice for gardeners with clay soil. Apricot rootstocks may hold some edge in promoting vigor.

Rootstocks with a dwarfing effect are common and popular. Dwarf (4 to 8 feet tall) and semidwarf (10 to 20 feet) trees take up less space, and picking and pruning a shorter tree is easier than dragging out the ladder to maintain a standard. Some downsizing occurs naturally. 'Goldcot', 'Puget Gold', and 'Harglow' are genetic semidwarfs that reach about 15 to 18 feet tall. 'Aprigold' is a naturally occurring genetic dwarf that stays at 4 to 6 feet tall even when grafted to standard, nondwarfing rootstocks.

Unless you garden in extreme conditions, such as very sandy soil or waterlogged clay, you need not worry about selecting the "right" rootstock. Suppliers of fruit trees want you to be successful at home fruit growing, so they graft their cultivars to rootstocks that grow well in most garden conditions. In nearly all cases, you can rely on the nursery to have chosen a suitable rootstock.

If you think your conditions may be marginal for successful apricot growing, it's a good idea to check with your county extension agent for advice. In very light soils, for example, you will be better off with a drought-tolerant rootstock, and one that is "well anchored," so that its roots will spread wide and deep to hold the tree solidly in the light soil. In these conditions, the commonly used Manchurian bush apricot rootstock is a good choice.

Your county agent will also be aware of any disease problems in your area that make particular rootstocks more desirable than others. Tomato spot virus, for example, which can affect fruit trees as well as tomatoes, is sometimes problematic in areas of New England and in the Great Lakes states. If you are in a virus-prone region, it would make sense to boost your chances by planting an apricot on 'Marianna 2624' rootstock, which has shown resistance to this (and other) diseases.

Asian apricots

In the 1930s, two small, tough, cold-hardy apricots arrived in America: the Siberian apricot *(Prunus armeniaca* var. *sibirica)*, and the Manchurian apricot *(P. armeniaca* var. *manshurica)*. Both are often referred to as Asian or Russian apricots. They resemble the European variety in their flowers and fruit but are shorter, reaching only 6 to 15 feet tall, and shrubby rather than treelike in habit. Asian apricots are usually grown on their own roots rather than grafted to a rootstock. They are reliably cold-hardy to zone 5, and a few particularly hardy selections can be grown to zone 4.

These trees are tailor-made for northern gardeners outside the range of European apricots. Their ancestry gives them the genetic gumption to withstand long, severe winters. They bloom, however, just as early as the European types, or even earlier, and their blossoms are just as easily damaged by unexpected cold following a warm spell. They are a poor choice for late-frost areas, and they languish in humid regions, showing a distinct susceptibility to rot, blight, and other fungal diseases.

Fruits are 1 to 2 inches in size, and the taste can vary from a delicious sweetness to mouth-puckering sour. The Manchurian holds more promise than the Siberian, which has poor quality fruit. Several Manchurian cultivars have been developed, including 'Sungold' and 'Moongold', a pair of selections from the University of Minnesota.

'Moongold', *a disease-free Manchurian apricot, does well in cold-winter areas.*

When grown as specimens or orchard trees, Asian apricots take more work than Europeans. Their shrubby habit means regular pruning is necessary to open the interior to light and air. On the other hand, the plants might also be used as a loose, low-maintenance hedge, with a bonus of flowers and fruit when weather permits.

Hybrids of Manchurian and European apricots, and selected Asian cultivars, show a wide range of plant habit. The selection 'Brookcot' is a tall, upright tree that branches poorly; the hybrid 'Sunrise' is bushy and compact. Read catalog descriptions carefully if the size and shape of your tree are important considerations.

What Apricot Should I Grow?

Commercial growers separate apricots into canning, preserves, and fresh-market types, depending on the taste, color, and keeping qualities of the fruit, and some cultivars for the home garden are targeted for the same uses.

Those differences don't matter, though, if you never get to harvest a piece of fruit. Almost any homegrown apricot will taste better than one that is store-bought, so choose cultivars for their suitability to your climate and for their disease resistance, then narrow your choices according to the use you intend. If, for example, you garden where summers are humid, you might choose the cultivar 'Hargrand', which resists brown rot, a common problem in steamy areas. If your winters are brutal, try 'Sungold' or 'Moongold', a couple of the many cultivars bred for cold tolerance. The large-fruited 'Perfection' is a good choice for mild-winter gardens. 'Puget Gold' sets fruit in cool, cloudy spring weather when others fail.

Some general rules regarding choices affected by climate are given in the box below. The list of recommended varieties, beginning on page 126, also notes the tolerance of climatic conditions and susceptibility to disease. It's always a good idea to consult with your agricultural extension agent or fruit specialist about which cultivars perform well in your area. If you can, buy trees grown at a nearby regional nursery; stock raised in British Columbia may not be adapted to conditions in New York. (Make sure the trees were raised at the nursery, not just shipped in from another region.) If you rely on mail-order catalogs, be sure to read descriptions carefully, looking for clues in the words ("early blooming," "late blooming," "cold-hardy") as well as between the lines (if it doesn't say "disease-resistant," it probably isn't).

When you've narrowed the list of cultivars to those that fit the bill for climate and disease resistance, you can weigh other factors in your choice. As a rule, apricots are fast growing and relatively short-lived. Europeans begin to bear at

Are winters mild and short?
Choose European cultivars with low chilling requirements.

Are winters cold and long?
Choose cold-hardy cultivars with Asian parentage.

Are summers hot and humid?
Choose disease-resistant cultivars.

Are springs cool and cloudy?
Choose cultivars like 'Puget Gold' that are good pollinators; plant more than one tree.

Is late spring frost after an early warm-up a distinct possibility?
Choose late-blooming cultivars.

about four to five years old; Asians may bear as young as age three. Even a young tree can bear several pounds of fruit, and an established standard cultivar can yield three to four bushels. Some apricot cultivars need two trees for cross-pollination, but many are self-fruitful. Read catalog nursery descriptions carefully so that you know which kind you are buying.

The tree's mature size is an important consideration, particularly if your space is limited. A standard-size tree will usually live for about 35 years. Genetic dwarfs such as 'Aprigold' and semidwarfs such as 'Goldcot' are generally as long-lived as standard-size trees. Most modern grafted dwarf cultivars, grown on rootstocks such as the peach-plum hybrid 'Citation', live nearly as long as standard-size trees.

When selecting a cultivar, you might consider fruit taste or size. Apricot fruit varies in size depending on the stock and the growing conditions. Many old "heirloom" trees of uncertain lineage receive little or no care and bear enormous quantities of small, $1^1/_2$-inch fruits, though only in alternate years. Most modern European cultivars for the home gardener in zone 6 or warmer regions bear reliable annual crops of fruit that is 2 inches or more in size, like a good-size plum but slightly flattened. Taste varies from the melting sweetness of cultivars such as 'Alfred' to the refreshing, slightly tangy 'Goldcot'. A few cultivars, including 'Hargrand' and 'Moorpark', bear oversize fruit as big as peaches. Cold-hardy Siberian and Manchurian apricots bear annual crops of small, plump fruit that varies in flavor from sweet ('Sungold') to decidedly tart ("Manchurian bush apricot" and other species seedlings).

Planting

Apricots are usually sold as one-year-old trees, about 3 to 5 feet tall. Those from mail-order sources are commonly shipped dormant and bare-root. Apricot trees at garden centers and nurseries may be sold bare-root but are frequently offered in containers and occasionally balled-and-burlapped, either dormant or in growth. (See the chapter "Planting Fruit Trees and Bushes" for a detailed discussion of planting trees.)

Choose a spot where the tree will receive full sun but be protected from prevailing winter winds, which can dry out or freeze the buds. If late-spring frosts are a problem in your area, plant the tree on a north-facing site to help postpone flowering. Apricots are vulnerable to verticillium wilt, a widespread disease of tomatoes and some other common plants. Avoid planting near brambles and strawberries and on sites where tomatoes, potatoes, and other nightshades have grown.

Deep, loose soil of average fertility is ideal. Apricots grow well in light soils if grafted onto peach or apricot rootstocks. Those grafted to plum rootstocks will also tolerate heavier soils. Good drainage is an absolute must. If you plant where water pools after a rain, you have signed the tree's death warrant. Avoid the temptation to lighten heavy soils by filling the planting hole with peat moss and other amendments; this just creates a sponge that soaks up rainwater and holds it in the root zone. If your soil is too heavy for good drainage, plant a dwarf variety in a wooden half-barrel or other large container.

If you are planting more than one tree, situate them with as much space between the trees as their expected height at maturity. In other words, plant dwarfs about 6 feet apart, semidwarfs about 15 feet, standards about 25. If a pollinator tree is needed, plant the trees side by side (at the recommended spacing) not on opposite sides of the garden.

Apricots also make good espalier subjects, especially when their ethereal pink or white blossoms and stark, bare-barked branches are highlighted against a brick or masonry wall. Train them in a simple fan shape. Where spring weather is unsettled, avoid espaliering an apricot against a south-facing wall; the added heat will only aggravate the early-blooming problem.

A low-care fruiting hedge of Manchurian or Siberian apricots may encourage visits from birds and other wildlife. Opossums, raccoons, and foxes may sample the fruit, and thrushes, tanagers, and orioles, among others, may be drawn to the bounty. Butterflies may come to eat overripe fruit, and you should be aware that yellowjackets and other wasps will also be attracted.

Training and Pruning

Standard and semidwarf apricots can be trained in the modified central-leader style, to keep the tree down to size and to open the interior to light and air. (See the chapter "Pruning for Fruits and Berries" for details.) But numerous backyard apricots have borne reliable crops without ever feeling the teeth of a pruning saw. Because many apricot varieties tend to grow in a strongly upright direction, you may want to keep fruit in easy reach by spreading young branches with a clothespin, as described in "Pruning for Fruits and Berries."

Most apricots are formed on one- to three-year-old fruiting spurs. These short, stubby branchlets produce fruit for only a few years, but new spurs are constantly forming from lateral buds on last year's growth, especially if branching has been encouraged by light pruning every year (or every few years) to thin out spent fruiting spurs. Asian apricots that retain their shrubby habit should be thinned, with branches removed to the trunk, to allow good air circulation. Prune all apricots just after flowering, when the still-leafless branches allow a good view. Pruning in winter or early spring, before flowering, will encourage early bloom.

Caring for Apricots

Apricots are one of the easiest fruit trees to maintain. But a few light chores performed each year will help keep your trees in good health.

Apricots need well-drained soil, but they are sensitive to drought. Water the trees deeply and often, at least once a week if rains are scarce, from the time of full bloom until you have harvested the fruit. The shoots of a well-watered, well-nourished apricot tree will grow about 15 to 20 inches a year. If growth is significantly less, even with generous watering, your soil may need a boost in fertility. You can spread a layer of well-rotted manure, about 1 to 2 inches thick, around the tree, or you can use packaged fertilizers. Apply enough fertilizer to equal a rate of about 1/4 pound actual nitrogen per tree. (See the chapter "Ongoing Care" for how to determine the amount of packaged fertilizer you'll need.) Apply all fertilizers in early spring, so that the new growth that is encouraged by the boost in fertility has plenty of time to harden before winter.

If spring weather is unreliable, pay attention to weather forecasts; a simple preventive measure may help ward off crop failure, at least in smaller trees. When frost or cold threatens, you can use a light blanket or sheet to provide some overnight protection. Weight the corners of the covering with stones (use rubberbands to hold the weights in place at the corners), then lift or fling the cover over the budding or flowering tree. Remove the cover as soon as the air warms the following morning.

Harvesting Fruit

If late spring frost hasn't robbed you of a crop, the fruit will be ready for harvest in midsummer, before most peaches and usually after sweet cherries — from early July through mid-August, depending on the cultivar and your location. You can even pick fruit in September from an unusual fall-ripening cultivar, 'Autumn Royal'.

Apricots are ready for picking when all traces of green have disappeared. Older varieties and seedling-grown trees (those growing on their own roots) often drop their ripe fruit all at once, but newer cultivars wait for you to pluck the fruit from the tree. A tree's fruit ripens over a period of about a week and a half. Be careful not to damage or pull off the spur, so that it can bear again next year. A slight upward twist will free the fruit quickly.

Many apricots are blushed with red, though some are a clear golden yellow color and others have spots or freckles of red. You can gauge their ripeness with a sniff and a squeeze — when they're ready to eat, the fruits yield to gentle thumb pressure, and they smell delicious. Taste a sample before you harvest the crop. The fruit will keep for a week or two in the refrigerator.

Apricot fruits are not overly juicy, so they're much neater for eating fresh than, say, peaches. The taste is sweet, with a tart edge, and somewhat plumlike, but the texture is drier and meatier. Most apricots are freestone; the meaty orange flesh slips away easily from the pit when the fruit is bitten or split in half. 'Harcot' and a few other cultivars show a tendency to cling to the stone. If you're planning to can or dry your harvest, be sure to select a freestone cultivar for easy processing.

Apricots are close kin to the almond, and you can eat pit and all of some specially developed cultivars. The apricot (or "alpricot") 'Stark Sweetheart', for example, bears fruits with large, sweet, edible pits inside the stony heart.

Controlling Pests and Diseases

Apricots are susceptible to a few troublesome insect pests and diseases, which vary by location. Most apricot pests and diseases do not kill the tree outright, but they can damage the fruit. Some pests cause unsightly holes or ruined flesh, while other problems can decrease the harvest. The most common problems and their treatments are identified below; for further information on pest control strategies, see the chapter "Ongoing Care."

Many home growers find out that they can harvest plenty of delectable apricots by doing no more than starting with disease-resistant stock and practicing good housekeeping. Ask your county extension agent for help choosing cultivars that are resistant to diseases and pests prevalent in your region. Promptly remove fallen fruit and dropped leaves. Snip out any diseased twigs or misshapen fruits when you notice them.

Plum curculio

These snout-nosed gray beetles cut the skins of tree fruits to lay their eggs inside. The crescent-shaped scars are unappealing cosmetically, and the developing larvae feed on the flesh of the fruit. Plum curculio can be a problem in all areas except California, the Rocky Mountain states, and the Pacific Northwest.

Fruits attacked by curculios often drop prematurely; remove and destroy them. No organic controls are effective. The chemical Imidan is effective, applied during and after the petals fall, generally mid-May.

Oriental fruit moth

Wilted leaves at the tips of twigs are often the first sign of infestation, marking the place where the half-inch adult moth laid eggs. The larvae tunnel into the twig tip, killing the twig. When adult, this first generation lays their eggs on fruit, where subsequent generations of larvae (three or four are common) burrow into the flesh around the pit.

Oriental fruit moths are widespread; they can be troublesome in all areas except Texas and the south-central states, the Pacific Northwest, and the Midwest.

Remove affected twig tips, cutting back to healthy wood. Ryania, an organic control, and the chemicals Imidan and Carbaryl are effective against oriental fruit moth. They are best applied from mid-July through mid-August.

Peachtree borer

Adult moths lay eggs near the base of the tree, and larvae climb and burrow into the trunks of apricot and other fruit trees, weakening the tree and making an entrance for other diseases and pests. If you see sawdust or sap oozing from a hole, insert a straightened paper clip to kill the borer.

Peachtree borers can be troublesome in New England and the mid-Atlantic states and in the Pacific Northwest. Hand removal by digging out the larva or stabbing it with an inserted wire are effective controls.

Brown rot

This fungal disease is especially troublesome in areas with hot, humid summers, including the South and Southeast. The afflicted fruits rot to brown mush inside, then shrivel and drop. White and brown fungus may grow on the fruit's skin.

If brown rot is a problem in your area, keep the fruits well-thinned, so that no two touch, and remove leaves so that air can circulate freely throughout the branches. To lessen the chance of future outbreaks, collect and remove all fruit, including dropped apricots, after harvest.

Wettable suphur, applied every week and a half if weather is wet, is an effective organic treatment from full-bud stage of flowers through early September. Make the last application no sooner than two weeks before harvest.

Verticillium wilt

Sudden wilting of an apricot tree may indicate infection by this fungal disease. Verticillium wilt can be avoided to some extent, but it cannot be cured. Be sure planting site is well drained; the fungus flourishes in wet soils. The disease also affects tomatoes, eggplant, peppers, potatoes, raspberries, and strawberries, and the disease-causing spores can survive in the soil for years. Avoid planting apricot trees where other susceptible plants have grown.

Verticillium wilt is widespread, and there is no effective control; plant resistant varieties.

Bacterial spot

Most common in the East, this disease is spread by bacteria that infect both leaves and fruit of apricots and other fruit trees. The first symptom is water-soaked black or brown spots on the undersides of the leaves. The spot may fall out of the leaf, leaving a hole outlined in red. Severely infected leaves drop, weakening the tree and possibly reducing the size of the fruit, as photosynthesis is restricted. When bacterial spot infects the fruit, the flesh appears sunken in spots or the skin may crack.

There is no sure cure for this disease. Maintain good hygiene, remove any affected leaves or fruit immediately, and plant resistant varieties if bacterial spot is prevalent in where you live.

■ RECOMMENDED VARIETIES OF APRICOTS

European Apricots

Aprigold
Fruit: Good-tasting, full-size fruit.
Zone/Tree Size: Zone 5; genetic dwarf.
Comments: Good small tree for cold-winter areas. Not recommended in coastal areas.

Autumn Royal
Fruit: Medium-size fruit.
Zone/Tree Size: Zone 5.
Comments: Self-pollinating. Only fall-ripening apricot; harvest in September. Good for canning or drying.

Blenheim (Royal)
Fruit: Medium to large fruit, freestone. Very sweet, juicy.
Zone/Tree Size: Zone 5.
Comments: Self-pollinating; good pollinator cultivar. Excellent

'Blenheim'

for canning. Early blooming. Standard California commercial variety.

Early Gold (Early Golden, Earligold)
Fruit: Highly flavored.
Zone/Tree Size: Zone 5.
Comments: Self-pollinating, but higher yield with a pollinator. Early-bearing tree, best where late frosts aren't a problem. Good for South and Southwest.

Floragold (Flora Gold)
Fruit: Full-size fruit, freestone.
Zone/Tree Size: Zone 6; genetic semidwarf.
Comments: Self-pollinating. About half the size of a standard tree. Fruit ripens early.

Harcot
Fruit: Firm, sweet fruit, somewhat clingstone. Edible kernels.
Zone/Tree Size: Zone 5.
Comments: Good in areas with late spring frosts or humid summers. Resistant to perennial canker, bacterial spot, and brown rot. Cultivars beginning with "Har" were developed at Harrow Research Station in Canada.

Harglow
Fruit: Sweet, firm, freestone.
Zone/Tree Size: Zone 6; genetic semidwarf.
Comments: Late-blooming. Resistant to perennial canker and, moderately, bacterial spot. Good for areas with late spring frosts or humid summers.

Hargrand
Fruit: Firm, freestone fruit, big as peaches.
Zone/Tree Size: Zone 6.
Comments: Resistant to brown rot, bacterial spot, and perennial canker. Good in areas with late spring frosts or humid summers.

Harval
Fruit: Large, freestone fruit.
Zone/Tree Size: Zone 6 (5 with protection).
Comments: Late-blooming. Disease-resistant to perennial canker, bacterial spot, and brown rot. Good for areas with late spring frosts or humid summers.

Henderson
Fruit: Large yellow fruit with red blush.
Zone/Tree Size: Zone 5.
Comments: Prolific. Good in north.

Moorpark
Fruit: Very large fruit, good flavor.
Zone/Tree Size: Zone 4; genetic dwarf, 8–10 ft. tall.
Comments: Vigorous, very hardy. Self-pollinating, but increased fruit set with pollinator.

Nugget
Fruit: Large fruit, good color and flavor.
Zone/Tree Size: Zone 8.
Comments: Only for mild-winter areas. Low chilling requirement.

Puget Gold
Fruit: Excellent flavor.
Zone/Tree Size: Zone 7; natural semidwarf.
Comments: Easy pollinating cultivar, good in cloudy coastal areas. Some disease resistance.

Royal Rosa
Fruit: Sweet, firm fruit.
Zone/Tree Size: Zone 6.
Comments: Self-pollinating. Bears young, very vigorous. Disease-tolerant.

Snowball
Fruit: White flesh, white skin with red blush.
Zone/Tree Size: Zone 8.
Comments: Early ripening. For mild-winter areas only.

Stark Sweetheart
Fruit: Good-tasting fruit. Large edible kernels.
Zone/Tree Size: Zone 5.
Comments: Good fresh or dried.

Wenatchee Moorpark (Wenatchee)
Fruit: Large, good-tasting fruit.
Zone/Tree Size: Zone 6.
Comments: Self-pollinating. Dwarf tree. Good pollination in rainy, cool springs; good choice for Pacific Northwest.

Asian and Hybrid Apricots

Brookcot
Fruit: Small fruits, can be clingstone.
Zone/Tree Size: Zone 4
Comments: Tall, upright Manchurian selection.

Moongold
Fruit: Sweet-tangy golden fruit.
Zone/Tree Size: Zone 4; under 20 ft. tall.
Comments: Manchurian selection for cold-winter climates. Needs pollinator. Disease-free.

Scout
Fruit: Golden, freestone fruit.
Zone/Tree Size: Zone 3; up to 12 ft. tall.
Comments: Manchurian seedling. Needs protected site. Bears more fruit with a pollinator. Disease-resistant.

Sungold
Fruit: Sweet, mild fruit.
Zone/Tree Size: Zone 4.
Comments: Manchurian selection for cold-winter areas. Needs a pollinator.

Sunrise
Fruit: Sweet, golden fruit.
Zone/Tree Size: Zone 4.
Comments: Manchurian/European hybrid. Compact, bushy tree.

Westcot
Fruit: Large, yellow to orange fruit.
Zone/Tree Size: Zone 4.
Comments: Mild-flavored Manchurian/European hybrid. Early bloomer.

Citrus

A dwarf tree, like this dwarf 'Valencia' orange, makes homegrown citrus possible for gardeners on the smallest properties.

Handsome evergreen foliage, fragrant spring flowers, colorful fruit, and a juicy harvest when few other fruit are in season make citrus highly desirable fruit trees. Oranges, mandarins (tangerines), grapefruit, lemons, and limes are the best-known members of this remarkably diverse group of plants. Less familiar to many are pummelos, kumquats, citron, and a range of hybrids with such exotic names as tangelo, tangor, and limequat. In addition to providing tasty fruit, citrus make handsome landscape specimens and effective hedges and screens.

As natives of tropical and semitropical areas, citrus can be grown outdoors year-round only in mild-winter climates (in general, where temperatures don't fall below 20°F). Fortunately for those whose winters are frigid, citrus are productive and striking container plants. A citrus tree grown in a pot or tub on the patio in the summer will enliven a sunny room through a harsh winter.

Because of concerns about spreading pests and diseases among commercial citrus plantings, there are numerous restrictions on shipping the fruit between states and even between counties within states. Gardeners living in regions where citrus is grown commercially will in all likelihood have to buy plants locally. Northerners who want to grow citrus in a container should be able to mail-order plants with little difficulty. (See "Sources of Supply.")

Climate and Adaptation

How hot it gets in the summer and how cold it gets in the winter determine not only whether you can grow citrus outdoors but what types of citrus and citrus varieties will do best for you.

The main citrus-growing regions of the United States all have mild winters — California, Arizona, southern Texas, the Gulf Coast, and Florida. But other factors such as heat and humidity differ greatly and, consequently, so do fruit characteristics and variety adaptation for each region. Even within a single region, differences in climate can have a dramatic effect on citrus fruit from one area to another.

Semitropical areas, such as Florida, are characterized by warm, humid summers, with only small fluctuations between daytime and nighttime temperatures. In these conditions, citrus produce thin-skinned, often unevenly colored, but very sweet low-acid fruit.

Subtropical areas, such as California, have warm, mostly arid summers, usually with wide fluctuations in temperatures from day to night. Inland from coastal California, it is not uncommon for daytime highs and nighttime lows to differ by as much as 30°F. There, citrus fruit is highly colored with thicker rinds. The fruit is sweet, but has a higher acid content — a combination some people think results in a more balanced flavor.

Heat requirements

To ripen properly, citrus require heat. How much heat varies by type. Grapefruit and some mandarins need the most heat. They are sweetest when grown in inland and desert California, Arizona, Texas, and Florida. Acid citrus, such as lemons and limes, which don't need to sweeten up, don't need as much heat and will do well wherever the climate doesn't exceed their tolerance for cold. Heat requirements are particularly important in California, where types that ripen properly in cool coastal areas are quite different from those that do so in warmer inland or desert regions.

Cold tolerance

Citrus suffers when temperatures fall too low. Fruit, leaves, shoots, or branches may be damaged, or the tree itself may be killed. Like heat requirements, cold hardiness varies by type. Least hardy are citron and Mexican lime, whose foliage is usually damaged if temperatures drop much below 30°F for more than an hour or two. True lemons are slightly hardier, followed in order of increasing hardiness by 'Bearss' lime, grapefruit, pummelo and pummelo hybrids, tangelo and tangor, limequat, sweet orange, most mandarins, 'Improved Meyer' lemon, Satsuma mandarins, sour orange, orangequat, and kumquat, which can usually withstand temperatures down to about 20°F.

Placing exact temperatures on citrus hardiness can be deceiving. A tree's hardiness often depends on the weather prior to damaging cold. For example, trees that have been "hardened off" by gradually decreasing temperatures should be able to withstand more cold than those subjected to sudden cold snaps. (But the longer temperatures remain low, the greater the risk of damage.) Late-season pruning or late-season fertilizing with nitrogen can also produce tender foliage that is more likely to be damaged by cold.

Unfortunately, ripening fruit is often less hardy than foliage. When it is close to maturity, most fruit will be damaged if temperatures stay below 27°F for more than an hour or two. Mandarin fruit, for example, can be ruined by cold weather while the foliage suffers little damage. In general, small thin-skinned fruit are usually harmed by cold first.

Microclimates

It is possible to stretch the limits imposed by your climate by planting a tree in a spot that is hotter in summer or warmer in winter than the immediate surroundings. Such spots, called microclimates, allow you to try citrus that would otherwise be too tender for your climate or that wouldn't receive enough heat to sweeten up. (We'll discuss how to recognize and use a microclimate when we talk about selecting a site.)

Choosing Citrus

You should consider a number of factors when deciding which citrus to plant. We can provide general guidelines here, but the best information about what is likely to do well for you will come from gardeners who grow citrus in your area, local nurseries that sell citrus plants, and from your cooperative extension agent.

Adaptation

As the previous discussion indicates, hardiness and heat requirements are important considerations. In northern Florida, along the Gulf Coast, and outside the Lower Rio Grande Valley of Texas, for instance, cold tolerance is a particular concern. There, hardy varieties like Satsuma mandarin, kumquats, and 'Meyer' lemons are excellent choices. In cool climates of coastal California, on the other hand, varieties with low heat requirements, such as lemons, 'Bearss' lime, and 'Valencia' orange are best adapted. The lists in this chapter indicate the regions for which each listed variety is best suited. (The regions are Florida, Gulf Coast, Texas, California and Arizona low-elevation deserts, inland California, and coastal California.)

Ripening dates

Citrus varieties ripen at different times during the year and are usually described as early, midseason, and late. Early usually refers to late October to December harvest; midseason is January to February; and late varieties ripen after February.

Climate, however, plays an important role in this timing — fruit ripens earliest in warmer areas. A 'Washington' navel ripening in the warm summer of inland California may be ready to eat in early December, while the same variety grown closer to the coast might not be ready until after February. (In Texas and Florida, navel oranges often dry out and lack juice.) In areas where cold temperatures threaten ripening fruit, select early varieties. Where low temperatures aren't a problem, plant a mix of early, midseason, and late varieties and enjoy fresh fruit for months.

Pollination

Most citrus are pollinated by insects, usually bees. Unlike some fruits and berries, most citrus varieties do not require cross-pollinization from another variety to set fruit. Some mandarin varieties may set more and larger fruit with another suitable source of pollen nearby, but the resulting fruit will be seedier.

Tree size and spacing

For most residential gardeners, size is a very important consideration when choosing a tree. As trees go, citrus are relatively small. Still, the tallest types — true lemons, grapefruit, pummelos, and 'Valencia' orange — can reach 20 to 25 feet high under ideal conditions. (Remember that height can

'Washington Navel' is one of the best oranges for fresh eating.

vary considerably depending on growing conditions.) Navel oranges and blood oranges are slightly smaller. Mandarins and mandarin hybrids usually reach 12 to 16 feet. Kumquats and kumquat hybrids usually grow 6 to 12 feet high. 'Meyer' lemons and limes reach 6 to 10 feet high. Taller types of citrus should be spaced at least 12 to 16 feet apart. Smaller ones can be as close as 8 to 10 feet, even less for a citrus hedge.

Rootstocks

Citrus are grafted onto a number of rootstocks to provide extra cold hardiness, adaptation to specific soil types, or disease resistance. Unfortunately, most retail nurseries do not offer gardeners a choice. (In fact, rootstocks are rarely even labeled.) However, nurseries that propagate citrus usually serve a particular region and tend to grow varieties on the rootstocks most suitable for that region.

Several rootstocks have a dwarfing effect on citrus, but under ideal conditions the resulting trees are seldom reduced in size by more than 20 to 25 percent. ('Flying Dragon', a truly dwarfing rootstock that reduces size by over 50 percent, is not widely available.)

Types of Citrus

When choosing a fruit tree for your garden or landscape, thoughts of ripening times, microclimates, and rootstocks are unlikely to be uppermost in your mind. Instead, you're probably considering the succulent sweetness of an orange, the tangy taste of a grapefruit, or the puckering punch of a lemon. The trick, of course, is to combine your taste preferences with the climatic preferences of the trees and the requirements of your landscape. To help make these decisions, here are brief portraits of the main types of citrus grown by home gardeners.

Sweet oranges

The most popular type of citrus, oranges come in three basic types (sweet oranges, blood or pigmented oranges, and bitter or sour oranges), which we'll discuss in turn.

Sweet oranges are the oranges familiar to most people. Of these, the 'Washington' navel orange and the 'Valencia' common orange set the standards of quality and are the most widely grown. Navel oranges are easy to peel and popular for eating out-of-hand. They are characterized by the small, secondary fruit that develops in the bottom end of the main fruit, and by the small hole — the "navel" — formed as a result. Of the many improved strains of navel oranges planted commercially in California, one of interest to home gardeners is called 'Lane Late', a late-ripening fruit that extends the harvest period into early summer.

The 'Valencia' is the most important and widely grown common orange. It is a late-ripening fruit that is primarily grown for juice and can be harvested well into summer. If left on the tree during summer, the rind usually regains chlorophyll and turns partially green. This "regreening" does not affect fruit quality, and summer 'Valencias' are usually wonderfully sweet.

Besides 'Valencia', a number of other common sweet oranges are grown primarily on a regional basis. In Arizona, for instance, the varieties 'Hamlin', 'Marrs', 'Diller', 'Pineapple', and 'Trovita' are often sold interchangeably as "Arizona Sweets." The same cultivars are also grown in Florida; with the exception of 'Trovita', they are not grown in California.

■ RECOMMENDED VARIETIES OF SWEET ORANGES

Diller
Season: Early.
Description of fruit: Small to medium-size. Few to many seeds. Juicy.
Adaptation: California and Arizona Low Elevation Deserts, Florida.
Comments: Usually juiced. Slightly later than Hamlin.

Hamlin
Season: Early.
Description of fruit: Small to medium-size. Few seeds. Juicy.
Adaptation: California and Arizona Low Elevation Deserts, Texas, Florida.
Comments: Popular juice orange. Usually ripens before cold weather.

Lane Late
Season: Late.
Description of fruit: Medium to large, seedless.
Adaptation: Coastal California, Inland California, California and Arizona Low Elevation Deserts.
Comments: Late-ripening navel.

Marrs
Season: Early.
Description of fruit: Medium-size. Few to many seeds. Juicy.
Adaptation: California and Arizona Low Elevation Deserts, Texas, Florida.
Comments: Juice orange. Small tree.

Pineapple
Season: Early.
Description of fruit: Small to medium-size. Few to many seeds. Rich and juicy.
Adaptation: California and Arizona Low Elevation Deserts, Texas, Florida.
Comments: Juice orange.

Robertson Navel
Season: Early.
Description of fruit: Medium to large. Easy to peel. Seedless.
Adaptation: Coastal California, Inland California, California and Arizona Low Elevation Deserts.
Comments: Early sport of Washington navel. Small tree produces at young age.

Shamouti

Season: Midseason.
Description of fruit: Medium to large. Few seeds. Easy to peel.
Adaptation: Inland California, California and Arizona Low Elevation Deserts.
Comments: Popular eating orange in Europe.

Trovita

Season: Early.
Description of fruit: Medium to large. Few seeds. Good fresh or for juice.
Adaptation: Coastal California, Inland California, California and Arizona Low Elevation Deserts.
Comments: Widely adapted navel seedling without the navel. Alternate-bearing.

Valencia

Season: Late.
Description of fruit: Medium to large. Few seeds. Very juicy.
Adaptation: Coastal California, Inland California, California and Arizona Low Elevation Deserts, Texas, Florida.
Comments: Most popular juice orange. Widely adapted. Holds well on tree.

Washington Navel

Season: Early.
Description of fruit: Large. Easy to peel. Seedless.
Adaptation: Coastal California, Inland California, California and Arizona Low Elevation Deserts, Texas, Florida.
Comments: Standard of excellence for fresh-eating orange. Best quality in California.

Blood oranges

Under proper conditions, blood oranges develop a red to purple internal color, and in some varieties, a dark red blush on the rind. They can also have a unique berrylike flavor, which makes them a favorite among gourmet cooks. When squeezed, blood oranges yield a beautifully colored, light pink to deep purple juice.

The exact conditions necessary for the development of the internal or external red color are not completely understood. The intensity of the color can vary from year to year, variety to variety, and even from one side of the tree to another. However, cold winters seem to produce the most intense coloration, with the best quality fruit found in interior valleys of California. 'Moro', the earliest variety, develops the deepest and most consistent coloration.

'Moro', a blood orange with deep red flesh, is a reliable producer.

■ RECOMMENDED VARIETIES OF BLOOD ORANGES

Moro
Season: Early.
Description of fruit: Large with deep red flesh and, some-times, rind. Few seeds.
Adaptation: Coastal California, Inland California, California and Arizona Low Elevation Deserts, Texas.
Comments: Deepest colored and most reliable blood orange. Best in inland California. Very thorny.

Sanguinelli
Season: Late.
Description of fruit: Small to medium-size. Egg-shaped. Moderate internal color; good blush. Few seeds.
Adaptation: Inland California, California and Arizona Low

Elevation Deserts, Gulf Coast and Northern Florida, Texas.
Comments: Attractive tree. Best exterior blush of the bloods.

Tarocco
Season: Midseason.
Description of fruit: Large fruit with light interior color; little blush. Few seeds. Excellent flavor.
Adaptation: Inland California, Texas.
Comments: Trees often take years to bear. Best flavor of bloods — truly berrylike. Very thorny.

Sour oranges

As the name suggests, sour oranges never sweeten up. The brightly colored, highly aromatic fruit is used to make marmalades, drinks, and perfumes. All sour oranges are very attractive landscape plants, especially two small-fruited varieties, 'Chinotto' and 'Bouquet de Fleurs'. Both are compact plants with distinctive foliage. They make excellent hedges, foundation plants, or container subjects. The large-fruited type, 'Seville', is one of the most popular varieties.

■ RECOMMENDED VARIETIES OF SOUR ORANGES

Bouquet de Fleurs
Season: Early.
Description of fruit: Small, acid fruit borne in clusters. Few to many seeds.
Adaptation: Coastal California, Inland California, California and Arizona Low Elevation Deserts, Texas, Gulf Coast and Northern Florida, Florida.
Comments: Grown as an ornamental for very fragrant flowers and handsome foliage. Small tree. Excellent hedge.

Chinotto
Season: Early.
Description of fruit: Small, colorful fruit with acid juice. Hang on the tree almost year-round. Few to many seeds.
Adaptation: Coastal California, Inland California, California and Arizona Low Elevation Deserts, Texas, Gulf Coast and Northern Florida, Florida.
Comments: Grown as ornamental. Compact, small tree with closely spaced leaves. Excellent hedge. Hardy.

Seville
Season: Early.
Description of fruit: Medium-size fruit with dark orange rind and acid juice. Few to many seeds.

Adaptation: Coastal California, Inland California, California and Arizona Low Elevation Deserts, Texas, Gulf Coast and Northern Florida, Florida.

Comments: Best in western climates. Grown as an ornamental, or for making marmalade.

Mandarins

A large group of citrus, mandarins offer a variety of flavors and landscape uses. They are hardy trees, generally withstanding temperatures as low as 23° to 24°F with little damage. The early ripening Satsuma mandarins, of which the 'Owari' is most common, are especially hardy and a favorite fruit in colder areas. Mandarins are smallish trees, reaching about 12 to 16 feet high, and many have a distinctive, nearly weeping habit that makes them attractive landscape specimens and container plants.

Mandarin fruits vary quite a bit. They offer a range of flavors, depending on variety and where they are grown. Some, such as 'Dancy', are rich and sprightly. Others, including 'Kinnow' and 'Page', are very sweet and aromatic. Some mandarins, such as the Satsumas, are easy to peel. 'Kinnow' and others have more adherent peels, though they're still easier to remove than that of a 'Valencia' orange. Some mandarins will store well on the tree, while others will begin to puff and dry out if left on the tree.

The name "mandarin" may be confusing to some readers because some mandarins are referred to as tangerines, a word with no botanical standing that was coined to market the brightly colored variety 'Dancy'. Technically, some mandarins could be considered tangelos because they have some pummelo or grapefruit parentage. But because they are usually sold as mandarins, they are listed as such here.

■ RECOMMENDED VARIETIES OF MANDARINS

Ambersweet

Season: Early.

Description of fruit: Medium to large with orange rind. Few to many seeds.

Adaptation: Inland California, California and Arizona Low Elevation Deserts, Florida, Gulf Coast and Northern Florida.

Comments: Often sold as an orange but really a mandarin hybrid. Recent introduction.

Clementine

Season: Early.

Description of fruit: Small to medium-size. Few to many

seeds. Easy to peel. Excellent flavor.

Adaptation: Inland California, California and Arizona Low Elevation Deserts, Texas, Gulf Coast and Northern Florida.

Comments: Also known as 'Algerian.' Pollinizer increases yield and seediness.

Dancy

Season: Midseason.

Description of fruit: Small. Many seeds. Rich flavor.

Adaptation: Florida, Inland California, California and Arizona Low Elevation Deserts, Gulf Coast and Northern Florida.

Comments: Known as the Christmas tangerine. Best in Florida.

Fairchild

Season: Early.

Description of fruit: Medium-size with brightly colored rind. Many seeds. Rich flavor.

Adaptation: Inland California, California and Arizona Low Elevation Deserts, Texas, Gulf Coast and Northern Florida.

Comments: Developed for desert regions. Pollinizer increases yields and seediness.

Fallglo

Season: Early.

Description of fruit: Medium to large. Many seeds. Easy to peel, brightly colored rind.

Adaptation: Florida.

Comments: Recent introduction. More cold-sensitive than other mandarins.

Honey

Season: Midseason.

Description of fruit: Small. Many seeds. Brightly colored with excellent flavor. Easy to peel.

Adaptation: Inland California, California and Arizona Low Elevation Deserts.

Comments: Not to be confused with the 'Murcott Honey' of Florida.

Kara

Season: Late.

Description of fruit: Medium-size with sprightly flavor. Many seeds. Doesn't hold well on the tree.

Adaptation: Inland California.

Comments: Best in inland California.

This container-grown 'Dancy' mandarin enlivens an entryway and provides a considerable crop.

Kinnow

Season: Midseason.

Description of fruit: Medium-size. Many seeds. Juicy, sweet, and aromatic.

Adaptation: Inland California, California and Arizona Low Elevation Deserts.

Comments: Strong tendency to alternate bear.

Murcott Honey
Season: Late.
Description of fruit: Medium-size. Excellent flavor. Many
   seeds.
Adaptation: Florida.
Comments: Tends to alternate bear. Not the same as 'Honey'
   mandarin grown in California.

Page
Season: Early.
Description of fruit: Small to medium-size. Few to many
   seeds. Sweet, aromatic.
Adaptation: Inland California, California and Arizona Low
   Elevation Deserts, Florida.
Comments: One of the best-tasting mandarins. Tends to al-
   ternate bear.

Pixie
Season: Mid- to late season.
Description of fruit: Small to medium-size. Easy to peel,
   bumpy rind. Seedless. Excellent flavor.
Adaptation: Inland California.
Comments: One of the best backyard varieties.

Ponkan
Season: Midseason.
Description of fruit: Small to medium-size. Few seeds. Easy
   to peel.
Adaptation: Texas, Gulf Coast and Northern Florida, Florida.
Comments: Tends to alternate bear. Does not hold well on
   the tree.

Satsuma 'Owari'
Season: Early.
Description of fruit: Medium-size fruit. Very easy to peel.
   Seedless.
Adaptation: Coastal California, Inland California, California
   and Arizona Low Elevation Deserts, Texas, Gulf Coast and
   Northern Florida, Florida.
Comments: Hardy, widely adapted tree. Does not hold on
   tree well. Owari is most common of the Satsuma type, but
   other strains are available.

Sunburst
Season: Early.
Description of fruit: Medium-size. Few to many seeds.
   Brightly colored.
Adaptation: Florida.

'Owari' is the most common of the early-ripening Satsuma mandarins.

Comments: Recent introduction. Pollinizer increases production and fruit set.

Lemons

There are a number of "true" lemons, but 'Eureka' and 'Lisbon' are by far the most commonly grown. They produce virtually identical fruit, familiar to any supermarket shopper. Commercial production is concentrated almost exclusively in the West. 'Lisbon' is preferred in inland areas, while 'Eureka' is grown in coastal areas, where it tends to bloom and produce fruit almost year-round.

True lemons are very vigorous trees, which often require regular pruning or shearing to keep them within bounds. They make attractive hedges with light green foliage and red-tinged new growth. They can also be trained as espaliers, but production will be greatly reduced. The trees are less hardy than most other citrus and will be damaged if temperatures drop much below 30°F.

The 'Improved Meyer' lemon is not a true lemon, but is thought to be a hybrid between a lemon and an orange, or a lemon and a mandarin. A hardy, very attractive small tree that rarely exceeds 10 feet high, it is ideal for containers or as a low hedge. The thin-skinned fruit is very juicy with a higher sugar content than true lemons. Although it is tart, it has a flowery flavor and bright yellow juice preferred by many dessert chefs.

Another hybrid, the 'Ponderosa' (a lemon-citron cross), produces very large fruit with a thick rind and little juice. It is grown primarily as an ornamental or an oddity.

■ RECOMMENDED VARIETIES OF SWEET LEMONS

Eureka
Season: Early.
Description of fruit: Medium-size. Few to many seeds. Some fruit borne year-round in coastal areas.
Adaptation: Coastal California, Inland California, California and Arizona Low Elevation Deserts.
Comments: True lemon. Supermarket lemon best adapted to coastal California. Vigorous tree. New growth and flowers tinged purple.

Lisbon
Season: Early.
Description of fruit: Medium. Few to many seeds. Very productive. Some fruit borne year-round in coastal areas.
Adaptation: Coastal California, Inland California, California and Arizona Low Elevation Deserts.
Comments: True lemon. Preferred in warmer areas. Vigorous tree. New growth and flowers tinged purple.

Improved Meyer
Season: Early.
Description of fruit: Small to medium-size. Few to many seeds. Thin rind. Very juicy. Sweeter (but still tart) than true lemons. Fruit borne year-round in coastal areas.
Adaptation: Coastal California, Inland California, California and Arizona Low Elevation Deserts, Texas, Gulf Coast and Northern Florida, Florida.
Comments: Lemon-orange or lemon-mandarin hybrid. Very hardy and ornamental. Small compact tree, ideal for containers.

Ponderosa
Season: Early.
Description of fruit: Large size with thick rind and little juice. Many seeds.
Adaptation: Coastal California, Inland California, California and Arizona Low Elevation Deserts, Texas.
Comments: Lemon-citron hybrid grown as an ornamental.

'Eureka', a true lemon familiar to supermarket shoppers,
produces fruit almost year-round in coastal areas.

'Improved Meyer', a hybrid of lemon with orange or
mandarin, is juicy and sweeter than true lemons.

'Star Ruby', a grapefruit with intensely red flesh, will color up even in cooler climates.

Grapefruit

These are large trees (to 25 feet high) with big, bold, glossy green leaves. The large fruit, usually borne in clusters toward the outside of the tree, combines beautifully with the foliage.

With the highest heat requirements of any citrus, grapefruit is best grown in the hot climates of the California and Arizona deserts, southern Texas, and Florida. In moderately warm areas, the fruit can be left on the tree into summer and will usually reach good eating quality. Cool-climate gardeners who prefer sweeter grapefruit should consider planting the pummelo-grapefruit hybrids 'Oroblanco' or 'Melogold'. Pink grapefruit varieties develop the deepest color in hot summer climates. Newer varieties with intense red interiors, such as 'Star Ruby' and 'Rio Red', will color nicely in cooler areas.

■ RECOMMENDED VARIETIES OF GRAPEFRUIT

Marsh Seedless
Season: Early to midseason.
Description of fruit: Large, bright yellow with white interior. Seedless. Holds well on tree.
Adaptation: Inland California, California and Arizona Low Elevation Deserts, Texas, Florida.
Comments: Standard white-fleshed grapefruit. Needs heat to sweeten up.

Redblush

Season: Early to midseason.

Description of fruit: Large, yellow, often with pink blush on rind. Few to no seeds. Interior light pink in hot climates. Holds well on tree.

Adaptation: Inland California, California and Arizona Low Elevation Deserts, Texas, Florida.

Comments: Identical to 'Marsh Seedless', but develops pink color in hot-summer climates.

Rio Red

Season: Early to midseason.

Description of fruit: Medium-size fruit with dark red interior and pink blush on rind. Few to no seeds. Holds well on tree.

Adaptation: Inland California, California and Arizona Low Elevation Deserts, Texas, Florida.

Comments: Very similar to 'Star Ruby', but fruit borne on more compact tree. Best in hot climates, but will color in mild climates.

Star Ruby

Season: Early to midseason.

Description of fruit: Medium-size fruit with dark red interior. Few to no seeds.

Adaptation: Inland California, California and Arizona Low Elevation Deserts, Texas, Florida.

Comments: Open, willowy tree, more frost-sensitive than other grapefruit.

Limes

Two types of true lime are grown in the United States. The Mexican lime, known as the Key lime in Florida, is a very frost-tender plant that can only be grown in the mildest climates, in containers, or in protected locations. A fine-textured, thorny plant, it bears small aromatic fruit often referred to as bartender's lime. (A thornless variety is sometimes available.) The tree is often grown on its own roots, so if it is frost-killed the roots may sprout and eventually bear fruit again.

Tahitian limes are slightly hardier and more widely adapted. Their handsome bright green leaves make them a beautiful container subject. The fruit is larger than Mexican lime, and very juicy, with good lime flavor. 'Bearss' is the most widely grown of the Tahitian limes. 'Rangpur' lime is most likely an acid mandarin with bright orange, sour fruit. It is much hardier than true limes and can be used as a lime substitute in cold climates.

'Bearss', *best lime for the West, is borne on a cold-tolerant and handsome tree.*

Limes are usually harvested when green, but the fruit turns yellow when fully ripe. In coastal areas, most lime trees will bloom and set fruit year-round.

■ RECOMMENDED VARIETIES OF SWEET LIMES

Bearss

Season: Early.

Description of fruit: Small fruit is greenish yellow when ripe. Can be picked green. Few to no seeds. Juicy. Some fruit borne year-round.

Adaptation: Coastal California, Inland California, California and Arizona Low Elevation Deserts, Florida.

Comments: Tahitian seedling discovered in California. More cold-tolerant than other limes. Very handsome tree. Best lime for the West.

Mexican

Season: Early.

Description of fruit: Small, aromatic fruit turns yellow when fully ripe. Few to many seeds. Some fruit borne year-round.

'Rangpur' lime, most likely an acid mandarin, is a good lime substitute in cold climates.

Adaptation: Coastal California, Florida, Texas.
Comments: Known as Key lime in Florida. Also called bartender's lime. Can be grown only in frost-free areas. Thorny, twiggy tree. Seedless variety is sometimes available.

Rangpur
Season: Early.
Description of fruit: Small to medium-size. Dark reddish orange with thin rind and acid juice. Many seeds. Some fruit year-round.
Adaptation: Coastal California, Inland California, California and Arizona Low Elevation Deserts.
Comments: Acid mandarin usually grown as an ornamental. Hardy. Can be used as a lime substitute.

Tahitian (also called Persian)
Season: Early.
Description of fruit: Small fruit turns greenish yellow when ripe. Few to no seeds. Some fruit borne year-round.
Adaptation: Florida.

Comments: Handsome, frost-sensitive tree suited to mildest climates of Florida.

Pummelos and pummelo hybrids

The largest of citrus fruit, pummelos sometimes approach the size of a volleyball. To eat the fruit, you peel off its thick rind, free the segments from a membrane and eat them alone or in a salad. The meat has a unique texture and rich, sweet flavor. Pummelo trees are large and vigorous with large, heavy-textured dark green leaves.

Two pummelo-grapefruit hybrids, 'Oroblanco' and 'Melogold', were developed by the University of California and are becoming very popular in that state. Segmented or eaten from the rind with a spoon, like grapefruit, the fruits have a mild, very sweet flavor without the tartness of grapefruit. They also have lower heat requirements than grapefruit.

■ RECOMMENDED VARIETIES OF PUMMELOS AND PUMMELO HYBRIDS

Chandler
Season: Early.
Description of fruit: Very large, yellow fruit with thick rind and pink flesh. Sweet flavor. Many seeds.
Adaptation: Inland California, California and Arizona Low Elevation Deserts.
Comments: Pummelo. California introduction. Large trees with big, dark green leaves.

Melogold
Season: Midseaon.
Description of fruit: Large fruit with thick rind and sweet, white interior. Seedless.
Adaptation: Coastal California, Inland California, California and Arizona Low Elevation Deserts.
Comments: Pummelo-grapefruit hybrid. Similar to 'Oroblanco' but heavier with thinner rind. Best flavor in inland areas.

Oroblanco
Season: Early.
Description of fruit: Large fruit with thick rind and sweet, juicy, white interior. Seedless.
Adaptation: Coastal California, Inland California, California and Arizona Low Elevation Deserts.
Comments: Pummelo-grapefruit hybrid with wonderful sweet flavor. Lower heat requirement than grapefruit.

Pummelos are the largest citrus, sometimes reaching the size of a volleyball.

Reinking

Season: Early.

Description of fruit: Very large yellow fruit with white interior. Many seeds.

Adaptation: Inland California, California and Arizona Low Elevation Deserts.

Comments: Pummelo. Similar to 'Chandler' but with white interior.

Tangelos and tangors

These are hybrids between mandarins and other citrus; both generally have high heat requirements. Tangelos' parents are mandarin-grapefruit or mandarin-pummelo hybrids, whose tree and fruit usually resembles one of its parents. 'Minneola', for example, resembles its mandarin parent, 'Dancy', more than its grapefruit parent, 'Duncan'. Tangors, hybrids of mandarins and orange, are most popular in Florida. Their flavor is rich and aromatic, more characteristic of a mandarin than an orange. The trees are vigorous with an open habit.

The tangelo 'Minneola' resembles its mandarin parent ('Dancy') more than the grapefruit side of its heritage.

■ RECOMMENDED VARIETIES OF TANGELOS AND TANGORS

Minneola (tangelo)
Season: Midseason.
Description of fruit: Large, deep orange fruit, usually with a distinct neck. Few to many seeds.
Adaptation: Inland California, California and Arizona Low Elevation Deserts, Florida.
Comments: Pollinizer increases crop and seediness.

Orlando (tangelo)
Season: Early.
Description of fruit: Medium to large fruit with deep orange rind. Few to many seeds. Juicy, sweet, and mandarinlike.
Adaptation: California and Arizona Low Elevation Deserts, Florida.
Comments: Leaves are cupped. Pollinizer increases yields and seediness.

Dweet (tangor)
Season: Midseason.
Description of fruit: Medium to large, with red-orange rind. Many seeds. Juicy.
Adaptation: Florida.
Comments: Doesn't hold well on the tree.

Tangors, like this one, are hybrids of oranges and mandarins, with rich aromatic fruit borne on vigorous trees.

Temple (tangor)

Season: Midseason.

Description of fruit: Medium to large fruit with deep orange-red flavor. Many seeds. Easy to peel. Excellent flavor. Juicy.

Adaptation: California and Arizona Low Elevation Deserts, Florida.

Comments: Often called Temple orange. Best in Florida. Not cold-hardy.

Kumquats and kumquat hybrids

Compact, small trees with fine-textured, dense foliage and an abundance of fruit, kumquats rank among the most attractive citrus, perfect for containers or as specimens. The small trees have tiny, compact leaves and bear fruit in abundance, handsomely displayed toward the outside of the tree. Trees are the hardiest among commonly grown citrus and are the ideal choice for colder climates within the citrus regions. As with all citrus, weather can affect the likelihood of a tree setting flowers and fruit. The small trees are easy to protect and therefore enhance chances of harvesting a crop.

Kumquat fruit is small and can be eaten whole, rind and all, or used in marmalade and sauces. 'Nagami' fruit is bright orange and oblong in shape; its rind is sweet but the flesh is tart. 'Meiwa' is round, bright orange, with sweet rind and flesh.

Kumquat hybrids combine the hardiness of the kumquat with fruit quality of popular types of citrus. All are very ornamental, with an abundance of fruit and good-looking foliage. Most useful are limequats, with small, green to yellow fruit that have the flavor and aroma of limes. The trees are a few degrees hardier than a lime, so they are a good choice in colder areas where limes won't produce without protection. Other kumquat hybrids include orangequats, which are very similar to kumquats but have larger fruit, and the calamondin, a very productive tree grown primarily as an ornamental. Its mandarinlike fruit is sour.

- ■ RECOMMENDED VARIETIES OF KUMQUATS AND KUMQUAT HYBRIDS

Calamondin (kumquat hybrid)
Season: Early to midseason.
Description of fruit: Small round fruit with acid juice. Few seeds. Some fruit year-round.
Adaptation: Coastal California, Inland California, California and Arizona Low Elevation Deserts, Texas, Gulf Coast and Northern Florida, Florida.
Comments: Commonly grown as an ornamental; grown indoors. Handsome, hardy tree. Fruits at a young age.

Limequats
Season: Early to midseason.
Description of fruit: Small yellow-green fruit with limelike flavor. Few to many seeds. Bears some fruit year-round.
Adaptation: Coastal California, Inland California, California and Arizona Low Elevation Deserts, Texas, Florida.
Comments: Handsome ornamental. 'Lakeland' and 'Eustis' have round fruit. 'Tavaras' has oblong fruit.

Meiwa kumquat
Season: Early to midseason.
Description of fruit: Small round fruit with sweet rind and flesh. Few seeds.
Adaptation: Coastal California, Inland California, California and Arizona Low Elevation Deserts, Texas, Gulf Coast and Northern Florida, Florida.
Comments: Best fresh-eating kumquat. Fine ornamental. Small tree. Hardy.

Nagami kumquat
Season: Early to midseason.
Description of fruit: Small oval fruit with sweet rind, sour flesh. Few seeds.

Possessing the flavor and aroma of limes, limequats can be grown in areas a little colder than limes will withstand. 'Eustis' shown here.

'Meiwa', the best kumquat for fresh eating, is also a handsome ornamental tree.

Adaptation: Coastal California, Inland California, California and Arizona Low Elevation Deserts, Texas, Gulf Coast and Northern Florida, Florida.

Comments: Most widely grown kumquat. Useful for candies and preserves. Hardy, attractive tree.

Citron

Historically, the citron is one of the most important citrus, having been cultivated by many cultures in which it played a role in a wide range of celebrations and religious ceremonies (such as the Jewish Feast of the Tabernacles).

The citron is a small, thorny, open shrub that doesn't match other citrus as an ornamental. It is most often grown for the aroma given off by the lemonlike fruit's thick rind, a fragrance that can fill a room. The fruit produces little juice, but the mildly sweet rind can be candied or pickled. Citron is very sensitive to frost and can be grown only in the mildest areas, in portable containers, or protected locations.

■ RECOMMENDED VARIETIES OF CITRON

Buddha's Hand

Season: Early to midseason.

Description of fruit: Large yellow fruit divided into fingerlike segments. Aromatic rind, little juice. Bears some fruit year-round.

Adaptation: Coastal California, Inland California, Florida.

Comments: Oddity grown for its unusual, aromatic fruit. Used as a decoration. Frost sensitive.

Etrog

Season: Early to midseason.

Description of fruit: Large, lemonlike fruit with thick, aromatic rind and little juice. Many seeds.

Adaptation: Coastal California, Inland California, Florida.

Comments: Used in the Jewish Feast of the Tabernacles. Thorny, twiggy tree is very frost-sensitive.

Selecting a Site for Citrus Trees

Citrus trees are relatively easy to grow compared to many other types of fruit trees. Annual pruning is usually not necessary, and if you site them carefully and water and fertilize appropriately, most citrus trees will remain productive for years. When selecting a site for citrus trees, you should consider soil, sunlight, and microclimate.

Citrons like 'Buddha's Hand' produce unusual-looking, but very fragrant, lemonlike fruit on thorny, open shrubs.

Soil and sun

Citrus trees grow well in soils ranging from sandy to clayey as long as the soil drains well. In poorly drained soils, citrus trees quickly succumb to a variety of soil-borne diseases. If your soil drains poorly, the easiest solution is to plant in raised beds or in containers.

Citrus prefer a slightly acidic soil. They adapt well to soils that are slightly alkaline, although they may require more frequent applications of micronutrients such as iron in those soils. Where soil is strongly alkaline, you can lower pH by adding sulfur, though you'll have to repeat the applications regularly to maintain a lower pH.

To ensure the highest quality fruit, plant citrus trees where they will receive at least eight hours of direct sunlight. Acid citrus, such as lemons and limes, and trees grown in very hot climates can tolerate some afternoon shade, but they'll be more productive in full sun.

Microclimate

As we mentioned previously, by planting trees where conditions are generally warmer than the surroundings, you can grow citrus whose heat requirements or cold hardiness might otherwise be questionable for your region. These areas, often called "microclimates," are not fail-safe havens for marginal plants, but they can allow you to harvest well-ripened fruit or to experiment with types and varieties of citrus you wouldn't ordinarily be able to grow.

Take advantage of reflected and stored heat. As the sun shines on solid objects like walls or paving, heat is either reflected or stored. Note how the area near a light-colored wall on the south or west sides of your home (the warmest exposures) is brighter and warmer than an area near a wall on the east or north sides. By planting citrus near south- or west-facing walls or light-colored paving, you can increase the heat the tree receives in summer. In winter, the heat stored in the surfaces (dark colors will store the most), will be released at night, raising air temperatures around the tree and providing some protection from cold.

Avoid areas where cold air collects. Like water, cold air flows and settles in low spots and accumulates at the base of objects (such as fences and walls) that block its path. A tree planted in such spots will be several degrees colder than one planted on higher ground nearby.

Planting and Caring for Citrus

Citrus trees are almost always sold in containers, although some plants to be grown indoors in cold winter climates are shipped bare-root. Citrus grown in containers can be planted any time of year. If possible, however, plant in early spring, after the last frost, so the trees can become established before the heat of summer and have an entire season to grow before being subjected to cold weather.

Plant citrus trees a bit on the high side (so the top of the rootball is an inch or two above the surrounding soil). If you make a basin to hold water, start it a few inches from the trunk to keep water from puddling against the trunk when you irrigate — a wet trunk encourages a variety of diseases. Other than removing dead or damaged roots and branches, no pruning is necessary when planting.

Watering

Citrus produce quality crops when soil is consistently moist but not waterlogged. Insufficient moisture results in small, poor quality fruit. Inconsistent watering, so that trees are allowed to go through wet and dry cycles, may cause fruit on some varieties of citrus, particularly 'Washington' navel oranges, to split.

How often you'll need to water depends, of course, on your soil type and climate. Trees in the arid West, for example, usually need at least two or three deep irrigations a month during the growing season. (In the hottest areas, trees are often watered weekly.) In the Southeast, on the other hand, irrigation is needed only to supplement rainfall. When you irrigate, remember to do so deeply, moistening the entire root zone (down 4 feet or so).

Fertilizing

Citrus trees need regular applications of nitrogen fertilizers to remain productive. Mature trees require 1 to 2 pounds of actual nitrogen per tree per year. Trees grown in western states are best fertilized on the lower end of that range; trees grown in the Southeast, on the higher end. (See the chapter "Ongoing Care" for the formula for determining how much fertilizer you need to apply to provide "actual" amounts of any nutrient.)

You can supply the nitrogen in three to four equal amounts over the course of the growing season. Make the first, and most important application in late winter (January or February) about six to eight weeks before the trees bloom. Don't make the last application any later than early August; nitrogen applied later can delay dormancy and force late growth that will be more susceptible to frost damage. Although you could apply all the nitrogen before bloom, spacing applications through the season is best in areas with sandy soils and frequent summer rainfall, where nitrogen can quickly be leached from the soil.

Young trees don't need as much nitrogen. Supply $1/10$ pound of actual nitrogen for a one-year-old tree; $1/5$ pound for a two-year-old tree; $1/3$ pound for a three-year-old tree; and $1/2$ pound for a four-year-old tree. (These are yearly totals; divide the amounts into doses as described above.)

Most soils contain sufficient amounts of phosphorous and potassium for citrus, so less expensive fertilizers that contain only nitrogen, such as ammonium sulfate (21-0-0) or calcium nitrate (15-0-0), are fine for most citrus. In some parts of the Southeast, however, citrus trees benefit from applications of phosphorous and potassium.

Citrus can also benefit from applications of micronutrients. Iron, zinc, and manganese are most commonly deficient, resulting in poorly colored foliage, low production, or poor quality fruit. Micronutrients can be applied in chelated or sulfate forms either as foliar spray or watered into the soil. Foliar applications are most effective when applied to young, expanding leaves.

A soil test is the best way to accurately assess your trees' needs for nutrients other than nitrogen. When you send your soil samples to the lab, be sure to specify the type of trees you're growing.

Pruning

Citrus trees do not require annual pruning to remain productive. Removing suckers, broken or diseased branches, and occasional wayward limbs is all that is usually necessary.

Citrus trees, however, respond well to pruning and can be shaped to control size (often desirable with more vigorous types such as lemons), opened up to create attractive specimens, or sheared as hedges. Heavy pruning will reduce yields, but trees are usually so productive the reduction is hardly noticeable.

The bark of citrus trees is very susceptible to sunburn, especially in the arid Southwest. Whenever pruning exposes the trunk or main branches to sunlight, paint them white for protection. Standard tree paint or a white latex paint, thinned 50 percent with water, work fine.

If parts of a tree have been killed by cold temperatures, it is best to prune out the dead wood the following summer when new growth will make it easy to distinguish the dead wood from the live. When you remove branches, make sure to cut back into living wood to reduce the chances of disease.

Harvesting

The best way to tell if citrus is ripe is also the simplest way — pick a fruit and eat it. Rind color is usually a poor indication of eating quality. Many citrus fruit are fully colored months before they are ripe. Others will have a tinge of green but still be delicious.

Unlike other fruit, many types of citrus can be "stored" on the tree for weeks or months after it is ripe. In fact, most varieties will improve in flavor. Once fruit starts to soften and the rind puffs, it is too mature and should be picked. (Citrus varieties that do not store well on the tree are noted as such in the variety lists.)

Cold protection

Sooner or later, no matter where you live, you'll probably have to protect your citrus trees from threatening cold temperatures. First, know when cold weather is coming. Be aware of the dates of the first frost in fall and the last in spring. Listen to local weather reports during frost season. Be observant; most frosts occur on clear, still nights when heat stored in the ground during the day can escape unimpeded to the sky above. Coldest temperatures are usually just before dawn.

One of the best ways to protect citrus from cold is to prevent heat stored in the soil during the day from escaping at night. You can trap the heat by covering individual trees with some type of material, such as clear plastic, floating row covers, tarps, burlap, or blankets. Support the cover with a framework of wood poles or PVC piping so the foliage does not come in contact with it. Leaves touching the cover are likely to be damaged. Stringing heat-producing Christmas lights in the tree will add even more heat under the cover. Unless temperatures are threatening, remove the cover during the day.

To maximize the amount of heat stored in the soil during the day, keep the ground around the tree moist, uncultivated, and clear of plants, such as weeds or turf. If you mulch, rake it back to expose bare ground.

You can also use sprinklers to increase the heat around citrus trees during cold weather. As the water cools, it releases heat, warming surrounding air by as much as two to three degrees. Start the sprinklers at least an hour before temperatures are likely to reach freezing and continue to run them until the threat is over. Even if the water freezes on the tree, the ice will provide insulation, keeping temperatures of the coated limbs from dropping much below freezing. Remember that too much ice build-up can break limbs.

Young citrus trees are particularly susceptible to damage from freezing, but their small size makes them easier to protect, especially with covers. You can wrap the trunks of young trees with an insulating material, such as commercial tree wraps, cloth rags, or even newspaper, to protect the bud union and preserve the scion variety. Make sure the wrap extends at least 6 inches above the bud union. For further protection, cover the wrapped trunk with loose mulch, such as compost or hay, or with mounded soil.

Growing Citrus in Containers

If your climate is cold or your soil poor, you need not despair of growing citrus. A container-grown plant can be moved to a protected location whenever there is a threat of cold weather — wheel it under the car port for a night or into a sunroom for the entire winter. And a container can be easily filled with fertile, well-drained soil if the heavy clay in the garden proves inhospitable to citrus. Even gardeners who can grow citrus in the ground can enjoy a well-groomed tree on the patio or near an entryway. Matched with a beautiful container, citrus leaves, flowers, and fruit combine for a wonderful display.

We cover most aspects of growing fruit and berry trees in containers in the chapter "Planting Fruit Trees and Bushes," so we'll just make a few comments here.

Any type of citrus can be grown in a container, though tree size and production will be retarded. Citrus trees will grow

'Mexican' lime, known as Key lime in Florida, bears small aromatic fruit and is a fine container plant.

in 12-inch pots (and even smaller) but are best grown in large containers of at least 15-gallon size. A half-barrel is ideal. Larger or fast-growing varieties will quickly outgrow any pot and be very difficult to keep healthy. Smaller types like kumquats, kumquat hybrids, 'Meyer' lemon, 'Bearss' lime, and some mandarins will stay healthy in containers for years. Other types and varieties grown on the 'Flying Dragon' dwarf rootstock are also ideal for growing in containers. Citrus that spend extended periods of time indoors may have problems setting flowers and fruit. You're likely to have more success producing fruit with 'Calamondin', 'Meyer' lemon, kumquats, and 'Bearss' lime.

'Calamondins' produce sour, mandarinlike fruit, but handsome trees that can be trained, like this container-grown specimen.

Like any container-grown plant, citrus will need more frequent watering and fertilizing (primarily nitrogen) than plants grown in the ground. In spring, foliar application of liquid fertilizers containing chelated iron, zinc, and manganese will keep plants deep green and healthy. You may need to root prune occasionally to control size.

Pests and Diseases

Citrus trees can be bothered by a number of insects and diseases. Specific problems vary from area to area, but common insects include aphids, mites, scale, thrip, and grasshoppers.

With the exception of scale, most insect pests are kept below troublesome levels by naturally occurring predators or parasites, and annual spraying of home garden trees is generally not required.

Several serious diseases attack roots and trunks of citrus trees. Most are caused or made worse by overly wet soil, poor drainage, or improper planting (setting trees too deep). Unfortunately, these diseases are difficult to diagnose without professional help. If you notice pitting, oozing sap, unusual wounds, or flaking bark on the trunk or on large branches, or if a tree appears in general decline, consult your local cooperative extension agent for assistance.

Scale

Various types of soft- and hard-shelled scales attack citrus and can become serious problems in most citrus-growing regions. The most difficult to control are the hard-shelled types, whose adult form lives under a protective, waxy plate that is difficult for pesticides to penetrate. Severe infestations of scales, which feed on plant juices, can weaken trees and cause leaf drop.

The individual scales appear as small white, red, yellow, brown, or black bumps on branches, leaves, and fruit. Several times a year the adult emerges from its shell, and it is during this mobile stage that it is most susceptible to sprays of summer oil or other pesticides. Beneficial insects can also help control scale. In western states, where red scale is a serious problem, the parasitic wasp *Aphytis melinus* is a very effective control.

European brown snail

A serious pest of citrus trees in most of California, the brown snail chews on foliage and sometimes fruit. You can keep them out of trees by wrapping copper barriers around the trunks (snails won't cross copper). You can also reduce snail populations in your garden by eliminating hiding places on the ground, such as boards, stones, debris, mulch, and weeds. You might also try handpicking at night, or trapping snails under boards or flower pots. In certain parts of California (mostly in the south), gardeners release decollate snails, which feed on European brown snails but usually not on citrus. (Check with your county extension agent to see if these snails can be used in your area.)

Gophers

These critters can kill citrus trees, especially young trees, in a very short time. The burrowing mammals feed on roots, causing a tree to wilt and, often, to die. You can reduce gopher damage by lining planting holes with wire mesh, which prevents the animals from reaching main roots. Some nurseries sell prefabricated wire baskets for use in planting holes. If you're persistent and follow instructions closely, you can control gophers with traps.

Other problems

Novice fruit growers are sometimes alarmed when trees drop leaves or fruit, produce split fruit, or bear lightly every other year. Usually, these are not symptoms of insect depredation or disease. Citrus trees naturally shed leaves over the entire year, most heavily with new growth flushes in spring. Lack of water, heavy insect infestations (particularly mites and scale), greasy spot fungus, and frost damage can also cause leaf drop.

Only a small percentage of citrus blossoms actually produce a mature fruit. During bloom, it is not uncommon for the ground beneath a tree to be covered with a white carpet of flowers. Even much of the fruit that does set will naturally drop off during the first couple of months after bloom. An especially heavy period of fruit drop, called June drop, usually happens during or after the first heat wave of late spring or early summer. If you think too much fruit is dropping, you may be applying excess nitrogen or watering inconsistently, both of which can increase fruit drop.

Inconsistent watering and sudden changes in heat or humidity can cause citrus fruit to split. This is most common with 'Washington' navel oranges in late summer and early fall. Other than watering properly, there is little you can do to completely prevent it. Usually, very few fruit are affected.

Some citrus, including 'Valencia' oranges, blood oranges, and some mandarins, tend to bear heavy crops of small fruit one year followed by light crops (or sometimes none) of large fruit the next. Alternate bearing can be evened out somewhat by thinning fruit after June drop in heavy-crop years.

Strawberries

'Earliglow', a disease-resistant June-bearer, is excellent for fresh eating, preserves, and freezing.

The sun-drenched sweetness of a ripe red strawberry is one of the great delights of the gardening season. Picked at the peak of perfection from a cultivar chosen to suit your taste buds, homegrown strawberries outshine even the best store-bought specimens.

For ease of growing, strawberries rank tops among fruit crops for the home garden. A well-chosen cultivar, properly planted and cared for, will produce an abundance of fruit in a relatively small area. You need no ladders for picking and pruning, no stakes or arbors to keep the plants in place. Gratification comes quicker than with most fruit crops — you'll be picking berries the first or second year after planting. And, by planting recently introduced "day-neutral" cultivars, gardeners in many parts of the country can harvest berries for months.

While strawberries can be easily grown in much of the United States, they are a challenge in the Deep South. A long growing season for berries also means a long growing season for weeds and pests. Southern gardeners must replant frequently and spend lots of time on maintenance.

With their attractive green leaves, white flowers, and vivid red berries, strawberries enhance an ornamental planting as well as a vegetable garden. Mass them as a ground cover among other ornamentals; plant them as an edging along a walkway or a flower bed. Strawberries are equally appealing grown in containers. Try a traditional strawberry jar (a clay pot with planting "pockets" puckering its sides) or a larger planter, such as a half-barrel. Remember that container-grown strawberries need careful attention to watering and fertilizing.

The Strawberry Plant

Strawberries grow from the arctic to the tropics, proof of their broad environmental tolerance. Two thousand years ago, the Romans knew of, and perhaps cultivated, two forms of strawberries that still exist today — the aromatic, small-fruited wood strawberry *(Fragaria vesca),* or *fraises des bois,* and the compact, continuously flowering alpine strawberry *(F. montana fraga).* The wood and the alpine strawberry, which Europeans began growing on a large scale in the 14th century, remained the primary cultivated strawberries until the 19th century. White- and red-fruited forms were popular in gardens of the 16th century.

The modern garden strawberry *(Fragaria × ananassa),* sometimes referred to as the "pineapple" strawberry for the aroma and flavor of the early hybrids, was developed in the 18th century from two North American species, the Virginia or scarlet strawberry *(F. virginiana),* and the Chilean or beach strawberry *(F. chiloensis),* a native of the western United States. Combined, they produce larger fruit, sweet flavor, and a distinct fragrance.

Strawberries, members of the rose family, are generally considered herbaceous perennials, though in some parts of the country strawberries are grown as annuals. A well-maintained, disease-free planting can do well for three to four fruiting years; beyond that, fruit quality and yield decline. Each strawberry plant consists of a crown, a compressed, modified stem from which fibrous roots grow downward and multiple stems grow upward, each topped with a three-parted leaflet. With their shallow roots, strawberries are sensitive to lack of water as well as waterlogged soils.

Individual strawberry plants ("mother" plants) spread by sending out runners — or stolons — long stems that extend over the surface of the soil. The runners produce new plants ("daughter" plants) along their length. By taking advantage of this fecundity, you can readily expand your initial planting.

One or more clusters of white five-petalled flowers form on short stems arising from the crown. Each flower produces a strawberry. Botanically speaking, the fleshy portion of the strawberry that we eat is the ripened receptacle, or base, of the flower. The hard, tiny tannish yellow or black dots on the surface of the strawberry, which we think of as seeds, are actually the true fruits of the strawberry, called achenes. Each achene contains a true seed.

Choosing Strawberries to Grow

All strawberry cultivars aren't created equal. They vary in flavor, suitability for different uses, disease resistance, tolerance of different climates, and harvest time. Each of these factors may influence your choice. Strawberries are self-fertile, so you can plant just one cultivar or many.

The flavor of strawberries ranges from sweet to tart. For comparisons, you might sample what your neighbors or local pick-your-own farms are growing. Decide what you want to do with your crop — liven up your morning cereal; make pies, jams, or preserves; or pop them in your mouth as you pick them. Some cultivars are better for one use than another. Soft-fruited cultivars, for instance, require eating soon after picking, while those with firmer fruit store better. Berry color, which covers a spectrum of reds, mostly matters for freezing or processing — cultivars with a uniform, deep red color are more visually appealing.

Selecting berries suited to your climate and resistant to diseases common in your area is particularly important. Before buying the most enticing cultivars from the list, consult the voices of experience. Ask local berry growers, knowledgeable nursery staff, or your cooperative extension agent which of these cultivars (or others) have proven themselves in your area.

Strawberry cultivars vary in the timing and duration of their crops according to their response to the number of hours of sunlight they receive at different times of the year. Horticulturists abbreviate this as a sensitivity to "daylength." In many parts of the country gardeners have the luxury of choosing when and for how long they want to pick berries. Cultivars are classified in one of three categories, based on their response to daylength.

June-bearers

The typical strawberry is a spring-bearer or June-bearer, so-called because it produces fruit in June. (In warmer climates, harvest may begin earlier.) Prompted by the short days of autumn, June-bearers form buds that flower and fruit the following spring, producing one large crop over about six weeks. Typically, June-bearers are spring-planted and not allowed to set fruit until the following season. You can expect a properly managed planting to fruit for two or three years.

If you want to pick lots of berries at once — for freezing, jam-making, or for an orgy of fresh strawberries and cream — June-bearers are a good choice. Avoid planting early-season June-bearers if your site is subject to late frosts, which can injure the blossoms.

Day-neutrals

Introduced about 15 years ago, day-neutrals are a strawberry-lover's dream. As the name implies, day-neutral strawberries don't respond to daylength. Instead, they flower and bear fruit more or less continuously for about five months, as long as temperatures are moderate (above 35°F and below 85°F), and they receive proper care. Day-neutrals do best in the northern half of the United States, from the mid-Atlantic to central California, and in higher, cooler elevation areas of the South. Typically, day-neutrals produce more berries in spring and fall than in hot summer weather.

A planting of day-neutrals is best grown for no more than one and a half to two years, as productivity and berry size decrease after that. But you'll enjoy ample fruit the first and second season. Depending on your climate and growing conditions, you'll harvest berries from spring until the first frost. Sometimes day-neutrals are grown as annuals.

If you want a long season of strawberry picking and live in a favorable climate, day-neutrals are a good choice. Compared to June-bearers, day-neutrals are more shallow rooted and plants are smaller, so they require some extra attention to watering and weeding. Day-neutrals also produce fewer runners.

Ever-bearers

The third type of strawberry, ever-bearers, produce two crops of berries, one in June and one in the fall. They form most of their flower buds during the long days of summer. Like day-neutrals, they produce few runners. Before the introduction of day-neutrals, ever-bearers were the only choice for a double crop. Today, however, day-neutrals are usually preferred over ever-bearers for their better fruit quality, higher yields, and hardiness. (In areas where consistently high temperatures seriously limit the yields of day-neutrals, consider growing June-bearers or ever-bearers instead.) For highest productivity, plantings of ever-bearers should be replaced after about three years in the ground.

Planting Strawberries

For best fruit production, strawberries need full sun. A deep, fertile, well-drained, yet water-retentive soil, such as a loam or sandy loam soil is ideal. On heavy soils with poor drainage, plant on raised beds. Strawberries perform best on slightly acid soil (pH of 6.2) and don't tolerate pH extremes (less than 5.5 or more than 7.0). Choose a site with access to water — strawberries are shallow rooted and require regular irrigation wherever you can't count on rainfall. Since strawberries bloom early in spring, avoid planting them in low-lying frost pockets.

To reduce the chance of verticillium wilt, a soil-borne fungal disease, avoid sites where other susceptible crops, such as tomatoes, potatoes, peppers, eggplant, raspberries, and blackberries have grown within the past three years. As added insurance, plant disease-resistant cultivars. Avoid planting strawberries in nematode-infested soil or in beds recently converted from lawn; sod can harbor grubs that eat strawberry roots.

Soil preparation

If possible, begin preparing the soil for strawberries a year before you plan to plant so that amendments have time to take effect. Eliminate all perennial weeds, then test and amend your soil for pH and nutrient levels. Digging weed-free organic materials, such as compost or manure, into the top 4 inches of soil will improve drainage and aeration in heavy clay soils and increase the water-holding capacity of sandy soils. If the organic material is well rotted, you can dig it in just before planting.

If you despair of improving your soil, or if your site is too wet (particularly where winter rains are heavy), plant on raised beds, 8 to 10 inches high. Make your own soil by mixing organic material with soil from the site, or buy good topsoil to fill the beds.

Into the ground

To minimize risk of disease, it's best to purchase virus-free plants from a reputable supplier rather than transplanting runner plants from an existing patch. (Garden plants may look perfectly healthy but could carry disease; if you decide to risk it, transplant runners in spring to give them the best shot at becoming established, and keep an eye out for problems.) Strawberries are usually sold in bundles of small, dormant plants with a mass of wiry roots. When the plants arrive, soak the roots in water for an hour or two (not much longer), then plant them right away. If you can't plant immediately, place plants in moist sawdust in a plastic bag and store them in the coolest part of the refrigerator.

Gardeners in cold-winter climates should plant strawberries as early in the spring as the ground can be worked — March or April in much of the United States. Fall planting (August through November) is a common practice in warm-winter climates. Plants then fruit in the winter months. In warm-winter climates, day-neutrals can be planted in fall or early spring.

A cool, cloudy day is ideal for planting; hot sun or drying winds are tough on transplants. Correct positioning of the crown is critical to success. (The crown is about 1 inch long and covered by overlapping buds from which the leaves develop.) The midpoint of the crown should be level with the soil surface — set too high, the roots can dry out; set too low, the crown can rot.

Dig the hole deep enough for the roots to extend straight down. If the roots are extremely long, you can cut them back to about 4 inches before planting. Trim and discard any moldy or black roots before planting. Positioning the crown at the correct height, set the roots into the hole and cover them completely with soil. (See drawing below.) Firm the soil and water thoroughly. Make sure the plants are well watered for the first two weeks after planting.

Planting Systems

People have long experimented with the number, arrangement, and density of strawberry plants in a bed to maximize production and make care and harvest easy. Several different "cultural systems" are popular; each offers advantages de-

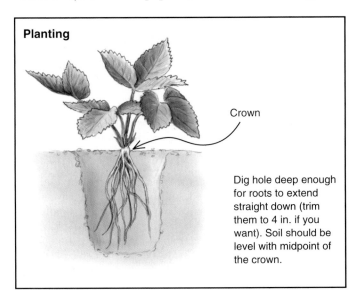

Planting

Crown

Dig hole deep enough for roots to extend straight down (trim them to 4 in. if you want). Soil should be level with midpoint of the crown.

pending on the type of strawberry, the conditions, and the needs of the grower.

Matted row

The easiest to maintain is the matted-row system, where runners are allowed to fill in a wide row. (See drawing below.) Set plants 12 to 15 inches apart in rows that are 48 inches apart. Let the runners spread and root to form a solid mat-

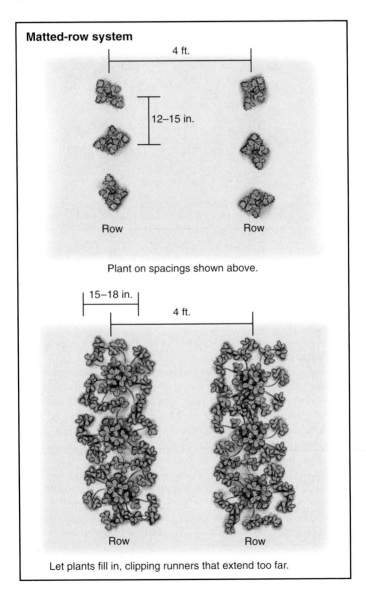

Matted-row system

4 ft.

12–15 in.

Row   Row

Plant on spacings shown above.

15–18 in.

4 ft.

Row   Row

Let plants fill in, clipping runners that extend too far.

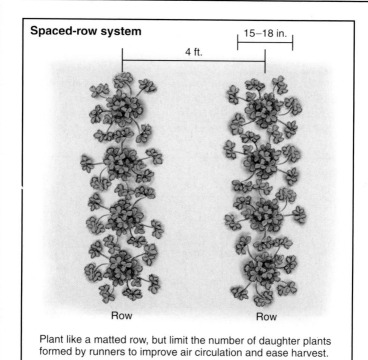

Spaced-row system

15–18 in.

4 ft.

Row   Row

Plant like a matted row, but limit the number of daughter plants formed by runners to improve air circulation and ease harvest.

ted row 15 to 18 inches wide, then clip off those extending farther. A row of this width is easy to weed and harvest, produces large fruit, and tends to minimize disease problems. To prevent matted rows from becoming too crowded, don't plant closer within the row than recommended or let the runners spread beyond the suggested row width.

Spaced row

In this system, you limit the number of runners per plant to direct more of the plant's energy into fruit production and to improve air circulation. (See drawing above.) As with the matted-row system, set plants 12 to 15 inches apart in rows 48 inches apart. When runners appear, cut off all but six to eight per plant, radiating from the mother plant at uniform spacings. Compared to the matted-row system, plants and berries in a spaced row grow bigger, the fruit is less likely to rot, and harvest is speedier because it's easier to spot the berries.

Yields vary, but under good growing conditions, each of the strawberry types will produce about a quart of berries per foot of matted or spaced row. A matted- or spaced-row system can be used on a raised bed, but doing so will make renovation, which we'll discuss later, more difficult.

Hill system

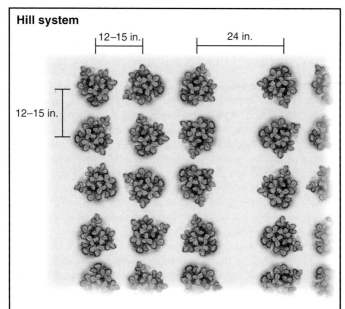

This is a triple-row hill system showing one bed and part of another; space plants as shown and remove all runners. Leave about 2 ft. between beds.

Ribbon row

In this system, plants are set 4 to 6 inches apart in rows spaced 3 feet apart, and all runners are removed the first and second years. With no runners to sustain, plants in ribbon rows tend to produce large berries. But the system requires more plants initially and more labor than the matted- or spaced-row system. (By the third year, it's hard to keep individual runners trimmed, so you can let them fill out into a narrow matted row.)

Hill system

There are several variations of the hill system; in each, all runners are removed. (Despite the name, plants are not necessarily set on "hills" or raised beds.) Typically, plants are set in a double or triple row bed, though single rows are sometimes used. (See drawing above.) Space plants 12 to 15 inches apart in rows spaced the same distance apart; leave $1\frac{1}{2}$ to 2 feet between beds. Remove all runners as they appear. The second year you'll have big plants, big fruit, and high yields.

Choosing a system

The choice of a planting system is dependent to a large degree on how freely a strawberry produces runners. June-bearers make many runners and can be successfully grown in several different planting systems; ever-bearers and day-neutrals, which produce fewer runners, offer fewer choices. The second criteria for selecting a system is more personal — do you want to limit your time caring for the berries, or do you want big berries? To grow big berries, you need to remove runners, which is time-consuming. Let the runners grow freely and you'll get smaller berries but more time to eat them.

June-bearers can be grown in any of the four systems described above. To take advantage of their prolific runner production, they are usually planted in a matted- or spaced-row system. Because you don't remove the runners, a matted row is the easiest system, but if the plants get too dense, the berries usually are smaller, fewer, and prone to rot. The other systems require time to remove some or all runners, but your efforts are likely to be rewarded with larger fruit and higher yields.

Ever-bearers and day-neutrals are better suited to a hill system rather than a matted row or spaced row, which they wouldn't fill in adequately. Day-neutrals also do well in a single ribbon row and are highly productive when planted in a special staggered ribbon-row system. Plant them on raised beds at least 8 inches high and 12 inches wide, inserting each plant through a covering of black plastic stretched over the bed. (Where summer temperatures are very warm, substitute white plastic.) Space the plants 6 inches apart in two staggered rows; leave $2^1/_2$ to 3 feet between the beds.

Caring for Strawberries

If June-bearers fruit the first year, their growth, runner production, and winter survival suffer, so it pays in the long run to remove all their flowers during that year. Cultivars that produce more than one flower cluster per plant may need this done several times. By the second year, your efforts will be rewarded with berries throughout the row. As an exception to the above practice, June-bearers planted in a ribbon row should be allowed to flower and fruit the first year. This system keeps plants small and productive, while discouraging runner formation, all of which are advantages in a high-density planting.

Remove all flowers from day-neutrals and ever-bearers for six weeks after planting; then let flowers form. You'll get larger plants and higher yields over the long haul.

Fertilizer
The amount of nutrients you'll need to provide depends on the fertility of your soil and the health of your plants. It's worth having a soil sample analyzed by your cooperative ex-

tension service lab or a private lab. If you tell them you're growing strawberries, they can give precise recommendations for fertilizer and amendments.

As a general guideline, however, for June-bearers or ever-bearers apply 2 pounds of a 10-10-10 or 12-12-12 formulation (or an equivalent, balanced fertilizer) per 100 linear feet of row six weeks after transplanting, and 2 pounds per 100 feet of row in late August or early September. In the second year and subsequent years, fertilize ever-bearers after harvest. (See Renovating below for second-year fertilizing of June-bearers.)

For day-neutrals, supply 2 pounds of 10-10-10 (or equivalent) per 100 feet of row every month, starting one month after planting and continuing through September. The second year, apply fertilizer beginning in May, at the same rate and frequency.

To avoid leaf and crown damage, fertilize when foliage is dry, then water it in. Avoid broadcasting fertilizer directly on crowns.

Irrigation

For maximum growth and yield, June-bearers and ever-bearers need 1 to $1\frac{1}{2}$ inches of water per week, supplied either by rainfall or irrigation. When June-bearers are fruiting, they need $1\frac{1}{2}$ to 2 inches per week. Provide day-neutrals with 2 inches of water per week. On sandy soil or in very hot weather, more water might be required. To minimize disease problems, avoid watering in late evening or very early morning. Soaker hoses or trickle irrigation are good choices for strawberries, because they keep the water off the leaves, which helps prevent problems such as gray mold.

Weed control

Weeds seriously compete with the shallow roots of strawberry plants, so keep the beds weed-free. You can pull weeds by hand, or remove them by shallow hoeing or cultivation, taking care to disturb the strawberry roots as little as possible. Remove any soil that gets tossed up onto the crowns while you're weeding. (Burying the crown can stunt the plant's growth.)

Mulch is an excellent aid to weed control, as well as a help keeping soil cool and moist and fruit clean. During the growing season, mulch with straw, sawdust, bark, or black plastic. In hot-summer areas, consider substituting white plastic for black, which causes fruit to burn when temperatures rise. To encourage growth, fall-planted berries in California are sometimes mulched with clear plastic, although this won't suppress weeds.

In slug-prone areas, mulch can provide the slimy little critters with a hiding place. Runners won't root through plastic, so it's best used with the hill system (cut the runners off even though they're not rooting) or where strawberries are grown as annuals. Straw is more effective than plastic for ribbon-row systems that you intend to convert to matted rows after a few years.

Winter protection

If you garden in a cold-winter climate, cover the plants with about 6 inches of clean straw in the fall when nighttime temperatures approach 20°F and plants are dormant (generally around Thanksgiving). The mulch prevents injury to crowns from cold temperatures and also helps keep soil temperatures stable, lessening chances of damage from cycles of freezing, thawing, and refreezing. Rake off the mulch into the paths early the following spring when the soil thaws (around the end of March in cold-winter climates) and the risk of severe cold has passed. Avoid straw mulch in areas with mild winter temperatures and extensive rainfall, such as western Oregon, because plants can break dormancy and begin growing under the mulch and rot.

In milder climates where some winter protection is needed, you can mulch with "floating" row covers of lightweight fabric instead of straw. Sold at nurseries or mail-order suppliers, row covers allow light to penetrate, producing higher berry yields than with straw mulch. Drape them over the plants in the fall and remove in spring before the plants flower to ensure good pollination.

Sprinkler irrigation can be effective temporary protection from early spring frosts. The heat released as the water freezes actually protects the berries from colder ambient temperatures. Set your sprinkler to cover the plants with a fine mist of water continuously from the time when the temperature drops below 33°F until the ice melts off the foliage in the morning.

Renovating June-bearers

Vigorous, relatively weed-free plantings of June-bearers can be "renovated" after their first productive year (the second year after transplanting) to maintain them for several more seasons. Because day-neutrals and ever-bearers produce into the fall, they aren't renovated. Renovation isn't mandatory for June-bearers, but removing leaves and keeping the plants from becoming crowded helps control diseases and insect pests. Because it reduces the number of runners, it increases the size of berries harvested.

To renovate, mow the foliage to about 3 inches high just

after harvest. (Don't cut back plants after the first, nonbearing year.) Whether you use a rotary mower or hedge clippers, take care not to damage the plants' crowns. Till the winter mulch you pulled off the plants in spring into the space between rows, narrowing matted rows (or third-year plantings of ribbon rows) to 12 inches wide. Apply a 10-10-10 fertilizer at the rate of 5 pounds per 100 feet of row. Then, to promote root development, spread an inch of soil over the mowed plants. Continue to irrigate as needed, and remove excess runners as they form. In early September, add another 3 pounds of 10-10-10.

Replanting

Strawberries don't produce well indefinitely, so they need to be replanted. June-bearers become less productive after two or three fruiting years, day-neutrals after one-and-a-half to two fruiting years, and ever-bearers after three years in the ground. Remove the entire planting and start again, if possible in a different location to minimize problems with soil-borne diseases. Because of the danger of disease, buy new plants rather than dividing existing ones.

Growing Strawberries as Annuals

Strawberries are often grown as fall-planted annuals in regions where the average January temperature stays above 50°F, including Florida, Alabama, and southern and central-coastal California. This approach entails a high-density planting system, much like the hill system described earlier. You set out freshly dug or partly chilled plants (depending on the cultivar and your location) closely spaced on plastic-covered raised beds. Depending on your location and the cultivar you choose, you might plant from August through early November and harvest three to six months later. You remove the plants in the spring and start the process again in the fall. 'Chandler' is often grown as a fall-planted annual, as are some day-neutral cultivars. Check with local nurseries for recommendations of cultivars suitable for annual planting in your region.

Several advantages make this method especially popular with commercial growers. Plantings are uniform. Plants grow in favorable winter temperatures and avoid the diseases, drought, and weed competition common in summer. Also, the time between planting and harvest is shortened, decreasing the amount of pre-harvest maintenance required. Home gardeners may also find some of these benefits tempting. Because of the method of growing strawberries as annuals, fruit quality decreases after the first harvest, so it isn't a good idea to try to switch an annual planting to a "perennial" one. You'll probably need to replant.

Gardeners in colder climates can also grow spring-planted day-neutrals as annuals, as do commercial growers of June-bearing cultivars who want a crop of day-neutrals to harvest later in the season. It might make more sense, however, for home gardeners to leave in a patch of day-neutrals for several years and plant a patch of June-bearers as well.

Alpine Strawberries

Alpine strawberries, often sold as *fraises des bois,* produce marble-size berries that release a burst of intense sweetness, a concentrated essence of strawberry flavor. First cultivated in the 18th century and popular in France where they are served with heavy cream or on tarts, alpine strawberries have become more popular in the United States.

Alpine strawberries are day-neutral, producing a small amount of fruit continuously throughout the growing season, perfect for an in-the-garden snack. Forming a neat mound, with no runners, they can easily be tucked among ornamentals, planted as a garden border or along a walk, or in a container. Their small white flowers and tiny pointed berries add a touch of refinement to the garden.

Alpine strawberries are easy to grow in full sun or part shade. You can buy plants bare-root, in pots, or as seeds, depending on the cultivar and source. Sow seeds indoors 10 to 12 weeks before the last spring frost date. Their cultural requirements are similar to those of day-neutrals. To encourage fruiting all summer, keep them well watered. Plants are long-lived; replace or divide them when they become less productive. The flavor of alpines can vary from garden to garden and year to year, so don't be discouraged if your first sampling tastes bland.

Several cultivars are available, including 'Charles V'; 'Rügen', with a flavor combining that of strawberries and roses; and 'Alexandria', which is similar to 'Baron Solemacher', a popular cultivar that is no longer available.

Harvest

Let your taste buds help you decide when to harvest — if the berries taste good, pick them. Berries ripen about 30 days after first bloom. For the sweetest, most flavorful berries for fresh eating, pick them a day or two after the entire berry turns fully red. For making jam, harvest slightly underripe berries. Pick the berries with the green caps on and about 1/2 inch of stem, pinching it off between your fingernails. To prevent decay, don't wash the berries until you're ready to use them. Pick all berries — overripe and rotting fruit left on the plant can encourage diseases and insects.

Pests and Diseases

Insects and diseases of strawberries vary with location; the symptoms and treatment for the most common ones are discussed here. Before you take action, properly identify the pest or disease, make sure the problem is significant enough to warrant control, and choose the least-toxic controls. (See the chapter "Ongoing Care" for more on this strategy.)

Verticillium wilt

This soil-borne fungal disease typically causes the outer and older leaves of affected plants to wilt, dry out, and turn red or dark brown between the veins and at the edges. If new leaves form, they're stunted. With a severe attack, many plants may die. This fungus can survive in the soil for many years and also infects tomatoes, potatoes, eggplants, peppers, raspberries, and blackberries.

There is no remedy for plants infected with verticillium, but you can take steps to avoid it. Don't plant in wet, low-lying sites. Plant resistant cultivars where susceptible crops have been recently grown. Start with healthy plants. Rotate the location of your strawberry plants every three to five years. Clean gardening tools before you use them.

Red stele

Young and old leaves of plants infected by this root-rot fungus lose their shiny luster and wilt during hot weather; plants eventually die. The center part (stele) of affected roots appears pink to red or brownish red, rather than a healthy yellowish white. Roots also may blacken and/or rot. To control red stele, plant resistant cultivars, grow them on well-drained soil, and plant in raised beds.

Gray mold

Gray mold, one of the most common fruit rot diseases of strawberries, is especially problematic with day-neutrals because they continuously fruit. Affected flowers turn brown; fruit develops soft, light brown spots that become covered with gray fungal growth, then they rot. Rainy and cool weather encourages spread of this fungus, as does handling healthy berries after touching infected ones. Pick and destroy infected berries to keep spores from spreading. As prevention, mulch early in the season to keep fruits off the ground and avoid planting on wet, low sites.

Leaf spots

Purple or reddish spots on the upper leaf surfaces indicate presence of one of several leaf diseases, which kill leaves prematurely and damage fruit. These diseases tend to be more serious problems on old, weak plants. Good air circulation and optimum growing conditions, along with renovation, minimizes problems. Resistant cultivars are also available.

Tarnished plant bug

This sucking insect, which is about 1/4 inch long and has yellowish and black spots, damages flowers. The resulting berries are small and nubby or twisted. Monitor for the small, green nymphs (the most damaging life stage) when plants start to flower. Tap leaves and flower clusters over a shallow, white dish. If more than two nymphs fall in the dish per foot of row, consider applying a least-toxic pesticide specific for their control. Remove misshapen berries. Clip down any ground cover for 5 to 10 yards around your berry patch to minimize hibernation sites for the adults.

Strawberry bud weevil

A major pest east of the Rockies, this dark, reddish brown weevil lays eggs in flower buds and cuts partly through stems, causing flower buds to fall over or off. Bud weevils hibernate in woodlots and nearby foliage, coming out in early spring. Destroy damaged buds, eliminate hibernation sites such as organic trash and nearby foliage, and/or apply a botanical insecticide registered for use on strawberries.

White grubs

These C-shaped beetle larvae, which are primarily a problem in the eastern United States, damage roots. Avoid planting strawberries on beds recently made from lawn; sod can harbor grubs. Beneficial nematodes or bacteria that cause milky-spore disease can be effective in reducing grub populations, as is cover cropping with deep-rooted legumes, such as clover.

Spider mites

Two-spotted mites, in particular, feed on strawberry plants. The undersides of the leaves turn brown in areas, then bronzed, and finally dry up and die. New growth appears yellowish and plants become stunted. Look on the leaf undersides for fine webbing and the very tiny pale yellow to green, eight-legged adults, usually bearing two dark spots. You might need a 10× hand lens to see them.

Hot dry weather favors spider mites. A forceful spray of water can reduce spider mite populations. If a stronger control is warranted, apply an insecticidal soap spray, making sure to cover the undersides of the leaves well. They are often controlled by their many natural enemies, such as predatory mites, especially if the beneficials haven't been killed off by insecticides. You can purchase and release predatory mites to aid the process.

Slugs and snails

These pests eat small, somewhat deep holes in berries, often leaving a dried-up, shiny trail of slime in their wake. To control them, eliminate nearby hiding places such as boards, stones, debris, mulch, and weeds. Handpick them regularly; nighttime forays, when snails and slugs are out in force, are most effective. Trap them under flower pots or boards. Commercially available copper barriers, buried a few inches below the soil surface and extending 6 inches above, are an effective deterrent.

■ RECOMMENDED VARIETIES OF STRAWBERRIES

Regions indicate where plant is well adapted. (See previous discussion of alpine strawberries for recommended varieties of that type.)

June-Bearers: Early Season

Chandler

Description of fruit: Very firm, moderately sweet; large; light red.
Resistance to red stele: Susceptible.
Resistance to verticillium wilt: Unknown.
Regions: South from North Carolina to Florida, along Gulf Coast (lower Mississippi, Alabama, Georgia) to Southern California. Grown as far north as New Jersey.
Comments: Excellent for fresh eating, preserves, and freezing. Resistant to rain and frost damage. Typically grown as annual on raised beds covered with black plastic.

Earliglow

Description of fruit: Firm; sweet, excellent flavor; medium-size.
Resistance to red stele: Good.
Resistance to verticillium wilt: Intermediate.
Regions: Northeast, upper Midwest, mid-Atlantic, mid-South (includes Kentucky, West Virginia, south to mid-Mississippi, Alabama, Georgia).
Comments: Excellent for fresh eating, preserves, freezing; cold-hardy.

Sequoia
Description of fruit: Medium-firm, very sweet; large.
Resistance to red stele: Susceptible.
Resistance to verticillium wilt: Susceptible to intermediate.
Regions: California and north to Oregon, Florida, Gulf Coast and lower South.
Comments: Excellent for fresh eating, preserves; fair for freezing.

Veestar
Description of fruit: Firm; sweet, excellent flavor; medium-size.
Resistance to red stele: Susceptible.
Resistance to verticillium wilt: Susceptible.
Regions: Northeast, Midwest, south to Arkansas.
Comments: Excellent for fresh eating, preserves. Very cold-hardy Canadian cultivar.

June-Bearers: Early Midseason

Honeoye
Description of fruit: Large, firm; tart, good flavor.
Resistance to red stele: Susceptible.
Resistance to verticillium wilt: Susceptible.
Regions: Northeast, Midwest, mid-Atlantic, mid-South, north-central, Pacific Northwest.
Comments: Excellent for freezing, good for fresh eating; very cold-hardy. May develop off-flavor on heavy clay soils or under hot temperatures.

Hood
Description of fruit: Firm; sweet; large.
Resistance to red stele: Resistant to certain races.
Resistance to verticillium wilt: Intermediate resistance.
Regions: Pacific Northwest.
Comments: Excellent for preserves, good for fresh eating. Not very winter-hardy.

Kent
Description of fruit: Firm; mild, subacid, excellent flavor; large.
Resistance to red stele: Susceptible.
Resistance to verticillium wilt: Susceptible.
Regions: Northeast, Midwest, mid-Atlantic, north-central.
Comments: Excellent for fresh eating, preserves, freezing. Very cold-hardy Canadian cultivar. Berries tend to lay on ground, so mulch to keep them clean.

'*Sequoia*'

Red Chief
Description of fruit: Firm; sweet, rich flavor; medium to large.
Resistance to red stele: Good.
Resistance to verticillium wilt: Good.
Regions: Northeast, Midwest, mid-Atlantic, north-central, mid-South.
Comments: Very good for fresh eating and freezing.

Surecrop
Description of fruit: Firm; sweet; large.
Resistance to red stele: Good.
Resistance to verticillium wilt: Good.
Regions: Northeast, Midwest, mid-Atlantic, north-central, mid-South, Gulf Coast.
Comments: Excellent for fresh eating, freezing. Drought-resistant.

June-Bearers: Midseason

Allstar
Description of fruit: Firm; sweet; large, light red.
Resistance to red stele: High.
Resistance to verticillium wilt: Intermediate.
Regions: Northeast to central Midwest; also mid-Atlantic, north-central, mid-South.
Comments: Excellent for fresh eating, freezing. Cold-hardy.

Benton
Description of fruit: Soft, sweet; medium to large.
Resistance to red stele: Intermediate.
Resistance to verticillium wilt: Susceptible.
Regions: Pacific Northwest, California.
Comments: Excellent fresh eating, good for preserves.

Cardinal
Description of fruit: Very firm; sweet; large.
Resistance to red stele: Susceptible.
Resistance to verticillium wilt: Susceptible.
Regions: Southeast, south-central (Arkansas and neighboring states east to Virginia, Carolinas), Florida and Gulf Coast; not consistent producer in North.
Comments: Very good for freezing, good fresh.

Shuksan
Description of fruit: Firm; sweet; large.
Resistance to red stele: Intermediate.
Resistance to verticillium wilt: Susceptible.
Regions: Pacific Northwest (recommended cultivar for colder areas of this region), north-central.
Comments: Excellent for freezing, good for fresh eating, preserves. Tolerates wet soils, alkaline conditions.

June-Bearers: Late Midseason

Glooscap
Description of fruit: Firm; sweet; large.
Resistance to red stele: Susceptible.
Resistance to verticillium wilt: Intermediate.
Regions: Northeast, upper Midwest, north-central, mid-Atlantic.
Comments: Very good fresh, good for freezing; very cold-hardy Canadian cultivar.

Jewel
Description of fruit: Firm; sweet, excellent flavor; large.
Resistance to red stele: Susceptible.
Resistance to verticillium wilt: Susceptible.
Regions: Nova Scotia to mid-Atlantic, Midwest; cooler, higher elevation southern areas, Alabama.
Comments: Excellent for fresh eating, freezing; very cold-hardy.

Lateglow
Description of fruit: Firm; sweet, excellent flavor; large.
Resistance to red stele: High.
Resistance to verticillium wilt: Intermediate.
Regions: Northeast, Midwest, mid-Atlantic; also some warmer-winter climates like Arkansas.
Comments: Excellent fresh, good for freezing. Cold-hardy.

Rainier
Description of fruit: Soft; sweet; medium to large.
Resistance to red stele: Intermediate.
Resistance to verticillium wilt: Intermediate.
Regions: Pacific Northwest.
Comments: Excellent for fresh eating, freezing, preserves. Highly recommended for fruit quality, disease resistance.

Sparkle
Description of fruit: Soft; mild, subacid, excellent flavor; medium.
Resistance to red stele: Good.
Resistance to verticillium wilt: Susceptible.
Regions: Northeast, Midwest, mid-Atlantic.
Comments: Excellent fresh; one of the best for preserves, freezing. Very cold-hardy.

Tioga
Description of fruit: Firm; sweet; medium to large.
Resistance to red stele: Susceptible.

Resistance to verticillium wilt: Susceptible.
Regions: California, Florida, Gulf Coast.
Comments: Excellent for preserves, good for freezing.

Day-Neutrals

Fern
Description of fruit: Firm; sweet; large.
Resistance to red stele: Susceptible.
Resistance to verticillium wilt: Intermediate.
Regions: Pacific Northwest, Midwest, mid-Atlantic.
Comments: Very good for fresh eating, good for preserves, freezing.

Hecker
Description of fruit: Firm; excellent flavor; large.
Resistance to red stele: Unknown.
Resistance to verticillium wilt: Good.
Regions: California.
Comments: Good for fresh eating, preserves, freezing.

Selva
Description of fruit: Firm; large. Flavor evaluations range from excellent to poor.
Resistance to red stele: Susceptible.
Resistance to verticillium wilt: Intermediate.
Regions: California, Florida, Gulf Coast, mid-South.
Comments: Good fresh, frozen, preserved.

Tillikum
Description of fruit: Firm; semitart, good flavor; small to medium; light red.
Resistance to red stele: Some.
Resistance to verticillium wilt: Susceptible.
Regions: Pacific Northwest.
Comments: Good for fresh eating, preserves. Produces all summer, even in high temperatures.

Tribute
Description of fruit: Firm; slightly tart, good flavor; medium to large.
Resistance to red stele: Good.
Resistance to verticillium wilt: Good.
Regions: Canada south to about Maryland; Midwest, upland areas of South, Pacific Northwest.
Comments: Good for fresh eating, freezing, preserves. Very cold-hardy.

Tristar

Description of fruit: Firm; sweet, excellent flavor; small to medium.
Resistance to red stele: Good.
Resistance to verticillium wilt: Good.
Regions: Range same as 'Tribute'.
Comments: Excellent for fresh eating, freezing. Very cold-hardy, bred for Northeast. Fall crop is heaviest.

Ever-Bearers

Fort Laramie

Description of fruit: Firm; sweet, excellent flavor, very aromatic; large to very large.
Resistance to red stele: Susceptible.
Resistance to verticillium wilt: Intermediate to good.
Regions: Grow in cold climates (except Alaska, where long days inhibit fruit production), also Pacific Northwest, California.
Comments: Good for fresh eating, preserves, freezing. Very cold-hardy.

Ogallala

Description of fruit: Soft, sharp, wild strawberry flavor; medium to large.
Resistance to red stele: Susceptible.
Resistance to verticillium wilt: Unknown.
Regions: Midwest, from Mississippi west through Mountain states.
Comments: Excellent for freezing, preserves. Very cold-hardy.

Ozark Beauty

Description of fruit: Medium-firm; sweet; large.
Resistance to red stele: Susceptible.
Resistance to verticillium wilt: Susceptible.
Regions: Midwest, Pacific Northwest, northern and southern mountain areas.
Comments: Excellent for fresh eating, freezing, preserves.

Quinault

Description of fruit: Medium-firm; sweet; large.
Resistance to red stele: Good.
Resistance to verticillium wilt: Intermediate.
Regions: Midwest, Alaska, Pacific Northwest.
Comments: Good for fresh eating, preserves; poor for freezing. 'Tillikum' has higher yields, better flavor.

Raspberries and Blackberries

'Tayberry' is a midseason Western trailing blackberry with soft, but very tasty fruit.

There is no better advertisement for growing raspberries in the home garden than a heaping bowl of fresh raspberries and cream. If your climate isn't extreme and you have reasonably good soil, a sunny planting site, and readily available water, you can grow these delightful berries.

Most people think "red" when they think of raspberries. But raspberries also come in black; in various shades of yellow, from off-white, to gold, to a slightly orange hue; and in purples that range from almost red to nearly black.

You'll find similar variation in flavor (from blah to exquisite), in firmness (mushy soft to dry and firm), in seediness, and in "drupelet cohesion," a five-dollar term that describes the berry's resistance to falling apart. (Raspberries are an aggregate fruit, composed of individual drupelets, held together by nearly invisible hairs. Each drupelet generally has a single seed, a few have two.) Raspberry canes can be arrayed with threatening hooklike spines or be nearly spineless. The former make excellent "security" hedges; the latter are friendlier to harvesters and young children.

While we're singing the praises of the raspberry, we shouldn't overlook its close relative, the blackberry. The two can be easily distinguished. When raspberries are picked, the stems and receptacles stay on the plant, and picked berries are hollow. Blackberries, on the other hand, retain their stems, and the picked berries are not hollow.

Though less popular with home and commercial growers alike, blackberries can be every bit as enticing. They have an exquisite flavor similar to, yet different from, raspberries. Picked slightly early, they're mouth-puckeringly tart. Left to ripen fully on the cane, they are deliciously sweet. Blackberries are also prolific, yielding on average at least half again as much as raspberries. And long after the summer raspberries are gone, there are blackberry cultivars still bearing.

With so much to recommend them, why aren't blackberries grown more widely? Mainly, the selection of cultivars is much narrower than for raspberries. And there are currently no cultivars that consistently produce where winter temperatures drop below -20°F, which eliminates about a third of the prime United States berry-growing areas. (On the other hand, blackberries will bear as far south as Ft. Myers, Florida.) Blackberry canes are much thornier and grow far more vigorously than raspberry canes, requiring more attention to keep them reined in. Finally, the berries are generally softer than raspberries and don't keep as well.

We'll discuss blackberries at the end of this chapter; because they are so similar to raspberries, it's worth reading the following material on raspberries first.

Raspberry Background

Raspberries can be found on all the continents, from the frigid arctic regions to the warm semitropics. In the arctic, mature plants are tiny, with gorgeous little flowers and very aromatic fruit. In the warmer regions, raspberries may form briar patches, a jungle of long climbing vines. In between are found the berries we're familiar with on cereal and in jams, the European and American species of red raspberry (*Rubus idaeus vulgatus* and *R. idaeus* var. *strigosus,* respectively), and the black raspberry *(R. occidentalis L)*. American raspberries are round, European are long and conical. Most of the berries on the market today are complex hybrids, having some of each type in their ancestry.

Although raspberries have been mentioned in literature for more than 2,000 years, they have been grown in Europe only since about Columbus's time. The first known sale of raspberry plants in North America wasn't until 1771. Serious commercial plantings in Europe and America date only from the last century. Today, the major commercial plantings in North America are along the northern California coast and certain valleys in Oregon, Washington, and British Columbia. Raspberries are grown in home gardens in all states, with the possible exception of Hawaii.

Categorizing things often makes understanding and remembering them easier. Raspberries can be classified in several ways, each of which highlights an important characteristic. Let's look at how raspberries differ according to the season in which the fruit matures, then at the characteristics of the berries themselves.

Season of maturity

Raspberry plants are an interesting blend of two common horticultural categories, perennial and biennial. The roots are perennial, but the aboveground growth, the leaf- and fruit-bearing canes, are biennial, each cane living only two growing seasons before dying.

Raspberries bear either in the fall or the summer. Fall bearers, called "primocanes," bear their crop on first-year canes; that is, on canes developed during the current growing season. Primocanes are the easiest raspberries to grow, especially if you prefer gardening organically. The moment snow is gone in late winter or very early spring, mow or prune off last season's canes just above ground level. New canes then grow and bear the crop in the fall — as early as mid-July to late November, depending upon the cultivar and your location.

Summer bearers, or "floricanes," on the other hand, form berries on canes that have overwintered from the previous season. This has three major implications, each of which adds to the care you must provide. First, the canes must be able to emerge from winter unharmed to bear a good crop. Second, while overwintered canes are trying to bear a summer crop, new canes are developing and competing for sunlight, water, and nutrients. Third, after bearing their crop, the second-year canes die and should be removed.

About berries

Easy-care, fall-bearing raspberries of good quality and acceptable yields are a recent development. So there is a much wider choice of color, size, flavor, and numerous other characteristics among the summer-maturing type.

If you're looking for purple or black raspberries — berries

you can't buy at most grocery stores — you have no choice. All currently available cultivars produce only summer crops. Be patient, though; within a decade or so the first fall-bearing black and purple raspberries are likely to appear in nurseries and on the market.

Black and purple berries are almost round. They tend to have a shorter season, are strongly flavored, and have seedier fruit than red raspberries. Purple berries have little eye appeal and are generally dull and soft. But, if you're making pie fillings, toppings, jams, syrups, and jellies, purple raspberries are ideal. They tend to outproduce the reds (at least east of the Rockies), pick much faster, and the color of the processed products is a very attractive, rich red. A few purple berries added to a simple dish like Jell-O or ice cream greatly enhances the flavor and visual appeal.

Yellow raspberries are mutations of red ones, so you'll find all kinds of them of both summer and fall-bearing types. Like red raspberries, they are round to conical in shape. Unfortunately, most yellow mutations are either very soft, or tasteless, or both. A few are extremely sweet and delicious but generally soft. Soft fruit does not ship, handle, and keep well. Yellow raspberries also tend to yield poorly. These are big problems for growers and marketers, but perhaps less so for home gardeners — a glass bowl full of yellow, black, and red raspberries is a delightful sight.

Although large berries frequently have a diluted taste, some people seem to taste with their eyes instead of their taste buds. The typical red raspberry at the supermarkets weighs about 2.5 to 3 grams, but some red cultivars can produce berries two, even three times that size. (Superior-tasting large red cultivars include 'Tulameen', 'Chilliwack', and 'Canby'.) Many of the purple cultivars tend to have berries about 50 percent larger than the average red ones. You can also increase the size of berries by thinning canes to concentrate the plant's energies in fewer berries.

Climate

The climate of the Pacific Northwest, with its long, mild growing season, is ideal for brambleberries (though it can be a little cold for some blackberries). Because plants must have sufficient cold to provide a minimal period of dormancy, brambles don't do well in the tropics (except for higher elevations). In addition, brambles, especially raspberries, do not like temperatures much above 75°F. Intense light and heat stress plants, and the fruit deteriorates. Individual drupelets may even sun-scald, becoming entirely white (but perfectly edible).

When selecting bramble cultivars, southern gardeners should pay particular attention to their chill-hour requirements. Some cultivars, such as 'Bababerry', can get along with fewer chill hours and with higher daytime temperatures. Southerners can also plant brambles in areas shaded from the heat of midday. Shade-cloth tents and misting can also reduce stress. (Don't mist in high-humidity areas; insufficient evaporation increases risk of disease.)

In cold regions, winter temperatures are of concern only with summer-bearing raspberries. Bramble roots will survive most anywhere; they can typically stand soil temperatures near 0°F, which is seldom reached even in the coldest regions. The fruit-bearing canes, however, must be able to weather the winter. The farther north you garden, the more limited your choice of climate-adapted cultivars.

If you can, site plants to protect them from winter damage. Place summer-bearing cultivars on a wind-protected northern slope. In late winter or early spring, temperatures can warm for several days, then suddenly drop. Canes urged from dormancy by the warm spell will freeze and their cells will rupture during subsequent cold nights. A cool north-slope location will lessen the chance of canes breaking dormancy prematurely.

Winter winds can also damage plants, mostly by desiccation. Protecting plantings from winter and summer wind-stress with windbreaks can increase yields considerably.

Since the canes of fall-bearing raspberries are removed in late winter, northerners need not be concerned with their winter hardiness. In the north, the main concern for fall-bearing cultivars is length of season. When do they ripen? If you select late-maturing cultivars, killing frosts may arrive before they ripen.

Pollination

Brambles are self-fertile, so you needn't plant different cultivars for cross-pollination. Raspberry flowers have a very sweet and attractive nectar, and lack of pollination is seldom a problem. Long periods of cold or cloudy, windy, and rainy days during flower time may hamper pollination, resulting in incomplete or crumbly fruit. The seed in each drupelet is the result of pollination. Without pollination there can be no seed, and without seed there will be no flesh around the seed.

Choosing a Raspberry Cultivar

Answering three questions will help you determine which types of berry suit your needs and climate best.

How do I plan to use most of my berries? If you're likely to eat them fresh out of hand, select cultivars providing intense flavor and eye appeal. Used fresh with cereals or special deserts, any color, or combinations of color, will do. For color accent, try a mixture of yellow, black, and red. Purple berries tend to look dull, an appearance occasionally heightened by a dusty "bloom" that is sometimes mistaken for fungicide residue.

   If you make preserves, texture and color after processing are important. Yellow berries can turn muddy when processed. Purples, on the other hand, are great for pastries and processed products. They have high yields and are large, easy and quick to pick, and provide good aroma, flavor, and sharp red color.

What suits my climate? For summer-bearing cultivars, northerners should select winter-hardy varieties. Black raspberries, such as 'Bristol' and 'Jewel', do well only where temperatures don't drop much below -20°F. 'Black Hawk' is hardier but also less desirable. Some purple cultivars ('Brandywine', 'Estate', and 'Royalty') will take just a little more cold. The most cold-hardy reds are 'Boyne', 'Nordic', 'Nova', and 'Killarney'. ('Latham' is very cold-hardy, but it is of poor quality and extremely susceptible to disease.) Gardeners whose winter temperatures never fall below -10°F can grow any black or purple cultivar and can therefore select for flavor, yield, and disease resistance. Good red cultivars in this range include 'Canby' and 'Chilliwack'.

   In the South, select summer-bearing cultivars according to the number of chill hours they need and the amount of heat they'll tolerate. 'Bababerry' is the first choice based on these criteria, and 'Willamette' is fair. (Neither tolerates temperatures below 0°F.)

   For fall bearers, in the northernmost regions (zones 3 to 4), 'Autumn Bliss', 'Redwing', and 'Summit' are good choices. If fall freezes don't arrive until early October (zone 5), choose cultivars such as 'Amity' or 'Heritage'. For a longer season yet (zones 6 to 7), try 'Rossana', an Italian cultivar of exquisite flavor and great yields. It has only recently appeared in North America, so you may have trouble finding it — and we haven't included it in the cultivar list for that reason — but it promises to be a terrific raspberry. Southerners should try 'Bababerry', which will bear an early crop in mid- to late May, perhaps, and another crop in August. (Grown in the north, 'Bababerry' bears only an early crop.)

When do I want to harvest? Summer-bearing varieties will produce for about three weeks. For an extended harvest,

'Autumn Bliss' is a very early, very hardy, and very tasty fall-bearing raspberry.

plant two summer bearers, one early and one late, and two in the fall, one early and one late. (Try 'Tulameen' to bridge the gap if your winters don't go below -5°F or so.) Those in zones 4 and colder can plant two summer bearers, but only an early fall-bearing type ('Autumn Bliss' or 'Redwing'), which will bear before fall frost puts an end to production.

Growing Raspberries

For growing, training, and pruning purposes, there are some differences between types of raspberries. First we'll discuss common aspects of cultivation, then their differences. All raspberries benefit from being trained to a support of some sort, which makes the canes easier to manage, reduces fungal diseases, and produces more berries, which are easier to pick. We'll discuss support systems after a look at the cultural requirements of the different types of berries.

Site, soil, and planting out

Plants do best in full sun, but in hot climates can be sited to take advantage of partial shade during the hottest parts of the day. Plants should be sheltered from hot summer and cold winter winds. Air movement is needed, however — particularly in humid climates — to help keep fungal diseases at bay.

Raspberries will do well in "good" garden soil that retains moisture but drains well; the roots die in waterlogged soil. Enriching your soil with organic matter, such as well-rotted compost and manure, aids fertility and improves water retention and drainage. Plants prefer a slightly acid soil, pH 6.0 to 6.7.

Brambles are sold as dormant, bare-root plants and can be planted in the spring in cold-winter climates or in the spring or fall in areas with mild winters. In heavy soil, cover the roots with about an inch of soil; in sandy soils, cover them with about 2 inches. The idea is to put the roots in the best soil and far enough from the surface to keep them from easily drying out.

Cut the canes down to the ground immediately after planting. If left, they will bear fruit in the summer, diverting energy from the developing plant. (See the chapter "Planting Fruit Trees and Bushes" for more on soil improvement and planting techniques.)

Water, weeds, and mulch

Make sure the plants have adequate water throughout the season — if nature doesn't supply it, you must. If your soil is rich in organic matter (3 to 5 percent on a soil test), plants need an inch of water every week or so. If your soil has less organic matter or is a light, sandy soil, they'll need an inch every four to five days. Wet canes are breeding grounds for fungal diseases; try to direct irrigation water to the roots, not the canes.

Mulch helps conserve water, suppresses weeds, keeps soil cool in hot weather, and generally improves the health and fertility of the soil. Well-matured compost is excellent mulch. It's easy to apply, looks good, and contains nutrients that are immediately available to the plant. In the spring, remove mulch from around the plants so the ground can warm and hasten emergence of young shoots. Later, when soil temperatures have risen, you can re-mulch to keep the soil cool and moist.

If you have good soil and healthy plants, the shade they create will discourage weeds. Those that struggle through can be pulled by hand, dislodged by shallow hoeing, or suffocated with compost.

Feeding

Reasonably good soil enriched with an inch or two of good compost or a moderate dose of balanced fertilizer each year should provide sufficient nutrients for your plants to thrive. Short of smothering your plants, good compost is hard to overdo. Unless your soil is truly awful, compost tends to correct almost all problems. This takes time, however, so if you know or suspect that you have soil nutrient or pH problems, have a soil test done and follow the lab's recommendations.

Berry lovers sometimes provide regular doses of foliar fertilizers to give their plants a boost. Absorbed by the leaves in liquid form, seaweed, fish emulsion, and similar organic materials in balanced formulations provide a broad spectrum of micronutrients. These liquid fertilizers, whether "home-brewed" or store-bought, can produce results in a few days. Foliar feeding must be done in late evenings, very early mornings, or on cool, cloudy days, otherwise the leaves can't absorb the nutrients. You can apply every 10 to 14 days from the time the plant emerges until it goes dormant. Avoid applying high-nitrogen fertilizers, especially after the plants have flowered. Potassium (K) is much more important in the formation of quality fruit with high sugar content and good shelf life. If your soil is slightly alkaline, you may also have to supply iron and manganese.

Remember that it is much better to underapply than to overuse chemical fertilizers. Too much fertilizer can easily upset the soil's chemical balance, affect its structure, porosity, and water-holding capacity, and wreak havoc with the important microbial life in the soil.

Fall-bearing raspberries

As we mentioned earlier, fall bearers are easy to grow. About all you need to do is control their tendency to spread where you don't want them and keep them tidy and pickable with a trellis. Providing adequate water (if nature doesn't), and regularly adding compost or fertilizer to provide nutrients completes your tasks.

Fall bearers multiply from the base of mother plants and

from root suckers, spreading 12 to 18 inches per year in all directions. If you want a solid row in a year, space new plants a foot apart. If you're willing to wait two years to fill in the row, space them 2 feet apart. To prevent your yard from becoming a jungle, you can limit their spread by placing wooden or plastic barriers in the ground. Dig down about 10 to 12 inches at the desired border and place the boards or plastic barrier vertically. If you don't use barriers, hoe, shallow till, or mow off any growth that appears where you don't want it.

As they grow, the canes will branch and spread to three or more feet. This is still narrow enough for you to reach in from both sides to harvest, but if you want narrower rows, limit the base to 12 inches wide or less. Some sort of trellising is necessary because the heavy load of ripening fruit tends to bend the canes down. (See Supporting the canes, below.) This makes them hard to find and reach and, if the canes rest on the ground, berries will rot or become so dirty they'll be inedible.

At the end of the winter, when the snow is gone, mow or cut all the canes down to the ground. If you have a wood chipper, grind them up and compost them. While it is possible to overwinter the canes of fall bearers and harvest a second crop the following summer, it isn't desirable. Because the second crop ripens toward the lower part of the canes, berries will be difficult to find and reach. And these berries won't taste as good, because they'll ripen in the shade. Most important, leaving the old canes for a second crop reduces the fall crop and increases the chances of disease. In short, if you want a summer crop, grow a summer variety.

Summer-bearing red and yellow cultivars

In most respects, these are treated like fall-bearing cultivars. The main difference is the need to remove second-year canes after they have borne a crop.

The moment you're done harvesting, prune off all spent canes. Prune when canes are dry to minimize spreading fungal diseases likely to be on the old canes. Cutting out these dead canes increases air circulation and light penetration for the new canes that remain and keeps the planting from becoming an impenetrable thicket. It's easy to distinguish old canes from new. Old canes are gray or brown and woody, new ones are green and succulent — less fibrous, with more water. Old canes have branches with yellowing leaves, the new are branchless with lush green leaves.

Check the new canes as you prune the old, removing any that are obviously diseased, spindly, or that are growing in awkward positions or angles. A newly pruned row may look a bit beaten up, but in two to three weeks, new growth will have filled the gaps.

In late winter or early spring, thin all summer-bearing red and yellow cultivars. Leave only the heaviest, sturdiest, and healthiest canes, reducing the total to about two to four canes per square foot of row. The result may look sparse, but leaving more has drawbacks. It can increase fungal diseases because crowded plants won't dry out; remaining canes will be thinner and weaker, the fruit smaller. If you leave too few, you'll have sturdy and healthy canes and extra-large fruit.

Some growers also "tip" canes at this time, removing the spindly top 6 inches or so. This has a number of advantages. It removes the thinnest wood, which produces the smallest berries, forces lower buds into growth, and doesn't reduce the harvest.

Black and purple summer bearers

These raspberries are, in some ways, easier to grow because they don't sucker and spread like the red and yellow cultivars. Weed control is also easier, because you can heavily mulch or hoe without worrying about covering or damaging emerging plants.

With few exceptions, these plants stay put. Plant them about 30 to 36 inches apart. Canes of black and purple cultivars tend to be larger in diameter and much longer than their red cousins. (Their spines are also larger, stiffer, and sharper.) This vigorous growth requires additional pruning of both first- and second-year canes.

For first-year canes, in late spring or early summer, when new canes have a good start on growth, remove all but the heaviest five or six new canes in each clump or cluster. Later, when the new canes are about waist high, cut off the top 3 to 6 inches of growth. This tip pruning forces each cane to produce numerous lateral branches, which will bear the fruit the following year. If you don't pinch back the young canes, they'll grow to unmanageable lengths of 12 feet and longer. (If the laterals are too high to pick the following year, adjust the height at which you prune them; experiment until you get results that are comfortable.)

Second-year canes (those that will bear the current season's crop) also need pruning. In late winter or early spring, before the buds swell, thin and cut back their lateral branches, which will have grown more than 6 feet by the end of their first season. Leave no more than eight to ten of the largest branches, and cut each branch back to no more than 8 to 12 inches in length. After pruning, these branches will not elongate again but will produce only short branches that bear flowers and fruit during the summer.

A simple, homemade T-stake for trellis comprising two strands of heavy monofilament or baling twine. Plants grow up between the strands, which keep them from sprawling. Wires are stretched taut between stout posts.

Thinning and cutting back determine the height, location, and number of berries on the plant. Fewer canes with fewer or shorter branches produce fewer but larger berries. As soon as possible after harvest, remove the spent, second-year canes.

Black raspberries are more susceptible to fungal diseases, so be particularly conscientious about applying lime sulfur in early spring (see Pests and Diseases on page 207) and cutting back canes to allow for free air circulation. If in doubt, leave less rather than more cane.

Supporting the canes

Volumes have been written about supporting brambleberries on trellises. While it is possible to allow less-vigorous red raspberry cultivars to grow as unsupported shrubs, most gardeners will welcome trellising. It allows you to make the plants grow how and where you want them and makes harvest much, much easier.

Good support systems share several characteristics. To encourage vigorous growth and berry production, a system should maximize the amount of sunlight reaching leaves and branches. It should also provide good air circulation, so that canes and leaves can dry off as fast as possible after rains, watering, fog, or dew. In addition, the canes should be more or less upright so you can come near the row to pick the fruit at a convenient height.

The drawings at right show two simple support systems suitable for home gardens. The single-fence trellis takes up

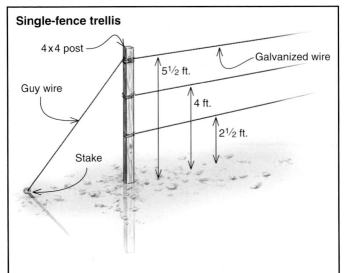

Single-fence trellis

4 x 4 post

Galvanized wire

5½ ft.

Guy wire

4 ft.

2½ ft.

Stake

Tie canes to wires with twist ties or twine; loop long canes around wires. Set posts 1½ to 3 ft. deep, depending on soil and climate.

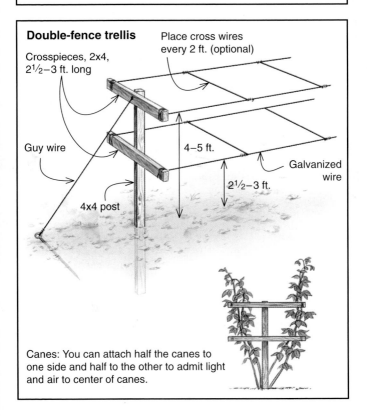

Double-fence trellis

Place cross wires every 2 ft. (optional)

Crosspieces, 2x4, 2½–3 ft. long

Guy wire

4–5 ft.

Galvanized wire

2½–3 ft.

4x4 post

Canes: You can attach half the canes to one side and half to the other to admit light and air to center of canes.

less space than does the double fence, but it also accommodates fewer canes. Canes and long laterals need to be attached to the single-fence trellis wires with twist ties or twine. You can loop long canes horizontally around the wires, too. The double-fence system forms a series of compartments that restrict canes, though you may want to loop or tie some in place, too. You can also omit the cross wires and tie canes and laterals directly to the four lengthwise wires, half to one side, half to the other, leaving space in the middle for light, air, and new canes to penetrate. This is a good system for all summer bearers, especially black and purple varieties, which grow so vigorously they always require trellising.

You can tie canes to wires with twist ties and loop canes around wires, or both. Keep up with the canes as they grow — it's easier to tie canes before the new foliage makes it hard to see the canes and wires. Keep tucking new canes to the inside of the trellis.

You can make these trellises with material available at local building centers. Preservative-treated wooden posts will last longer than those that aren't treated; galvanized metal is even more durable. You can sink the posts 18 to 36 inches deep, depending on your soil and the length of row they support. At each end post, guy wires attached to stakes or anchors will provide additional strength.

Baling wire, heavy twine, or strong monofilament will all support canes. The monofilament is about $1/8$ inch in diameter, about the same as 14-gauge wire. It is lightweight, has great tensile strength, does not conduct electricity, doesn't rust, and can be cut by pruning shears. But it is expensive. For twine, use the kind made for large round bales; it is thick and has good tensile strength. You can stretch wire tight with turnbuckles. With tall cultivars and in mild climates, you may need taller supports and more tiers of wire or twine.

Harvest

Summer bearers may be ready to pick as early as May or as late as July depending on your location. Fall bearers can be harvested until frost. If the first frost comes early, cover the plants for a night or two with plastic or other sheeting material.

Ripe raspberries do not keep well on the plant — a day or two too long and quality deteriorates rapidly — so monitor berries closely as they ripen. Pick berries as early in the day as possible, but not before the dew has dried off, unless you use them immediately. Wet berries deteriorate rapidly. Cool picked berries and store them as close to freezing temperature as you can. Rinse them just before use.

It is useful and fun to record the dates when your plants flower and when they're ready to harvest. (In general, they take 40 to 45 days from bloom to mature berries.) Record your observations and reactions to each cultivar you grow. Note which plants have too many canes, or changes you'd like to make in the trellis to match the cultivar's habits. These notes will be valuable when you make plans during the winter.

Lengthening the Season

It wasn't much more than a decade ago that you could harvest fresh raspberries for only a few weeks in the summer and a few weeks in the fall. Today, you can plant early, mid, and late varieties of both summer- and fall-bearing raspberries. Gardeners in milder climates (winters above 0°F) can also grow the newly released 'Tulameen', a late-season berry that bridges the gap between the late-summer and early-fall varieties. Its harvest can last as long as six weeks in some areas. Aficionados who select cultivars carefully can have fresh home-grown raspberries from May (in climates like Southern California) or early July (in climates like Minnesota) until the frost puts an end to production in the fall.

Several cultural tricks also extend the raspberry season. For fall cultivars, plant on a southern or southwestern slope and, if possible, plant on sandy ground. Both measures capture spring heat, so plants emerge and mature the crop ahead of colder soils and fields. You can gain a week or ten days in maturity with these techniques.

Gardeners in cold climates, such as upstate New York, Wisconsin, and Minnesota, can partially bridge the gap between summer and fall crops. After you've mowed down the old canes of fall-bearing varieties in the spring, cover early fall-bearing varieties like 'Autumn Bliss' and 'Redwing' with clear plastic. Bury or weight the edges of the plastic to form a mini-greenhouse, allowing enough slack for the new plants to grow inside. (Such an arrangement is called a floating row cover.) Make sure to prevent excessive heat from building up inside the cover; temperatures over 75 to 80°F will stress the plants and retard growth. Remove covers when plants are knee-high or when temperatures inside the cover repeatedly come near 80°F. By forcing early growth under the cover, you can gain as much as two weeks on harvest time.

Pests and Diseases

Raspberries, particularly black ones, are susceptible to fungal, bacterial, and viral diseases. The home gardener can do little about viral diseases beyond buying virus-clean stock. Bacterial and fungal diseases can be difficult to diagnose correctly. If you husband your soil with compost and natural amendments, provide good air circulation, and water carefully, you should avoid many of the problems that plague commercial monocultures.

Prudent home growers will also spray to prevent fungal problems. When the first leaves have emerged 1/4 to 1/2 inch, spray all the canes thoroughly with lime sulfur. The material is a natural product, stinks like rotten eggs, and is the best preventive measure you can take against all three major fungal plant diseases: anthracnose, cane blight, and spur blight. Timing is critical. If you do it too early, the spray won't be as effective. If you do it too late . . . well, don't worry about it too much. The spray will be very effective but you may also burn back the larger leaves a bit.

Blackberries

Blackberries are so closely related and so similar in many respects to raspberries that most of the information you'll need to grow them is covered in the preceding section. Here, we'll highlight how blackberries differ from raspberries in their preferred climate, culture, and cultivar selection.

Generally speaking, blackberries are less cold-hardy than raspberries but can tolerate considerably more heat. That's why you'll find them in greater abundance in warmer climates, whether in central and southern states or along the milder Pacific coast. Extreme heat, however, will shorten the life of the plants and reduce the yield and the quality of the fruit.

As the name suggests, blackberry fruits are mostly black, but you can encounter variations to reddish purple. There are no fall-bearing blackberries, only summer-bearing ones, which typically ripen later in the summer than raspberries do. ('Chester', a new cultivar, has such a late and long season, that you'll still be picking its berries in late August and September while harvesting early fall-bearing raspberries.)

Horticulturists distinguish between erect and semierect Eastern types and trailing Western types of blackberries. We'll discuss the Eastern first. Eastern types differ among themselves, and the easiest way to distinguish these differences is according to whether the canes bear thorns (thorny) or not (thornless). In general, thorny blackberries are sweeter than the thornless ones. Yields, on average, are about the same. There is a much greater difference from cultivar to cultivar, among both thorny and thornless, than there is between the two basic types.

Thorny blackberries

Thorny blackberries are less cold-hardy than black raspberries but hardier than thornless blackberries. They are generally safe down to -5°F. (One newly introduced cultivar, 'Illini Hardy', produces quite well even after winter temperatures drop down to -20°F.) Blackberries, like summer-bearing raspberries, bear fruit on the previous season's canes, which die after bearing fruit. The canes must survive the winter in good condition in order to produce abundant berries.

Treat thorny blackberries much like black or purple raspberries. When first-year canes are about 36 to 48 inches high, cut off the top few inches. This not only forces branching, but also stiffens the cane. Cut the new lateral branches way back in late winter, down to about a foot in length. Remove thin laterals altogether. Thorny blackberry canes are sturdier than black and purple raspberry canes, and some gardeners don't trellis them. But they look neater and are easier to manage when trellised, much like black raspberries. Train canes as high as possible so that the ripening berries will be located above the new growth.

Thornless blackberries

More sensitive to cold than their thorny cousins, thornless blackberries are generally safe to about 0°F, with several cultivars good to considerably lower temperatures.

Thornless blackberries are vigorous, erect or semierect plants and should be planted 4 to 6 feet apart in the row — much wider spacing than for black or purple raspberries. When you train them to a trellis you can either weave fruiting canes around the top trellis wire or cut them back to the top wires of a four-wire trellis, tying half the laterals to the wires on one side, half to wires on the other to admit light and air into the center of the row.

Shorten first-year laterals to 12 to 18 inches long and remove spindly ones entirely. In late winter, thin canes to allow four to six canes per crown. ('Waldo', the only thornless trailing cultivar currently available, should be trained as described below for Western trailers.)

Hybrid Western trailing blackberries

Gardeners in northern California and the Pacific Northwest have a number of blackberries to choose from. (Blackberries are less commonly grown in Southern California.) These berries are usually lumped into the general category of Western trailing blackberries or sometimes simply dewberries. As a group, they have aromatic, highly flavored, soft fruit that keep poorly — eat them right off the plant or process them immediately. Trailing blackberries yield fewer berries than erect or semierect types. (Gardeners in the region have also had success with 'Chester', a semierect thornless blackberry, and 'Cherokee', an erect, thorny variety.)

Western blackberries are more cold-sensitive than their Eastern relatives (they lose flower buds at temperatures below about 15°F) and do best along the Pacific coast and in mild valleys inland from the sea where the soil hardly ever freezes. Most have trailing, rather than upright, growth habits and are most conveniently grown on trellises. (Some varieties trail in their first season, then become semierect or erect in the second.) Almost all are thorny; a few thornless cultivars may revert to thorny growth after injury. Trailers are vigorous plants and may prove too much so for gardeners without a lot of space. As with other blackberries, they bear in summer on canes in their second year of growth.

Plant trailing types 6 to 8 feet apart and train them to a big, strong trellis. Just let first-year laterals grow; prune only the diseased and weak canes of trailers. The best way to train them is to tie each cane to the trellis individually. But this requires a lot of work. Commercial growers weave a bundle of canes along the top trellis wire, then turn the canes back toward the crown, weaving them along the bottom wire. This "bundle" type of training increases the chance of fungal problems and can make harvesting berries more difficult, but it's much faster.

There are large commercial plantings of trailing blackberries in the Pacific Northwest, and home gardeners also grow these varieties. 'Marion' is the most popular, with more acreage than all other blackberries and hybrids combined. 'Olallie', 'Evergreen', 'Boysen', and 'Logan' are also quite popular, and 'Kotata' is highly recommended. (Many readers will have seen some of these in supermarkets sold as boysenberry, loganberry, and so on.) Varieties such as 'Sunberry', 'Tayberry', 'Tummelberry', and others are actually hybrids between raspberries and blackberries. 'Logan' bears earliest, 'Marion', 'Kotata', 'Boysen', and 'Tayberry' are early midseason, and 'Evergreen' is late.

In general, gardeners outside the Pacific Coast region should avoid Western trailing blackberries unless they have similar conditions. Because of its superior flavor, many eastern gardeners have tried to grow 'Tayberry'. Its soft fruit isn't suitable for commercial production, so the only way to have it is to grow it at home. If you're in doubt about the winter survival of the canes (roots and plants will almost always survive), train them at an angle on the trellis, then untie and drop them to the ground in winter, covering them with straw. Retie to the trellis when the plant begins to break dormancy in the spring.

'Logan' is an early-bearing hybrid Western trailing blackberry.

'Olallie', a hybrid Western trailing blackberry, grows best in the Pacific Northwest.

■ RECOMMENDED VARIETIES OF RASPBERRIES

All entries have good flavor; exceptional flavor is noted. Unless otherwise noted, all are quite spiny. Minimum temperatures are those below which canes suffer serious damage. Zones are the coldest where cultivar generally does well.

Floricane or Summer-Bearing: Red and Yellow Raspberries

Algonquin
Season: Midseason.
Description of fruit: Red; medium to large; very good taste.
Disease resistance/susceptibility: Resists root rot, mosaic virus, spur blight, bushy dwarf.
Comments: Few spines. To -25°F.

Bababerry
Season: Early.
Description of fruit: Red; large.
Disease resistance/susceptibility: Susceptible to crown gall.
Comments: The most heat-tolerant cultivar. Better flavor in warm than cold climates. Produces late spring and late fall crops in warm climates. To -10°F.

Canby
Season: Very early.
Description of fruit: Light red; very large; excellent taste.
Disease resistance/susceptibility: Resists mosaic virus; susceptible to crown gall, root rot, bushy dwarf.
Comments: Very few spines. To -20°F.

Chilliwack
Season: Midseason.
Description of fruit: Red; extra large; excellent taste.
Disease resistance/susceptibility: Resists root rot, mosaic virus, spur blight, bushy dwarf; susceptible to crown gall
Comments: Few spines. To -15°F.

Killarney
Season: Early.
Description of fruit: Red; large.
Disease resistance/susceptibility: Resists root rot, mosaic virus, bushy dwarf.
Comments: Very spiny. To -35°F.

Latham
Season: Medium to late.
Description of fruit: Red; medium-size.

Disease resistance/susceptibility: Resists root rot, bushy dwarf; susceptible to mosaic virus, powdery mildew, spur blight.
Comments: Few spines. To -40°F.

Newburgh
Season: Midseason.
Description of fruit: Red; medium to large; very tasty.
Disease resistance/susceptibility: Resists root rot, mosaic virus.
Comments: To -20°F.

Nova
Season: Late.
Description of fruit: Light red; medium-size.
Disease resistance/susceptibility: Resists root rot, cane diseases.
Comments: Few spines. To -30°F.

Titan
Season: Medium to late.
Description of fruit: Red; extra-large. Flavor bland if picked immature.
Disease resistance/susceptibility: Susceptible to crown gall, root rot, mosaic virus, bushy dwarf.
Comments: Few spines. To -25°F.

Tulameen
Season: Very late.
Description of fruit: Red; extra-large; excellent.
Disease resistance/susceptibility: Resists mosaic virus; susceptible to bushy dwarf.
Comments: Long late season overlaps with early primocanes in some areas. To -5°F.

Floricane or Summer-Bearing: Black Raspberries
All are very spiny. All susceptible to anthracnose.

Black Hawk
Season: Midseason.
Description of fruit: Large.
Disease resistance/susceptibility: Resists bushy dwarf.
Comments: To -25°F.

Bristol
Season: Early.
Description of fruit: Very large; very tasty.
Disease resistance/susceptibility: Resists powdery mildew, bushy dwarf.
Comments: To -20°F.

Cumberland
Season: Early.
Description of fruit: Very large; very tasty.
Disease resistance/susceptibility: Resists bushy dwarf.
Comments: To -20°F.

Haut
Season: Midseason.
Description of fruit: Very large; very tasty.
Disease resistance/susceptibility: Resists botrytis root rot; susceptible to orange rust, anthracnose.
Comments: To -20°F.

Jewel
Season: Early.
Description of fruit: Extra-large; very tasty.
Disease resistance/susceptibility: Least susceptible of blacks.
Comments: To -25°F.

Floricane or Summer-Bearing: Purple Raspberries

Brandywine
Season: Very late.
Description of fruit: Very large.
Disease resistance/susceptibility: Susceptible to crown gall.
Comments: Very spiny. To -25°F.

Estate
Season: Very late.
Description of fruit: Very large.
Disease resistance/susceptibility: Resists powdery mildew.
Comments: Very spiny. To -25°F.

Royalty
Season: Late.
Description of fruit: Extra-large, very tasty conical. Tart when red, sweet when dark purple.
Disease resistance/susceptibility: Resists root rot, mosaic virus; susceptible to crown gall.
Comments: To -25°F.

Primocane or Fall-Bearing
All are red or yellow raspberries. Hardiness zone indicates the northernmost zone in which fruit will be likely to mature before fall frost.

Amity
Season: Early to midseason.
Description of fruit: Red; medium-size.
Disease resistance/susceptibility: Resists root rot, spur blight; susceptible to mosaic virus.
Comments: Few spines. Zone 4.

Autumn Bliss
Season: Very early.
Description of fruit: Red; very large; very tasty.
Disease resistance/susceptibility: Resists root rot, mosaic virus; susceptible to bushy dwarf.
Comments: Zone 3.

Bababerry
Season: Very late.
Description of fruit: Red; large.
Disease resistance/susceptibility: Susceptible to crown gall.
Comments: Very spiny. Zone 6.

Goldie
Season: Midseason.
Description of fruit: Yellow; medium-size.
Disease resistance/susceptibility: Resists powdery mildew.
Comments: Zone 5.

Heritage
Season: Midseason.
Description of fruit: Red; medium-size.
Disease resistance/susceptibility: Resists powdery mildew.
Comments: Zone 5.

Redwing
Season: Very early.
Description of fruit: Red; medium-size, very tasty.
Disease resistance/susceptibility: Resists bushy dwarf, mosaic virus.
Comments: Zone 3.

Ruby
Season: Late.
Description of fruit: Red; very large.
Disease resistance/susceptibility: Resists powdery mildew; susceptible to crown gall, root rot, mosaic virus.
Comments: Zone 5.

Summit
Season: Very early.
Description of fruit: Red; small.

Disease resistance/susceptibility: Resists root rot; susceptible to mosaic virus.
Comments: Zone 3.

■ RECOMMENDED VARIETIES OF BLACKBERRIES

Thorny Blackberries
All are erect plants.

Brazos
Season: Very early.
Description of fruit: Large with good flavor, but tart.
Comments: Disease-resistant; leading southern cultivar for many years. Zone 7–8.

Cherokee
Season: Early.
Description of fruit: Medium to large sweet berries.
Comments: Zone 5.

Cheyenne
Season: Early.
Description of fruit: Very large; superior flavor.
Comments: Zone 6.

'Darrow'

Choctaw
Season: Early.
Description of fruit: Large tasty berries.
Comments: Resists orange rust, anthracnose, root rot. Zone 6.

Darrow
Season: Very early.
Description of fruit: Fair-tasting.
Comments: Zone 5.

Illini Hardy
Season: Midseason.
Description of fruit: Medium-size.
Comments: Hardiest to zone 4 (-20°F).

Shawnee
Season: Late.
Description of fruit: Largest, highest yielding blackberry. Good flavor, soft fruit.
Comments: Somewhat disease-resistant. Zone 6.

Thornless Blackberries

Arapaho
Season: Earliest.
Description of fruit: Medium-size; superior flavor.
Comments: Erect bush. Zone 6.

Chester
Season: Latest.
Description of fruit: Very large; very sweet.
Comments: Semierect. Very long season, very productive. Hardiest: zone 5 (-10°F).

Dirksen
Season: Midseason.
Description of fruit: Large; excellent flavor.
Comments: Semierect. Consistent producer. Resists anthracnose, leaf spot, mildew. Zone 5.

Hull
Season: Late.
Description of fruit: Very large; sweet fruit.
Comments: Semierect. Zone 5, slightly less hardy than 'Chester'.

Navaho
Season: Very late.
Description of fruit: Medium-size; excellent flavor.
Comments: Erect. Resists orange rust, rosetting, anthracnose, root rot. Zone 5.

Blueberries

Fresh from the bush, blueberries are a treat eaten out-of-hand or with cereal, ice cream, or in fruit salad.

Plentiful, portable, and delicious, blueberries have been prized by North Americans for thousands of years. The berries are sweet, plump, and just the right size to pop into your mouth for a perfect summer treat. Gardeners with a little more patience can bake them into pies, muffins, and other treats. Preserved by drying, as Native Americans have long done, or by canning or freezing, blueberries can also be enjoyed right through the winter.

Blueberries are perfect for laissez-faire gardeners. The plants are vigorous, usually untroubled by disease or insects, and require no rigorous pruning. Even plants that feel the hand of the gardener only at harvest time deliver a bountiful crop. The bushes are particular about soil pH, but if azaleas thrive in your soil, so will most blueberries. Those whose soil pH isn't right may be able to alter the pH with natural amendments or avoid the problem by planting in containers.

Besides the delicious berries, these shrubs can contribute handsomely to your landscape, offering beautiful fall foliage, suffused with red, and in the spring, numerous waxy white flowers that dangle from branches like tiny bells. Their natural form is as appealing as many other landscape shrubs, and their general unfussiness makes them well suited for maintenance-conscious gardeners. Although blueberries need little or no pruning for good fruit production, you can shape them to any size or form you desire, from a low hedge to a tree shape. Try a grouping of highbush blueberry shrubs in an informal planting, backed by a clump of tawny ornamental grass and with a mat of ground-hugging, evergreen bearberry *(Arctostaphyllos uva-ursi)* at their feet. Or weave a few bushes among the rhodies and azaleas that front your house, where the blueberries' understated white flowers will be a restful contrast to their knock-your-eye-out neighbors.

In a wildflower or natural garden, lowbush blueberries can run at will, forming a colony that's appealing to wild visitors as well as the gardener. Unusual varieties of blueberry can be used in place of more familiar ornamentals. 'Bloodstone', for example, a cultivar of the creeping, evergreen blueberry *Vaccinium sempervirens,* is an interesting alternative to run-of-the-mill ground covers.

Taming the Wild Blueberry

Known as huckleberries, whortleberries, and of course blueberries, members of the genus *Vaccinium* have long thrived in the northern hemisphere. The three main types of cultivated blueberry — lowbush, highbush, and rabbiteye — still grow wild in North America, along with dozens of other species that fill various ecological niches and provide pleasant afternoons of berrying.

So plentiful were the berries in the wild that efforts to domesticate and improve the blueberry began in earnest only early in this century. Starting with selections of the large-fruited, sweet-tasting highbush types chosen for superior size, abundant crops, and adaptability to cultivation, breeders later turned to lowbush blueberries of the frigid north for their extreme cold hardiness and the intense flavor of their berries. Rabbiteye blueberries held promise for southern and western gardeners, who needed a plant that could withstand the rigors of heat and drought.

Today's blueberry aficionado can choose from scores of cultivars suited to all kinds of gardens. There are cultivars that hunker down under the extremes of a far north winter, and those that bake without complaint in the heat of the summer sun. Low-growing types are perfect for gardeners with limited space, while 12-foot-tall upright blueberries make the perfect good-neighbor fence between boundaries.

Most blueberries sold in garden centers and by mail-order nurseries for home fruit production are cultivars of highbush blueberries, with rabbiteye running a close second, especially in milder areas. Lowbush blueberries and other, less well known "wild" species, many of which make fine ornamentals, expand the offerings. In an interesting example of how gardening goes full circle, unimproved species of blueberries are increasingly popular among back-to-basics gardeners.

All blueberries are, to some extent, self-pollinating. But if you cross-pollinate with another blueberry, the fruit will be larger, ripen earlier, and have fewer seeds. All types cross-pollinate with each other — a highbush cultivar can pollinate a lowbush and vice versa, a rabbiteye can pollinate a highbush, and so on. Blueberries begin ripening in early summer and continue over several weeks, not all at once. If you have the room, you can plant early, midseason, and late-fruiting cultivars that will keep you in berries from June through late August. Remember to plant pollinators that bloom at the same time — an early-season blueberry with another early cultivar, a late-season with another late-season.

Because of the variety of available cultivars, it's important to read the fine print in catalogs and on nursery tags when selecting blueberries so that you choose the cultivar best suited to your climate and your conditions. The cultivars 'Northland' and 'Berkeley', for example, are both hardy to at least zone 4, but 'Northland' has strong, pliable branches that withstand the heavy weight of snow without snapping or cracking, while 'Berkeley' has brittle canes that snap easily. The list beginning on page 232 notes some of these characteristics, but the best help in making decisions is likely to come from your county extension agent and blueberry growers in your area.

Highbush blueberries

Big berries with sweet, mild flavor, and plenty of them, make highbush blueberries *(Vaccinium corymbosum)* the perennial favorite for home growers. Cold hardiness varies, but many cultivars flourish as far north as zone 3. In the South and other warm-winter regions, highbush blueberries are limited by their winter-chill requirement, a certain period of time at cool temperatures needed by the plant to break dormancy in spring. (See the chapter "Growing Fruits and Berries at Home" for more on winter chill.) Most highbush cultivars need about 700 chill hours. In milder winter areas, rabbiteye blueberries are often a better choice, though the so-called Southern highbush types, such as 'Cape Fear' and 'Georgia Gem', extend the highbush range well into the South.

In the wild, highbush blueberries thrive in both wetlands and on drier upland wooded slopes from Nova Scotia west to Wisconsin, south to Georgia and Alabama. In their natural habitat, the bushes reach 5 to 15 feet in height. In the home garden, most cultivars grow to 6 to 12 feet tall.

Highbush blueberries are upright growers. The handsome well-branched plants make a lovely informal shrub planting, or a good addition to a shrub border. They also make an attractive hedge, with the bonus of tasty fruit. 'Collins' is a good candidate for a hedge. It reaches 4 to 6 feet tall, and its red-barked canes are attractive in all seasons. The medium to large berries are intensely flavored, yielding about 10 to 15 pounds per plant. Fall color begins early and is vivid and long-lasting.

Rabbiteye blueberries

These are an excellent choice for gardeners in the Deep South, Southern California, and other mild-winter climates including the Atlantic coast and coastal Alaska. They will grow as far north as Boston, if winters aren't extreme. Rabbiteye blueberries *(Vaccinium ashei)* are tall, upright bushes. They thrive in hot, humid summers and tolerate drought much better than other blueberries, but they are cold-hardy only to zone 6 or 7, depending on cultivar. Well-mulched plants may survive the rare dip in the thermometer to as low as -20°F, though branches may be killed to the ground.

Rabbiteyes are less finicky than highbush types about soil pH and will flourish at slightly higher pH levels. The bushes grow rapidly, reaching 10 to 25 feet, depending on cultivar. Such height makes protecting the crop with netting difficult, not to mention the difficulties of harvesting. Many gardeners prune their rabbiteyes to keep them within arm's reach.

The berries of unimproved plants may be small and gritty with seeds, but improved selections and cultivars have put the fruit of rabbiteyes on almost equal footing with the fruit of highbush types.

Lowbush blueberries

Lowbush blueberries are big on flavor, but small in size of both berries and plants. They're extremely cold-hardy, growing in the wild as far north as Arctic North America. Lowbush blueberries reach only 1 to 2 feet tall, but the fruit is prolific, and the spreading plant provides an increasing yield.

Lowbush species include the low sweet blueberry *(V. angustifolium),* found from the Arctic to Minnesota and the

Species lowbush blueberries carpet a naturalistic planting.

mountains of New York and New Hampshire, and the sour-tasting velvet-leaf blueberry *(V. myrtilloides),* which grows wild throughout New England and west through zone 2. In their natural habitat, these super-hardy plants spread by underground rhizomes to create extensive colonies called "blueberry barrens." Wild colonies are managed and harvested for commercial use in jellies and jams and for freezing and canning. The bushes are burned off every few years in late winter, while the ground is solidly frozen. Burning removes weedy undergrowth that might compete with the berry bushes, and new growth is vigorous, although fruit is not produced until the following year.

Home gardeners grow lowbush blueberries because of their cold hardiness (to zone 2) and their flavor, which many fanciers prefer to that of other blueberries. They grow best in areas where summer heat is not intense. Zone 7 is about the limit of their endurance. You can plant lowbush blueberries in naturalistic, free-form plantings, or you can line them out in a row, which will soon fill out to a vigorous low, dense hedge. A single plant generally produces 1 to 2 pints of berries.

Improved cultivated varieties of lowbush blueberries are far fewer in number than highbush or rabbiteye cultivars, and they are not necessarily superior to species plants, which are a fine choice for the home gardener who wants a taste of wild blueberry flavor. 'Tophat' is a dwarf cultivar that turns blazing red in fall. It makes an excellent container plant and is right at home in ornamental plantings, where its prolific white bell-shaped flowers last for weeks. The sweet, medium-size berries are almost a bonus.

Blueberry hybrids

Breeders cross species to produce hybrids that, at their best, incorporate desired traits of each parent. A major incentive for crossing highbush and rabbiteye blueberries was to produce plants with fruit that ripened early and would grow in southern or mild-winter climates. These hybrids will usually grow well in northern climates, but the buds are not hardy and will often suffer frost damage.

Lowbush/highbush crosses have also been tried. 'Bluehaven' combines the large berries and taller size of its highbush parent with the flavor of the lowbush side of the cross. It bears large, firm, light blue fruit with good flavor on a vigorous, upright plant that thrives in zones 5 through 7. A similar cross, 'Northblue' also keeps its "wild berry" flavor, but it grows well as far north as zone 3, having retained more of the cold hardiness of its lowbush parent than did 'Bluehaven'.

Species and ornamental blueberries

Little-known native blueberries are a taste of the wild for an adventurous gardener. The fruit is tempting to wildlife and decorative on the plant. Of course, the gardener can also enjoy the berries, which are often small but rich in concentrated flavor.

Native plant nurseries and specialty fruit growers or edible landscaping nurseries are the best sources for species and cultivars. (See "Sources of Supply" at the back of this book.) You may want to import your own region's wild blueberries to your garden, or you might like to branch out with other kinds. Consider such plants as the creeping blueberry, *Vaccinium crassifolium,* and the evergreen, prostrate *V. sempervirens.* The unusual 'John Blue', a cultivar of *V. darrowi,* boasts cool blue leaves. 'Blue Ridge' is an ornamental cultivar of the yellow-barked *V. pallidum,* with excellent fruit. *V. occidentalis,* the western blueberry, is a wild favorite from British Columbia to central California and west to the Rockies. The delectable black highbush blueberry, *V. atrococcum,* is found from southeastern Virginia to eastern South Carolina. The evergreen blueberry *V. myrsinites* is a southern species that thrives into Florida.

Soil: Persnickity pH

Blueberries have a reputation for being particular about soil acidity, but the trait is more complex than that. They are not "acid-loving" per se, but their specialized requirements are best met in a soil of low pH, about 4.0 to 5.5. (Rabbiteye blueberries tolerate slightly higher pH than this.) As we mentioned earlier, if azaleas and rhododendrons flourish in your garden, blueberries will, too.

It's safest to test your soil to make sure of its pH level. If your soil is outside the desired range, it's no good crossing your fingers and planting the bushes anyway. The plants will soon decline. If your soil registers over 6.2 on the pH scale, it will be very difficult to reduce the pH sufficiently with amendments; you're better off growing blueberries in mounded beds of amended soil or in containers. If your soil pH measures in the 5.3 to 6.0 range, however, amendments can usually do the job.

It's not as difficult as you might think to provide blueberries with the soil conditions they need. Recent research shows that altering pH with organic amendments is better for blueberries than doing so with powdered sulfur, an old-time favorite for the task. Powdered sulfur will lower the pH, but it also combines with water to form sulfuric acid, which kills off the soil microorganisms that have been found to be vital to the blueberry plant's growth.

Amending the soil

Mixing an acidic natural material with the soil will lower its pH. Peat moss is the traditional pH modifier, but because harvesting this material destroys the fragile ecology of ancient peat bogs, many environmentally concerned gardeners are turning to readily available local substitutes. Composted leaves are an excellent pH modifier, as are pine or hemlock needles. Oak, beech, and chestnut leaves, as well as the bark from these trees, are high in tannic acids that lower pH. Both hardwood and softwood sawdust are also ideal. In the South, bald-cypress leaves and composted cypress bark are excellent alternatives.

For best results, whatever material you choose should be shredded, chopped, or chipped to a very small size before you mix it with the soil. Nitrogen deficiencies, usually shown by slow growth and yellowing, then reddening leaves, can result from amending soil heavily. Apply dry manure, cottonseed or blood meal, or packaged high-nitrogen fertilizers to counteract. Also be sure to keep close tabs on moisture levels in amended soil. If you allow peat, sawdust, and other finely ground materials to dry out, they will repel rainwater instead of soaking it up.

Amending soil for blueberries need not be a laborious task. The plants have shallow roots, so you don't need to dig deep when incorporating the amendments. The type of soil you start with will determine how much material you need to work in. You want to end up with a "soil" that is light, loose, and moisture-retentive, with a crumbly texture, like natural woodland soil. In clay soils you may need to replace up to half the soil with organic amendments; in loam, a quarter to a third by volume may do the trick. As with many gardening techniques, amending with natural materials is more a matter of feel and experience than of formulas. Organic materials vary greatly in their effect on pH; when in doubt, be over-generous.

Assuming an "average" soil, you'll need about a half-bushel of amendments for each plant. The day you plant, spread the material over a 2- to 3-foot-diameter circle of cleared soil. With a garden fork, work the amendments into the soil to a depth of about 8 inches (the depth of the fork). The resulting mix should be half to two-thirds amendment and half to one-third native soil. The amended soil will be mounded, which helps provide the drainage so important for blueberries.

Your heavy dose of soil amendments will work for years, often for the life of the plant. A 4- to 5-inch-thick annual mulch of acidic natural materials (the same ones you dug into the soil, with the exception of peat) will keep the pH at the level you want, as earthworms and microorganisms work their magic of decomposition.

Drainage

Blueberries have shallow fibrous roots that do best in well-drained but constantly moist soil. In the woodsy areas where blueberries naturally grow, the soil is light, even sandy, and humusy. It drains well after a rain, so that the bushes don't sit in soggy soil, but it holds moisture because of its high content of organic material. This is the ideal you're aiming for in home blueberry growing.

Organic material will help light soils hold moisture. Heavy, poorly drained soils can be difficult to fix. Digging in a lot of organic matter can loosen them up and improve drainage. If that doesn't seem to do the trick, you can plant cultivars that are adapted to clay, such as the highbush 'Patriot'. Or plant the bushes in containers or build high raised beds to keep the roots out of the water.

Mulch is the key to keeping the soil cool and moist. Keep a thick layer of it around your plants all year long, renewing it as it decomposes. If you're adjusting pH, remember to mulch with acidifying material.

Container growing

Where soil pH is beyond levels for effective alteration, or space is limited, you can still grow blueberries as container plants. They adapt well to the confines of a large container if they are kept well watered and well fed with regular doses of high-nitrogen fertilizers.

A pair of wooden half-barrels, one plant in each, work well for blueberries in the garden or on the patio. (Two different cultivars ensure cross-pollination.) Fill with a sufficiently acid soil mix to within 6 to 8 inches of the rim, so that you have room to add a thick layer of moisture-preserving mulch. If you are planting in plastic tubs, it's a good idea to add a few heavy rocks or bricks before filling with soil mix, so that the container isn't prone to topple in wind.

You can make a good all-purpose mix for blueberries by mixing two parts garden soil, one part compost, two parts composted chopped leaves or peat, and two parts sand. Use coarse builder's sand rather than "sandbox" sand, which is so fine it hardens when dry and may contain a lot of pulverized alkaline shell fragments. "Soilless" mixes, such as three parts sand, three parts peat moss or sawdust, and two parts composted chopped leaves, are also a good planting medium for blueberries, but you'll have to fertilize during the growing season to keep plants healthy.

Gardeners in cold-winter areas should haul containers to an unheated garage or porch for the winter. Mulch the roots with a thick blanket of leaves and wrap the plant in burlap for extra protection if temperatures are extreme. Be sure to water container-grown plants during the winter months whenever they need it; don't let the soil become bone-dry.

Planting and Caring for Blueberries

Apart from their stringent pH requirements, blueberries present no unusual problems. (See the last three chapters for general information on planting and maintenance; we'll summarize procedures here and comment on aspects specific to blueberries.) The plants do best when located in full sun. If you want to gamble on a cultivar that is marginally cold-hardy for your area, you can boost your chances of success by choosing the planting site with care. Avoid planting in "frost pockets," where cold air settles, such as at the foot of a hill. After the ground freezes, mulch heavily and swath the plant in burlap.

Blueberries are sold as two- or three-year-old plants, usually in containers. In cold-winter areas, plant in early spring; fall or early winter planting is best in areas with mild climates. Handle plants carefully when you transplant them.

Don't let the roots dry out or freeze, and don't expose them to sunlight. The ultraviolet rays will kill the small fibrous roots. Protect bare roots with a damp, light-proof covering.

Plant highbush cultivars 3 feet apart to create an informal hedge. If you are using blueberries in naturalistic groups, space the plants 4 to 6 feet apart. For easiest picking, planting 6 to 8 feet apart allows room for access on all sides. Space rabbiteye plants up to 8 feet apart, or closer for a hedge. Plant lowbush blueberries 2 to 3 feet apart, or 1 to 2 feet apart for a ground cover (the plants will sucker and fill in).

Blueberries have shallow roots, which makes them sensitive to drought and easily damaged by cultivation. Instead of tilling, hoeing, or even hand-cultivating around the plants, use mulch to prevent weeds and preserve moisture. An acidic mulch, such as oak or beech leaves, or pine or hemlock needles, will help the soil maintain proper pH levels. To avoid disturbing the roots, hand-pull any weeds that may sprout in the mulch. Don't rake up dropped blueberry leaves — their decomposition will help maintain correct pH levels.

Supplementary watering is often necessary, because the top few inches of soil, where the roots are concentrated, dry out quickly, even under a mulch. Pull aside the layer of mulch and wiggle your finger into the soil to check moisture levels during a dry spell. (Remember that rabbiteye types can take some drought.)

Fertilizing

Provided insufficient nitrogen, blueberry bushes grow slowly and berries will be small, although still tasty. If your soil needed no amendments to correct pH, a yearly application of high-nitrogen fertilizer should be all you need to keep the plant growing vigorously. To make sure your blueberries are getting enough nitrogen, make it a regular routine to pull back the mulch around each plant in spring and apply $1/2$ to 1 pound of a high-nitrogen fertilizer, such as dry manure, cottonseed or soybean meal, or a high-nitrogen packaged organic fertilizer. Any fertilizer formulated for azaleas or rhododendrons makes a good blueberry fertilizer too. Blueberries tolerate only small amounts of nitrogen at a time, so use a little less fertilizer than recommended for azaleas or rhododendrons.

The high-carbon soil amendments that correct pH also tie up available nitrogen as they decompose. If the soil in the planting hole is heavily amended, it's a good idea to keep an eye on the plants for signs of nitrogen deficiency. If the bush is not putting out plenty of healthy, vigorous new growth, or if berries are small or few, apply a supplemental feeding of high-nitrogen material.

A serious nitrogen deficiency will elicit signs of stress — leaves turning yellow and eventually red during what should be the green and growing season. Slow, stunted growth usually confirms the diagnosis. Apply a high-nitrogen liquid fertilizer, such as manure tea, augmented with a fast-acting foliar spray to plants exhibiting signs of stress.

Pruning

Blueberries are the perfect choice for the low-maintenance gardener. The bushes are naturally well shaped. Highbush blueberries grow in an upright to slightly spreading shape, with the several stems producing side branches almost to the ground. Rabbiteye plants have more of a bare-legged look, with the stems branching only near the tops. Lowbush blueberries are naturally short and spreading in shape, with branching almost to the ground. All will bear well for years without ever feeling the cut of the pruning shears.

Pruning established plants is done for several reasons, most of them for the convenience of the gardener rather than the health of the plant. (For the first two or three years after planting, blueberries need no pruning at all.) Keep in mind that blueberries bear their fruit on year-old and older wood (which fruit growers call canes and gardeners call branches). If you are overzealous about cutting back, you won't have much of a crop. Late winter is the time to prune. The following pruning tips apply to highbush and rabbiteye blueberries. Lowbush types need no pruning, but if you like, you can thin out older, less productive canes.

- After the plants are established, you can begin pruning to control the height of taller varieties. Cut back the young stems of rabbiteyes in particular to encourage low branching, which places the fruiting branch tips in reachable distance.
- When the bush is bearing abundantly and the plant seems crowded with branches, you can prune to open the interior for better plant health and easier access to berries. Weak or old unproductive canes should be the first to go. Check for fruit buds to judge how valuable an older, thicker cane still might be.
- Blueberries bear abundantly, but the berries are larger when there are fewer of them. Some gardeners selectively snip fruit bud–bearing branch tips, reducing the size of the crop, causing the remaining berries to swell to a larger size. Fruit buds are easy to distinguish from leaf buds: the fat, round fruit buds develop at and near the branch tips; the smaller, more pointed leaf buds appear farther down the stems.
- Occasionally, a severe winter will kill off some or even all of a blueberry's branches; prune off these winter-damaged

branches at an outward-facing node where healthy wood begins.

- As blueberries get older, the canes become less productive, and their tips become twiggy from years of fruit-bearing. Cutting back the twiggy ends of older branches will give you more and bigger berries in years to come. It's also a good idea to occasionally thin out six-year-old and older canes, to open the bush and make room for younger, more productive canes.

Harvesting

Most blueberry cultivars will bear fruit beginning at the age of three years (the first year in your garden if you've planted three-year-old bushes.) The plants are long-lived and can continue to bear for up to 40 years.

Depending on type and cultivar, and on your growing area, blueberries ripen from mid- to late summer. The berries do not ripen all at one time. Most ripen over a period of two weeks or longer; the 'Bluecrop' season lasts a full month. In the home garden, several rounds of picking are usually not a problem.

Turning blue is a sign of ripening, not a sign of ripeness. Most blueberries turn blue one to two weeks before they are ready to pick. Ripe berries twist off the stems easily. A taste test is another sure way to decide if picking time has arrived.

Pests and Diseases

Large blueberry plantings like those of commercial growers may be invaded by insect pests attracted to the monoculture, but home growers are rarely troubled. Two types of insect larvae, the cherry fruit worm and the blueberry maggot, are occasionally troublesome.

Diseases are also rare among homegrown blueberries, but they can occasionally cause problems in warm, moist areas such as the South. Although seldom encountered by the home blueberry grower, mummy berry is a common enough ailment that breeders have developed some cultivars resistant to this disease. Viral diseases that cause the slow decline and death of a plant are sometimes seen; they have no cure. Your county extension agent can alert you to potential virus problems in your area and make suggestions about resistant cultivars.

Protecting the harvest from other berry eaters is the number-one concern of most home-garden blueberry growers. Keeping the berries for yourself often takes more work and forethought than growing healthy fruit. Birds are eager to share a crop of blueberries, and they will outwit every protective measure short of physical barriers.

'Coville', a highbush cultivar, is the top commercial blueberry; it is also excellent, and attractive, in the home garden.

Birds and animals

Birds will be the worst enemy of your blueberry harvest. Interestingly, blueberries are a favorite of sandhill cranes, which breed in the heart of blueberry country near the Canadian border and feast on a menu of grasshoppers and blueberries before the late-summer migration.

Thrushes and other songbirds are more likely to be a problem than cranes. Some blueberry growers resort to building a permanent cage for their plantings, but plastic mesh bird netting works just as well. Drape it over the bush, making sure there are no gaps or openings, and secure it to the base of the canes. If birds reach through the mesh, suspend it on a frame a foot or so above the berries.

Blueberries, both wild and cultivated, are also appreciated by bears and small mammals. Most home gardeners won't have to worry about encountering foraging bruins in their blueberries. They'll more likely confront deer and rabbits browsing on the leaves and twigs. If animals become pesky, a fence or cage is the surest solution.

Blueberry maggot

These larvae burrow into and feed on ripening blueberries. Like the cabbage worms that infest broccoli, blueberry maggots are well camouflaged; they're often the same color as the pulp. Because the berries are usually popped in the mouth without close inspection, blueberry eaters may get a little more protein than they bargained for. Luckily for squeamish eaters, the maggots are infrequent in home plantings. If an infestation reaches extreme levels, affecting more than a few berries, pick and destroy fruit and dust plants with rotenone.

Cherry fruit worm

The larva of a half-inch nondescript mottled brown moth, the cherry fruitworm feeds inside blueberries until full grown. Adults hibernate over winter, emerging in late spring to lay eggs on developing fruit. Destroy any infested fruit. If larvae infest more than a few berries, pick and destroy fruit and dust the plants with rotenone.

Mummy berry

This fungal disease causes blueberries to rot, shrivel, and fall off. Like other fungi, it thrives in warm, moist areas without good air circulation. Destroy any infected fruit. Prune selectively to thin out the branches and open the plant to light and air. If mummy berry is a problem in your area, choose a resistant cultivar, such as highbush 'Spartan'.

■ RECOMMENDED VARIETIES OF BLUEBERRIES

Highbush
Most cultivars grow 6–12 ft. tall.

Berkeley (Berkley)
Season: Midseason.
Description of fruit: Very large, light blue berries with mild, sweet flavor.
Zones: 4–8.
Comments: Yellow canes are brittle; will break under snow load. Best in light, sandy soil.

Bluecrop
Season: Midseason.
Description of fruit: Large to very large, bright light blue berries with good flavor, a bit tart.
Zones: 4–7.
Comments: Top commercial cultivar; excellent in home gar-

den. Heavy bearer. Needs 800 hours chilling. Attractive as ornamental.

Bluejay

Season: Midseason.

Description of fruit: Medium to large, light blue berries with mild flavor, slightly tart.

Zones: 4–7.

Comments: Resistant to mummy-berry disease.

Blueray

Season: Midseason.

Description of fruit: Large, medium blue, very sweet berries with a hint of tartness.

Zones: 4–8.

Comments: Good for hot climates, but needs 800 chill hours. Brilliant red fall color.

Cape Fear

Season: Early to midseason.

Description of fruit: Large, firm, light blue fruit with good flavor.

Zones: 6–10.

Comments: Low-chill cultivar for mild-winter areas. Moderately vigorous upright and productive bush.

Collins

Season: Midseason.

Description of fruit: Medium to large, light blue fruit with rich flavor. Sweet to sweet-tart.

Zones: 5–7.

Comments: Red-barked canes; good, long-lasting red fall color. Reaches 4–6 ft. tall, good for hedge.

Coville

Season: Late.

Description of fruit: Large to very large, medium blue berries with intense, aromatic flavor.

Zones: 5–8.

Comments: Excellent ornamental with waxy leaves and vivid red fall color.

Darrow

Season: Late.

Description of fruit: Large, light blue fruit with excellent flavor.

Zones: 5–7.

Comments: Good for Pacific Northwest.

Earliblue

Season: Early.

Description of fruit: Medium to large, light blue fruit with excellent flavor; sweet and mild.

Zones: 5–7.

Comments: Good in northern areas.

Georgiagem

Season: Early.

Description of fruit: Large, mild-flavored berries.

Zones: 7–9.

Comments: Low-chill highbush for mild climates. Early ripening.

Ivanhoe

Season: Early.

Description of fruit: Large to very large, medium blue fruit with excellent, sweet-tart flavor.

Zones: 5–7.

Comments: Vigorous, tall-growing bush.

Jersey

Season: Late.

Description of fruit: Small to medium, light blue berries. Juicy but bland flavor.

Zones: 5–8.

Comments: An old favorite, from 1928, and still popular although other cultivars offer better flavor. Excellent yellow fall color.

O'Neal (O'Neill)

Season: Early.

Description of fruit: Large fruit.

Zones: 7–9.

Comments: Good in mild-winter gardens. Needs only 200 hours of chilling.

Patriot

Season: Early to midseason.

Description of fruit: Large, medium blue fruit with very good flavor.

Zones: 3–7.

Comments: Tolerates wet soil and clay; resists root rot.

Sierra

Season: Early to midseason.

Description of fruit: Very large berries with fine flavor.

Zones: 4–7.

Comments: Introduced in 1989.

Spartan
Season: Early.
Description of fruit: Large to very large, powder blue berries with superb flavor.
Zones: 5–7.
Comments: Partially resistant to mummy-berry disease. Fussy about soil conditions; requires light, well-drained soil.

Lowbush

All grow well in zones 2–6. Plants grow 1 to 2 ft. tall. Berries are small, rich-flavored, and usually dark blue. Species plants (Vaccinium angustifolium) *are fine for a naturalistic garden. Only a few cultivars are available, including 'Augusta', 'Brunswick', 'Chignecto', 'Leucocarpum' (which bears white fruit), and 'Tophat', a dwarf that turns blazing red in fall. 'Bloodstone', a selection of the species* V. sempervirens, *is a good ground cover because of its trailing habit.*

Hybrids

All are crosses between highbush and lowbush; all are hardy from zones 3–7 (except where otherwise noted); all ripen in midseason.

Blue Haven
Description of fruit: Large, firm, light blue berries.
Comments: Vigorous, upright plant. Zones 5–7.

Northblue
Description of fruit: Large, sweet fruit with superb wild-berry flavor.
Comments: 20–30 in. tall. Shiny, dark green leaves with good fall color; good in ornamental plantings. Easy-to-pick fruit with all the flavor of a wild berry.

Northcountry (North Country)
Description of fruit: Medium-size fruit with some degree of wild flavor.
Comments: Light blue flowers on a low, 18–24-in.-tall plant.

Northland
Description of fruit: Small, wild-type berries with superb flavor.
Comments: 3–4-ft.-tall bush; pliable branches resist damage from heavy snows.

Northsky

Description of fruit: Small to medium, light blue berries with excellent wild flavor.

Comments: Very low plant, reaching 10–18 in. tall and spreading to as much as 3 ft. Dense foliage colors dark red in fall. Hardiest of the hybrids, surviving temperatures of -40°F.

Rabbiteye Blueberries

Most need a pollinator; check with your supplier for recommendations.

Beckyblue

Season: Early.

Description of fruit: Medium to large, light blue fruit with sweet flavor.

Hardiness zones: 6–9.

Comments: 6–10-ft. upright-spreading bush.

Bluebelle

Season: Midseason.

Description of fruit: Very large fruit with superb flavor.

Hardiness zones: 6–10.

Comments: Ripens over a period of 3 to 4 weeks.

Brightwell

Season: Early to midseason.

Description of fruit: Medium to large, light blue berries with sweet taste.

Hardiness zones: 7–9.

Comments: 8–12-ft. upright bush.

Briteblue

Season: Late.

Description of fruit: Large, very sweet berries.

Hardiness zones: 6–10.

Comments: Tolerant of a wide range of growing conditions, including heat and drought.

Centurion

Season: Late.

Description of fruit: Medium to large, good-tasting fruit.

Hardiness zones: 6–9.

Comments: Good hedge plant; dense foliage.

Choice
Season: Mid- to late season.
Description of fruit: Medium-size berries with good taste.
Hardiness zones: 6–9.
Comments: 8–12-ft. upright, slightly spreading bush.

Climax
Season: Early.
Description of fruit: Medium to large fruit with sweet taste.
Hardiness zones: 7–9.
Comments: 6–10-ft. upright but open bush.

Delite
Season: Late.
Description of fruit: Medium to large fruit with very sweet flavor.
Hardiness zones: 6–10.
Comments: 6–10-ft. upright bush.

Garden Blue
Season: Early to midseason.
Description of fruit: Light blue, medium-size fruit with fine flavor.
Hardiness zones: 6–9.
Comments: Vigorous plant.

Powder Blue
Season: Late.
Description of fruit: Medium to large, very sweet fruit.
Hardiness zones: 6–9.
Comments: 8–12-ft. upright bush.

Premier
Season: Early to midseason.
Description of fruit: Light blue fruit with excellent flavor.
Hardiness zones: 6–9.
Comments: Upright plant with attractive foliage. Highly productive.

Tifblue
Season: Mid- to late season.
Description of fruit: Medium to large, sweet, full-flavored berries.
Hardiness zones: 7–9.
Comments: 8–14-ft. upright bush. Vigorous grower, productive. A favorite among rabbiteye growers.

Gooseberries and Currants

Prized in Europe, gooseberries are a rare delight in North America.

For those in the know, gooseberry pie and currant jam rank high among life's delights. North Americans, however, are largely ignorant of these tasty berries, which are far more popular in Europe. (After strawberries, more currants are grown around the world than any other berry.) Fresh gooseberries and currants are almost impossible to find at markets on this side of the Atlantic.

The solution, of course, is to grow your own. If you live where summers aren't scorching, gooseberries and currants are among the easiest berries to grow and offer a range of choices for berry size, color, and flavor. The bushy plants can be integrated into a home landscape or sited in a "production" plot with other fruits, berries, and vegetables. In the future, there are likely to be even more cultivars available, thanks to the establishment in 1989 of the International Ribes Association, a group of professional and amateur enthusiasts devoted to the genus *Ribes* — gooseberries, currants, and jostaberries.

A Troubled Past

If these berries are so delicious and easy to grow, why, you may ask, are they not grown more often? In addition to their many virtues, some members of the genus *Ribes* (black currants in particular) host white pine blister rust, a fungal disease that can be fatal to white pines. Accidentally imported into North America in the early 1900s, the disease became such a threat to the timber industry that thousands of acres of gooseberries and currants were destroyed in an effort to control the spread of the fungus, which must spend part of its life on the leaves of a member of the *Ribes* clan. So serious was the problem that military troops were employed to eradicate the bushes.

Some states continue to ban or control the importation of *Ribes* plants; in addition controls may also be imposed by counties or towns. You can check with your local extension agent to determine if *Ribes* are prohibited in your area. Mail-order nurseries may not ship plants to areas where bans are in effect. Even in areas where *Ribes* are permitted, you should be aware of the problem. If a white pine (five-needled) grows within 1,000 feet of your property, plant rust-resistant cultivars.

Ribes Profile

Left on their own, gooseberries and currants form bushy plants, with additional stems arising each year from underground buds or sprouts on the plant's crown. Americans often allow the plant to take this bushy habit, thinning it once a year. European gardeners, on the other hand, radically restrict the plant's growth habit, training it to a single stem, or cordon, and lateral branches. We'll discuss the pros and cons of these methods later.

In Europe, black currants are widely grown and used primarily for juice, but few are offered by North American nurseries. Here, you can choose from red cultivars (most common) as well as white, various shades of off-white (light yellow, amber, gold), and pink. Gooseberries come in a rainbow of colors, from green to white, red, and yellow, and a myriad of combinations in between. There are few cultivars available of the American gooseberry *(Ribes hirtellum)*. Its European cousin, *R. uva-crispa,* offers a much wider choice.

Trained like little trees along a double-wire trellis, these gooseberries resemble a miniature orchard.

They are also larger, more productive, and better tasting, though a bit less winter-hardy and more prone to disease — particularly powdery mildew, the prime gooseberry problem.

Gooseberry berries vary greatly in size, from those no larger than small blueberries to those the size of a plum. They are borne on fruiting shoots, one, two, or three to a shoot. Currants are half the size of gooseberries or smaller ($1/4$ to $1/2$ inch in diameter) and are borne on racemes or sprigs of about six to thirty berries.

Flower buds form in midsummer and continue developing throughout the winter. On black currants, buds form mostly on one-year-old wood, while on other currants and gooseberries they form mostly on spurs of two- to three-year-old wood. Yield starts dropping on wood older than four years, necessitating the constant renewal of fruiting wood. Gooseberries and currants are insect-pollinated, and all but some black currants are self-fertile. (While cross-pollination isn't necessary, it is beneficial, aiding fruit set and fruit size.)

Currants and gooseberries are long-lived plants. Requiring four to five years to get into full production, they may provide respectable quantities of berries for 20 years or more.

Climate and Conditions

Gooseberries and currants are very winter-hardy, but they don't appreciate hot summers. They can stand winter temperatures of -20° to -30°F, need a minimum of 120 to 140 frost-free growing days, and do best where soil is cool. Day-time temperatures that are frequently in excess of 85°F stress the plants, causing defoliation and damage to the fruit. Be very selective if you live in hot-summer areas, choosing a heat-tolerant cultivar such as the gooseberry 'Glendale'. Fortunately, gooseberries and currants will tolerate some shade (commercial growers used to plant them between rows of orchard trees), so gardeners in hot-summer areas can moderate temperatures to an extent. Remember, too, that plantings along the north side of your home will do much better than those on the south side. (The farther south you live, the more important this becomes.) If your area is prone to late-spring frosts, a northern exposure is also safer — many of the cultivars tend to bloom very early in the season, so planting on the north side of the house or on a north-facing slope delays blooming and lessens chances of damage from a late frost.

Gooseberries and currants, like other berries, love well-drained soil high in organic matter (on a soil test, up to 5 percent humus or organic matter). If your soil falls short, add as much organic matter as you can, particularly high-quality, well-matured compost. Soil high in humus provides necessary air in the root zone; good water penetration, retention, and drainage; and the capacity to hold and release plant nutrients.

Planting and Care

Most nurseries and mail-order suppliers in North America will sell bare-root plants, usually a single stem with several lateral branches. Plants may be one or two years old, though nurseries may sell plants by size rather than age.

Gooseberries and currants can be planted on their own or in rows, or they can be trained as a simple espalier or a single cordon. Currants are quite attractive as privacy fences and look great along property lines when planted as hedgerows. Though somewhat more labor intensive than the others, espaliers are often chosen by farmers and gardeners who appreciate symmetry and the aesthetics of clean lines and orderliness. This form, and the related single cordon, allows for best light interception, maximum air circulation, the production of the largest racemes (clusters) and berry size, and makes picking a breeze, even with thorny gooseberries. We'll discuss training and pruning in detail later.

If you choose to grow gooseberries or currants as bushes, plant short cultivars at least 3 feet apart in a row (or 3 feet from neighboring plants if planted singly), more for larger cultivars. Space multiple rows 7 or more feet apart.

Set plants at least an inch deeper than they were growing in the nursery. (Look on the stems above the roots for a change in color, which marks the soil line.) Shallow-set plants are more prone to drying out, so err on the deep side. Plants set deeper develop additional roots, producing a strong, vigorous plant. Some gardeners trim roots to encourage them to branch and to stimulate root growth.

At planting time, cut young single-stemmed plants down to three or four buds, no more. (If your plant has more than one stem, cut off all but the healthiest-looking.) If you purchased a large branched plant, cut it down to about half its height, leaving just a few good lateral branches. This drastic pruning may seem merciless, but the aboveground portion of the plant must be balanced with the root system or the plant will suffer. A normal plant will have as much or more growth underground as it has aboveground. When plants are dug at nurseries, most of the roots are left in the soil or trimmed for convenient handling, bundling, packaging, storage, and shipping. It's up to you to trim the top growth to match.

Once planted, pamper gooseberries and currants and they will reward you. Mulch the drip zone (or root area) with several inches of compost, well-aged manure, or weed-free straw each year. In addition to providing nutrients, suppressing weeds, and improving the health of the soil, mulch will cool the soil — these plants do not grow well in hot soil. If soil tests show you need to supplement nutrients, in early spring apply a 10-10-10 fertilizer to each bush as follows: 4 ounces for one-year-old plants; 6 ounces for two-year-olds; 8 ounces for three-year-olds; and 10 to 12 ounces for plants four years old and older. Don't apply any more than those amounts. Be particularly careful of nitrogen — too much produces excessive vegetative growth which attracts insects and is susceptible to powdery mildew. Never apply nitrogen after fruit set; it lowers fruit quality and flavor. Cut fertilizer quantities by at least half for single-cordon plants. If possible, build up the fertility of your soil over time with compost and manure.

If your soil lacks organic matter and doesn't hold water well, plan on supplying gooseberries and currants with an inch or more of water per week if nature doesn't do it for you. Drip irrigation is best because it keeps the water off the plants, thereby reducing chances of fungal diseases.

Training and Pruning

The traditional system for commercial farms and home gardens, hedgerow cultivation is by far the most common. The pruning practices that follow are the same whether you plant a single bush or several bushes in a row. This type of pruning is a good choice if the time you can spend on maintenance is limited. If you're planting only one plant, be sure to allow enough room between it and other plants so you can approach, care for, and harvest the plant from all directions (7 to 10 feet apart should do).

In late winter or early spring following the plant's first growing season in your garden, cut off all but four of the healthiest new stems. These may have arisen from underground buds or have grown as lateral branches on the stem

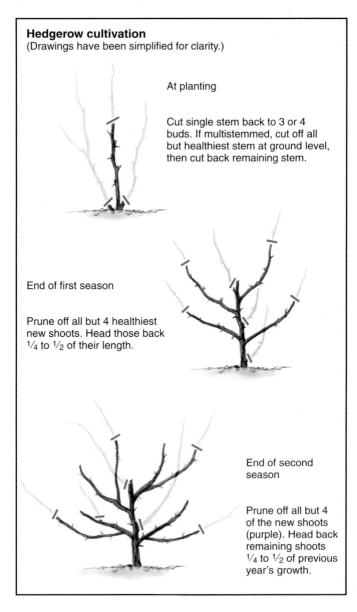

Hedgerow cultivation
(Drawings have been simplified for clarity.)

At planting

Cut single stem back to 3 or 4 buds. If multistemmed, cut off all but healthiest stem at ground level, then cut back remaining stem.

End of first season

Prune off all but 4 healthiest new shoots. Head those back ¼ to ½ of their length.

End of second season

Prune off all but 4 of the new shoots (purple). Head back remaining shoots ¼ to ½ of previous year's growth.

you planted. Choose those with the largest diameters; if they are lateral branches, choose those that form a wide angle with the main stem and are evenly spaced around it. (See the drawings below.)

Depending on your preference, you can train the bush on a single stem, allowing only lateral branches to grow, or you can retain stems arising from underground buds as well. The

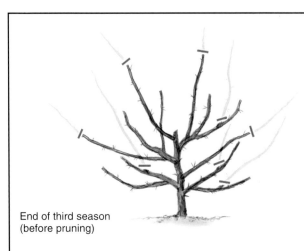

End of third season
(before pruning)

Prune off all but 4 of the new shoots (blue). Head back remaining shoots $\frac{1}{4}$ to $\frac{1}{2}$ of previous year's growth.

End of fourth
season

Remove all 4-year-old growth. Prune off all but 4 of the new stems (red). Head back remaining shoots $\frac{1}{4}$ to $\frac{1}{2}$ of previous year's growth. Repeat this each year.

former will be a somewhat tidier bush than the latter. The amount and size of the fruit won't be affected though — that results from restricting the number of bearing stems, regardless of whether they're lateral branches or arise from underground buds.

In the spring of the following two years, after the second and third growing seasons, once again remove all but four of the most vigorous of the new stems or lateral branches.

At the end of the fourth year, your plant will have a single stem that just finished its fifth growing season. (It was already at least one year old when you bought the plant.) There will also be four stems or branches that are four years old, four that are three years old, four two years old, and all the new shoots formed during the past growing season. Now remove all the four-year-old stems or branches, which will be flagging in health and production, and remove all but the four healthiest of the new, one-year-old stems or branches.

Repeating this practice each year will keep the bush at a productive peak. No shoots will be older than four years, with groups of three-, two-, and one-year-old shoots coming on to replace the four-year olds that are removed. Leaving just four shoots in each year's group produces a healthy bush that is manageable to care for and harvest. You could leave a few more new shoots, but remember that a crowded bush will produce smaller berries and be more prone to disease.

When you're thinning out stems in the spring, it's a good idea to reduce the length of the stems you keep. Cut off one-quarter to one-half of last year's growth, depending on the plant's vigor. Remember, don't cut half of the total length, but only half of the growth that occurred the previous year. This strengthens the branches and stems, produces larger berries, and creates a less "junglelike" habit.

Simple espalier

The goal of this training is to produce a plant with a single vertical stem and a few selected side branches (laterals) resembling arms that reach out along trellis wires, as shown in the drawings on pages 248–249. Espaliered plants will yield large fruit that is easy to pick — even on thorny gooseberry cultivars. With no branches closer than 15 to 18 inches to the ground, fruit will be cleaner, in clear sight and easy reach, and foliage will be healthier.

This system is most labor intensive to train, but least demanding of space and effort for harvest. It is ideal for growing gooseberries or currants in small yards or in a narrow plot by a wall or patio. It is excellent for organic gardeners. Exposed to optimum amounts of sunlight and circulating air, the plants are far less susceptible to fungal diseases, so chemical controls can be avoided. Restricting growth to a single stem and a few branches also makes weeding, mulching, composting, and fertilizer application easier.

Begin by installing a three- or four-wire trellis. Wire (14-gauge) or strong monofilament (about $1/8$ inch in diameter) work well for the trellis. Monofilament is lightweight (though more expensive), easy to handle, does not rust, and will not transmit electricity. Space the trellis lines 15 to 18 inches apart. If you choose 15-inch spacing, for example, start the first strand 15 inches above the ground and set the others at 30, 45, and 60 inches aboveground.

Set new plants in well-prepared soil beneath the trellis. Space plants about 20 to 24 inches apart. Remove all but the healthiest stem emerging from the soil, and rub off all buds and side shoots up to a height of 6 inches above the soil. (See the drawing on page 248.) Next, prune this stem, called the leader, to half its height, cutting it $1/4$ inch above a bud. Tie the leader loosely to a stake or strong bamboo cane; jute works well for a tie.

When the remaining buds push out shoots, choose the healthiest and tie it to the stake to extend the leader. Remove the others. This shoot will itself produce side shoots, called laterals. On each side of the stem, select one strong lateral, growing a few inches beneath the first wire, and prune off others. As the chosen laterals grow, train them to the wire, one growing to the left, one to the right. When the leader reaches subsequent wires repeat this procedure. As the growing season progresses, remove buds or shoots as they appear on the leader, forcing all energy and growth into your chosen laterals. Some gardeners also leave shortened laterals between the longer ones that are tied to the wires.

If the leader doesn't reach a wire in a season, cut it back in late winter or very early spring, removing about one-fourth of the previous year's growth, then train the strongest shoot to extend the leader as described above. Repeat as necessary until the leader has reached the top wire. This will develop a stronger leader and force more branching.

Each year, in late winter or early spring, cut back growth arising from the wire-trained laterals to three new nodes on the previous season's growth. (Also remove any growth from the leader, unless you need a new shoot to replace a damaged lateral.) These nodes will form shoots and fruiting spurs that will bear in subsequent years. Observant gardeners adjust the number of nodes retained according to the vigor of the plant, the density of the foliage, and the size of the fruit. If the plant threatens to get too large or too tangled, you can remove branches (not the wire-trained laterals) entirely. It can sometimes be difficult to distinguish new growth from old. Differ-

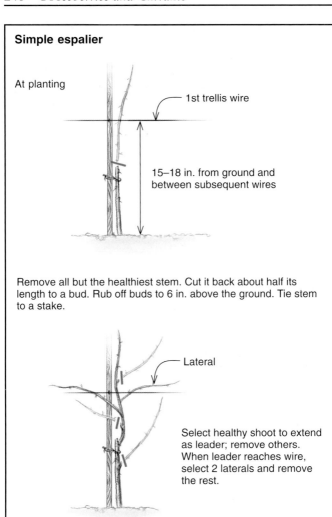

Simple espalier

At planting

1st trellis wire

15–18 in. from ground and between subsequent wires

Remove all but the healthiest stem. Cut it back about half its length to a bud. Rub off buds to 6 in. above the ground. Tie stem to a stake.

Lateral

Select healthy shoot to extend as leader; remove others. When leader reaches wire, select 2 laterals and remove the rest.

ences in the distances between nodes is a great help. In the spring, when growth is vigorous, nodes are farther apart than in the late summer when growth slows. These "up-tight" nodes signal where growth ended one year and began the next.

It will take about four years to achieve a fully formed simple espalier. Because vigor and yields decline on fruiting wood more than three to four years old, you'll need to have replacements for over-the-hill spurs and laterals. Plan ahead to stagger the replacements, one this year, another the next, so you won't lose too much production.

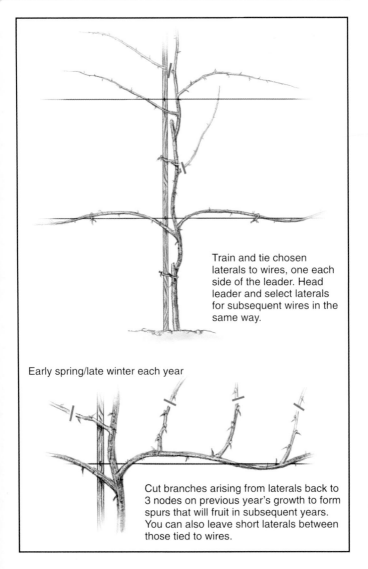

Train and tie chosen laterals to wires, one each side of the leader. Head leader and select laterals for subsequent wires in the same way.

Early spring/late winter each year

Cut branches arising from laterals back to 3 nodes on previous year's growth to form spurs that will fruit in subsequent years. You can also leave short laterals between those tied to wires.

Single-cordon training

Currants, typically, are stronger plants than gooseberries and can be grown in a single-cordon system that is even more compact than the espalier. (See the drawings on pages 250–251.) Single cordon is ideal for pot or tub culture; plant in a good-quality commercial soil mix in a 4- to 5-gallon (minimum) container. Remember that you must be especially attentive to the water and nutrient needs of plants grown in containers. To protect roots from heat in summer, cover the pots entirely with straw, wood chips, or mulch; to keep them warm

Single-cordon training

Planting (fall or spring):
Cut leader back about half
its length. Cut existing
shoots back to about 1 in.
from the stem. Train leader
to stake and let shoots
grow during the first
summer.

First winter: Cut lateral shoots
to 3–4 nodes. Head leader
back to a bud, leaving about
half of last year's growth.

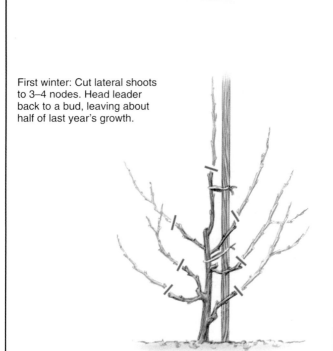

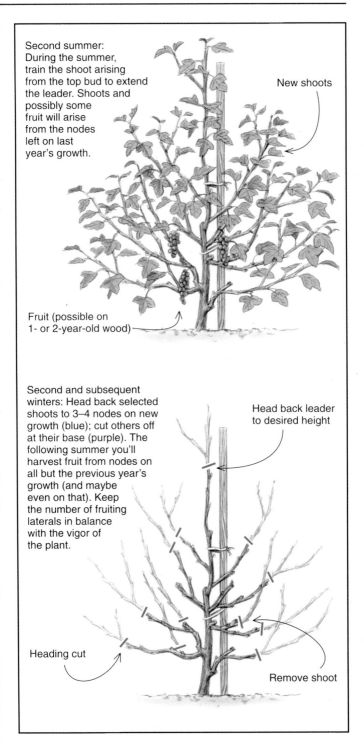

Second summer: During the summer, train the shoot arising from the top bud to extend the leader. Shoots and possibly some fruit will arise from the nodes left on last year's growth.

New shoots

Fruit (possible on 1- or 2-year-old wood)

Second and subsequent winters: Head back selected shoots to 3–4 nodes on new growth (blue); cut others off at their base (purple). The following summer you'll harvest fruit from nodes on all but the previous year's growth (and maybe even on that). Keep the number of fruiting laterals in balance with the vigor of the plant.

Head back leader to desired height

Heading cut

Remove shoot

in winter, cover with snow. Heat is as deadly to roots as extreme cold.

The training is very similar to that described for espalier, but instead of training laterals on wires to form permanent arms, you prune selected laterals back each winter, leaving only about three or four nodes on each, as shown in the drawings on pages 250–251. After a number of years the laterals will be extended from the trunk and their fruiting will begin to lag. Remove extended, unproductive laterals and select new shoots arising either on or near the trunk as replacements. As your plant matures, you can adjust the number of laterals to match its vigor and capacity for fruit production. You'll know that you've got too many laterals, or laterals that have grown too long, when you begin to harvest shorter clusters of smaller berries. (Too much growth also makes it difficult for the fruit and foliage to dry off, increasing the danger of powdery mildew and other fungal diseases.)

Harvest

Gooseberries and currants will be ready to harvest early to midsummer — late June to mid-July for most cultivars in most of North America. Taste and color, with some experience, will alert you to the prime time to pick them. For fresh consumption, they're best left to ripen fully. For jams and jellies and some other preserves, you may want to pick some of the crop on the immature side. Don't hesitate to leave some berries on the plants for maturing beyond prime. Gooseberries and currants can be "stored" on the plant, and this often improves flavor and increases sweetness. A week one way or the other, unless you get heavy rains, will not matter much. By protecting currants from rain in plastic tunnels, growers in mild climates like the Netherlands and Belgium used to keep their currants on the bush six to eight weeks and more after maturity.

Pests and Diseases

If your summers aren't too hot and you keep the soil cool with a cover of mulch, and don't let the plant get overgrown, your gooseberries and currants should be relatively free of problems. Powdery mildew is the main problem for gooseberries, particularly for European cultivars; it is less of a problem for currants. White pine blister rust is a big problem for black currants — plant only resistant cultivars where white pines are grown. If you want to grow European gooseberry cultivars, choose ones resistant to powdery mildew. If you're concerned that conditions on your property (high humidity, lack of air circulation) are conducive to powdery mildew, grow plants on a trellis and prune them for best light interception and air circulation.

Currant aphid

These critters love succulent new growth and are apt to be a problem in early spring just as leaves are emerging, particularly on plants fed with too much nitrogen. Control with an insecticidal soap; picking excess succulent growth can help. Be vigilant — aphids multiply very rapidly. Aphid and other insect problems can also be controlled by applying dormant oil in early spring.

Imported currant worm

This voracious pest can defoliate a plant within days. It is an immature sawfly caterpillar, about an inch long, green with numerous black spots. Control with a natural insecticide at first sighting.

Currant fruit fly

White maggots hatch from eggs deposited in fruit and feed on surrounding tissue. Destroy infested berries to prevent the maggots from pupating in the soil and reinfesting next year's crop.

Anthracnose

This and other fungal problems can often be controlled by a thorough application of lime sulfur at bud break. Rake up and destroy infected leaves.

■ RECOMMENDED VARIETIES OF GOOSEBERRIES

Unless otherwise noted, all varieties listed withstand temperatures as low as -20° to -30°F and do best where temperatures are not regularly above 85°F.

American-type Gooseberries

Captivator
Season: Early to midseason.
Description of fruit: Small, purple-pink berries with good
  flavor.
Comments: Thornless. Resists powdery mildew.

Glendale
Season: Early.
Description of fruit: Small, purplish red fruit with good
  flavor.

Comments: Best for hot climates. Resists powdery mildew and leaf spot.

Houghton
Season: Late.
Description of fruit: Small dark red fruit with good flavor.
Comments: Vigorous, productive bush.

Josselyn (Red Jacket)
Season: Early.
Description of fruit: Medium-size red fruit with excellent flavor.
Comments: Vigorous bush. Resists powdery mildew.

Oregon Champion
Season: Early.
Description of fruit: Medium-size green fruit.
Comments: Resists white pine blister rust.

Pixwell
Season: Midseason.
Description of fruit: Small pale pink fruit, fair flavor.
Comments: Productive. Few thorns. Resists white pine blister rust.

Poorman
Season: Late.
Description of fruit: Medium-size red fruit, excellent flavor.
Comments: Few thorns. Resists white pine blister rust.

'Pixwell'

'Welcome'

Ross
Season: Mid- to late season.
Description of fruit: Medium-size red fruit.
Comments: Very spiny, dense bush. Susceptible to powdery mildew.

Sylvia
Season: Midseason.
Description of fruit: Medium-size pinkish red fruit with excellent flavor.
Comments: Susceptible to powdery mildew.

Welcome
Season: Early to midseason.
Description of fruit: Light red medium to small fruit.
Comments: Few spines, long season.

European-type Gooseberries

Achilles
Season: Late.
Description of fruit: Large, elliptical red fruit with superior flavor. Good keeper.
Comments: Highly susceptible to powdery mildew. Very high yield. Upright bush.

Careless

Season: Midseason.
Description of fruit: Large, pale green fruit with good flavor.
Comments: Susceptible to powdery mildew.

Clark

Season: Midseason.
Description of fruit: Very large copper red fruit.
Comments: Resists powdery mildew; susceptible to leaf spot.

Colossal

Season: Midseason.
Description of fruit: Very large green fruit with mild flavor.
Comments: Heavy bearer.

Early Sulfur

Season: Very early.
Description of fruit: Small gold-yellow berries with superior flavor.
Comments: High yielding.

Fredonia

Season: Early to midseason.
Description of fruit: Large, good quality red fruit.
Comments: Very thorny open spreading bush. Susceptible to powdery mildew.

Hinnonmakis Red

Season: Early to midseason.
Description of fruit: Medium-size red fruit with good flavor.
Comments: Small compact bush. Resists powdery mildew, leaf spot.

Hinnonmakis Yellow

Season: Midseason.
Description of fruit: Small to medium-size yellow fruit with very good flavor.
Comments: Low compact bush. Susceptible to powdery mildew and leaf spot.

Hoenigs Frueheste

Season: Very early.
Description of fruit: Medium-size gold-yellow fruit with superior flavor.
Comments: High-yielding.

Invicta

Season: Early to midseason.
Description of fruit: Very large, round, pale green berries with good flavor.
Comments: Very high-yielding. Resists powdery mildew and leaf spot. Wicked thorns.

Keepsake

Season: Midseason.
Description of fruit: Very large, oblong, yellow-green fruit with very good flavor.
Comments: High-yielding. Highly susceptible to powdery mildew.

Leveler

Season: Midseason.
Description of fruit: Very large yellow-green fruit with good to superior flavor.
Comments: Highly susceptible to powdery mildew.

May Duke

Season: Very early.
Description of fruit: Large red fruit with good flavor.
Comments: High yield, but will crack with heavy rains. Susceptible to powdery mildew and leaf spot.

Whinham's Industry

Season: Midseason.
Description of fruit: Large round to elliptical dark red fruit with good flavor.
Comments: High yield. Susceptible to powdery mildew and leaf spot.

Whitesmith

Season: Midseason.
Description of fruit: Medium to large yellow-green oblong fruit with superior flavor.
Comments: Resistant to powdery mildew and leaf spot.

■ RECOMMENDED VARIETIES OF CURRANTS

Unless otherwise noted, all varieties listed withstand temperatures as low as -20° to -30°F, and do best where temperatures are not regularly above 85°F.

Red Currants (Ribes rubrum, R. sativum)

Cascade
Season: Early.
Description of fruit: Very large, very good fruit.
Comments: Vigorous plant. Good choice for early crop.

Cherry
Season: Midseason.
Description of fruit: Medium-size fruit with good flavor.
Comments: Medium yields. Resistant to powdery mildew.

Jonkheer van Tets
Season: Early.
Description of fruit: Very large fruit with good flavor.
Comments: Very productive. Resistant to powdery mildew.

Laxton's No. 1
Season: Midseason.
Description of fruit: Large, bright red fruit with superior mild flavor.
Comments: High-yielding, vigorous bush.

Minnesota 71
Season: Mid- to late season.
Description of fruit: Medium to large berries with good flavor.
Comments: Vigorous upright plant.

Perfection
Season: Early.
Description of fruit: Extra-large fruit with good sweet flavor.
Comments: Resists white pine blister rust and powdery mildew.

Red Lake
Season: Midseason.
Description of fruit: Medium to large, light red berries; easy to pick.
Comments: Very productive. One of the most popular red currants in the world.

Wilder
Season: Late.
Description of fruit: Small berries.
Comments: Susceptible to powdery mildew.

'Red Lake'

'Wilder'

White Currants (Ribes rubrum, R. sativum)

Primus
Season: Early.
Description of fruit: Light yellow, good aroma.
Comments: Upright habit. Very popular in Europe.

Blanca
Season: Late.
Description of fruit: Yellow berries, very good flavor.
Comments: Very long sprigs of berries. High-yielding.

White Imperial
Season: Early.
Description of fruit: Medium-size, very sweet.
Comments: Resistant to powdery mildew.

Translucent white currants make a striking contrast to their shiny red cousins.

White Versailles
Season: Very early.
Description of fruit: Medium to large aromatic fruit.
Comments: Disease-resistant plant.

Black Currants (R. nigrum)

Ben Connan
Season: Early to midseason.
Description of fruit: Large fruit.
Comments: Compact bush, high yield. Resistant to powdery mildew.

Ben Sarek
Season: Very early.
Description of fruit: Large fruit.
Comments: Compact bush, high yield. Resistant to powdery mildew.

Consort
Season: Early to midseason.
Description of fruit: Small to medium-size berries.
Comments: Resistant to white pine blister rust. Susceptible to leaf spot; very susceptible to powdery mildew.

Crusader
Season: Mid- to late season.
Description of fruit: Small to medium-size berries with fair flavor.
Comments: Very vigorous plant. Resistant to white pine blister rust. Requires cross-pollination.

Crandall *(R. odoratum)*
Season: Late.
Description of fruit: Medium to very large berries make fabulous jams, pies, and preserves.
Comments: Not true black currant, but has beautiful yellow flowers; bears in great abundance. Resistant to powdery mildew.

Wellington
Season: Early.
Description of fruit: Great flavor.
Comments: Heavy yields.

Grapes

'Suffolk Red' is a handsome seedless American grape produced by a highly disease-resistant vine.

Grapes, of all fruits, resonate the deepest with humankind. Eaten fresh or dried, squeezed as juice or fermented as wine, grapes have for thousands of years been our companion in revelry and reverence. Small wonder that even gardeners with no interest in growing other fruits and berries can be found lovingly tending a grapevine.

Grapes are accommodating plants. Though the image of a sunny, warm hillside springs to mind at the very thought of a vineyard, grapes will grow almost anywhere there are gardens. And, from the heavy purple clusters of the time-honored 'Concord' to the newest French hybrids, there are grapes of all descriptions for almost any garden. Full sun and protection from late spring frosts are the essential elements for successful grape growing. It's true that grapes do best in deep, friable, well-drained soil, but there's no need to despair if you garden in heavy red clay. Just plant a miniature vineyard in a permanent planter, wooden half-barrel, or other large container filled with your own custom-made soil mix.

Grapevines make excellent ornamental plants. The canes are quick to cover a raw new arbor, trellis, or fence. In spring, their clusters of greenish flowers scent the air with sweet perfume, and in summer, their big leaves provide cool, shifting shade. Some cultivars offer special attractions. Among the wine grape species, *Vitis vinifera,* for example, the cultivar 'Purpurea' boasts dramatic red or purple-tinged leaves and excellent fall-colored foliage, while the leaves of the unusual 'Incana' are covered with dense white down that creates an almost cobwebby look. 'Apiifolia' and 'Ciotat' have lacy, deeply cut leaves.

A trained, well-pruned vine is also a handsome addition to a formal or traditional garden scheme. Backing a border, trained to a fence, or centering an island bed, the carefully clipped vine gives a feeling of permanence to the garden. In the quiet season of winter, the shreddy bark of a grapevine's trunk and branches and its knotted, gnarled form catch the eye of garden visitors. Grapes appeal to other creatures as well. The dense branches attract nesting catbirds, thrashers, and other birds, and the fruit is a magnet for birds, raccoons, opossums, and other animals.

If grapevines are so handsome and easy to grow, why don't more gardens include them? The problem may be simple intimidation. Grapes have acquired a reputation for needing complicated pruning, a procedure so daunting to many gardeners that they give up before they get started.

Overcoming Fear of Pruning

The truth about pruning, as any owner of a neglected decades-old backyard vine can tell you, is that, strictly speaking, you don't need to do it. Most grapes will bear some fruit whether or not they ever feel the blade of the pruning shears.

But pruning has such benefits for both vine and grower that few gardeners will ignore it. Pruning and training keeps the vine healthier by promoting air circulation through the plant, avoiding the creation of a jungle of leaves and canes in which powdery mildew and other maladies thrive. For the grower, it enables the production of lots of fruit in limited space. And pruning keeps the harvest near at hand — no ladders or backhand stretching required.

Training and pruning do require some knowledge and commitment, but most people can learn to do it without undue stress, and many will even find the process interesting and enjoyable. Few gardeners have the patience to snip out branches according to diagram, and that may be part of the reason why grapes often seem like just too much trouble. But mastering pruning technique is not a test of how well you can read and clip at the same time. It's more a matter of acquiring a basic understanding of how grapes grow and fruit. Once you know where flower buds can be expected to appear on your vine, you can clip away to suit your own aesthetic sense and the strength and size of your arbor. And if you mess up, you won't have to live with it very long. Like a bad haircut, most pruning "disasters" are soon camouflaged by new growth. The quick-growing branches of the vine will offer you ample opportunity to hone your pruning techniques. (We'll discuss training and pruning in detail later in the chapter.)

Grapes for Good Eating

With a history of cultivation that dates back millenia, the grape embraces an immense extended family of cultivars. Grapes for the garden come from four different lines of parentage: American, European, American hybrids, and muscadine. While 90 percent of all grapes cultivated in the world belong to the European class, that figure is heavily weighted by the preponderance of the European grape in vineyards. In backyard gardens in this country, the scale is probably tipped more in favor of the cold-hardy Americans and American hybrids. Which type you plant depends upon where you live and what your garden conditions are.

American grapes

Represented by the quintessential 'Concord', American grapes are cold-hardy types that tolerate humid summers and are more resistant to disease than European grapes. They are often heavily aromatic and usually have an intense "foxy" flavor, like bottled grape juice. Depending on the cultivar, they can be grown in zones 4 through 8.

Unlike European grapes, American varieties part easily with their skins, allowing you to swallow the fruit skin and all, or swallow only the juicy flesh and spit out the tart, tougher skin. Because of this easy separation of skin from pulp, American grapes are known as "slipskin."

American grapes include a large number of native species that fill various ecological niches from the canyons of Texas to the banks of Louisiana bayous, from the rocky mountain outcrops of the Appalachians to the woodlands of New England. Those grown in home gardens are mostly descendants and selections of *Vitis labrusca*, the fox grape native to the eastern half of the country.

Native peoples appreciated and gathered American grapes long before the first Europeans arrived, eating the fruit fresh or drying it for later use. Europeans were delighted to find a familiar food in the New World, albeit with smaller fruits and more athletic vines than those back home. Surrounded by wild grapes, they nevertheless set about establishing vineyards of their own familiar varieties of European grapes. Franciscan monks planted rows of European grapes in California as early as 1769 and soon began producing tolerable wine.

But outside of California and Mexico, the European grapes were out of their element. The winters were brutally cold, fungal diseases were rampant in the humid summers, and phylloxera root aphids devastated the plantings. Repeated attempts to establish vineyards with European grapes in less serendipitous areas of the New World were disappointing.

Noting the hardy, vigorous American vines that surrounded their failed plantings, some settlers began to experiment. By grafting European cultivars to native rootstocks, they obtained a natural resistance to phylloxera and greater cold tolerance on plants bearing familiar fruit. Breeders also began selecting the best of the wild vines for propagation, cultivation, and possible improvement.

Among the most rewarding was the fox grape or skunk grape *(Vitis labrusca)*, a vine that scrambles into the tree tops in search of sun. The fruits had a distinctive musky flavor, described as "foxy" in those days when people knew what a fox (or fox den) smelled like. In 1843, the intensely flavored 'Concord', still the standard for bluish black grapes, was introduced, having been selected from plants grown from seeds of a wild fox grape in Concord, Massachusetts. Although some still say this grape tastes "foxy," its intense, rich flavor is the essence of grapes for many people. If you've drunk bottled grape juice, you know the taste of 'Concord'.

V. labrusca also served as the parent of the white grape 'Niagara' and the coppery red 'Catawba', as well as dozens of other cultivars. The sweet, full-flavored 'Catawba', which shares the rich grapey flavor of its parent, is today the leading grape for American wine and juice, although it also makes a fine table grape. 'Niagara', introduced in 1882, has a more delicate, tangy flavor and is a favorite for home arbors. *V. labrusca* cultivars are well suited to gardens in the Northeast, Northwest, and central states, and many, including the old cultivar 'Champanelle' and the newer 'Fredonia', will also thrive in gardens south of the Mason-Dixon line.

Other American species have been used in breeding attempts, but with less success than *V. labrusca*. The riverbank grape *V. riparia*, a native species impervious to cold, has lent that trait to its progeny, including 'Beta' cultivars that are

This colorful harvest of grapes includes the European varieties 'Tokay' and 'Thompson Seedless', the American standby 'Concord', and others.

excellent for gardeners in New England, northern Michigan, and other areas where the thermometer sinks to well below 0°F in winter. With the proliferation of native-plant nurseries, many gardeners are rediscovering the "wild grapes" of southern riverbanks and eastern woodlands. Usually small-fruited but prolific and intensely flavored, such species as the shrubby mountain grape of the Ozarks and the Appalachians *(Vitis rupestris)* and the eastern United States fox grape *(V. vulpina)*, which needs cold to sweeten it up, are moving into the garden.

Native grapes are excellent landscape plants, quickly covering a fence or the wall of a garage, and they are superlative for attracting wildlife. Many are high climbers, and although the clusters of fruit are often out of reach for easy picking, any berries that fall do make a tasty nibble for the gardener. Foraging animals, including raccoons, foxes, opossums, squirrels, and mice, have an easier time reaching the fruit, and birds are drawn to this banquet from miles around. Many of the "wild" native grapevines are full of ripened fruit during fall migration, when such birds as rose-breasted grosbeaks, tanagers, thrushes, thrashers, and others seek out the fruit. Any grapes that hang on into late fall and winter are welcomed by cedar waxwings, bluebirds, mockingbirds, yellow-rumped warblers, and other fruit-eaters.

European grapes

These are the classic wine and dessert grapes, best for areas with a long, warm growing season and no extreme winter cold. Cultivars and selections of *Vitis vinifera*, they are not as cold-hardy as American or American-European hybrids, growing best in zones 7 through 9 depending on cultivar. They are often prone to disease, and they usually require dedicated attention to produce a good crop. The fruit is sweet and winy-tasting, and the skin adheres to the flesh. The green 'Thompson Seedless' grape found in every supermarket is a European cultivar.

European grapes like it hot. As early European settlers soon found out, most of them thrive only in areas with a long, warm growing season, and they suffer in humid summers or in winters when the temperature dips near 5°F. The long, high heat of California's Central Valley is ideal. European grapes will also grow well in parts of Arizona and the Southwest and in parts of Washington and Oregon, where the season is long and warm and winters are not too cold.

If your climate is suited to growing these grapes, you can take your pick from hundreds of cultivated varieties. The names of some European cultivars are already familiar, thanks to the California winemakers' tradition of naming their wines after the grape that produced them, rather than after a vineyard or region, as with French wines. You won't find a 'Beaujolais' grape cultivar or a 'Champagne', because these are French wines. But you will find grapes named 'Chardonnay', 'Chenin Blanc', 'Zinfandel', and so on. The namesake of the popular Chenin Blanc wine is a very vigorous vine with juicy, whitish green grapes.

A few European cultivars are cold-hardy enough to grow as far north as zone 5. They're planted in vineyards (in New York and other states) more often than home gardens, because the fruit is best suited for wine. If you want to try your hand at making wine from French grapes, you might like to experiment. The bluish black wine grape 'Baco Noir', an older French hybrid, tolerates heavy soils and temperatures down to 0°F. 'Chancellor' is another hardy European red-wine grape. This heavy bearer will stand temperatures as low as -10°F.

European grapes have another drawback for the home gardener. They are susceptible to the ravages of several diseases and insect pests, some of which can be fatal to the vine. The severity of these problems varies by location, and from year to year. A regular program of spraying is often necessary to prevent problems. If you are considering planting European grapes, get in touch with your county extension agent to find out what to guard against in your area. European grapes also need more attention to pruning than American or hybrid grapes, both for disease prevention and to restrict fruiting, which prevents exhaustion from overbearing and produces sweeter fruit.

If you have the ideal climate and the time to dedicate to keeping the vines healthy, European grapes can produce heavy loads of wonderful fruit, great for eating fresh from the vine and perfect for your own try at a respectable homemade Chardonnay.

American hybrids

Combining the best of old and new worlds, these crosses join the superb fruit of the European vines with the disease resistance and hardiness of the American species. Also known as American-European hybrids, American-French hybrids, and French hybrids, the plants show a variety of traits, depending on how the genes work out. In most cases, American hybrids exhibit better disease resistance, cold hardiness, and tolerance for humidity than European grapes. Depending on cultivar, they can be grown from zones 4 through 9; many are hardy to at least -10°F. The flavor of the fruit may taste like the winey European side of the family, or it can show the decidedly grapey flavor of its American heritage.

The American hybrids include some of the best grapes for home growers. 'Himrod', for instance, offers the delicious seedless flesh and delicate flavor of its European parent, 'Thompson Seedless', but the vine tolerates temperatures in zone 5, two full zones colder. Even better is the incredibly cold-hardy 'Reliance', a seedless pink-red grape that is unharmed in temperatures as low as -34°F. The vigorous vine resists anthracnose and powdery and downy mildew, and the fruit is superb — tender skin, firm flesh, and outstanding sweet flavor.

Muscadine grapes

These American natives of the South and Southeast are the practical choice for gardeners in the Deep South (zones 7 through 9). Fat dull-purple muscadine grapes get their common name from the French word *musc,* meaning "musk scent," for the musky flavor of their pulp. (The European muscat grape is named for a similar character.) To many grape eaters, the flavor of muscadines takes a little getting used to. It's a woodsy, smoky taste, not the rich, grapey flavor or mild sweetness our palates have become accustomed to.

Muscadine grapes are derived from the species *Vitis rotundifolia,* which grows in the wild from Delaware to Florida and west to Kansas and Mexico. Cultivated varieties of muscadine grapes are grown mostly in the Cotton Belt, a stretch of the Deep South from Georgia to Texas where the climate is mild and the summers muggy. (The plant's botanical name comes from its rounded or oval-triangulate, mostly unlobed leaves — an unusual attribute among grapes.)

The muscadine classification includes the famed 'Scuppernong', one of the oldest and still most widely grown varieties of muscadines. (The whole class is sometimes referred to as scuppernong grapes.) The large, aromatic 'Scuppernong' fruits have an unusual color that ranges from greenish amber to reddish bronze, depending on how much sun the fruit receives, and they are dotted all over with russet speckles. The pale flesh is sweet and almost plum-flavored. Favored for fresh eating as well as a sweet golden wine, scuppernongs take their name from a river and lake in North Carolina.

Unlike American and European grapes, which usually ripen all at once or over a short period, many muscadine cultivars ripen over an extended length of time. Instead of "feast or famine," when the kitchen is piled with bushels of quick-to-spoil grapes, the harvest of muscadines can be enjoyed for fresh eating at a more leisurely pace, over the space of several weeks. The very productive 'Magnolia', for example, which can yield a bushel of lovely bronze fruit from just one vine, ripens from September to early October.

Choosing the Right Grape

Grapes have been tinkered with for so long that cultivars exist to fit almost any growing conditions. This is both good and bad news. The good news is that, with proper selection, almost all gardeners can enjoy their own grapes. The bad news is that the plethora of cultivars means you will need to take some extra care when making your selections, to be sure of getting a grape that is adapted to the climate and conditions in your area.

Matching cultivars to conditions necessitates weighing a number of factors. In the Pacific Northwest, for example, the sweet blue-black 'Price' American grape is a good choice because it ripens well even in cool weather; 'Scuppernong' is all wrong for this area because it fails to ripen under these conditions. 'Concord' performs to perfection in areas with cool or humid summers, but in the Southwest and other dry, hot summer areas, this venerable American grape is a disappointment. In such climates, 'Champanelle' is a much better choice, offering full 'Concord' flavor with the necessary heat tolerance that the older cultivar lacks. The familiar 'Thompson Seedless' European grape fills many a fruit basket in warm areas such as California's Central Valley and parts of Arizona; in cooler areas of California, the earlier, not quite so sweet 'Perlette' is a reasonable substitute.

Susceptibility to pests and diseases is a crucial quality. Always be sure to check the fine print in catalogs and care notes for any information on pest and disease susceptibility or resistance. Look for cultivars that are resistant to the diseases prevalent in your region. Some cultivars may be resistant to one or a number of diseases, yet particularly vulnerable to another. If black rot isn't a problem in your area, for instance, the outstanding 'Reliance' may be a good choice, even though it shows susceptibility to that disease. Many cultivars, such as the meaty, seedless 'Suffolk Red' and the sweet-tart, golden 'Interlaken Seedless' are generally disease-resistant.

As for all plants, cold hardiness is always a big consideration, and we've included hardiness zones or minimum temperatures for most of the cultivars in the list, beginning on page 291. But because grapes are so selectively bred for so many different climates and conditions, just finding the right zone number doesn't mean you've made a good match. Ask your nursery owner or call your county extension agent to confirm whether a cultivar that catches your fancy is one that will do well in your garden. Refer to the regional recommendations on page 272 for some guidelines on suggested cultivars.

Faced with all these considerations, a beginner may despair of being able to make a good choice. As usual, however, the most reliable way of finding out what grows well in your area is to ask your local extension agent, a knowledgeable person at a local nursery, or an experienced local grape grower. Reputable mail-order suppliers also keep up on what does well where. As a rough guideline, the chart below lists some cultivars that are proven performers in these regions. Even so, check them out with a local expert before buying.

Regional Recommendations

Northeast, Central:

'Buffalo'
'Canadice'
'Captivator'
'Catawba'
'Concord'
'Delaware'
'Fredonia'
'Moore Early'
'Niagara'
'Ontario'
'Steuben'
'Van Buren'
'Worden'

European grapes

'Aurore'
'Baco Noir'
'Chancellor'
'Foch' ('Marechal Foch')
'Seyve-Villard'
'Verdelet'
'Villard Blanc'

South:

'Blue Lake'
'Champanelle'
'Doreen'
'Fredonia'
'Fry'
'Higgins'
'Ives'
'Jumbo'
'Lake Emerald'
'Magnolia'
'Portland'
'Pride'
'Scuppernong'
'Stover'

Northwest:

'Campbell Early' ('Island Belle')
'Diamond'
'Fredonia'
'Glenora'
'Himrod'
'Interlaken Seedless'
'Moored'
'Seneca'
'Suffolk Red'

North:

'Beta'
'Edelweiss'
'Fredonia'
'King of the North'
'Reliance'
'St. Croix'
'Worden'

California Arizona and other hot-summer mild-winter areas:

'Black Monukka'
'Cardinal'
'Emperor'
'Flame Seedless'
'Golden Muscat'
'Niabell'
'Perlette'
'Thompson Seedless'
'Tokay'

Rootstocks and pollination

Grapes may be grown on their own roots from cuttings of the parent vine, or they may be grafted onto other rootstocks for better disease resistance or hardiness. Fortunately, you needn't become a rootstock expert but can trust the judgment of the growers to have selected the appropriate rootstock. (You won't have a choice in most instances anyway.)

American and European grapes and their hybrids are self-fruitful, with the exception of a very few cultivars. Muscadine types usually need a second muscadine cultivar for pollination. Read the catalog or hangtag carefully so that you know whether you will need to buy a pollinator variety and which pollinator is recommended. 'Magnolia' is a good pollinator for many muscadines.

Site and Soil

Choose a planting site in full sun, sheltered from cold winter winds. A south-facing slope is the perfect place to plant grapes. Grapes grow best in loose, deep soil at a pH level of about 5.5 to 7.0. Good drainage is a must — grapes will not survive with "wet feet." Avoid planting in a low-lying "frost pocket" where cold air collects.

Grapes grow well on a fairly lean diet, and supplemental fertilizer is almost never needed, unless your soil is severely deficient in nutrients. Given the commitment you're making to the plant (grapes live for years), it is best to test your soil and amend it if necessary the year before planting. Rather than amending the small amount of soil in the planting hole, improving a larger area will allow the roots to spread widely. See the chapter "Planting Fruit Trees and Bushes" for a discussion of soil preparation; if you have insurmountable drainage or soil problems, consider growing a grapevine in a container, also as described in that chapter. Because grapes need to be supported, a container-grown plant must be positioned permanently in one spot.

The Support System

Grapevines need support. Before you plant, and as a consideration in selecting your site, think about the kind of support structure you want. As you might imagine for a plant that's been grown intensively for thousands of years, there are many support systems. We'll describe a simple one that will work for the training systems we cover later.

Grapevines need a single, sturdy stake to support the main stem — a 2 × 2 or metal fence post will do. A simple arrangement of horizontal wires strung between firmly set 4 × 4 wooden posts spaced 8 to 10 feet apart will support the fruiting branches. Some vines are trained to one wire, with a branch called an "arm" or "cordon" extending out from the trunk in each direction along the wire. Another popular system requires two wires to support four cordons (the "four-armed Kniffin" system). Supports can go higher, for example if you wanted to cover the wall of a building, though this makes it more difficult to tend and harvest the vine. Because of the shade cast by the upper branches, the lower cordons of a multiple-cordon vine will not bear as much fruit as those at the top.

Bury the wire-support posts at least 2 feet into the ground. (Height above ground is determined by the number of wires you choose.) You'll need at least 8 feet of horizontal support (4 feet either side of the main stem) for a single vine. Muscadine grapes are extremely vigorous and require 12 to 20 feet on which to ramble.

Use heavy galvanized wire (12-gauge) for lateral supports, and wrap it securely around each end post, stapling with heavy-duty fasteners to any posts in between. If you train the vine against a wall, the wires should be 8 to 12 inches from the wall, and they must also be sturdy enough to support the vine and its crop.

Position the first wire about 3 to 4 feet above the ground, which is a convenient height to tend the vine, and space subsequent wires at 2- to 3-foot intervals — the wider spacing provides more air and sun to the plant and more room for you to maneuver when planting.

Many gardeners integrate grapes into their landscape, growing them on a fence or arbor — hung with grapevines, an arbor offers a focal point for the garden and welcoming shade for seating underneath. Whatever structure you choose, build it to last — anchor it firmly and make sure it will be able to support the weight of a mature fruiting vine. Here again, advice from local experts is indispensable. Finally, build the support structure before you plant vines. Sinking posts or stakes after planting may shear off roots or disturb the smaller feeder roots, slowing the progress of the new vine.

Buying and planting grapevines

Grapes are sold as dormant, one-year-old (sometimes two-year-old) vines in early spring, usually bare-root, although garden centers may also pot up bare-root plants for sale. Bare-root plants are often in peat or coarse sawdust wrapped in plastic packaging. Buy them early in the season while the roots are still fresh. Packaged bare-root plants that languish at garden centers well into spring may show signs of life on top, but the roots can be in poor shape.

In some areas, such as California, dormant grapevines may be sold loose (their roots kept moist in wood chips or sand) as well as in packages. If you have the opportunity to examine the roots, choose a plant with well-developed roots growing all the way around the joint at the bottom end (the "basal node") rather than a plant with roots on only one side.

Planting

The best time to buy and plant grapes is in late winter or early spring before "budbreak," the time when leaf buds swell and begin to open. (If your just-purchased grapevine is already leafing out, be especially careful to keep the soil moist after planting to prevent the leaves from withering.) Unwrap the package and shake the roots free of any packing material, then carefully undo any rubber bands, wire twist-ties, or other fasteners.

About an hour before you plant, soak the roots in a bucket of water and clip the vine back to leave just two live buds. While the plant is soaking, dig the planting hole, positioning it along your support wires (remember to space two or more vines 8 feet apart; muscadines 12 to 20 feet). The hole should be wide enough for you to comfortably spread out the roots.

Plant the vine at the level it grew in the nursery; look for discoloration on the stem to indicate the previous soil line. If your vine is grafted — you'll see a visible scar of the graft union — be sure to keep the graft joint aboveground, otherwise the top graft will set roots and you'll lose the benefit of the rootstock.

When the hole is ready, drive a support stake about 2 to 4 inches from where the stem of the vine will grow. The stake should be as tall as the height you plan for the plant's head. (See the training discussion below.) If you're planting next to an arbor or trellis, position the hole and stem the same distance from a sturdy vertical support post. Fill soil around the roots; when the hole is half-full, soak it with water, let it drain thoroughly, and add the remainder of the soil. Form a shallow basin around the vine to catch rain and irrigation water. Grapes like it dry, and many growers leave bare soil around the plants. If you mulch, do so lightly.

Training and Pruning

These are two separate processes. You train the vine to establish the trunk against a vertical support and create the basic framework of bearing cordons. Then you prune it each year, cutting back the canes of the vine to keep it in check and to boost the quality of the fruit. The training described here takes three years and your first harvest comes in the fourth.

All training and pruning methods have similar aims — to rein in the otherwise rampant growth of the plant, to concentrate energy into fruit production (bigger and sweeter grapes), to keep the fruit easily accessible, and to minimize the pest and disease problems associated with crowded growth. The methods are rooted in the way the plant grows.

Grapes are borne on new shoots that sprout from growth that began the previous season. In a single year, a new shoot may reach 3 to 15 feet long. During the shoot's first year, leaves sprout from nodes along its length. Tucked behind each leaf (in the "leaf axil") is a compound bud. When growth resumes the following spring, each compound bud pushes out a new shoot. At the base of these shoots clusters of small, greenish yellow, often fragrant flowers form. (Created by the fruiting part of the compound bud.) Depending on cultivar, vigor, and exposure to sun, the vine may produce from one to four clusters of flowers at each node, which will then mature into delicious grapes.

A vine's growth is almost all concentrated in its one-year-old canes. (After its first winter, the matured shoot is called a cane.) Latent buds scattered along the length of older canes can sprout, but they do so much less often. So each year the new growth — and fruit — on an unpruned vine will occur farther and farther away from the trunk. Training and pruning seek to keep the formation of new canes, and therefore, the fruiting buds, close to the plant's trunk.

Training and pruning are also aimed at providing as much sunlight as possible to the fruiting parts of the vine. Grapevines need sun to produce flower buds. Wild climbing grapes, like the small but sweet frost grape *(Vitis vulpina)*, usually go to the birds because they bear only when the vine manages to scramble into the treetops, where it can feel the warmth of the sun. Sun also gives the ripening grapes good color. Some varieties fail to develop their final color if they hang in shade. 'Scuppernong', for example, stays a greenish-yellow rather than developing its more usual translucent copper-glazed color. Some growers go so far as to pinch off interfering leaves that shade the clusters, especially in an overcrowded vine. This is a good idea if you don't carry it to extremes; removing several leaves on a healthy, well-growing vine won't dent its vigor.

Training for structure

Here, we'll describe training to a wire support structure. With minor differences, you can use the same technique for training along a fence, or against a trellis or an arbor. In this method, all vines are trained in the same general way for their first three years of growth. (See drawings on pages 278–279.)

The first year. Let the newly planted vine grow unrestrained, free of the support stake. Water is vital in the first year for the development of good, strong roots. Keep the soil moist (but never soggy); it should feel damp when you wiggle a finger into the surface. A soaker hose does an admirable job, and a light blanket of mulch will prevent rapid evaporation. Cut back on watering beginning in late summer, to give the vine time to harden off for the coming winter. After mid-August, water only if the leaves begin to wilt.

With vines trained on two wires and neatly mulched with wood chips and manure, this little vineyard is both handsome and productive.

In average soil, grapes don't usually need fertilizing, which encourages leafy growth at the expense of fruit. Some cultivars are slow to get going; if growth is less than vigorous, test your soil (if you haven't already) before running for the nitrogen.

The first winter. Actual training begins now, in late winter, with the selection of a trunk for your vine. It takes just a minute or two. During its first growing season, a newly planted vine will usually throw out several canes, each about 1 to 2 feet long. Choose the thickest, most vertical shoot. With a pair of hand pruners, nip this cane back just above the third bud from the cane's connection to the trunk. Cut off any other shoots.

The vine, which is now a short three-budded cane, will look very much like it did just after planting. As you make the cuts, draw solace from the knowledge that the first season's growth has produced a solid root system. When growth starts up again in spring, your little vine — bolstered by those healthy roots — will take off like a shot.

Occasionally, a vine may grow extra-vigorously its first year, producing canes 3 or 4 feet long. If yours is one of these fast growers, select the strongest cane, stretch it vertically above the base of the plant and fasten it loosely to the support post. Then cut it to a bud between 2 and 3 feet above the ground. Then train its top shoot to extend the trunk as pictured on the next page.

Basic training

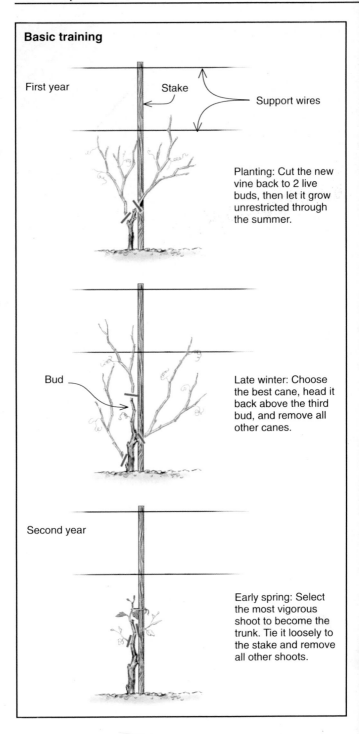

First year

Stake

Support wires

Planting: Cut the new vine back to 2 live buds, then let it grow unrestricted through the summer.

Bud

Late winter: Choose the best cane, head it back above the third bud, and remove all other canes.

Second year

Early spring: Select the most vigorous shoot to become the trunk. Tie it loosely to the stake and remove all other shoots.

Summer: Tie the growing shoot to the stake at intervals. When it reaches head height (here, just below the first wire) pinch off its growing tip.

Summer: Form cordon arms by training 2 vigorous shoots to the wire on either side of the trunk. Remove all other shoots arising from the trunk.

Third year

Allow new shoots to form on the cordons, but pinch out all (or most) flower clusters when they appear.

The second year. During this year, you support the trunk as it grows to its final height, and you begin developing the cordons arising from it.

When the vine breaks dormancy in its second spring, new shoots will sprout from the buds on the short, sturdy cane you selected during late winter. Wait until the shoots achieve about 6 to 8 inches of new growth, then select the strongest, most vigorous, most upright shoot to become the trunk. Tie it loosely to the support stake and snip off all other shoots. (Where damage from extreme cold is a possibility, growers often select and tie up an additional shoot as insurance. Tie this shoot lower than the others.) As the shoot extends during the growing season, tie it loosely to the support stake at intervals of about a foot.

When the shoot grows to within about 6 inches of the support wire, pinch off its growing tip with your thumb and forefinger — just like you'd pinch back a chrysanthemum. This establishes the trunk's final height, called its "head," and encourages shoots to form below, which will be trained along the wire. The height of a vine's head depends on the support against which it is grown. In our example, we're training to a single wire, so the head comes just below the wire. A good height for a vine grown against a 4-foot-tall fence is about 3½ feet, high enough to allow the cordon arms to be trained to run along the top of the fence. A vine reaching for the top of an arbor may need a head 6 feet or more aboveground. If your grapevines will be trellised up a ladder of wires, its head should be about 6 inches below the last wire.

Soon after pinching, new side shoots will sprout from the trunk. When they reach pencil thickness, choose two of the strongest and guide each horizontally along the wire (or trellis or arbor), so the vine forms a T shape. Remove any other shoots on the trunk. As they grow, loosely tie the cordons to the lateral supports at intervals; occasionally weave them around the wire supports. Don't damage the leaves sprouting along the length of the arms, but remove any growth as it arises from the trunk, and cut off below ground level any suckers at the base of the plant. If shoots as well as leaves sprout from the cordons, pinch them back to about 8 to 10 inches in length.

The second winter. Remove any shoots that have grown from the cordons, and neaten up the trunk if necessary, so that all that is left is the basic T-shaped vine. If the cordons have grown vigorously during the summer, cut them back to about 10 to 12 buds each. If your goal is a multitiered vine, with four, six, or more arms, you'll need to allow the main trunk to extend to the top support, which may take an additional season or two. Head back the trunk each season to a vigorous-looking bud, then select a strong shoot to train upward. Meanwhile, select shoots to train as arms on the wires or other supports below. When the trunk reaches its final height, in winter, cut through its top bud to prevent further upward growth.

The third year. With the trunk and cordon arms established, the third year is easy. The compound buds on the now one-year-old arms will produce new shoots and may produce flowers. Unfortunately, bearing fruit would stress the still-young plant, so pinch the flowers off and think of harvests to come. (If you can't wait, settle for just a few clusters of grapes this year.) Don't damage the shoots when you're pinching off flowers — you'll need them next year.

Training is complete. From now on you'll be pruning. How you handle the vine in the coming winter will depend on whether you're cane pruning or spur pruning, which we'll discuss next.

Pruning for fruit

Working on the compact structure created by training, pruning limits the amount of fruit the vine produces, which creates larger, better-quality grapes and preserves the strength of the vine. A well-pruned vine is less vulnerable to disease, because air circulation is good and the relatively sparse vegetation allows you to see any problems in their early stages.

For the cordon-trained vine we've created, you can choose between two time-tested methods: cane pruning and spur pruning. For all grapes except muscadines, pruning is done in winter or late winter before the plant breaks dormancy. Muscadines are pruned in summer when the rampant-growing vine has settled down after its flush of spring growth and pruning is less likely to initiate new growth. Muscadines are usually trained to an arbor, where the vines are allowed to dangle after they reach the top.

American grapes, most American hybrids, and a very few European cultivars (including 'Thompson Seedless') usually do not bear fruit on the first two or three nodes of a cane, called the basal buds. Instead, clusters of grapes are borne farther out on the canes. Because of this trait, these vines are usually cane pruned, a style that allows long canes to develop. Almost all European grapes, on the other hand, bear fruit on shoots that grow from basal buds. Spur pruning, which keeps the vine compact, works well for these cultivars.

Cane pruning

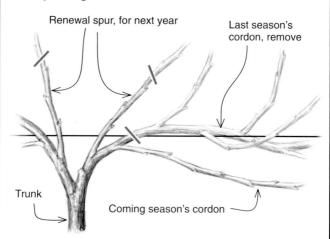

Renewal spur, for next year

Last season's cordon, remove

Trunk

Coming season's cordon

Third winter: On each cordon arm, select 2 robust, dark canes growing near the trunk. Remove the old cordon and tie the new cane that is farthest from the trunk to the wire — it is the coming season's cordon. Cut the second selected cane back to 2 or 3 buds. Head back each new cordon arm to 10 or 12 nodes (or however many nodes your vine can support).

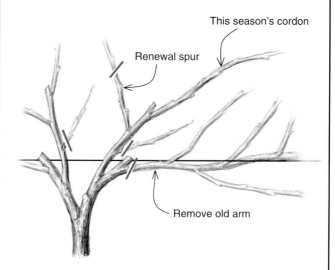

This season's cordon

Renewal spur

Remove old arm

Fourth and subsequent winters: Choose healthy canes for new cordons and renewal spurs and repeat procedure.

Cane pruning

This method produces a heavy crop of fruit from many buds formed on long arms. Because fruit is produced only on one-year-old wood, new fruiting canes must be brought along each year to replace those that are removed after they've produced a crop.

Picking up where we left off training, our vine has just finished its third season, its head is at the desired height, and shoots arise along the length of both arms. (See drawing at left.) The arms, prohibited from fruiting last season, will not fruit again, so you need to remove them and choose two new arms from among last season's shoots to replace them.

In late winter, on each cordon choose the two darkest and thickest canes that arise near the trunk. The dark color shows that the cane received plenty of sunlight last year; these canes will bear best. On each cordon, the selected cane farthest from the trunk becomes the fruit-bearing arm for the coming season. Cut away the old cordon and tie the new one loosely to the wire. The other selected canes, the ones closest to the trunk, become the "renewal spurs" for each cordon. Cut them back to two or three buds. These buds will produce shoots during the coming season, providing a crop of one-year-old wood from which to select fruiting canes next winter. With grapes, you're always thinking two years ahead.

Remove all other canes, then head back the new cordons to a length appropriate to the age and vigor of the vine. An average vine can support about 8 to 12 nodes on each arm. As your vine matures and you get to know it, you can vary the number of nodes, even the number of cordons, according to its health and productivity and the space you have available. If fruit is small and sparse, reduce the number of nodes; if the vine is particularly vigorous, you might increase the number.

In subsequent winters, cut back the old cordons to the renewal spurs, each of which will now have two or three new canes growing from them. Choose the two darkest, thickest new canes on each spur and repeat the process of creating a new cordon and renewal spur outlined above. Snip off any other canes produced by the renewal spur.

Spur pruning

This method keeps vines at a more compact size than cane pruning. The fruit is borne on short, two-budded fruiting branches or spurs that arise from two permanent cordons. This is an easy method for home gardeners, because the arms remain the same year after year. It works best for European grapes. Spur pruning grapes that do not fruit on basal buds will result in meager harvests.

Spur pruning

Summer: Each 2-bud spur will produce 2 new shoots and 1 to 4 clusters of grapes.

Late winter: To maintain the same amount of fruiting wood, on each spur remove 1 fruiting cane (purple) and cut the other (blue) back to 2 buds. Next year, each bud will form a shoot and 1 or more clusters of fruit. Repeat the process each year.

Again, picking up where our discussion of training ended, your vine has just finished its third season, its head is at the desired height, and shoots arise along the length of both arms. (See drawing at left.) In late winter, select three to four of the healthiest of the shoots arising from each arm, spaced about 6 to 10 inches apart, and remove all others. Head back the selected shoots to form spurs by leaving only two buds on each. In spring, each bud will produce a shoot and one to four clusters of flowers, and soon you'll have grapes.

During the growing season, remove shoots arising from the trunk and any suckers sprouting from the base. In late winter, on each spur, cut off one of the fruiting shoots at its base. Shorten the remaining shoot to just two buds, and the cycle repeats itself. This procedure keeps the number of fruiting spurs constant. You can increase that number according to the health and productivity of your vine by heading both canes on a spur to two buds; or you can decrease it by removing both canes entirely on selected buds.

Head training

This is the simplest training method, creating a compact single trunk that can be pruned to produce canes or spurs depending on the type of grape you're growing and the amount of space you have available. We mention it last because it is used mostly for wine grapes, and only in dry summer areas. Where summers are humid, the dense ball of growth at the head of the vine is ripe for the proliferation of pests and diseases.

Training is almost the same as previously described through the first two years, except that during the second growing season instead of choosing two shoots to train as arms, you let all the shoots grow. (See drawings on pages 286–287.) Then, in late winter, choose four or five canes that arise near the top third of the trunk. Cut these back to two buds and remove all others. As the season progresses, remove any other growth from the trunk and any suckers that appear at its base. You should have eight to ten good canes at the end of the season.

To cane prune, in late winter, tie two or three of the now one-year-old shoots to the support wire, cutting them back to 10 to 12 buds each. Head back two or three of the other canes to two or three buds (shoots arising from them will provide candidates for next year's canes). Cut the remaining canes off flush at their bases. Repeat this process each year.

To form spurs, cut no more than five of the canes back to two buds in late winter. Then treat each spur as described previously, cutting one or both fruiting canes back to two buds each winter depending on the vigor of the plant. A ma-

Head-training basics

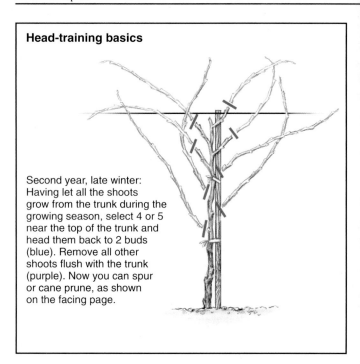

Second year, late winter: Having let all the shoots grow from the trunk during the growing season, select 4 or 5 near the top of the trunk and head them back to 2 buds (blue). Remove all other shoots flush with the trunk (purple). Now you can spur or cane prune, as shown on the facing page.

ture spur-pruned, head-trained vine needs no lateral supports, and the plants can be grown closer together.

Training and pruning on an arbor

Grapes on an arbor are often left to their own devices. If you're concerned more with a lush look than with yield, you can allow the grapes to follow their own path. But if you want to pick more than an occasional nibble, you can train the grapes, then employ a modified style of cane pruning.

For arbors, choose a fast-growing, vigorous variety. For rapid coverage, plant one vine at each of the arbor's corner posts. After planting, train as described above for the first two years. You can let the shoot you've selected for a trunk reach to within 6 inches of the top of the arbor (usually about 7 feet) before pinching out its growing tip to make it branch. Then, instead of tying the cordons horizontally, let them meander over the arbor at will, or with gentle guidance. Cane prune the vine so you will always have a good supply of fruitful year-old wood. When the vine becomes too dense for sunlight to ripen the grapes, be ruthless. Cut out as much as needed, preserving the main, older branches. It will quickly grow back.

Keep in mind that an arbor covered with fruiting grapes will attract wasps when the fruit is ripe. You'll probably want

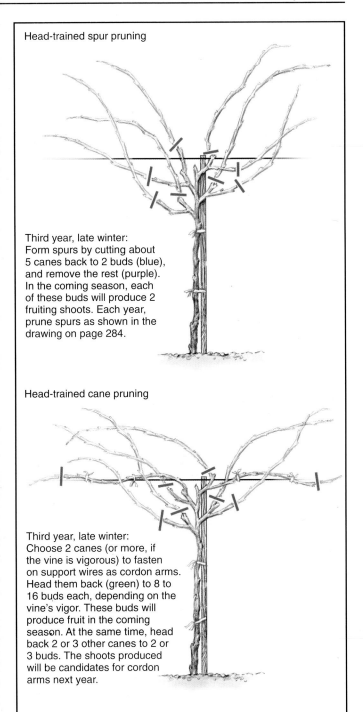

Head-trained spur pruning

Third year, late winter:
Form spurs by cutting about
5 canes back to 2 buds (blue),
and remove the rest (purple).
In the coming season, each
of these buds will produce 2
fruiting shoots. Each year,
prune spurs as shown in the
drawing on page 284.

Head-trained cane pruning

Third year, late winter:
Choose 2 canes (or more, if
the vine is vigorous) to fasten
on support wires as cordon arms.
Head them back (green) to 8 to
16 buds each, depending on the
vine's vigor. These buds will
produce fruit in the coming
season. At the same time, head
back 2 or 3 other canes to 2 or
3 buds. The shoots produced
will be candidates for cordon
arms next year.

to find another spot to enjoy your lemonade until after the harvest. If you're tempted to allow a vine to ramble over an arbor, remember that left to its own devices a grapevine will quickly produce a dense tangle of canes, the fruit yield will drop, and ripening will be delayed. Pests and diseases will cause more problems for a "natural" vine, and fruit will be difficult to protect from critters as well as harder to harvest.

Caring for Grapes

Once established in the ground with a good root system and aboveground with a sturdy trunk, grapevines can live for decades with minimal care.

Like most young plants, grapevines need extra watering in the first year to encourage fast, strong root growth. In subsequent years, water when the leaves show signs of wilting or when natural rainfall is scarce. Too much water as berries are ripening can swell the fruit and cause it to crack. A light layer of bark chips, chopped leaves, or other organic mulch around the vine will keep soil moist and hold weeds down. Renew mulch as necessary during the season.

Grapes do best on a fairly lean diet. Overfertilizing will produce lots of leaves and vines that don't know when to quit, but it won't do much to improve the fruit. If growth falls off, or leaves become discolored and you suspect a nutrient deficiency, have your soil tested.

Winterkill

If you have chosen a cultivar adapted to the climate of your area, you probably won't have any problems with winterkill. But extreme cold in any climate, or swings of temperature extremes can cause damage. You can help prevent winterkill by wrapping the vine in burlap or hilling snow over the roots. The shaggy canes are impervious to a fingernail, so you can't do the scratch test to check for green wood. If you suspect your grapevine has suffered winterkill, wait until any surviving buds have leafed out. By that time, any dead buds will be brittle and brown and crumble at your touch. Prune back dead wood to the first live bud.

Pests and Diseases

A rogues' gallery of pests and diseases can threaten grapes, but not all problems occur every year or in every location. We discuss the most common below, but others may be prevalent in your area. As we mentioned earlier, educate yourself before selecting types and varieties. Call your county extension agent, trusted nurseryman, or local grape growers to find out what insects and diseases cause trouble in your area, what cultivars do well in your area, and what controls are effective.

Choosing disease-resistant stock is prudent. With so many kinds of grapes available, it's only common sense to choose those cultivars that will be least affected by the bad actors detailed below. Also be sure to choose nursery stock that is certified virus-free. Although they may be susceptible to one or another problem, a number of the varieties in the list are generally disease-resistant, including the American grapes 'Canadice', 'Concord', 'Edelweiss', 'Kay Gray', 'Lake Emerald', 'Ontario', and 'Steuben'; the muscadines 'Carlos' and 'Doreen'; and the European grapes 'Aurore', 'Baco Noir', 'Foch', and 'Seyval'.

You'll also note that sulfur spray controls black rot, bunch rot, and several mildews that afflict grapes. Applied first when shoots are about 6 inches long and repeated every two weeks until harvest, a program of sulfur spray should keep all of these in check.

Japanese beetles

An invasion of beetles can make lacework out of grape leaves in no time. Introduced into the United States in 1916, Japanese beetles are now found in all states east of the Mississippi and have recently appeared in California and elsewhere. It's probably only a matter of time before everyone has to deal with these attractively iridescent but destructive critters.

Japanese beetles are easy to control on a restrained vine. Fill a can or other container with a few inches of ammonia and patrol the vine. When you spot a beetle, hold the can beneath it and gently tap the leaf or beetle. It will drop right into the death trap. More serious infestations may require a campaign involving the entire neighborhood, as beetles roam over a fairly large territory. Special beetle traps sold at garden centers may be effective if placed on the perimeter of a large area. Several natural controls, including milky spore disease bacteria (sold under several different commercial names), are also available to kill the grub stage of the beetle.

Black rot

Black rot disease begins as rusty brown-colored spots on the leaves. In moist weather, black dots of spores arise in the rusty spots and infect the fruits, turning them first brown then hardening into black "mummy berries."

If black rot is problematic in your area, plant resistant cultivars. Remove and destroy any infected fruit or leaves. Prune with a heavy hand to open the plant to light and air. Apply sulfur sprays throughout the season for control. Dust or spray the vine with sulfur when shoots are about 6 inches long, then repeat about every two weeks until harvest.

Botrytis bunch rot

This disease makes berries soften and turn brown, until eventually the entire cluster is covered with powdery brown mold. It can also cause leaf spots, and it can affect the flowers. Control it like black rot, with thorough hygiene and the same program of sulfur spray.

Downy mildew

If you notice lighter-colored patches on leaves, with a fine white powder on the underside of the leaf, you are looking at the first signs of downy mildew. The disease may progress until young shoots and even fruit clusters are covered with the white powder. European types are much more vulnerable to mildew than American grapes.

Prevent problems by planting resistant cultivars. If downy mildew appears, prune to increase air circulation. Dust the vine with sulfur when shoots are about 6 inches long, repeat treatment at 15 inches, then reapply about every two weeks until harvest.

Powdery mildew

This disease usually appears first on the canes rather than the leaves. Look for blotches of gray or white powdery mold on the canes in the first stages of the disease; it then spreads rapidly to leaves and finally to fruits, which either split open or stop dead. European types are much more prone to mildew than American grapes.

Prevent problems by planting resistant cultivars. If mildew appears, remove infected parts if possible. Powdery mildew can cause infection even in the absence of moisture, so pruning for better ventilation isn't always a surefire preventive. Apply sulfur as for downy mildew.

Stinging insects

Bees, wasps, and other stinging insects that are attracted to grapes aren't a threat to the fruit or the plants, but they can be a nuisance to grape pickers. Honey-sweet grape flowers attract bees and other insects, and the ripe and especially overripe fruit often attracts bald-faced hornets and other wasps. These insects are usually absorbed in feeding and are not generally aggressive; however, they will sting in self-defense. If children stumble into a fruiting vine or if you reach for a handful of fruit without looking, the encounter may not be pleasant. If you or someone in your family has an allergy to bee stings, be sure to plant your grapevine well away from paths and walkways in the garden, and pick the ripe grapes with care.

The beautiful saddleback caterpillar, the larva of a nondescript brown moth, is occasionally encountered on grapevines. This striking creature is bright leaf green with a brown saddle and venomous spines that can cause a bee-stinglike effect when brushed against with bare skin. Look before you reach.

■ RECOMMENDED VARIETIES OF GRAPES

American and American Hybrids
Unless otherwise noted, all can be grown in zones 5–8 and are cane-pruned.

Alden
Description of fruit: Big clusters (up to 1 lb. each) of reddish and purplish black fruit. Solid, sweet, delicate, somewhat musky flavor.
Comments: Hardy to -20°F. Nonslipskin, texture more like European grapes. Prolific; should be thinned to prevent biennial heavy/light crop tendency.

Beta
Description of fruit: Small blue-black fruit with tart taste of wild grape.
Comments: Hardy to -40°F. Use for jelly, juice; too tangy to eat fresh; fruit ripens in as little as 110 days. Good in cool-summer areas.

Blue Lake
Description of fruit: Dark blue fruits with tangy-sweet flavor.
Comments: Disease-resistant. Good for southern gardens. Zones 5–9.

Buffalo
Description of fruit: Medium-size blue-black fruit with spicy-sweet flavor and grapey aroma.
Comments: Disease-resistant. Prolific.

Campell Early (Island Belle)
Description of fruit: Deep black-purple fruit with heavy bloom, excellent taste.
Comments: Best in fertile soil. Resists downy mildew; moderately prone to powdery mildew.

'Concord'

Canadice

Description of fruit: Red, seedless fruit with outstanding grapey flavor.

Comments: Excellent fresh-eating grape. Moderately resistant to black rot; somewhat prone to mildews. Vigorous, reliable. Zones 5–7.

Captivator

Description of fruit: Large orange-red fruit with lilac-colored bloom. Good taste with a hint of musk.

Comments: Usually healthy vine. Hardy to -5°F. Needs moderately long growing season. Usually grown in Mid-Atlantic or Midwest, where summers are long, hot, and humid.

Catawba

Description of fruit: Coppery red fruit with excellent sweet flavor.

Comments: Superb for jellies and wine. Used in New York and Ohio for "Catawba" wine. Susceptible to mildew. Hardy to -10°F; zones 5–7.

Champanelle

Description of fruit: Large black fruit with fine flavor when fully ripe.

Comments: Vigorous vine. Good for jelly and wine. Good for South, through zone 9.

Concord
Description of fruit: Large blue-black fruit with whitish bloom; excellent grapey flavor.
Comments: The standard of excellence in blue-black American grapes. Vigorous, hardy, prolific vine. Susceptible to black rot. Hardy in zone 4.

Delaware
Description of fruit: Small red fruit with pale bloom and very sweet flavor, sometimes a hint of muskiness.
Comments: An old favorite, still used for white wine in the East. Plant closer than usual; vine only moderately vigorous. Susceptible to powdery mildew. Hardy to -10°F.

Diamond (White Diamond)
Description of fruit: Golden yellow grapes with sweet-tart flavor.
Comments: Excellent juice grape, also good for wine. Old variety introduced in 1870. Hardy to -10°.

Edelweiss
Description of fruit: Greenish white to yellow fruit with mild, sweet flavor.
Comments: Very good disease resistance. Hardy to -35°F. Vigorous, heavy-bearing vines.

Fredonia (Early Concord)
Description of fruit: Large blue-black fruit with bloom, intense spicy grape flavor.
Comments: Resists black rot. Moderately susceptible to downy mildew. Vigorous, productive vine. Hardy to -40°F; zones 4–9. Does well in South.

Glenora
Description of fruit: Seedless, blue-black grape with sweet, rich flavor.
Comments: Mildew-resistant. In some years, fruit may be musky; other years, firm and meaty like European grapes. Moderately cold tender (-8°F or so).

Golden Muscat (hybrid)
Description of fruit: Large, pale golden yellow fruit with distinctive muscat flavor.
Comments: Prone to powdery mildew. Needs long season.

Himrod (hybrid)

Description of fruit: Seedless golden yellow fruit with excellent, crisp flavor.

Comments: Superb for fresh eating, also makes good raisins. Moderately disease-resistant. Hardy to -15°F.

Interlaken Seedless (hybrid)

Description of fruit: Solid golden yellow fruit with crisp, sweet flavor.

Comments: Less vigorous and has smaller berries that ripen earlier than related 'Himrod'. Generally disease-resistant.

Ives

Description of fruit: Black fruit with spicy flavor.

Comments: Old cultivar from about 1850. Prolific.

Kay Gray

Description of fruit: Very firm, white fruit with mild, somewhat musky flavor.

Comments: Highly disease-resistant. Good fresh or for wine.

King of the North

Description of fruit: Blue fruit with tart flavor.

Comments: Disease-resistant. Good for jelly, juice, wine. Productive. Zone 4.

Lake Emerald

Description of fruit: Green fruit with fine flavor.

Comments: Highly resistant to disease. Good for fresh eating. Zones 7–9.

Lakemont

Description of fruit: Yellow-green fruit with sweet, crisp flesh.

Comments: Similar to 'Himrod' and 'Interlaken'. Vigorous, heavily productive.

Mars (Mars Seedless)

Description of fruit: Seedless crimson fruit turns blue when ripe; sweet with mild muskiness.

Comments: Not for colder areas. Moderately resistant to disease and mildew. Fine all-purpose grape. Reliable and productive.

Moore Early (Moore's Early)

Description of fruit: Very large, blue-black fruit with good flavor.

Comments: Prolific. Hardy to zone 4.

'Niagara'

Moored
Description of fruit: Large red fruit with musky flavor.
Comments: Productive vine.

Niabell
Description of fruit: Large, blue-black fruit with good flavor.
Comments: Good substitute for 'Concord' in hot areas, where 'Concord' fails. (Zones 5–9.)

Niagara (White Concord)
Description of fruit: Very large, light green to white fruit with tangy, slightly musky flavor.
Comments: Good for fresh eating or wine. Hardy to -15°F; zones 5–7.

Ontario
Description of fruit: Small, white to light yellow fruit with sweet, distinctive flavor, some muskiness.
Comments: Highly disease-resistant. Zones 6–8.

Portland
Description of fruit: Large greenish white fruit with good flavor.
Comments: Excellent wine grape.

Price

Description of fruit: Blue-black fruit with sweet, grapey flavor.

Comments: Excellent fresh and juice grape. Ripens even in cool weather; good for Pacific Northwest. Hardy to -10°F.

Reliance (hybrid)

Description of fruit: Firm, seedless pinkish red fruit with outstanding mild, sweet flavor.

Comments: Highly disease-resistant. Susceptible to black rot. Hardy to -34°F.

Schuyler (hybrid)

Description of fruit: Blue-black fruit with very sweet flavor with a slight tang.

Comments: Disease-resistant. Susceptible to powdery mildew. Excellent for fresh eating, juice, wine. Prune hard to prevent overbearing. Zones 7–9.

Seneca (hybrid)

Description of fruit: Greenish to golden berries with sweet-tangy, very grapey flavor.

Comments: Prone to powdery mildew. Fruit of this hybrid has European-grape firmness and texture. Zones 7–9; not hardy when young.

St. Croix

Description of fruit: Red fruit with sweet, grapey flavor.

Comments: Good for wine making. Hardy to -40°F.

Steuben

Description of fruit: Very large, blue to purple-black fruit with sweet-tangy flavor.

Comments: Resistant to mildew and rot. Excellent fresh-eating grape, also good for wine and juice. Hardy to -20°F. Thin grapes for best quality.

Stover

Description of fruit: Light green to golden fruit with mild flavor.

Comments: Disease-resistant. Vigorous vine. Hardy only to zone 7.

Suffolk Red (hybrid)

Description of fruit: Seedless, red to pink fruit with tangy-sweet taste.

Comments: Highly disease-resistant. Susceptible to mildews. Prune foliage at fruit clusters for good color. Not fully cold-hardy.

Van Buren
Description of fruit: Purple-black fruit with sweet flavor.
Comments: Good for poor soil. Very vigorous vine. Hardy to -20°F.

Worden
Description of fruit: Large black fruit with good flavor.
Comments: Highly resistant to insects and disease. Good all-purpose grape. Outstanding cold hardiness, to well below 0°F.

Muscadine
Good for the South, muscadines withstand humidity better than other grapes. Unless otherwise noted the varieties below can be grown from zones 7–9.

Carlos
Description of fruit: Medium to small bronze fruit with pleasant flavor. Excellent for wine and juice.
Comments: Hardy. Self-fertile, weeping habit. Prolific bearer.

Doreen
Description of fruit: Light bronze fruit with sweet flavor.
Comments: Disease-resistant. Very productive late-season vine. Self-fertile.

Fry
Description of fruit: Very large bronze fruit with excellent flavor.
Comments: Susceptible to black rot.

Higgins
Description of fruit: Very large, pink to red-bronze fruit with good taste.
Comments: Heavy-bearing. Moderately disease-resistant. Susceptible to black rot.

Jumbo
Description of fruit: Very large purple-black fruit of fair quality.
Comments: Disease-resistant. Vigorous, productive. Needs pollen source.

Magnolia
Description of fruit: Bronze fruit with sweet flavor.
Comments: Prolific, vigorous, hardy vine. Self-fertile.

Nesbitt
Description of fruit: Large purple-black fruit of excellent quality.
Comments: Disease-resistant, hardy, self-fertile vine.

Noble
Description of fruit: Small purple-black fruit, excellent for processing.
Comments: The industry standard black-fruited variety for processing, including juice and wine. Self-fertile.

Scuppernong
Description of fruit: Reddish bronze with russet dots. Sweet to tart, foxy flavor.
Comments: Resists pests and diseases common in humid climates. Will not fruit in Northwest. Vigorous, productive. An old favorite.

Sterling
Description of fruit: Medium to large bronze grapes.
Comments: Very hardy, ideal for colder muscadine areas. Self-fertile.

Sugargate
Description of fruit: Very large purple-black grape. Very sweet, excellent eaten fresh.
Comments: Early ripening. Needs pollen source.

Summit
Description of fruit: Large bronze, very sweet grape.
Comments: Mid- to early season. Very productive vine. Susceptible to black rot, but still reliable producer. Needs pollen source.

Triumph
Description of fruit: Medium to large bronze grape.
Comments: Early season. Self-fertile.

European
Need long warm summers and mild winters. These will grow in zones 7–9 unless otherwise noted. All are spur-pruned. Interspecies hybrids are also included here.

Aurore
Description of fruit: White fruits with pink blush; very sweet.
Comments: Resistant to powdery and downy mildew. Very

'Baco Noir'

productive. Important white wine grape in Finger Lakes region. Also good for eating fresh. Hardy to -10°F. Hybrid.

Baco Noir
Description of fruit: Bluish black fruit in small clusters, good flavor.
Comments: Resistant to downy mildew. Extra-vigorous vine. Grows well in heavy soil. Hardy to 0°F; zones 5–7. Hybrid.

Black Monukka
Description of fruit: Oval, reddish black grapes with crisp, sweet flesh; mostly seedless.
Comments: Excellent fresh eating, or for wine, jelly. Among the hardiest of European cultivars. Zones 5–8. Needs 100 chill hours.

Cardinal
Description of fruit: Dark red fruit with few seeds, crisp flesh.
Comments: Good for fresh eating. Vigorous, prolific vine. Needs 100 chill hours.

Chancellor
Description of fruit: Blue-black fruit with tart taste.
Comments: Good for wine. Heavy producer. Ripens early,

'Chancellor'

good for short-season climates. Hardy to -10°F. Susceptible to downy mildew. Hybrid.

Chardonnay

Description of fruit: Green-white fruit.
Comments: Used in wine. One of the most cold-hardy white
European grapes. Good in cooler regions.

Chenin Blanc

Description of fruit: Oval, whitish green fruit.
Comments: Wine grape. Extra vigorous, very productive vine.
Best in cool to moderate climates. Needs 100 chill hours.

De Chaunac

Description of fruit: Bluish black fruit.
Comments: Wine grape. Disease-resistant, very vigorous.
Hardy to -10°F. Hybrid.

Emperor

Description of fruit: Large red to purple fruit with good
flavor.
Comments: Good for fresh eating.

Flame Seedless (Flame)

Description of fruit: Light red seedless grapes with crisp, sweet taste.

Comments: The red seedless grape of supermarkets. Superb for fresh eating, also makes good raisins. Zones 7–10.

Foch (Marechal Foch)

Description of fruit: Blue-black fruit with cherry-flavored juice.

Comments: Good for juice or wine. Hardier than most Europeans. Good disease resistance. Zone 7. Hybrid.

Perlette

Description of fruit: Small to medium-size seedless light green to yellow-green fruit with excellent flavor.

Comments: Good for eating fresh. Needs 100 chill hours.

Seyval (Seyve-Villard)

Description of fruit: White fruit.

Comments: Wine grape. Good disease resistance. Hardy to -5°F. Hybrid.

Thompson Seedless

Description of fruit: Well-known white seedless, very sweet fruit.

Comments: Excellent fresh eating, good for raisins. Zones 7–9.

Tokay (Flame Tokay)

Description of fruit: Large pale to dark red fruit with crisp flesh.

Comments: Good for fresh eating or wine. Needs 100 chill hours.

Verdelet

Description of fruit: White to golden fruit with sweet flavor.
Comments: Excellent fresh eating. Hardy to -5°F. Hybrid.

Villard Blanc

Description of fruit: White to golden fruit with sweet, mild flavor.

Comments: Good for fresh eating. Vigorous vine. Hardy to zone 6. Hybrid.

Zinfandel

Description of fruit: Reddish black fruit.

Comments: Wine grape. Heavy-bearing. Needs 100 chill hours.

Other Hardy Fruits

'Smyrna', one of the best quinces, with large, mild-tasting tender, aromatic fruits, is esteemed for desserts and preserves.

The hardy fruits in this chapter are among gardening's best-kept secrets. The sweet smoothness of a pawpaw, the spicy-tart bite of a fresh quince, the juicy pleasure of a handful of mulberries provide ample reward for the adventurous gardener willing to try something different. And the effort required is minimal — most of these plants need no pampering, thrive in average soil, and fend off pests and diseases.

A hundred years ago, many hardy fruits and berries were better known, sought and savored by those who lived close to the land and knew how to make the most of the wild offerings around them. Persimmons were baked into dense, spicy puddings, mulberries fermented into fragrant wines, and cranberries studded into quickbreads. Early European settlers thought enough of the native pawpaw to ship the trees back to England.

Today, you're more likely to find winter strawberries flooding into your supermarket from the Southern Hemisphere than local specialties like persimmons. But enterprising small-scale fruit growers have begun introducing unusual fruits to specialty stores, and specialty nurseries are beginning to offer North American natives as well as hardy imports, such as the kiwi from New Zealand. Even mainstream catalogs and garden centers are catching on.

Hardy fruits can be eye-catching as well as taste-tempting. One look at the huge, tropical-like leaves of the pawpaw tree and you can understand why it has moved from the river bottoms of the South to a commanding spot in some ornamental gardens. The slim, graceful persimmon tree, with its checkered bark and clear yellow fall foliage, is beautiful in a mixed planting with viburnums and emphatic ornamental grasses. The sand cherry's attractive fountain shape and silvery green leaves make an exciting alternative to standard-issue suburban yews. Some hardy fruits are also perfect for trouble spots. Elderberry, a shrub with creamy flower clusters that are as showy as any hydrangea and delightfully fragrant, grows vigorously in wet soil. Sand cherries are well suited to light, dry soils.

Best Bets for the Home Garden

In this chapter we provide a selection of the many hardy fruits that are less often grown in home gardens. We've included some old-fashioned fruits that were once favorites and some that are relatively new here (though quite well known elsewhere in the world). Many of the fruits are good for fresh eating, some are best for cooking. All are tasty. Most of the plants do double duty in the landscape. You can plant them as hedges, in informal groups, and with other plants. A few make good shade trees. We've also chosen plants for ease of growing. Only the vining kiwi requires regular pruning, and then only to keep its vigorous growth in bounds. All are tough customers when it comes to fighting off pests and diseases. No regimen of spraying or other preventive care is necessary to harvest a fine crop.

The selection begins with the better-known fruits — persimmon, kiwi, pawpaw, mulberry, and quince, moving then to the jujube (a plant being rediscovered), and a handful of native fruits. Strictly speaking, not all these are hardy — oriental persimmons are limited to zones 7 through 10, and the kiwi *Actinidia deliciosa* can't take temperatures below 10°F. We include them here along with their cold-hardy relatives. Given limitations of space, we have provided brief portraits, which we hope will at least pique your interest. Special cultural requirements are discussed; otherwise consult the last three chapters for general advice on planting and care. Advice from an experienced grower in your area or your local extension agent will prove invaluable — perhaps even more so for these plants than for the other plants in this book — and we encourage you to seek it before deciding which fruits to grow.

Finally, one of the reasons unusual hardy fruits are not more widely grown is the difficulty gardeners have obtaining them. If you get to know aficionados in your area, you may be offered cuttings or seedlings from a special tree that grows the biggest mulberries, or the meatiest Chinese dates, or the heaviest heads of elderberries. While growing these local favorites can be fun and rewarding, if none are available there are other sources. Some of the fruits discussed here may be available at a local nursery, but don't give up if they're not. All can be obtained through specialty suppliers, a number of which are included in "Sources of Supply" at the back of this book. These folks are also likely to know a great deal about growing the plants and are usually happy to help beginners.

Persimmons

Lusciously sweet and mildly spicy, persimmons belong to the genus *Diospyros,* which aptly translates into "food of the gods." The two types, American and Oriental, deserve equal

The hardy American persimmon is a prolific producer.

place in the divine order of fruit, but they differ in size of tree and fruit, and in cold hardiness. A small and slim tree, American persimmon is hardy to at least -25°F and thrives in areas as warm as zone 8. Its Oriental cousin is a larger, more tender tree that does best in zones 7 through 10. Its fruits are immense compared to its American counterpart.

Persimmons bear best in full sun, although the trees will also grow in light shade. They thrive in a variety of soils, from heavy clay to lighter soils, where their taproots are able to reach deep for water. Generally pest- and disease-free, persimmons are very long-lived trees. Some venerable Oriental trees count their age in centuries, and a few American trees that have survived logging can make the same claim.

American persimmons

The American persimmon *(Diospyros virginiana)* is most commonly found along roadsides, fencerows, and at the edges of fields and woods in the lower Midwest and the Southeast, but its natural range covers a wide area from New Jersey to Florida west to Nebraska and Texas, extending into New York and Connecticut. You can easily identify the tree in the wild by its unusual checkered bark, which is split into a pattern of squares like alligator hide. Persimmon is a member of the ebony family, and its dark, dense, and very heavy wood was prized for golf-club heads and tool handles before metal and carbon-fiber substitutes came along.

Brought in from the wild, the American persimmon is an outstanding small tree for landscape use. It has widely spaced, gently curved branches and a slim trunk. The slow-growing tree usually matures at about 20 to 35 feet tall, although some oldsters have reached as high as 50 and even 100 feet. 'Pieper', a dwarf cultivar that reaches about 15 feet tall, is a fine plant for ornamental groupings, perhaps underplanted with kneehigh clumps of little bluestem grass *(Schizachyrium scoparium),* which turns a soft orange-red in fall and winter. 'Garrettson', an ultimately full-size tree which takes years to reach 20 feet, has an almost contorted branching structure that is striking in the winter garden against a light-colored wall or fence.

The American persimmon is also an excellent choice for a naturalistic wildlife garden. The prolific fruits dangle decoratively along the bare branches well into winter and are irresistible to many animals and birds. Elegant taupe-gray cedar waxwings are just as fond of the sweet fruits as opossums, foxes, coyotes, and raccoons. Possums, it is said, will walk miles to reach a fruiting persimmon tree.

The round, usually orange fruit ranges in size from about

that of a large cherry tomato up to 2 inches in diameter. A sweet, delectable mouthful with a hint of spiciness when eaten fresh, the fruit is delicious when steamed or baked in "puddings," which have the texture of carrot cake. Flavor intensifies when it is dried like prunes or raisins. Native American peoples preserved persimmons this way, and both the Algonquin word *persimmon* and the Cree *pasiminan* mean "dried fruit."

Persimmons ripen so late in the year that northern gardeners must be sure to choose an American cultivar that has time to mature before days shorten and cold sets in. Once fruit has reached full size and color, cold actually sweetens the flavor of the soft pulp. 'Meader', the standard-bearer among American persimmons, ripens over weeks from September through October and is very cold-hardy. Shaped like a narrow pear tree, it has very sweet fruit. Northerners can nudge the season up even a few more weeks by planting 'Early Golden', a selection of 'Meader'.

The sex life of American persimmon trees would fit right in on any TV talk show. Suffice it to say that trees usually need to be planted in pairs, one male, one female, to ensure pollination. Seedless varieties, however, are self-pollinating and will produce fruit on their own. (Pollinated by a seeded variety, a seedless tree may produce seeded fruit.) To be sure of what you need to do, consult the nursery that is supplying the plants.

Oriental persimmons

Also known as kaki persimmon, from the species name *(Diospyros kaki)*, these are attractive trees usually 20 to 30 feet tall, with spreading branches and gorgeous autumn foliage of red, yellow, or bronze, depending on the variety. If space is limited, look for a small cultivar like 'Oriental', which reaches only 10 to 15 feet tall. Kaki persimmons are self-fruitful, so you only need one tree.

Less cold-hardy than the American species, kaki persimmons grow from zone 7 through 10, though a few, such as the seedless, very sweet 'Hira Tanashi', do well as far north as zone 6. Kakis bear well without a long period of winter chill. 'Oriental' flourishes even in frost-free areas.

The heavy, smooth-skinned fruits of the kaki persimmon fit into the palm of the hand like a good-sized peach. Japanese breeders have been tinkering with the fruit for centuries, creating such wonders as the seedless, meltingly sweet 'Saijo', which can be enjoyed all winter long when dried like dates, and the very large, juicy 'Giant Fuyu', with flesh so firm and smooth textured that the fruit can be munched like an apple.

Planting and care

Persimmon trees are usually sold potted at nurseries and bare-root when bought through mail-order. Both are likely to be two to three years old (though some are year-old seedlings) and $1^1/_2$ to 2 or 3 feet tall. Persimmons are grown on their own roots — as seedlings or from cuttings — or they can be grafted to a rootstock. You can trust a reputable nursery to select an appropriate rootstock, but some background can be helpful. American persimmon is a common choice for rootstock because it thrives in diverse conditions and is cold-hardy. But its taproot is sensitive to disturbance and finicky about transplanting, and it has a tendency to sucker. Non-suckering oriental persimmon rootstock is popular in California; it does well in moderately moist soils, but it lacks cold hardiness and, like the American, has a sensitive taproot structure. A related species with fibrous roots, the date plum *(Diospyros lotus)* provides an easily transplanted rootstock that thrives in dry soils, though it shows more susceptibility to disease.

Persimmons bear best when planted in full sun, although the trees will also grow in light shade. Just about any soil will do. The large Oriental persimmons call for spacing about 20 feet apart, but you can space slim American persimmons as close as 10 feet in landscape groupings. All persimmons should be planted well away from walks and drives, where slippery, squashed fallen fruit could cause a problem. A ground cover will disguise the dropped fruit, but a mulch of wood chips or chopped leaves give you a better view of the wildlife that comes to dine on the windfall.

Persimmon roots are sensitive to disturbance and have a reputation for being difficult to transplant. Roots of plants dug for bare-root shipment often suffer in the process. Those with fast-growing fibrous roots quickly overcome any root damage. Taprooted plants are slower to reestablish themselves when transplanted; if the taproot is broken it may do very poorly or die. It's best to plant taprooted trees when they're very young and the root is a manageable size. Unlike field-grown plants, those grown in pots are likely to suffer less on transplanting, as the root hasn't been disturbed by digging it up and is cushioned and protected by the soil. Whether bare-root or container-grown, regular watering of the slow-growing roots for at least the first two years is vital to establishing a young persimmon tree. With soil of average fertility, fertilizing isn't usually necessary.

Harvest

Persimmon trees usually begin to bear fruit two to five years after planting, depending on cultivar. The waxy white flowers appear late, well after frosts, and are hardly noticed among the leaves. Fruit is generally ready to pick about four to five months later, in early or late fall depending on cultivar.

Soft and sweet, ripe persimmons are luscious. But bite into an American persimmon before its time, and the unripe fruit packs more pucker-power than a sour lemon. It's easy to discover this too late, because persimmons turn color long before they are ripe. The fruit is ready when it feels soft to a gentle squeeze and separates fairly easily from the calyx, the cap to which the stem is attached. While many varieties can be eaten when they turn soft, for others you must wait until a few frosts have wrinkled the skin and softened the flesh to pick the fruit. One taste will tell you if your timing is right.

Gauging ripeness is trickier, if less risky, with Oriental persimmons, because the fruit is often still firm when ripe and does not separate easily from the calyx. Thankfully, the unripe fruit is usually nonastringent, so you can safely taste-test one. Unripe fruits are insipid in flavor, like a green banana. (Some Oriental cultivars, including the superb 'Chocolate', are just as astringent when unripe as their American cousins and become delectable only when they are well softened.) To harvest the fruit, clip it off with a small section of attached stem. If your timing is a little off and the fruit has not reached full flavor, you can ripen Oriental persimmons by putting them in a brown paper bag with an apple for a few days.

Pests and diseases

American and Oriental persimmons are largely exempt from disease and pests. Scale can infest twigs but is not seriously detrimental. Anthracnose and, in mild-winter areas like the warm South, citrus mealybug and persimmon psylla are occasional pests. Rarer still, the persimmon borer can damage roots and kill the tree.

Anthracnose. Anthracnose is a serious fungal disease. It causes small black, dead, sunken spots on foliage, with a characteristic raised border. Pink or brown rings may form around the spot. As the disease spreads to the wood of the tree, it can kill major branches and eventually the entire tree. Various forms of the disease affect sycamores, dogwoods, persimmons, garden bean crops, and other plants.

Several cultivars of Oriental persimmons, including 'Fuyu', show susceptibility to anthracnose. Call your county extension agent to find out if the disease is a problem in your area, and plant resistant cultivars such as 'Runkwitz' if it is. To control the disease, remove infected parts as soon as you notice them. There is no organic control, and chemical measures are often ineffective.

Persimmon psylla. Somewhat similar to pear psylla, these tiny insects suck sap and excrete "honeydew," a sticky substance that provides a breeding site for a sooty mold that can blacken foliage and twigs. They can also carry viral diseases. The insects are nearly invisible to the naked eye, but if you see signs of sooty black mold, remove and destroy the affected leaves and twigs and check other leaves carefully for droplets of sticky honeydew.

A severe infestation of persimmon psylla will require a more aggressive approach, because it can reduce the crop and weaken the tree. To control a severe outbreak, spray the tree with dormant oil in early spring, while the tree is well dormant, and then again when the buds show green. Insecticidal soap spray can help control persimmon psylla during the growing season.

Citrus mealybug. Resembling tiny tufts of cotton, these white insects hide under leaves and on stems, sometimes clustering together. They rarely cause serious damage to persimmons. To treat a small tree, moisten a cotton swab in rubbing alcohol and use it to dab up any mealybugs within reach. Insecticidal soap spray is a good general-purpose remedy for a larger tree.

■ Recommended Varieties of Persimmons

American Persimmons
Unless otherwise noted, trees need a pollinator for best fruit set; check with supplier for recommendations. Zones 4–8 unless otherwise noted.

American Persimmon *(Diospyros virginiana)*
Description of fruit: Species trees produce small, yellow-orange fruit, reddening when ripe.
Comments: Hardy to -25°F. Drought-resistant and adaptable.

Early Golden
Description of fruit: Large, sweet fruit with large seeds.
Comments: Commercial favorite. Resistant to anthracnose. Ripens a few weeks before 'Meader'.

Evelyn
Description of fruit: Large, intense orange fruit, often without seeds. Sweet.
Comments: Prolific. Early.

Garrettson (Garretson)
Description of fruit: Large, sweet fruit, medium-size seeds.
Comments: Selection of 'Early Golden'. Fruit ripens early. Anthracnose-resistant. Good ornamental in the landscape because of unusual, somewhat contorted branching.

John Rick
Description of fruit: Largest fruit of all cultivars, with excellent flavor.
Comments: Most popular cultivar. Ripens early. Plant 'Yates' as a pollinator.

Lena (Mitchellena)
Description of fruit: Large, sweet fruit.
Comments: Bears abundantly. Ripens early.

Meader
Description of fruit: Small, very sweet fruit, usually seedless.
Comments: The persimmon standard-bearer. Self-fruitful; no pollinator needed. Hardy to -35°F. Ripens early over a long period, from September through October.

Pieper
Description of fruit: Small, astringent fruit.
Comments: Dwarf tree.

Pipher
Description of fruit: Large fruit, fine flavor.
Comments: Resistant to anthracnose. Grown commercially for canning.

Runkwitz
Description of fruit: Medium-size, good-tasting fruit.
Comments: Midseason. Bears abundantly. Anthracnose-resistant.

Wabash
Description of fruit: Small fruit, seedless.
Comments: Ripens early.

Yates
Description of fruit: Very large, sweet fruit, seedless if grown without a pollinator.
Comments: Ripens very early. Some anthracnose resistance.

Oriental Persimmons

All are self-pollinating, usually seedless fruit. Generally pest-and disease-free. All grow well in zones 7–10, unless otherwise noted. Need at least 200 hours of chilling.

Oriental Persimmon (*Diospyros kaki*, Kaki, Kaki Persimmon, Hachiya)

Description of fruit: Species trees produce large, somewhat flattened, acorn-shaped fruits with orange pulp, few seeds. Sweet even when not fully ripe.

Comments: Tree grows 10–15 ft. tall; excellent ornamental qualities.

Chocolate

Description of fruit: Small to medium fruit, red skin and brown flesh, excellent flavor.

Comments: Astringent until soft. Prolific.

Eureka

Description of fruit: Large, deep red-orange fruit, excellent flavor.

Comments: Often bears in its third year. Prolific. Fruit occasionally seedless.

Fuyu (Apple Persimmon, Jiro)

Description of fruit: Medium to large, orange-red fruit, sweet.

Comments: Late-ripening. Good for areas with cool summers. Hardy to zone 8.

Fuyugaki (Winter Persimmon)

Description of fruit: Medium-size, dark red skin with light pulp, blue blush when ripe. Excellent flavor.

Comments: Most popular commercial persimmon in Japan.

Giant Fuyu

Description of fruit: Very large fruit, almost half-again the size of regular Fuyu. Sweet, juicy.

Comments: Hardy to zone 8. Adapts to hot or cool summers.

Great Wall

Description of fruit: Small orange fruit, very sweet.

Comments: Prolific, very early. Hardy to zone 6.

Hachiya

Description of fruit: Large, acorn-shaped orange fruit.

Comments: Flesh sweet even when unripe. Superb for fresh eating; good for drying. Leading commercial variety in U.S.

'Fuyu'

Beautifully shaped tree makes excellent small shade tree with red, bronze, and yellow fall foliage. Zones 7–9.

Hana-Fuyu (Winter Flower)
Description of fruit: Very large, excellent flavor.
Comments: Dwarf tree.

Oriental
Description of fruit: Nearly seedless, orangish gold fruit.
Comments: Nonastringent even when unripe. Great for fresh eating; good dried. Tree grows 10–15 ft. tall. Zones 7–9.

Saijo (Mr. Elegant)
Description of fruit: Small, yellow-orange fruit, very sweet when soft.
Comments: Astringent until soft-ripe. Good for drying. Hardy to zone 6. Variety at least 600 years old. (*Saijo means* "The very best one.")

Sheng

Description of fruit: Medium to large fruit, often seedless; excellent flavor.

Comments: Dwarf tree. Hardy to zone 6.

Smith's Best

Description of fruit: Small to medium-size, dark or brown flesh, very sweet.

Comments: Small, compact tree. Prolific. Does well with minimal attention.

Tanenashi (Tani Nashi)

Description of fruit: Large or very large, orange with yellow flesh, seedless, excellent flavor when soft-ripe.

Comments: Prolific. Hardy to zone 8.

Quinces

When they hear "quince," many gardeners think immediately of the lovely Japanese or flowering quince (*Chaenomeles* spp.) and the masses of delicate pink and white flowers that burst along the length of its bare branches in early spring. Fruit connoisseurs, on the other hand, think of a different genus and species altogether. The true or orchard quince, *Cydonia oblonga*, is a small tree with interesting crooked branches and the less distinctive habit of flowering from the tips of its leafy stems. It has been cultivated for its fragrant, golden fruit for thousands of years.

The fruits of the true quince are large (up to 5 inches), firm, and shaped like apples or pears. Quince usually tastes better cooked than raw, although some cultivars, such as 'Champion', are sweet enough to enjoy fresh. The round, white-fleshed 'Pineapple' has a tart, fruity taste for zesty fresh eating. Quinces can be simmered for preserves and jellies, or baked like apples, with brown sugar and lemon. The very large fruits of the cultivar 'Orange', up to a pound in weight, have beautiful orangish yellow flesh that is wonderful baked, cooked into a clear, gem-colored jelly, and in all kinds of cooking. 'Smyrna', considered one of the best by quince connoisseurs, bears large, pear-shaped golden yellow fruits with mild-tasting tender, aromatic flesh. It is esteemed for desserts and preserves. The flesh of most quinces turns pink when cooked.

Native to western Asia, true quince is hardy in about the same regions as peaches (zones 6 to 9). Its branches can suffer dieback when temperatures fall below -15°F, although the root (which may be grafted) may survive. Reaching about 15 to 20 feet tall, the quince is a lovely tree to add at a wide curve in a mixed border. Its angular branches are striking in winter. The large but delicate pink or white flowers are appealing, especially if the tree is accented with nearby plantings of late-spring-blooming, low-care perennials such as blue phlox *(Phlox stolonifera* or *P. divaricata)*. The leaves flash a silvery underside when a breeze stirs the branches. The down-sized 'Dwarf Orange' reaches about 10 feet tall and can be trained as a lovely tree for the small garden.

If you are as interested in flowers as fruit, you might try the gorgeous flowering quince *Chaenomeles speciosa*, 'Rubra Grandiflora'. Covered in spring with masses of crimson blossoms, this shrub has very tart fruit that makes a fine-flavored jelly. 'Cameo' offers pretty double peach flowers and a harvest of yellow edible fruits. The Chinese quince *(Cydonia sinensis)* is grown as an ornamental shrub or small tree in zones 6 to 9. But in areas with long growing seasons, its large fruit (up to 6 inches) has time to ripen.

Planting and care

Quinces are sold as one- or two-year-old plants, either as unnamed seedlings or as cultivars that are grafted to an appropriate rootstock (usually 'Angers'). They are self-pollinating, so only a single plant is needed for a good crop. Flowering quince is self-sterile and requires two plants for pollination.

True quince has shallow roots, so it does best in a moderately heavy soil that stays moist. ('Pineapple' tolerates wet soils.) Plant in full sun, and to retain moisture, surround the tree to within 4 inches of the trunk with a thick layer of wood chips or other mulch. Quinces prefer a lean diet. High-nitrogen fertilizers can cause suckering and increase susceptibility to fire blight, as the plant responds with tender new growth. If your quince sprouts suckers from the roots, forming a brushy stand of young plants, snip off these shoots at ground level and avoid applying fertilizer.

Quinces demand no pruning beyond removal of dead, diseased, and damaged branches. Some gardeners prefer to prune out inner branches, creating a more open structure which makes the fruit easier to reach and the branching patterns more interesting. The trees begin to bear fruit one to two years after planting. Fruits are borne on young, short lateral branches. Cutting back long shoots will encourage more of these fruiting spurs to sprout.

Harvest

The fruit ripens from about early September until well into October, depending on cultivar. Harvest quince fruits after the skin changes from green to a rich yellow. Some types ripen late in the season; light frost will not damage the fruit. Although the flesh of quinces is quite firm, it can be easily damaged by rough handling. Carefully place the quinces into a basket as you pick to avoid bruising. If you will not be using them right away, store quinces in the fruit bin of your refrigerator, where they will keep well for about a week.

Pests and diseases

Quinces are susceptible to many of the same problems that affect apples and other tree fruits.

Fire blight. If young, tender shoots suddenly wilt and die back, and leaves turn black or brown as if singed by fire, your tree is likely infected by fire blight. The bark may split and ooze watery liquid, and the tree may weaken and die.

No cultivars are resistant. If fire blight develops, cut off infected stems about a foot below the diseased area and destroy them; the disease spreads internally before external symptoms develop. Disinfect your pruning shears between cuts by dipping into a sterilizing solution.

Oriental fruit moth. Wilted leaves at the tips of twigs are often the first sign of infestation, marking the place where the half-inch adult moth laid eggs. The larvae tunnel into the twig tip, killing the twig. When adult, this first generation lays their eggs on fruit, where subsequent generations of larvae (three or four are common) burrow into the flesh around the pit. Oriental fruit moths are widespread. They can be problematic along the eastern seaboard, in all areas except Texas, the south-central states, the Pacific Northwest, and the Midwest.

Remove affected twig tips, cutting back to healthy wood. Ryania, an organic control, and the chemicals Imidan and Carbaryl are effective. They are best applied from mid-July through mid-August.

Borers. If you see holes oozing sap or sawdust in your quince stems, borers could be the cause. Adult moths lay eggs near the base of the tree, and larvae climb and burrow into the trunk, weakening the tree and making an entrance for other diseases and pests.

Insert a straightened paper clip into the hole to stab the larva; prune off below the borer hole if the damage is in a smaller branch; or dig or cut out the affected area in thick branches or trunks to remove the pest.

'Pineapple' is a tart, fruity-tasting quince for zesty fresh eating.

■ RECOMMENDED VARIETIES OF QUINCES
All quinces are self-pollinating. Zones 6–9 unless otherwise noted.

Common Quince *(Cydonia oblonga)*
Description of fruit: Large, deep yellow fruit, round to oblong. Pink flowers.
Comments: Grows 12–20 ft. tall.

Champion
Description of fruit: Golden yellow, sweet fruit. White flowers.
Comments: Very hardy. Reliable bearer.

Dwarf Orange
Description of fruit: Large yellow fruit with orangish flesh. Excellent flavor.
Comments: Small tree or shrub to 10–15 ft. Prolific.

Orange
Description of fruit: Very large fruit, often more than 1 lb. Bright yellow with orangish pulp, superb flavor.
Comments: Hardy to zone 5. Low chill requirement makes it suitable through zone 10. Early-ripening. Very old cultivar.

Pineapple

Description of fruit: Large, round, yellow fruit with tart white pulp. Pink-tinged white flowers.

Comments: A Burbank cultivar. Good for areas with late spring frosts; blooms late. Tolerates wet soils. Zones 5–10; 200 chill hours.

Smyrna

Description of fruit: Very large golden fruit, excellent flavor.

Comments: Old cultivar dating to 1897. Zones 5–10; 200 chill hours.

Jujubes

Had you gardened a hundred years ago, you might have exchanged fruit or seedlings from your favorite jujube trees with your neighbor over the garden fence. These "Chinese dates" *(Ziziphus jujuba)* named for their origin in ancient China and their small oval fruits that look and taste something like meaty dates, are enjoying a comeback. Thriving in zones 5 through 10, the tree takes almost anything nature can throw at it, including pests, disease, drought, extreme heat, and wide swings in temperature. It is an equally excellent choice for arid southwestern gardens and steamy southern ones. In more northern gardens, the shorter growing season may prevent fruit from ripening. Planted in average soil, in full sun, and provided with a long hot summer, your tree will be healthy and produce good fruit. Trees are self-pollinating, so you only need one.

An excellent ornamental specimen, this small, deciduous tree reaches only 25 feet in height and brings a gnarled, drooping character to the garden. The leaves are a glossy green and the bark light gray. Plants vary in habit, depending on heritage; some are spiny, especially when young, and some sucker readily from the roots. 'Ming Tsao' is a small tree with no spines but with suckers. 'Hu Ping Tsao' is a large-fruited cultivar without spines that produces only a few suckers.

Although some seedling trees can produce bland fruits, the fruit of the best jujubes is of fine flavor. Many of the heirlooms, including the excellent Alabama variety 'Davis', are enjoying a new burst of popularity. Among the fine cultivars are 'Tigertooth' and 'Silverhill', two similar types with long, thin, extra-sweet fruit. 'Lang' is a large-fruited cultivar with reddish brown fruits, and 'Li' offers large, round fruit with a small pit. 'Wuhu Tsao' is a "seedless" variety in which the usual hard pit is a soft, easily swallowed kernel.

Jujubes bear abundant clusters of fruit on trees adapted to a wide range of conditions. 'Lang' is shown here.

Trees bear fruit at a very early age — sometimes as soon as the year after planting. The fruit hangs, like dates, in abundant clusters from the branches and turns from green to mahogany brown as it ripens, usually over a month or more beginning in early fall. A single tree can produce a hundred pounds of fruit, which can be eaten several ways — fresh, dried, or even brandied. The dried fruit, popular in Asian and Mideastern countries, will keep at room temperature for months, just like dates.

■ Recommended Varieties of Jujubes

Jujubes are self-pollinating; they thrive in both arid and humid conditions and are generally untroubled by pests and diseases. All listed will perform well in zones 5–10.

Jujube species (**Ziziphus jujuba**)
Description of fruit: Small oval fruits of seedling trees vary in quality and taste.
Comments: Grow well in Southwest, and Southeast to Pennsylvania.

Davis
Description of fruit: Excellent flavor, good production.
Comments: Local heirloom variety from Alabama.

Hu Ping Tsao
Description of fruit: Large fruits.
Comments: Spineless, nonsuckering tree.

Lang
Description of fruit: Large fruits, $1^1/_2$–2 in. long × $^3/_4$ in. wide.
Comments: Ripens September to October.

Li
Description of fruit: Large, almost-round fruits, 2 in. in diam. Small pit. Sweet.
Comments: Self-pollinating.

Ming Tsao
Description of fruit: Small, sweet fruit.
Comments: Small erect tree that suckers. No spines.

Sherwood
Description of fruit: Large, excellent quality.
Comments: Good for Deep South.

Silverhill (Silverhill Round)
Description of fruit: Plum-shaped, white flesh, sweet.
Comments: Ripens in September.

So
Description of fruit: Round, sweet.
Comments: Tree has attractive zigzag branching.

Tigertooth
Description of fruit: Long, thin fruits, ripen to crinkly brown.
Comments: Harvest when brown and crinkly.

Pawpaws

The "Hoosier banana" has a lush tropical look and taste, though it is hardy to zone 5 and thrives through zone 9. The plump, sausage-shaped fruits look and taste like bananas, though their high content of unsaturated fat gives them a creamier texture, like a thick pudding, that melts on the tongue.

The huge, drooping leaves of the pawpaw tree *(Asimina triloba)* reach 12 inches long, an unusual size for a tree that reaches only 10 to 25 feet tall. Pawpaws are slim-trunked understory trees, growing in moist riverbottoms beneath taller gums and oaks from Pennsylvania into the northern parts of the southern states, west to Nebraska, and in the Great Lakes region. "POP-aw" is the common pronunciation in many areas where the trees grow wild.

Bare-root plants, 1 to 2 feet tall, are sold at one to two years old to avoid damage to the long, brittle taproot that soon develops even in young trees. Potted plants are occasionally available and are easiest to transplant. Where the plants grow wild, you can always count on someone who knows where to find seedlings of the tastiest pawpaws, but buying a named cultivar from a nursery assures excellent flavor. 'Sunflower' is a reliable favorite with large, thick fruits of superb flavor. Pawpaws need a second tree as a pollinator.

In the home garden, pawpaws do well in shade or part shade, in rich, moist soil. The trees are moderately fast growing and fairly short-lived, although a new crop of plants is always coming along, thanks to the suckering nature of the roots. In the wild, pawpaws often form small colonies. The plants require no pruning.

The unusual maroon-purple, bell-shaped flowers resemble those of wild ginger but are often overlooked because of their quiet color. They are borne on wood of the previous season and are followed in late summer by the irregularly cylinder-shaped fruits, which grow in clusters of three to seven fruits. Fruit set may be unreliable even in the presence of a pollinator. If your trees produce plenty of flowers but few fruits, you can try hand-pollination to boost the crop, gently dusting one flower against the others so that the pollen coats the smooth, shiny stigma.

Pawpaws are delicious eaten fresh. As they ripen, the 3- to 5-inch-long green fruits first turn yellow like bananas, then deepen to black, becoming soft at maturity. Some people eat them when they're just beginning to turn black. You can just peel and eat them, although a plate and spoon will make for less mess. Unlike bananas, pawpaws are full of brown seeds the size of lima beans, but your tongue will easily separate them from the sweet pulp. The pulp can also be used in cakes, puddings, and other treats.

Pawpaws are generally untroubled by insects and disease. Fall webworm may be troublesome. The webs appear in late summer, festooning the branch tips, while caterpillars defoliate the leaves. Clean off the webs as soon as they appear. A horde of four-legged pests will also try to beat you to the crop. Raccoons, opossums, squirrels, and bears relish the sweet custard flesh, and even wild turkeys will exert themselves to reach any fruits they can. If animals come to dine, a secure fence is the only solution.

■ RECOMMENDED VARIETIES OF PAWPAWS

All listed will do well in zones 5–9. Pawpaws require a second tree as a pollinator.

Pawpaw species (*Asimina triloba*, Banana Tree, Custard Banana, Nebraska Banana, Hoosier Banana)
Description of fruit: Greenish yellow, 3–5 in. long, black when ripe with yellow pulp. Banana-custard flavor.
Comments: Seedlings of species may vary in flavor depending on parent tree.

Mango
Description of fruit: Large roundish fruit with excellent flavor.

Mary Foos Johnson
Description of fruit: Medium-size fruit with good flavor.

Mitchell
Description of fruit: Large roundish fruit with fine flavor.

Overlease
Description of fruit: Large roundish or oval fruit with outstanding flavor.
Comments: Bears a reliable crop yearly.

Sunflower
Description of fruit: Very large, thick fruit with sweet banana flavor.
Comments: Small tree.

Sweet Alice
Description of fruit: Large fruit with sweet, rich banana flavor.

Taylor

Description of fruit: Small green fruit with yellow pulp; typical banana-custard flavor.

Wilson

Description of fruit: Medium-size yellow fruit with sweet, rich banana flavor.

Mulberries

Beloved by kids, scorned by parents, mulberries are a part of the landscape of childhood. A testimony to their tough constitution, the trees spring up in every nook and cranny of the countryside, suburbs, and city and produce abundant sweet berries despite drought, bone-chilling cold, the worst heat and humidity, compacted soil, or city pollution. There always seem to be enough half-inch, blackberry-shaped berries for every neighborhood child, bird, squirrel, and other fruit eaters.

Somewhere between childhood and adulthood the consensus on mulberries changes from "Mm-mm-good" to "What a nuisance!" The ripe fruit stains everything it touches a lasting purple that spreads from walks and drives to shoes and entrance rugs. Birds patronizing a fruiting mulberry contribute to the mess with purple splotches on cars, patios, and laundry on the line.

In the right place, however, a mulberry can be an asset to the landscape as well as a delight to children. The vigorous tree is adaptable to all except the wettest soils, so it can be placed in just about any sunny site that keeps the fallen fruit out of foot traffic. (Keep them away from flower beds and ground covers, too — fallen berries soon sprout, and even very young mulberry seedlings are tough to pull out.) Planted as a hedge, mulberries turn a natural border with your neighbors into a feeding trough for the kids. You can't curb the birds, but you avoid the stains they let fly by planting a white-fruited cultivar, such as 'Beautiful Day' or 'Sugar Drop'.

The three most common "wild" mulberry species include two western Asian species, black mulberry *(Morus nigra)* and white mulberry *(M. alba)*. Red mulberry *(M. rubra)* is a native of North America from the mid-Atlantic states to Florida and west to Nebraska and Texas. The two Asian species were introduced to North America in attempts to farm silkworms, first in colonial Virginia, then in 19th-century industrial Massachusetts, and even in frontier Nevada City, where the cheap labor of Chinese immigrants brought in to build the railroad was exploited by silkworm entrepreneurs. The silk industry wasn't a big success, but the mulberry trees flourished.

All three species are 20- to 40-foot trees so similar in leaf shape and fruit size as to be confusing. Even the ripe fruit of the "white" mulberry is often purple or black-purple. The main reason to distinguish among them is the slight difference in cold hardiness. The white mulberry is hardiest, to zone 5. The black species is more tender and does best in areas without severe winter cold, although it may languish in the humidity of the Deep South. Red mulberry flourishes in the eastern United States as far as the Gulf Coast, where the shorter, often shrubby Texas mulberry *(M. microphylla)* takes over and grows throughout the Southwest. Some mulberries are self-pollinating, but even those that aren't are usually taken care of as the wind blows pollen in from trees somewhere in the vicinity.

For home fruit gardeners, the named selections are the best choice. An interesting new selection called 'Pakistan' bears purple-red fruit an incredible 3 inches long. Hardy to zone 7, it thrives in dry climates. 'New American', actually a very old cultivar, bears heavy crops of large, tasty black-purple fruit. 'Downing', a mulberry brought down to home-garden size, grows to about 15 feet tall and bears large, sweet pink berries. The very hardy 'Black English', which thrives in zones 4 through 9, bears sweet, purplish black fruit and grows quickly to its mature height of 15 feet. 'Persian Dwarf' is a pint-sized version that reaches only 8 to 10 feet tall. It is hardy to 0°F. The white-fruited 'Beautiful Day', a bountiful, medium-size (25 to 30 feet) tree, bears pure white berries that are delicious when eaten fresh and like white raisins when they are dried.

Mulberries are generally untroubled by insect pests and disease. Scale and cankers are occasional but slight problems, soon overcome by the vigorous tree. Popcorn disease, an odd and unusual affliction of the fruit, can cause them to look like grotesque kernels of popped corn. If this happens, remove and destroy all infected fruits. The fruits are so attractive to birds that mulberry trees are sometimes planted as a decoy crop to distract birds from other ripening fruits.

■ Recommended Varieties of Mulberries

Beautiful Day
Description of fruit: Medium to large, pure white. Sweet.
Comments: Zones 6–8. Prolific. Dried white mulberries are tasty.

Black English
Description of fruit: Large, purple-black. Very sweet.
Comments: Zones 4–9. Prolific. Self-pollinating.

Black Mulberry *(Morus nigra)*
Description of fruit: Red to purple-black. Sweet to tart, depending on tree.
Comments: Zones 5–9 (depending on place of origin of seedling stock). Native to Asia.

Downing
Description of fruit: Large, pink. Sweet.
Comments: Maintenance-free. Prolific. To 15 ft. tall.

Everbearing
Description of fruit: Large, good-tasting fruit.
Comments: Zones 4–8. Large main crop in early summer; second, smaller crop in late summer.

Illinois Everbearing
Description of fruit: Large, black, nearly seedless. Sweet-tart.
Comments: Zones 5–8. Self-pollinating. Harvest lasts over two months from spring through summer. Hardy to -25°F.

Korean
Description of fruit: Medium-size sweet red fruit.
Comments: Native to Korea, tree grows to 18 ft.

New American
Description of fruit: Large, tasty black-purple fruit.
Comments: May be same variety as Wellington.

Pakistan
Description of fruit: Very large, red to black berries up to 3 in. long. Sweet.
Comments: Zones 7–9. Excellent in dry climates.

Persian Dwarf
Description of fruit: Black fruits. Mild flavor.
Comments: Dwarf tree reaches 8 ft. Hardy to 0°F.

Red Mulberry *(Morus rubra,* American Mulberry)
Description of fruit: Large, red to purple. Tart to sweet.
Comments: Zones 5–8. Native to eastern North America.

White Mulberry *(Morus alba)*
Description of fruit: White fruit, tinged with pink or lavender when ripe. Mild, sweet.

Comments: Zones 4–8 (to -25°F). Dried fruit is staple in Asia. Makes a good early trap crop to distract birds from cherries or other prized fruits. Native to China; silkworm food.

Shangri La
Description of fruit: Large, black. Mild.
Comments: Zones 7–9. Good for warmer regions, including the South.

Sugar Drop
Description of fruit: White, tinged with lavender when ripe. Extremely sweet.
Comments: Zones 5–8. Dried fruit is an excellent sweet treat.

Wellington
Description of fruit: Large sweet black fruit.
Comments: Zones 5–9. Prolific bearer.

Kiwis

If you garden in zones 8 and 9, chances are good that you can successfully raise your own fuzzy brown-skinned kiwis *(Actinidia deliciosa),* just like the ones you see in the supermarket. If you garden in colder regions of the country, you can enjoy two reasonable facsimiles, the hardy kiwifruits, *A. arguta* and *A. kolomikta.* The smooth-skinned fruits of hardy kiwi may be much smaller than their fuzzy green-fleshed cousin — about the size of a big grape — but these sweeter, smooth-skinned fruits can be popped into the mouth skin and all.

Except for a few self-fruitful cultivars, all three species need both a male and a female plant to produce fruit. The vines are sensitive to temperature swings, especially when the weather warms in midwinter and then plummets again to frigid cold — a common occurrence in many parts of the Southeast and Midwest, where growing kiwis can be an iffy proposition.

Once called Chinese gooseberry and renamed "kiwi fruit" in a stroke of New Zealand marketing genius, the tender *A. deliciosa* (also known as *A. chinensis*) can be grown as far north as zone 7 if temperatures do not fall below 10° to 15°F. At the same time, the plant requires a period of winter chill to break dormancy. If you garden in an area where temperatures do not fall below 50°F for at least 30 days or more, you might try the low-chill cultivars, such as the female cultivar 'Gracie', which extends the kiwi into areas with warmer winter.

Commonly called "hardy kiwifruit," *A. arguta* withstands cold to -25°F and grows well in zones 4 through 7. The fruits need about five months to ripen. The rampant vines can be difficult to manage in the home garden, twining to at least 40 feet in length. You'll need to prune them regularly and severely to keep them confined to a trellis or other support. If the prospect of pruning is worrisome, try the less-vigorous, self-pollinating cultivar 'Issai', which often bears in its second year, though the fruit is not as tasty.

The hardiest of the kiwifruits, *A. kolomikta,* is sometimes called "Arctic Beauty" kiwi for its lovely pink and white foliage. The vine is smaller and slower growing than *A. arguta,* but must still be controlled in the home garden by pruning. The small, smooth-skinned fruits of this super-hardy kiwi need less than 19 weeks of growing season to ripen. The fruit tends to drop when ripe, but the cultivar 'Clara Zetlan' holds its fruit longer than most.

Planting and care

One-year-old kiwi vines are usually sold as potted plants for spring planting. (Some mild-climate nurseries carry potted plants year-round.) They like well-drained soils of pH 5.0 to 6.5. *Actinidia deliciosa* and *A. arguta* do best in full sun, although they'll also tolerate partial shade, especially in hot-summer climates. *A. kolomikta* prefers light shade.

You can tame the rampant growth and keep the plant somewhat fruitful if you attack it with pruning shears only once a year. When the vine is dormant, trim back all branches that have fruited and any long nonfruiting shoots to about 18 inches from the branching point. If a thoroughly neglected vine threatens to overrun your ankles as you walk to the mailbox, you can whack it back drastically to return it to its allotted boundaries.

For a tidier plant and fewer but bigger fruits, you can train a kiwi in a manner similar to grapes. Support the plant on a sturdy trellis or arbor anchored by 4-inch-square posts, and develop a strong base structure and fruiting arms. When you plant the vine, cut it back immediately to four or five buds, which will grow into shoots. Select the sturdiest shoot to be the main trunk, and tie it to the arbor, then remove the other shoots. When the trunk reaches the top of the arbor, cut it off at the tip so that new side branches are produced to grow along the arbor.

Once a month, all summer, every summer, you'll need to prune each shoot of new growth back to four or five buds. This regimen produces a dense, short-limbed vine, which will bear abundantly in its second or third year and thereafter. (See the chapter on grapes for more information on training.)

Fruit is borne near the base of this year's new shoots. *A. chinensis* is ready for picking when the skin turns brown and the seeds turn black (cut one open to check). Ripe hardy kiwis will either drop of their own accord or will twist off easily in the hand. Pick them with their stems attached.

Kiwi vines are untroubled by most pests. Japanese beetles can be pesky but don't cause serious damage. To control them, knock the beetles one by one into a small open container of ammonia or soapy water. Kiwi vines can succumb to crown rot if planted in heavy, often waterlogged soil. A well-drained site will avoid the problem.

■ RECOMMENDED VARIETIES OF KIWIS

Unless otherwise noted, kiwis need both a male and female plant to ensure fruit; male plants seldom bear fruit.

Hardy Kiwi: Actinidia arguta

Also known as Arctic Kiwi, Bower Actinidia, Hardy Kiwi, Siberian Gooseberry, Tara Vine, Yang-Tao. All will do well in zones 4–7 unless otherwise noted.

Actinidia arguta species plants
Description of fruit: Smooth 1-in. lime green fruits. Very sweet.
Comments: Grapelike deciduous vine reaches 30–50 ft. Bears fruit in 3–4 years. Hardy to -25°F.

74-49
Description of fruit: Large, smooth, round fruit. Sweet, aromatic.
Comments: Ripens in fall. Zone 5. Female plants only.

74-55
Description of fruit: Medium to large round fruit. Sweet.
Comments: Fast-growing vine, prolific. Hardy to -25°F. Female plants only.

Ananasnaja (Ana, Anna, Anna Kiwi, Annasnaja, Manchurian Pineapple)
Description of fruit: Smooth, light green fruit to 1 1/2 in. Very sweet.
Comments: Insect- and disease-resistant. Hardy to -30°F. Plants are male or female.

Dumbarton Oaks
Description of fruit: Smooth fruit. Sweet.
Comments: Zone 5. Found in Georgetown, Washington, D.C., garden. Plants are male or female.

Warm-winter gardeners can grow fuzzy-skinned tender kiwis, like the ones at top, while those in colder climes can try the smaller, but sweeter, hardy kiwi, like those above.

Issai
Description of fruit: Smooth fruit up to 1¾ in. long. Moderate flavor.
Comments: Self-pollinating; fruit set increases when planted with an *A. arguta* male of another variety. Fruit is seedless if no pollinating male. Bears in second year. Flourishes in almost any conditions except wet soils. Zone 5.

Meader
Description of fruit: Medium-size, smooth fruit. Sweet.
Comments: Good pollinator for Ananasnaja. Ripens earlier than most varieties. Hardy to -28°F. Plants are male or female.

Hardy Kiwi: Arguta kolomikta
Zones 3–7, unless otherwise noted.

A. *kolomikta* species plants
Description of fruit: Small, smooth fruits on female plants.
Comments: Vine reaches 10–12 ft. Not as rampant as other kiwis. Hardy to -40°F. Good for shade. Zones 4–7. Plants are male or female.

Arctic Beauty
Description of fruit: Smooth ¾-in. fruits. Very sweet.
Comments: Good in shade. Variegated leaves, especially eye-catching in pink-white-green males. Hardy to -40°F. Male and female.

Clara Zetlan
Description of fruit: Large sweet fruits.
Comments: Holds ripe fruit longer than most cultivars of *A. kolomikta*. Female plants only.

Krupnopladnaya
Description of fruit: Flavor like a cross of kiwi/pineapple.
Comments: Prolific. Ripens mid-August. Female plants only.

Tender Kiwi: Arguta deliciosa
Also known as A. chinensis, *Chinese Gooseberry, Kiwi Berry, Yang-Tao. Zones 8–9, unless otherwise noted.*

A. *deliciosa* species plants
Description of fruit: Fuzzy brown fruit with green flesh. Mild, gooseberry-like.
Comments: Fruit ripens in late October. Hardy in zones 7–9. Plants are male or female.

Abbott
Description of fruit: Medium fruit, densely furred. Good taste.
Comments: Prolific. Female plants only.

Blake
Description of fruit: Small to medium, pointed fruit. Ripens early October.
Comments: Very large leaves. Male and female flowers on same plant.

CC Early
Description of fruit: Male plants only, no fruit.
Comments: Blooms early. If flowers are damaged by frost or cold, it reblooms.

California
Description of fruit: Male plants only, no fruit.
Comments: Pest- and disease-resistant. Good pollinator for female Hayward. Hardy to 10°F.

Gracie
Description of fruit: Long fruit tapered at stem end. Good taste.
Comments: Low chill requirement. Female.

Hayward
Description of fruit: Standard commercial type. Fuzzy brown 3-in. fruit with green flesh. Sweet-tart taste.
Comments: Hardy to 5°F. Best in areas with warm summers. Female.

Vincent
Description of fruit: Medium-size fruit.
Comments: Low chill requirement; only needs 100 hours. Female.

Elderberries

Elderberries offer two edible treats: berries and flowers. Heavy clusters of glistening, tiny purple-black berries make delicious juice, wine, and jelly, and the flowers can be turned into scrumptious elderberry fritters. The American elder (*Sambucus canadensis*) is most commonly cultivated, although some gardeners plant the taller, less cold-hardy European species (*S. nigra*).

Both the American and European species are easy-to-grow, pest-free bushes that bear so abundantly that you can easily sacrifice a few flower clusters in the spring for fritters. The American elderberry reaches 6 to 10 feet tall and expands into an ever-growing clump by producing suckers. It is hardy to zone 3 and grows well through zone 8. The European species, which can reach 30 feet, grows best in zones 5 through 8. Improved selections of the American species, such as the old favorites 'York', 'Adams', and 'Johns', offer bigger berries and better flavor.

Plant elderberries in full sun, in moist soil high in organic matter. Although the bushes are somewhat self-pollinating, the yield can increase dramatically if another cultivar is planted nearby. To allow room for harvesting the fruit, plant the bushes 5 feet apart.

The berries ripen in late summer, turning from green to shining purple-black. Their complex flavor is a fruity blending of grape and blackberry, tart-sweet with the faintest hint of bitter. The fruits are too small to eat fresh, though they're good for an occasional nibble while you're in the garden. Besides, you'll want to save the bounty for those jewel-colored homemade jellies and wines.

Birds are less able to restrain themselves. They are so fond of elderberries that they'll settle on a bush of ripe berries and strip each cluster bare. To protect the crop, throw large sheets of plastic bird netting over the bushes, fastening it to the stems with wire twist-ties. Although some intrepid birds may still try to reach the fruit through the netting, most are too wary of becoming entangled in the net to settle.

■ RECOMMENDED VARIETIES OF ELDERBERRIES
All will grow as far south as zone 8 unless otherwise noted.
All require cross-pollination unless otherwise noted.

American Elderberry (species) *Sambucus canadensis*
Description of fruit: Black-purple fruit clusters.
Best use: Jelly, pie, wine.
Comments: Hardy to zone 3. Grows 6–10 ft. tall.

Adams (Adams No. 1)
Description of fruit: Huge fruit clusters.
Best use: Jam, preserves, juice, pie, wine.
Comments: Prolific, easy to grow. Pest- and disease-free. Hardy to zone 4.

Ebony King
Description of fruit: Black berries with waxy coating.
Best use: Jelly, wine, pie.
Comments: Hardy to zone 3.

The Western red elderberry (Sambucus callicarpa) bears abundant clusters of berries on a tree or bush that is hardy to zone 7.

Hardy to zone 4, the Western blue elderberry (Sambucus caerulea) bears big clusters of dark blue berries.

Hidden Springs
Description of fruit: Large clusters of fruit ripen evenly.
Best use: Jelly, wine, syrup.
Comments: Grows to 15 ft. Zone 6 and south. Good choice for hot-summer gardens.

Johns
Description of fruit: Immense fruit clusters.
Best use: Jam, jelly, juice, pie, wine.
Comments: A more vigorous bush but slightly less productive than 'Adams'.

Nova
Description of fruit: Large fruits.
Best use: Jelly, wine, pie.
Comments: Hardy to zone 4. Pollinate with York.

Tarheel
Description of fruit: Large clusters of berries.
Best use: Wine, jelly.
Comments: Plant can grow 6 ft. in first year.

York
Description of fruit: Purplish black clusters of very large berries.
Best use: Jam, jelly, juice, pie, wine.
Comments: Hardy to zone 4. Last of varieties to ripen. Cross-pollinate with Nova.

European Elderberry *(Sambucus nigra)*
Description of fruit: Large clusters of shiny, purplish black berries.
Best use: Jam, pie, wine.
Comments: Hardy to zone 5. Reaches 30 ft. tall.

Native Specialties

Native American fruits offer a welcome treat to hikers and berrying parties from the Atlantic to the Pacific. As word spreads of their good taste and adaptability, the plants are finding a home in gardens both in and outside their natural range.

Buffaloberries

This extremely hardy (to zone 2) deciduous shrub or small tree gets its name from the American Indian practice of pounding dried berries together with buffalo meat to make pemmican. Buffaloberry *(Shepherdia argentea)* is a unique nitrogen-fixing shrub, able to thrive in the poorest dry or rocky soils. It also does well in general garden conditions. Growing to 18 feet tall, the thorny-stemmed plant is a good choice for a hedge impenetrable enough to keep pets and other animals in or out of an area. Its oblong leaves are silvery on both sides. Oval red or yellow fruits about a quarter of an inch across hang in clusters like currants. The berries are sour when eaten fresh but make superb jelly, jam, or relish. The cultivar 'Xanthocarpa' has yellow berries. 'Russet' is a thornless cultivar, with leaves and twigs coated with an unusual coppery "fur."

Buffaloberry can be severely damaged by Japanese beetles; handpick for control as described for kiwis. Late-spring frosts can damage blossoms and buds; plant on north-facing exposures to delay bloom where spring weather is unpredictable.

Chokecherries

The "choke" in chokecherry comes from the astringency of the fruits — they are just as mouth-puckering as unripe persimmons in spite of their fruity, spicy aroma. You can turn the tempting aroma and fruity flavor to wonderful advantage in jellies or wines of sparkling deep red color.

The chokecherry *(Prunus virginiana)* is another super hardy native (to zone 2). A fast-growing tree reaching 20 to 30 feet tall, it does best in full sun, in poor to average soil. Heavy clusters of reddish black fruits ripen in July. The cultivar 'Canada Red', also known as 'Redleaf' and 'Red Flame', has bluish purple fruits and is hardy through zone 3. Chokecherry fruit is irresistible to vireos, tanagers, and other fruit-eating birds, making the small tree an excellent addition to a hedgerow or "natural" landscape.

Sand cherries

Like the chokecherry, the sand cherry *(Prunus besseyi)* is a good addition to an edible or natural landscape. Birds like the fruits, but save some for yourself, too. The sweet, fleshy, purplish black fruits make delectable pies, jams, and jellies. Hardy to zone 2 and drought-tolerant, this deciduous Great Plains native is an attractive fountain-shaped shrub 4 to 6 feet tall, with glossy silver green leaves and fragrant flowers. The purpleleaf sand cherry *(Prunus × cistena)* has glowing reddish purple foliage from spring through fall. In frost-prone areas, the late-blooming sand cherry ensures more fruit than most cherries.

Highbush cranberries

A compact, upright bush hardy to zone 3, the deciduous cranberry *(Viburnum trilobum)* reaches 6 to 12 feet tall. It grows well in almost any moisture-retentive soil and will tolerate wet sites.

Its showy white blooms develop into clusters of bright red fruit, which ripen in late July and persist all winter long unless eaten by gardener, bird, or beast. Though the berries vary in tartness from one seedling plant to another, the best are sweet enough to eat fresh, and even the most bitter redeem themselves in jellies and sauces. As an added attraction, the leaves turn vivid red in fall. 'Wentworth' and 'Phillips' are two of the best-tasting cultivars.

Huckleberries

If it looks like a blueberry and tastes like a blueberry, but it's small and dark and grainy with seeds, it's a huckleberry. Members of both the blueberry genus, *Vaccinium* spp., and the huckleberry genus, *Gaylussacia* spp., are commonly known as huckleberries. Depending on species and conditions, huckleberry shrubs can reach 4 to 8 feet in height. Dwarf huckleberry *(Gaylussacia dumosa),* which ranges from Florida to Newfoundland, is a creeping shrub that reaches only 18 inches high. Evergreen or California huckleberry *(Vaccinium ovatum),* a compact shrub with small shiny foliage, reaches 6 feet tall and 2 to 3 feet wide in the shade. Grown in the sun its reaches only about 2 feet tall.

Like blueberries, huckleberries will fail to thrive on alkaline soils, preferring those with a pH range of 4.5 to 5.2. The twiggy, deciduous bushes need a shady location in sandy or peaty soil. They make appealing landscape shrubs, especially in fall when their foliage turns a striking bronzy red.

Juneberries

Juneberry, serviceberry, shadblow — this native American tree or shrub answers to a litany of common names. The small, shaggy-petaled blossoms open in soft white drifts in April woodlands, about the time that the bony fish known as shad are returning from the ocean to their freshwater spawning grounds, hence "shadblow."

Juneberries *(Amelanchier* spp.) range from graceful single-trunk trees up to 40 feet tall *(A. laevis)* to multistem shrubs as small as 3 feet *(A. alnifolia,* which can also grow much larger). All have showy white flowers. Hardy from zones 3 to 8, there are many cultivars, some selected for ornamental attributes, such as their autumn leaf color, and others for better fruit. 'Autumn Sunset' turns a vivid deep orange in fall and 'Cole's Select' is outstanding for its brilliant red-orange autumn foliage.

The dark blue or purple fruits, which look vaguely like blueberries, ripen on the tree in early summer. They are sweet in flavor, but gritty with small seeds that are pleasantly bitter when bitten. Though the fruits of the unimproved species plants are very small, selected cultivars offer berries as big as three-quarters of an inch. A single bush of 'Smokey', a selection of the western serviceberry *(A. alnifolia)* can yield more than 80 pounds of large, very sweet fruits. 'Moon Lake' bears large fruits better than half an inch across. 'Honeywood' has slightly smaller fruits but bigger crops. 'Thiessen' is renowned for its fine-flavored fruit. 'Regent' is a productive shrub reaching about 3 feet. 'Ballerina', an English ornamental, offers tasty red fruit and decorative bark on a beautiful small tree.

Cactus fruits

The fruits of several cacti are venerable native food, prickly pears (*Opuntia* spp.) being among the most flavorful. The flat, round pads of the prickly pear are studded with spines, but the fruit is usually spineless.

Although cacti usually bring visions of the hot southwestern deserts to mind, several prickly pears are hardy plants. The prostrate, yellow-flowered *O. compressa* flourishes in zones 4 through 10. The purplish, 2-inch fruit is improved in flavor by remaining on the plant all winter. *O. phaecantha*, hardy in zones 5 through 10, has large pads, to 8 inches long, and big red fruits in autumn. *O. humifusa, O. fragilis,* and *O. goldhillea* are other hardy species.

The fig-shaped fruits of a tender, spineless prickly pear, the tuna or Indian fig *(O. ficus-indica)*, have a sweet, watermelon flavor. The 2-inch fruits may be maroon, peach, or green in color, depending on cultivar. The species is not hardy below 20°F.

Other Tender Fruits

With handsome leaves, flowers, and fruit, mangoes are good landscape plants in frost-free climates.

Lush in looks and taste, semitropical and tropical fruits are fast-growing productive ornamentals. Figs and bananas are the best known of these tender fruits. But no less delectable are guavas, papaya, and a whole market basket of exotic tastes that English can describe only by analogy. A feijoa tastes like a minty pineapple, a mango like a flowery peach.

Where winters are mild, most of the tender fruits in this chapter will flourish with such vigor that they can be grown as landscaping shrubs and trees, offering homeowners a bounty of tropical looks and taste. Northern gardeners can grow these plants in containers, though fruit production depends on how much heat and light you can provide. (See "Planting Fruit Trees and Bushes" for details on how to grow fruits in containers; the chart on page 340 offers brief comments on overwintering container-grown plants.)

Overwintering Container-Grown Tender Fruits

Unless otherwise noted, all plants are also suited for greenhouse growing.

Fruit	Comment
Avocado	Smaller or well-pruned avocados can be grown in containers. (A 20-gallon tub may eventually be needed.) Grow them as houseplants in bright light, or grow outdoors and winter over in a greenhouse or sunroom.
Banana	Select a short cultivar for container growing. Overwinter in sunroom or greenhouse.
Feijoa	Overwinter potted feijoa in a cool (45°–55°F) sunporch, garage, or greenhouse. Plant will go dormant until moved back outside in spring, then will bloom and fruit the following growing season.
Fig	In winter, move a potted fig to a cool garage, basement, or porch for the winter, where it will go dormant.
Guava, strawberry	Strawberry guavas bloom and bear almost all year. Cut them back as needed for indoor culture.
Guava, tropical	Tropical guavas must have steamy heat and bright light all year.
Loquat	Place a potted loquat in a bright window or sunroom and be sure to keep moisture levels high. Fruit sets in fall and ripens the following spring.
Mango	Must have warm, dry conditions to set fruit. Choose small cultivars for container growing.

Climate Considerations

The tender fruits in this chapter are native to the tropics and semitropics. Only the southernmost part of the continental United States, including Florida, southern Texas, a bit of Georgia and South Carolina, and a strip along the Gulf Coast, comes close to matching the even, humid heat and abundant moisture required for many of them to flourish. But tender fruits have also adapted well to the drier heat of semitropical California, Arizona, and southwest Texas, with some protection from intense afternoon sun and regular watering when rainfall is scarce.

Cold tolerance

Frost-free areas of the United States, zones 9 and 10, are the general limits for the tender fruits in this chapter. Unfortunately for interested northern gardeners, the blossoms and fruit of these plants are usually more frost-tender than their roots and foliage. Many tender fruits will suffer when temperatures fall below 20°F, even if their leaves and roots are hardier to colder temperatures. What's more, some of the otherwise fairly hardy plants bloom during the cold months or hold their fruit through winter. Bananas, for example, take up to eight months to ripen. Protecting the unripe fruit from the cold is a major concern for gardeners even in zones 9 and 10, where a freak bout of frost can wreak havoc with the harvest.

Zone 8 is a borderline range for a few tender fruits. Gardeners in the warmest parts of this zone are often tempted to risk their harvest and their hearts growing the more tender types, hoping that the winter will be mild or that the plants will somehow survive any cold snaps. Choosing the hardiest cultivars can make a big difference, especially in the Southeast and the western regions of zone 8, where winter temperatures can fall to 10°F.

If you garden in zone 7 or colder regions, most tender fruits are out unless you move them indoors for the winter. But you needn't give up altogether on the idea of growing tender exotics outdoors. Some cultivars of figs and feijoas are tougher than most when it comes to cold. The old favorite 'Brown Turkey' fig and the sweet 'Tennessee Mountain' fig can be grown in zone 7. Some cultivars of the pretty silvery-leafed feijoa will survive temperatures as low as 7°F.

Heat requirements

Many tender exotics are not only susceptible to frost but need heat and sun to ripen and sweeten their fruit. Even within frost-free zone 10, temperatures and sunshine can vary greatly, making some areas more favorable than others for tender fruit production. For example, north in zone 10 along the California coast the climate is generally frost-free, but the Pacific cools the air all year long. Some tender fruits need more heat and sun to ripen than this region can provide. And a few of the most tender plants, like papaya, will thrive only in the hottest parts of zone 10 — southern Florida and southern California.

Winter chill requirements

Most of the fruits in this chapter are native to subtropical regions. They grow year-round with no period of winter dormancy, renewing leaves a few at a time. The feijoa and fig have somewhat different requirements, which will be discussed below.

Microclimates

It is possible to stretch the limits (either hot or cold) of your climate by planting in a site that is slightly warmer or cooler than the surroundings, or by altering the climate around the plant. We've summarized the main points here; see the chapter "Planting Fruit Trees and Bushes" for details.

Where the climate is a bit too cold, take advantage of reflected and stored heat when selecting a site. An area near a light-colored wall with a south or west exposure will be brighter and warmer than elsewhere. Avoid low spots where cold air collects.

The strength of the sun in desert gardens may be a little overwhelming, especially for plants that have been pruned to an open shape, allowing sunlight to penetrate the center of the plant. If you garden in an area of searing sun, plant your tender fruits where they can rest in light afternoon shade. Some growers paint the trunk and exposed branches with commercially available tree paints to prevent sunburn, which can weaken the tree.

Tender Exotics for Home Gardens

The fruits included here are useful as ornamentals as well as for providing generous quantities of tasty fruit. As with other plants, the farther removed from conditions to which these tender fruits are adapted, the more difficult it becomes to grow them. When grown in appropriate climates, they are generally low-maintenance plants. They are usually untroubled by insects, and resistant cultivars reduce disease problems. All will do well in ordinary garden soil, as long as it is well drained. Grow them in raised beds of imported or amended soil if you're stuck with heavy clay.

Watering is important with subtropical fruits, particularly when the plants are young. Avocados, bananas, tropical guavas, mangos, and papayas need 1 to 2 inches every week or two until they're well established. Figs, strawberry guava, and loquat need an inch every three to four weeks. Make a rain-catching basin about 4 feet in diameter around the newly planted tree by mounding organic mulch 3 to 4 inches deep to form a small dyke. As the tree grows, so should the catch basin, out to as much as 12 feet in diameter. If rainfall is scant, supplement it with irrigation. After three years, trees need 1 to 2 inches of water every two to four weeks.

Because tender fruits are demanding when it comes to climate, your safest bet is to buy from local nurseries, since they usually stock only plants that perform well in your region. But if you're ready to branch out from the run-of-the-mill, want to buy from mail-order nurseries, or have papaya seeds or an avocado sprout ready at hand, you'll need to read on about the individual fruits in this chapter and consult your county extension service about plants suitable for your climate and conditions.

Cold Hardiness
General range of the fruits in this chapter.

Avocado	Zones 8–10
Banana	Zones 9–10
Feijoa	Zones 7–10 (requires up to 100 hours of chill)
Fig	Zones 7–10 (requires less than 100 hours of chill)
Guava	Zones 9–10
Loquat	Zones 8–10
Mango	Zones 9–10
Papaya	Zone 10

Avocados

This fast-growing evergreen tree *(Persea americana)* produces oval fruits that can be green or black, thin-skinned or bumpy, and weigh as little as a few ounces or as much as 2 pounds. Peel away the skin, though, and all avocados have the same smooth, buttery consistency and taste.

Two types of avocados are most familiar to North Americans, the thin-skinned green or black Mexican avocados and the thick, bumpy black-skinned Guatemalan types; both are named for their place of origin. Avocados flower in winter, and frost will damage the flowers, destroying the crop. As for the plants themselves, some Mexican cultivars and hybrids are hardy to about 22°F and tolerate heavy soil. The Guatemalan tolerates no frost (zone 9 or warmer). A third, even more tender type is the smooth, yellow-skinned West Indian avocado. You're likely to find it only in southern Florida and Hawaii. (Hybrids of Guatemalan and West Indian avocados are hardy to zone 9.) Most avocados are partially self-pollinating — one tree is all home gardeners will need for a good crop.

Avocado trees grow from 20 to 60 feet tall, but most reach about 30 feet tall and 25 feet wide. For small gardens, dwarf cultivars are available that reach only 8 to 10 feet. With so many types to choose from, you can find an avocado that is the right size for your garden, well adapted to your climate and soil, and resistant to diseases in your area. If you garden in the Southeast, for example, you may have trouble with the West Indian avocado, but you'll triumph with the Mexican, which is hardier and more tolerant of heavy soil. No sense, either, trying to grow the Guatemalan avocado 'Gwen', which will blacken in temperatures below 26°F, when the hardier 'Jim' or 'Mexicola' can take a little cold.

Planting and care

It's easy and tempting to sprout an avocado seed from last night's dinner salad. But you'll have to wait years until the seedling bears fruit, with no guarantee of quality. If you want fruit as well as the avocado's big, attractive leaves, a better bet is to plant nursery stock.

Nursery stock is usually sold as grafted young trees in containers. Most are self-pollinating, and a single tree will give you all the avocados you need. Plant the young tree in spring in full sun in soil of pH 5.5 to 6.5. A well-drained site is critical. Heavy waterlogged clay is certain death, and so is a site where the water table is high in winter. Even mature plants need an inch of water weekly. Let the leaves that avocados drop through the year lie as a mulch to retain moisture. No pruning is necessary for good fruit production, but you can cut back the tree at any time to keep it in bounds. Never cut back more than one-third of the total growth at once.

An avocado harvest is a long-term production. From pollination to ripe fruit can take as long as 14 months. Most avocados bear a heavy crop one year and a light crop the next. The fruit ripens year-round, some earlier, some later, depending on cultivar. You can tell a mature avocado by its color. Green avocados develop a slight yellowish tinge to the skin; black ones darken from green to black when they're ready for picking. The fruit softens slightly when ripe. Very soft fruit is overripe and tastes "off," so to be safe, you can pick the fruit while it is still hard but matured, and ripen it off the tree. Snip the fruit with pruners, taking care to leave a bit of the long stem attached. Handle carefully to avoid bruising.

Avocados are free of pests but are subject to diseases in some regions. In California, avocado root rot can be a major problem. The disease causes leaves to yellow and drop, leading to the eventual death of the tree. There is no cure, but you can avoid the problem by planting certified disease-free stock and never planting a new tree where an old tree has grown before. In the Southeast, fungal diseases, including powdery mildew and scab, are common. Scab-resistant cultivars are available. For mildew, remove the infected parts and dispose of them immediately. Check with your county extension agent about diseases in your area.

■ RECOMMENDED VARIETIES OF AVOCADOS

All on this list are partially self-pollinating (a single tree will give you all you need) and hardy to zones 9 and 10, unless noted otherwise.

Avocados for Florida

Choquette
Description of fruit: Very large, green fruit ripens November to February.
Comments: Resistant to scab.

Gainesville
Description of fruit: Small green fruit ripens July to August.
Comments: Cold-hardy to 18°F.

Hall
Description of fruit: Large to very large green fruit ripens November to January.
Comments: Prolific.

Mexicola
Description of fruit: Small dark purple fruit ripens July to August.
Comments: Cold-hardy to 18°F.

'Mexicola', hardy to 18°F, bears small fruit prolifically.

Monroe

Description of fruit: Large green fruit ripens November to
January.
Comments: Cold-hardy to 26°F.

Pollock

Description of fruit: Very large green fruit ripens July to September.
Comments: Scab-resistant.

Waldin

Description of fruit: Medium green fruit ripens September to
October.
Comments: Scab-resistant.

Avocados for California

Anaheim

Description of fruit: Large to extra-large green fruit ripens
June to August.
Comments: Upright, medium-size tree.

Bacon

Description of fruit: Medium green fruit ripens November to
March.
Comments: Bears young.

'Bacon'

Fuerte
Description of fruit: Medium green fruit ripens November to January.
Comments: Popular California cultivar.

Hass
Description of fruit: Medium black fruit ripens February to October.
Comments: Very popular, superb flavor.

Jim
Description of fruit: Small to medium purple-black fruit ripens October to January.
Comments: Hardy to 24°F. Bears young.

Mexicola
Description of fruit: Small dark purple fruit ripens August to October.
Comments: Prolific. Hardy to 18°F.

Pinkerton
Description of fruit: Large green fruit ripens January to April.
Comments: Heavy-bearing. Small seed.

Reed
Description of fruit: Medium to large green fruit ripens July to September.
Comments: Heavy-bearing. Upright tree.

Dwarf Avocados

Gwen
Description of fruit: Medium to large green fruit ripens March to November.
Comments: 12–14 ft. Small compact tree.

Whitsell
Description of fruit: Small green fruit ripens March to July.
Comments: 10–12 ft. Bears heavy one year, light the next.

Wurtz (Little Cado)
Description of fruit: Medium green fruit ripens May to September.
Comments: 8–10 ft. Bears young, may be light crop in alternate years.

Bananas

Commonly called trees, bananas are really herbaceous perennials, although they can reach 25 feet tall. They grow from underground rhizomes that form a fleshy stalk sheathed with enormous, broad leaves and a striking cluster of fruit that can weigh as much as 100 pounds. These fast-growing plants do best where temperatures do not fluctuate greatly. Their growth may stop altogether when the heat rises above 100°F or drops below 53 °F, and it slows down as temperatures approach these levels.

Most bananas for fresh eating are hybrids of *Musa acuminata,* used for its sweet-tasting fruit, and *M. balbisiana,* chosen for its vigorous growth. The plants are self-pollinating and untroubled by insects or disease. A banana will produce fruit at an age of 1 to $1^1/_2$ years, if conditions are right. The plant needs 10 to 15 months of temperatures around 70°–80°F to produce a flower stalk, and then another eight months of slightly warmer weather for the fruit to mature. The fruit is usually carried through the winter, ripening after warmer weather sets in. The stalk dies after fruiting, but new stalks grow from the rhizome to replace it.

Northern growers aren't likely to get the plant to fruit, but thanks to their gigantic leaves and fast growth, bananas make a dramatic display in areas where the weather is too cold for the fruit but not for the tree. Banana roots are hardy to about 22°F. 'Dwarf Cavendish' and other smaller types are adaptable to life as container plants. Set out after the soil and air have warmed, they add a tropical look to a poolside setting or make a striking centerpiece for a bed of annuals. The dwarf trees can be moved indoors to bright, diffuse light to overwinter or grown year-round in a greenhouse.

Planting and care

Suppliers sell semidormant, bare-root rhizomes or container-grown suckers. Choose a site in a sheltered spot but in full sun. A hedge, fence, or trellis will provide protection from the brunt of the wind, which can tatter the broad leaves or topple the plants. Plant in deep, well-drained, fertile soil of pH 5.5 to 6.5.

During the warmest time of year, bananas need plenty of water and fertilizer to support their fast, lush growth. Supply an inch or two of water each week if nature doesn't, and mulch to conserve soil moisture. Apply about $^1/_2$-pound of high-nitrogen fertilizer each month for a young plant, and $1^1/_2$ to 2 pounds for a plant older than 10 months.

Grown as ornamentals, bananas require no pruning, but for fruiting, you'll want to direct all the plant's energy into one main stalk. As soon as you see them, break off suckers

'*Dwarf Cavendish*'

that arise during the growing season. When the main stalk is six months old, let one vigorous sucker grow for next year's crop. Harvest the stalk when the bananas at the top of the cluster begin to turn yellow. Cut the remains of the fruiting stalk to ground level a few weeks after harvest.

■ RECOMMENDED VARIETIES OF BANANAS

Dwarf to Medium-Size Plants (under 15 feet tall)
All are self-fruitful.

Apple (Dwarf Apple, Santa Katrina)
Description of fruit: 3–4-in.-long yellow fruits with apple-sweet taste when ripe. Chalky, astringent taste when green.
Comments: 10–15 ft. tall.

Dwarf Cavendish (Dwarf Chinese)
Description of fruit: 5-in. yellow fruit with sweet flavor.
Comments: 5–7 ft. tall. Excellent pot plant. Hardy only in zone 10.

Golden Pillow
Description of fruit: 3–4-in. fat fruit, very sweet.
Comments: 10–12 ft. tall.

Largo (Bluggoe)
Description of fruit: 7–9-in. yellow fruit with mild pink flesh.
Comments: 8–10 ft. tall.

Nino (Sucrier, Honey)
Description of fruit: 4-in. golden fruit with very sweet flavor.
Comments: 8–12 ft. tall.

Valery (Taiwan)
Description of fruit: 7–10-in. yellow fruit with fine flavor.
Comments: 6–7 ft. tall. Wind-resistant.

Williams (Williams Hybrid)
Description of fruit: 7–9-in. yellow fruit with very good flavor.
Comments: 6–8 ft. tall. Fruiting clusters weigh up to 150 pounds. Wind-resistant.

Tall Plants

Brazilian (Brazilian Apple, Park-Yuk, Pome)
Description of fruit: 4–5-in. yellow fruit with sweet, mild flavor.
Comments: 18–20 ft. tall. Wind-tolerant with strong roots and massive trunk.

Hamaku (Bungulan, Monte Cristo, Pisang Masak Hijau)
Description of fruit: 6–9-in. pale yellow fruit with sweet flavor.
Comments: 15–25 ft. tall.

Ice Cream (Java Blue)
Description of fruit: 5-in. silvery blue skin turning to pale yellow when ripe; snowy flesh with sweet flavor.
Comments: 14–18 ft. tall. Wind-resistant thanks to strong roots.

Lady Finger (Ney Poovan)
Description of fruit: 4–5-in. pale yellow fruit with sweet flavor.
Comments: 20–25 ft. tall.

In addition to a warm climate, you need a lot of room to grow a tall banana.

Red Cuban (Colorado, Cuban Red, Red, Spanish Red)
Description of fruit: 5-in. purple fruit turning red when ripe; creamy flesh with good flavor.
Comments: 20–25 ft. tall.

Feijoas

Known also as pineapple guava, the waxy, blue-green fruits of feijoas have the same rounded-oval shape as guavas and are 1 to 3 inches in size. Feijoa fruit is eaten fresh, by cutting it in halves or quarters and eating the soft, mildly pineapple-flavored jellylike flesh with a spoon. They fall from the shrub when ripe, from early autumn to early winter, depending on the cultivar. The fruit's dull coating can be made more appealing by shining it with a soft cloth.

Feijoa tastes of the tropics but is tougher than most when it comes to cold. The species *(Feijoa sellowiana)* comes from the cooler regions of Brazil and Argentina. Instead of the steamy heat preferred by subtropical plants, feijoas do best where summers are moderate, with temperatures below 90°F, and winters are cool, with temperatures above 15°F. (It can be grown where temperatures dip to 7°F.) Be careful when choosing cultivars if you garden in a marginal zone. Some cultivars, including 'Coolidge', require winter temperatures no lower than 18°F. Some growers notice that less than 100 hours of winter chill results in a smaller crop, which usually isn't a problem because the plants bear so generously. Flowering is sporadic in southernmost Florida, where there may be only 50 hours of chill.

This handsome evergreen shrub makes a versatile low-maintenance landscape plant, with leaves that flash their silver undersides when a breeze stirs the foliage. It is practically disease-free and needs no pruning, though an energetic gardener can shape it to fit a variety of landscaping needs — trim it into a lovely hedge, train it as an espalier, or limb it up to a small tree. Left alone, it grows as a multistemmed shrub, reaching 25 feet tall and as wide if not killed back by frost. Its feathery flowers are an intriguing combination of white petals surrounding a brush of brilliant red stamens. If you work carefully, you can pluck the edible white petals for use in salads without sacrificing later fruit. The petals have a spicy, almost cinnamon taste.

The fruit of species plants can vary in quality. For predictable results, it's best to stick to named selections such as 'Nazemetz' and 'Trask', which have been chosen for their fine flavor.

Planting and care

Young plants are usually sold grafted onto a rootstock or grown from cuttings. Plant feijoas in well-drained soil of pH 5.5 to 7.0. They do best in full sun unless summer heat is regularly in the 100°F range. In hot climates, place the plants where they receive some afternoon shade. Feijoas bear fruit two to three years after planting.

Feijoa's attractive flowers produce tasty, pineapple-flavored fruits (hence the common name, pineapple guava). The flower petals are also edible.

■ RECOMMENDED VARIETIES OF FEIJOAS (PINEAPPLE GUAVAS)

All these will grow in zones 8–10 unless otherwise noted. Need 100 chill hours for reliable production. All are self-fruitful except where noted.

Apollo
Description of fruit: 3–4-in. fruits with excellent flavor.
Comments: Ripens early.

Coolidge
Description of fruit: 1–3-in. fruits with good flavor.
Comments: Usually flowers the first season. Hardy to 12°–18°F.

Edenvale Improved Coolidge
Description of fruit: 3–4-in. fruits with fine flavor.
Comments: Productive.

Edenvale Supreme
Description of fruit: 2–3-in. fruits with excellent flavor.
Comments: Good choice for cool coastal areas.

Mammoth
Description of fruit: 3–4-in. fruits with fine flavor. Yields are increased if planted with pollinator.
Comments: Hardy to 18°F. Ripens late, from October to November.

Nazemetz
Description of fruit: 1–4-in. fruits with good flavor. Yields are increased if planted with pollinator.
Comments: Hardy to 18°F.

Pineapple Gem
Description of fruit: 1–3-in. fruits with very good flavor. Yields are increased if planted with pollinator.
Comments: Hardy to 7°F.

Trask
Description of fruit: 2–3-in. fruits with fine flavor. Needs a pollinator.
Comments: Midseason variety.

Triumph
Description of fruit: 1–3-in. fruits with excellent flavor. Needs a pollinator.
Comments: Late ripening, into December.

Figs

The venerable fig *(Ficus carica)* has beautiful silvery bark and dramatic lobed foliage that make it an outstanding landscape plant. It can reach 15 to 30 feet tall in home gardens, with spreading branches and a wide crown that casts dense shade. The stout trunk and thick branches take on a gnarled look with age, but even when young, the framework is attractive in the winter garden after the deciduous leaves have dropped. The exotic pear-shaped "fruits" are actually fleshy receptacles housing many minute flowers and undeveloped true fruits, the source of the distinctive "seed" crunch in the mouth. In the fig's native lands a specialized wasp pollinates the flowers by climbing through the tiny opening at the end of the receptacle. The varieties available here bear edible fruit without pollination, so one tree will do. They are quick to bear fruit, often producing a small crop the first year after planting.

Centuries of breeding have produced more than 200 fig cultivars, with varying characteristics of hardiness, low-chill requirements, crops per season, and ripening times. Being Mediterranean plants, figs are adapted to long, hot summers and go dormant in winter. The dormant tree is hardy to 12°–15°F, and the roots may be hardy to 0°F. They are excellent in desert climates and moderately drought-tolerant (though fruit quality is better with some irrigation). Figs generally need at least 100 chill hours to produce a reliable crop, though cultivars do well in subtropical Florida.

Many cultivars thrive in zone 9, and a good selection, including 'Magnolia' and 'Osborne Prolific', are hardy in zone 8. Some have hardier dispositions, such as 'Texas Everbearing', which regrows after a freeze and is hardy to at least zone 7. A few tough customers, such as the sweet, meaty 'Brown Turkey' and the plump, violet-skinned 'Celeste', will fruit as far north as zone 5, provided the fruiting branches are protected in winter. (We'll discuss methods to protect fig trees below). Smaller cultivars make good container plants.

Figs are borne singly along the length of branches; some cultivars hold the fruit erect on short stems, others are pendant. Depending on cultivar and climate, figs bear one short crop or two crops of fruit each year. The first, or "breba crop," is produced from June to July on the previous season's growth. A second crop may be borne on this season's growth, ripening from late August to November. In the Southeast, where long, hot summers allow plenty of time for the main crop to ripen, look for cultivars such as 'Alma', which bear a light breba crop from June to July and a heavy crop from late August to November. An excellent choice for areas with shorter, cooler growing seasons is the cold-hardy 'King', which produces a good breba crop but no main crop.

Planting and care

Plant figs in ordinary, well-drained garden soil. Because dropped fruit can be messy, choose a site away from walks, patios, or driveways. Figs need regular watering until they're well established. In dry climates, or when rainfall is scarce, water deeply at least every two to four weeks. Mulch to conserve soil moisture. Older plants are moderately drought-tolerant.

No pruning is necessary for a crop, but figs are vigorous growers that sprout suckers from the roots and may need pruning to keep them in bounds. Use a shovel to behead any unwanted suckers, or dig them up and share them with friends.

Figs are disease-free but are bothered by a few pests. Pocket gophers are a problem in California. A tree's roots can be protected from these underground dwellers by placing a big basket fashioned from chickenwire or fencing in the planting hole before setting in the young tree. Birds and ants may be attracted by the sweet fruits. Use plastic netting to keep away birds, and brush off the ants before you eat the fruit. In the Southeast, the dried fruit beetle, which enters through the "eye" on the end of the fruit, may be problematic. "Closed-eye" cultivars, such as the yellow-skinned 'Excell', are the solution.

Figs are ready for plucking when they're slightly soft and beginning to bend at the neck. When ripe, the fruit will detach easily from the branch. Don't wait for it to fall from the tree, which can bruise the tender flesh. It's a good idea to wear gloves while working around a fig tree or harvesting the fruit, because the milky sap can be irritating to bare skin.

Figs don't continue to ripen once they're picked, and the fruit stays good for only a few days, so peeling and eating the fresh fruit is a pleasure that's short and sweet. The rest of the bounty can be dried, canned, or made into jams for a winter treat. Figs dry in about five days in the sun and will keep for as long as eight months.

Winter protection

The fig tree's outstanding appearance and fruit have inspired gardeners to go to great lengths to grow it far north of where it is usually hardy (roots die at about 0°F). To protect the tree through cold winters you can either uproot it and bury it in a trench or bury it in place under leaves and straw. For the first method, prune the tree back to about 6 feet in late fall. Wrap it in heavy plastic and carefully loosen the roots, tipping the tree into a prepared trench the same length as the tree, about 2 feet deep, and lined with boards. Pile straw and dry leaves around the tree, place a board on top and mound soil over the whole thing.

For the roots-in-place method, some advance planning is necessary. You'll have to train the tree from a young age to a short trunk (about 1 to 2 feet tall) that is low enough to cover well, with only two fruiting branches. In the spring, prune away all but two strong shoots, one on each side of the trunk, for this year's crop. During the growing season, select two other strong shoots, at right angles to the original two, to bear next year's crop. After harvest in late fall, remove the two branches that bore fruit. Pile straw or leaves around the tree, and stretch out the two remaining branches on top of the insulation, weighing them down so they are nearly horizontal. To coax reluctant branches down, tie a brick near the end of each one. Layer more leaves or straw over the branches and the top of the trunk, add a sheet of insulating microfoam material, a sheet of plastic, and finally a thick layer of soil or sod. Keep the tree buried until the spring weather is reliably settled. Figs are quick to break dormancy when the weather warms, and the new foliage is easily damaged by an unexpected return to cold.

■ RECOMMENDED VARIETIES OF FIGS

All are self-pollinating. Unless otherwise noted, all are hardy in zones 8–10. Fruit production is best with 100 hours of winter chill, though some fruit will be produced with no chill.

Alma

Description of fruit: Medium-size, light yellow skin with extremely sweet golden-tan pulp. Light breba, heavy main crop. Fresh, dried.

Comments: Needs long, hot summer. Good in Southeast. Less than 100 chill hours.

Black Mission (Mission, Franciscan, California Large Black)

Description of fruit: Medium to large, purple-black skin with red flesh. Full-flavored, not overly sweet. Two heavy crops. Fresh, dried, canned.

Comments: Large tree; needs less than 100 chill hours. Introduced by Franciscan missionaries in 1769.

Blanche (White Marseille, Lattarula, Italian Honey Fig, Lemon)

Description of fruit: Large, yellow-green fruit with sweet lemony-tasting pulp. Use fresh or dried.

Comments: Good in short-season areas with cool summers. Introduced in 1992.

'Brown Turkey' Fig

Brown Turkey (San Piero, San Piero Black, California Large Black)

Description of fruit: Medium to large, maroon-brown fruit with sweet juicy-tasting pulp. Ever-bearing. All-purpose fruit.

Comments: 10 ft. tall, bushy. Bears as far north as zone 5. Excellent container plant.

Celeste (Blue Celeste, Celestial, Honey Fig, Malta, Sugar Fig, Violette)

Description of fruit: Small to medium, violet fruit with extremely sweet, juicy white pulp. Good fresh or dried.

Comments: Hardy to 0°F with winter protection.

Excell

Description of fruit: Medium yellow fruit with sweet amber pulp. All-purpose fruit.

Comments: Introduced in 1975. Resists splitting.

Green Ischia
Description of fruit: Small to medium, green-yellow fruit with red pulp. Heavy breba crop. Fresh or dried.
Comments: Good for containers. Old cultivar.

Kadota (White Kadota, Dottato, Florentine)
Description of fruit: Medium yellow-green fruit with sweet white to amber-pink pulp. Two crops. All purpose.
Comments: Vigorous. Needs long, hot summer to ripen. Less than 100 chill hours. Very old variety; noted by Pliny. Commercial canning cultivar.

King (Desert King)
Description of fruit: Green skin with white flecks; violet-pink pulp. One crop. Fresh or dried.
Comments: Hardy roots regrow after a freeze.

Lattarula (Italian Honey Fig)
Description of fruit: Yellow-green fruit with tasty golden pulp. Two crops. Fresh, dried, canned.
Comments: Popular in Northwest.

Magnolia (Madonna, Brunswick)
Description of fruit: Large coppery brown fruit with reddish pink pulp. Small first crop of large fruit; large second crop of medium-size fruit. Fresh or canned, not dried.
Comments: Hardy to 5°F with winter protection. Good for gardeners with short growing season.

Marseilles
Description of fruit: Large, green to yellow fruit with rich-tasting translucent pulp. Good fresh.
Comments: Grown by Thomas Jefferson at Monticello.

Negronne
Description of fruit: Small black fruit with excellent-tasting red pulp. Two crops. Fresh or dried.
Comments: Zone 8; good for cooler areas. Needs 100 chill hours.

Osborne Prolific (Neveralla, Archipel)
Description of fruit: Medium to large, dark purplish brown fruit with very sweet white to golden pulp. Two crops. Fresh.
Comments: Zone 8. Good for cool coastal areas and other regions with short summers.

Texas Everbearing (English Brown Turkey)
Description of fruit: Medium to large, brown-purple fruit
  with reddish pulp. Ever-bearing. Jam, preserves.
Comments: Good in cool areas of South, Southwest, and
  areas with short growing season.

Guavas

These evergreen shrubs with fragrant white flowers and pleasant tasting fruits thrive only in the warmest parts of the country, generally zones 9 and 10. The strawberry guava *(Psidium
cattleianum)* can tolerate temperatures as low as 24°F, but the
tropical guava *(P. guajava)* will drop its leaves at about 26°F.
Both are self-fruitful.

The strawberry guava is smaller and shrubbier than the
tropical guava, making it a perfect low-maintenance edible
hedge or screen, or a good choice in mixed plantings. Where
the climate isn't frost-free, it adapts well to life in a container.
Its glossy green leaves emerge bronze. The plant bears fragrant flowers and small (an inch or two in diameter) round
fruits that turn from red to dark red then almost black when
ripe. The white flesh tastes both sweet and tart, with some
suggestion of pine. Species plants can produce excellent fruit,
although it can be variable in quality. There are no named
cultivars available; 'Lucidum', which has yellow fruit, may be
a hybrid or a botanical variety.

The tropical guava reaches 25 feet tall and can be a shrub
or small tree. Its long leaves, which sometimes drop in early
spring, have noticeable veins and a matte finish. New leaves
on some cultivars are a pretty salmon color. Tropical guava
fruits reach 1 to 4 inches in diameter and are oval to pear-
shaped. They have a sweet, pleasant flavor with a bit of acid
for balance, and sometimes a hint of muskiness. The seeds inside have a soft, pleasant texture and are swallowed right
along with the fruit. Unnamed tropical guavas vary in flavor
from plant to plant. Named selections such as 'Mexican
Cream' will assure you of quality.

Plant guavas in full sun, in well-drained soil with a pH of
5 to 7. Strawberry guava needs less fertilizer than the fast-
growing tropical guavas, which benefit from an annual dose
of high-nitrogen fertilizer (½ pound actual nitrogen for a mature tree).

The plants begin to bear 2 to 3 years after planting and
ripen over a long period, sometimes from spring to fall, and
sometimes almost a year. Ripe fruit turns from green to yellowish green and, for some cultivars, has a musky perfume.

A few pesky insects in Florida can cause problems that will

threaten your harvest. Ask your extension agent about prevalence and control of guava whitefly, guava moth, and Caribbean fruit fly.

■ RECOMMENDED VARIETIES OF TROPICAL GUAVAS

Varieties will grow only in zones 9 and 10. They are evergreen small trees or large shrubs 15 to 25 ft. tall. All are self-fruitful.

Hong Kong Pink
Description of fruit: Medium to large fruit, sweet pink flesh.

Indonesian Seedless
Description of fruit: Firm, white flesh with good flavor.

Mexican Cream
Description of fruit: Small fruit with sweet white flesh.

Red Indian
Description of fruit: Small to medium fruit with red flesh, little muskiness.

Ruby
Description of fruit: Medium-size fruit with sweet red flesh.

Supreme
Description of fruit: Large fruit with sweet white flesh.

White Indian
Description of fruit: Small fruit with tangy flavor, white flesh.

Loquats

Known also as Japanese medlar or plum, loquats more closely resemble apricots and taste like orangy pears. Although they do best in areas with mild winters, you can grow them as far north as zone 7 if you give them a sheltered spot. Temperatures below 20°F will damage the foliage, while the tree itself can withstand 12°F. The oval or pear-shaped, 1- to 2-inch fruits of loquats may be white or yellow inside. As a rule, white-fleshed cultivars do best in areas with cool summers, while yellow-fleshed fruits thrive in areas with warm summers. Where summer sun is intense, plant yellow-fleshed loquats in light shade to avoid sunburned fruit.

Like other tender fruits, loquat trees *(Eriobotrya japonica)* are often grown as ornamentals. Their regular, round-headed form reaches about 15 to 30 feet tall in the landscape, although the trees can be kept pruned to smaller size in containers for at least several years. They have unusual bold evergreen leaves, with prominent veins and toothed edges, glossy on top and covered with rust-colored down on their light green undersides.

To be sure of getting good-quality fruit, choose grafted young trees of named cultivars. Plant them in well-drained soil, in full sun or partial shade. The woolly, fragrant flowers smell good to gardeners and bees alike, and the plant hums with all kinds of nectar-seeking insects when in flower, something to keep in mind if you're planning to grow them near your picnic table or swingset. Established trees will shrug off drought, but young trees need an inch of water every two weeks. No pruning or training is necessary.

Most loquats are self-pollinating and bear in four to six years after planting. Borne in clusters at the tips of branches, the round fruits are aromatic and sweet-tart in taste, with large seeds in the center. As they ripen, they change from green to yellow or orange, depending on the cultivar.

Fire blight can be a problem for loquats. If you see signs of scorched-looking foliage and dying twig tips, remove them by cutting the stem back 12 inches past the point of damage. Destroy the blighted clippings and sterilize your shears between cuts.

■ RECOMMENDED VARIETIES OF LOQUATS

Self-fruitful unless otherwise noted. All here can be grown as far north as zone 7. Trees are hardy to 12°F; foliage damaged below 20°F; flowers damaged by frosts. White-fleshed cultivars do best where summers are cool; those with yellow flesh need more warmth to increase the sugar content of the fruit.

Advance
Description of fruit: Medium to large white-fleshed fruit with good flavor.
Comments: Needs pollinator.

Big Jim
Description of fruit: Large oval orange fruit with sweet orange flesh.
Comments: Upright habit.

Bradenton
Description of fruit: Large, light yellow, sweet-tart fruit with white flesh.
Comments: Vigorous tree, upright habit.

Loquat is a handsome evergreen tree bearing small apricotlike fruit that tastes like an orangy pear.

Fletcher Red
Description of fruit: Large oval orange-red fruit with reddish flesh and fine flavor.
Comments: Upright habit. Best in warm-summer areas.

Gold Nugget
Description of fruit: Small round orange fruit with sweet-tart yellow-orange flesh.
Comments: Vigorous upright tree.

MacBeth
Description of fruit: Extra-large yellow fruit with creamy flesh.
Comments: Vigorous tree.

Premier
Description of fruit: Light yellow oblong fruit with very sweet white flesh.
Comments: Small, slow-growing tree.

Tanaka (Tanakas)
Description of fruit: Large golden fruit with sweet-tart orange-yellow flesh.
Comments: Vigorous tree.

Mangoes

The "peach of the tropics" is unfortunately one of the most tender fruits. Flowers and fruit are killed at less than 32°F, young trees at 28°F, and mature trees at 25°F. If you don't live in a frost-free climate, you can try a mango in a pot; smaller cultivars are available, and a combination of pruning and the dwarfing that occurs from restricted root systems will keep the tree a manageable size.

Mango trees *(Mangifera indica)* are evergreens that usually reach about 20 to 30 feet tall in cultivation. They have a wide-spreading crown and dense, narrow leaves, with new growth often tinged red. Creamy yellow to red flowers are borne in long sprays at the end of each branch, with hundreds of flowers in each cluster. The fruits dangle on long "strings," an eye-catching arrangement. They're good landscape plants in frost-free climates if you plant them where ripe, dropped fruit won't cause a nuisance.

Fruit quality and ripening time are considerations when choosing cultivars. Many mango fanciers prefer cultivars with fiberless or nearly fiber-free flesh; some excellent ones are included in the list of cultivars, beginning on page 366. In

Mangoes dangle from long stems and taste like flowery peaches.

Florida and Hawaii, where anthracnose is a problem, look for the spring- and summer-ripening anthracnose-resistant Indian types. Early cultivars like 'Earlygold' are ready for picking from May to June. 'Tommy Atkins' and later cultivars are ripe from July to August. In California, where anthracnose is usually not a problem (except in some areas near the coast), gardeners grow Indo-Chinese types, which ripen in fall and winter. 'Kenny' ripens in October and 'Reliable' in January.

Plant young grafted trees in well-drained soil of pH 5.5 to 7.5, in full sun. The trees anchor themselves with a taproot, which means they must be given extra care during transplanting. Mangoes need thorough watering (at least 1 inch) once a week to produce a profusion of flowers and a bounty of fruit. Many trees show a tendency to bear heavily one year and lightly the next. There isn't much you can do about it, because the tree will replace pinched flowers.

Ripe fruit turns hues of green, yellow, purple, and red, depending on cultivar. To test for readiness, cup a mango in your hand and squeeze lightly with your thumb as you would to test a peach. The fruit is ready for eating when soft to the touch. An easy way to eat a mango is to peel the skin a bit at a time with a paring knife and cut chunks or slices of the juicy flesh away from the large flat seed. The flesh is firmly attached to the seed so you won't get it all off. But kids love to suck the seed clean. Fruit that isn't devoured on the spot can be stored in a cool dry place, above 55°F, for up to three or four weeks.

■ RECOMMENDED VARIETIES OF MANGOES

Mangoes for Florida
Fruits have nonfibrous flesh unless otherwise noted.

ANTHRACNOSE-RESISTANT CULTIVARS

Earlygold
Description of fruit: Medium-size yellow-green fruit. Early.
Comments: Small tree. Light crops.

Parvin
Description of fruit: Large pink-red fruit. Flesh almost free of fibers. Very late.
Comments: Light producer.

Saigon
Description of fruit: Small yellow-green fruit. Midseason.
Comments: Upright tree.

Tommy Atkins
Description of fruit: Large yellow-red fibrous fruit. Midseason.
Comments: Moderate resistance to anthracnose.

ANTHRACNOSE-SUSCEPTIBLE CULTIVARS

Adams
Description of fruit: Small red fruit. Midseason.
Comments: Upright, lightly spreading tree.

Carrie
Description of fruit: Medium-size yellow-green fruit. Midseason.
Comments: Small tree.

Kent
Description of fruit: Large multicolored fruit. Late.
Comments: Small seed.

Palmer
Description of fruit: Large yellow-red almost fiber-free fruit.
Late season.
Comments: Open tree.

Mangoes for California
Except where noted, all are susceptible to anthracnose, a disease usually not prevalent in California.

Aloha
Description of fruit: Variable size (small to large) red fruit.
Almost fiber-free. Midseason.
Comments: Light producer.

Kenny
Description of fruit: Small multicolor fruit. Early.
Comments: Light producer.

Reliable
Description of fruit: Variable size (small to large) red-yellow
fruit. Almost fiber-free. Late.
Comments: Domed crown.

Villasenor
Description of fruit: Medium pink and green fruit. Late.
Comments: Spreading tree. Anthracnose-resistant.

Planting Fruit Trees and Bushes

Fruits and berries are working plants. Domesticated for centuries, they have been bred for bigness. The baseball-size apple of today is descended from fruits the size of peas. Strawberries, whose wild ancestors would fit three to a thimble, now rival plums in size.

Breeding has not only increased the size of fruits but also the size of crops. A strawberry plant the breadth of a dinner plate can have at any moment half a dozen fruits of different ages that outweigh the leaves and stems twentyfold. An apple tree can yield one 4-inch fruit for every eight leaves.

To nurture and support this bounty, fruits and berries need good growing conditions. All the elements responsible for growth — sun, fertile soil, and water — have to be present in generous amounts. In this chapter we'll discuss locating your plants so that they receive all the sun they need and avoid damaging encounters with frost and wind. We'll examine how to prepare the soil and set the plants in the ground to give them a good start in life. (Providing supplementary water and fertilizer are covered in the chapter "Ongoing Care.")

This discussion is, of necessity, general. Most of the plants in this book can be treated as described here. Special requirements are discussed in the chapters on individual fruits and berries. It is also a good idea to consult with a knowledgeable person at a local or specialty mail-order nursery or with your extension agent to see if there are any local conditions that affect planting and care of specific fruits and berries.

Sun

Location, location, location — it's just as vital when planting fruit trees as it is when buying real estate. The more sun, the greater the crop. Like all plants, fruits and berries convert sunlight into the sugars and starches that build roots, stems, leaves, and fruits. They do best in unfiltered, unobstructed sunlight, morning to evening, from the beginning of the growing season right through to harvest. Grown in full sun, the plant forms stout stems and branches and is compactly branched according to its natural habit.

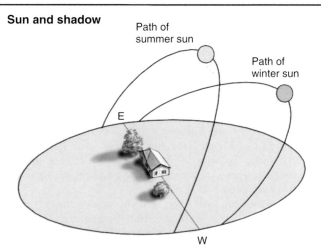

Sun and shadow

Path of summer sun

Path of winter sun

E

W

Site your fruit trees and bushes so they receive ample sun. You can anticipate shadows by thinking of the path of the sun during different times of year, as shown here. In summer, the sun travels slightly north of an east-west line through your property. In winter, the sun is much lower, traveling south of the same line.

Survey your property for a site with full sun. First, look for places that have open views to the southern half of the sky. Note the trees and buildings to the east, south, and west, and their distance from the site you have in mind. Then picture where their shadows will fall throughout the day.

For reference, imagine an east-west line running through the site. (See the drawing opposite.) In spring and fall, when the day is only eight to ten hours long, the sun rises and sets south of the line. It tracks across the sky at a low angle, reaching about 45 degrees above the horizon at midday. In midmorning and late afternoon, trees and buildings cast long shadows. By summer, the sun is rising and setting north of the line, tracking higher in the sky, and passing almost overhead at midday. The day lasts 14 hours or more and the shadows are far shorter in midmorning and late afternoon.

When you have a good idea where the shadows of trees and buildings fall throughout the growing season, note the site or sites with the most sun. Then consider exposure, frost, and soil as discussed below before making final decisions.

Partial shade

Fruits and berries in partial shade grow less vigorously than they would in full sun. Shoots elongate, becoming thinner and weaker, flowering is reduced, and so is the subsequent harvest. Plants have smaller reserves of energy to fuel their growth in early spring, a critical time when many fruits and berries flower and set fruits. And what fruit is produced may taste insipid, or worse, having been scanted on sugars ordinarily produced by a full ration of photosynthesis. Shaded leaves also stay wet longer after a rain or a watering, increasing chances of diseases like scab and mildew. Plants have less energy to ward off these diseases and damage from pests. Finally, they may have too little energy to bear a full crop year after year. Often, plants in partial shade bear a reasonable crop one year, a light crop the next, and so on.

Nevertheless, if you have no areas of full sun on your property, don't give up hope. A few fruit trees, including American persimmons and sour cherries, will bear well in light, partial shade. It is also possible to raise reasonable crops of other fruits and berries on a site that has less than full sun. But there are limits. The plants must have direct sun for at least six hours during the middle of the day (from 9:00 or 10:00 A.M. to 3:00 or 4:00 P.M. in summer) when the sunlight is most intense. Try only fruits that mature in the summer and fall — raspberries, blackberries, apples, peaches, pears, plums. What they lack in sun from day to day, they can partly make up over a long growing season. Plants that yield harvests in spring and early summer, like strawberries, will be setting and ripening fruits when the sun is still low in the sky. They need more than six hours of weak sunlight to do the job.

Exposure

Shelter from the cold, drying winds of winter and the last frosts of spring sometimes makes the difference between a full crop of fruit and a modest or even meager crop. If you chose fruits and varieties that are hardy in your region, they'll emerge from most winters unscathed. But now and then, in an extreme winter or a late frost, they may suffer enough damage to limit the crop. Shelter provides a margin of insurance.

Fruit trees vary widely in hardiness. The most cold-hardy varieties of apples, pears, and cherries will flower and fruit without a sign of distress after winters as cold as -30°F and even -40°F. On the other hand, few peaches can tolerate temperatures lower than -10°F. But no matter how hardy the tree, when the temperature nears the limit of its tolerance, protection from wind will help the buds survive.

As fruit plants awaken from their winter sleep, they rapidly lose their winter hardiness. Long before they break dormancy, they are vulnerable to freezing temperatures that would have left them unfazed just weeks earlier. As the buds of fruit trees open, and as flowers appear, both can be killed outright by temperatures in the mid-20s. The emerging shoots of brambles likewise can be killed by late frosts (the plants will send up new shoots eventually, but the harvest will be later and smaller).

Shelter

You can't do much to change the weather, but you can position your fruit trees and bushes to take advantage of variations in its local manifestations. Fences, windbreaks, trees, and buildings offer protection from winter winds, or shade from blast-furnace sun on summer afternoons. These small enclaves are sometimes called "microclimates" because conditions in them can differ in significant ways from those in adjacent, unprotected areas.

Consider planting heat-loving fruits, such as grapes, against a masonry wall or near the house, where the mass of the building releases heat. A south-facing slope, wall, or niche in a building wall may heat up days earlier than spots with northern exposures.

A sunny south or southeast exposure can jump-start spring, but that's not always a good idea. If your spring weather is fickle, and late spring frosts are a possibility, you're better off planting on a north-facing slope or the north side of your house, away from the teasing warmth of the early spring sun. Planted in a cool spot, the tightly furled buds of an early bloomer such as peach or apricot may avoid decimation when that unexpected blue norther whirls down out of Canada and turns the delicate pink buds opening on trees in sunny southern exposures into brown mush.

Frost pockets

Cold air sinks to the low spots in a landscape just like cold water settles to the bottom of a lake. A little valley in your garden may look like the perfect location for a fruit tree, its sheltering sides offering respite from wind, but this inviting locale could be a trap. The cold air that drains downhill on clear spring nights will settle and pool there, possibly lowering temperatures enough to damage buds and flowers. Hedges, fences, and buildings on a slope can also interrupt and prevent cold air from flowing downhill.

To keep your fruit trees and bushes out of harm's way, plant them above frost pockets in the landscape or situate them on an unimpeded slope. When planting on a hill, it's best to plant near the top rather than at the bottom, where cold air may collect. If you want to plant near a solid fence that might trap cool air, you could redesign the fence to allow air to move through or under it.

Soil

Just as fruits and berries need sun to yield well, they also need a steady supply of nutrients and water. They grow best in soil that is reasonably fertile, moisture-retentive, and well drained. Fortunately, most fruits are very adaptable when it comes to soil and will grow in conditions that fit a great number of gardens in North America.

Drainage

Except for elderberries, fruit trees and bushes do not like wet feet. Roots need air in the pores of the soil around them to grow and take up water and nutrients actively. If water saturates the soil, driving out the air, the roots grow less active. In prolonged wet spells they may even die, suffocated by lack of oxygen or killed by root rot and other fungal problems that are exacerbated by wet conditions.

Soils that drain too quickly also cause problems. If the soil dries out, even briefly, when fruits are small and growing rapidly, the crop suffers. The fruits stop growing temporarily and never reach the size they would have with uninterrupted moisture.

Deep, loose soil high in organic matter drains well but holds sufficient water and is excellent for fruit plants. Most fruits will also thrive in clay soils, although heavy clay can slow the growth of trees. Sandy, fast-draining soils may not hold enough water to support the tree or its crop of fruit.

To find out what kind of soil you have, trowel up a handful. Rub some between your fingers. If it feels greasy or slippery, your soil has lots of clay. It's likely to drain slowly. If the soil feels gritty, there's sand in it, and drainage is likely to be good, or even fast. Or squeeze a handful of soil. When you open your hand and the soil holds together tightly, even if you poke it, the chances are the soil has a lot of clay in it. If it falls apart without poking, it has a lot of sand in it.

Testing drainage

If you're uncertain about the drainage on the sunny site that seems best for your plants, test it. Let the garden hose run slowly in the middle of the site for an hour, until the ground is saturated. Then dig a narrow hole on the spot, about 9 inches wide and 9 inches deep. Fill the hole with water and time how long the water takes to drain into the soil completely.

If the time is less than one hour, your soil is so well-drained that you will have to water your plants every few days during any spell of dry, warm weather. If the time is more than four hours, the soil is likely to become saturated during a long wet spell, and your plants may suffer. If the time falls between one and four hours, your soil holds moisture well but is also reasonably well drained. It's fine for fruits and berries. In heavy soils, a gentle slope can hasten water movement through the soil.

Soil that drains too quickly or too slowly can sometimes be improved with amendments (outlined below). More severe problems may require installation of drain lines, or you may decide to plant in raised beds or containers. If you think drainage poses a big problem, professional advice is often well worth the expense.

Soil fertility and pH

Most fruit and berry plants will do just fine in soil of average fertility. If other shrubs and trees grow well on your property, fruit and berry plants are likely to do so, too. Moderate to slow drainage is another sign that the soil has enough fertility for fruits and berries.

The best way to determine soil fertility is to test it. Call the local office of the state extension service and ask for a soil-test kit. The instructions that come with the kit will tell you how to take a soil sample and send it to the testing laboratory run by the extension service. (If the extension service doesn't have a lab, ask them to recommend a private one.)

Tell them what fruits and berries you'd like to grow, and the lab will send you a report that tells how much of the main nutrients (nitrogen, phosphorus, and potassium) you need to apply to the soil to grow them. You can add this as commercial fertilizer or use organic amendments such as compost and aged manure. (See the discussion below.)

The lab will also report the pH of your soil, the measure of its alkalinity or acidity. Sometimes it seems as though gardeners pay more attention to pH levels than plants do — if common plants flourish in your garden, you'll most likely have no problem growing fruit trees and most berry bushes.

Acidity and alkalinity are indicated by pH on a scale from 0 to 14, with 7 being neutral. Numbers above 7 indicate alkaline soil, those below, acid. Soils in the Pacific Northwest and the East are likely to be moderately acidic, with a pH of 5.0 to 6.5 (pH 4.0 is the acidity of orange juice). Midwestern soils are mostly near-neutral (pH 6.5 to 7.5). Soils of the dry West may be moderately to severely alkaline (pH 7.5 to 8.0 are mildly alkaline; ammonia has a pH of 11.5).

If your soil pH proves problematic, or if you need to cater to the finicky pH preferences of blueberries, you can alter pH with amendments. Ground limestone, or lime, is used to tone down highly acid soils; acidic elemental sulfur is commonly used to temper extremely alkaline soils. Changing the pH level of your soil is a tricky business, because amounts of amendments vary depending on soil type as well as the starting point of the pH. Follow the recommendations of the lab test for best results. (See the chapter on blueberries for specific recommendations for that plant.)

Soil amendments

Small fruit and berry plants can be planted, just like their ornamental cousins, grouped in large, specially prepared beds in which the soil has been dug and amended with compost and other organic material. Trees and larger bushes are usually planted in individual holes. Gardeners have long been encouraged to "improve" the soil in these holes. The idea was to fill the hole with a generous dollop of compost, a shovelful of fine peat moss, a few scoops of rich, well-aged manure to produce a wonderful mix that any roots would thrive in.

According to recent research, however, such pampering actually causes problems. Roots may like the amended soil so well that they are reluctant to reach out into the less hospitable soil beyond the planting hole. A planting hole dug in hard impervious soil and filled with fluffy absorbent material may create a sink that draws in and holds water just like a sponge. Some growers call this the "sponge-in-a-teacup" effect. In the short run, extra nitrogen in a rich mix of amendments can cause a spurt of succulent new growth that is inviting to aphids and other insect pests and certain diseases.

But what if your soil is dry and loose or heavy and compacted? Digging in compost, humus, rotted manure, or other organic matter certainly improves the tilth and drainage of clay or sandy soils. You just need to improve a much larger area than the planting hole. Think big right from the start — work on an area that is at least half as big as you estimate the full grown tree will require. Many roots of a standard apple tree, for example, will occupy an area within about a 20-foot radius of its trunk. So you should improve an area with at least a 10-foot radius. Sow and till under a crop of "green manure," such as ryegrass, the year before planting. Add abundant amounts of compost, decomposed leaves, aged manure, and other organic materials. You may need to incorporate as little as 5 percent organic matter or as much as 50 percent, depending on the condition of your original soil.

Raised beds

Where soils are very poor, very acidic, or very alkaline, or where drainage proves an insurmountable problem, you can often grow fruits and berries in raised beds. (If raised beds won't work either, try growing plants in containers; see the discussion at the end of this chapter.)

The fastest way to make a raised bed is to dump a lot of compost and organic material on your soil, till or dig it in, and rake the amended soil into a mound. A raised bed 18 to 24 inches high and 3 to 4 feet wide should be adequate for dwarf fruit trees and small to moderate-size berry bushes. On very waterlogged soil, raised beds should be 2 to 3 feet deep. To keep beds tidy, you may want to enclose them with retaining walls, in effect making very large bottomless containers.

Lacking abundant supplies of compost, most gardeners buy topsoil and organic amendments by the truckload for raised beds. Most plants will do well in a mix of half garden soil or imported topsoil, one-quarter compost and one-quarter manure. Some plants, such as blueberries, have very specific soil requirements. Since you're going to all the trouble of making your own soil, tailor it for the plants you wish to grow.

Buying Plants

Many gardeners prefer to buy plants locally rather than from mail-order nurseries. At a trusted local nursery, you can personally select vigorous, generously sized specimens and receive advice from staff who know what grows particularly well in your area.

Unfortunately, many local nurseries and garden centers carry only a handful of varieties and may not carry some types of fruits and berries at all. If you want a wider choice, explore the offerings of mail-order nurseries specializing in fruits and berries. (See "Sources of Supply" in the back of this book.) They offer a mouthwatering selection — 20 kinds of plums, a hundred kinds of apples, 50 different grapes. Some of the fruits just gaining popularity, such as pawpaws and edible cacti, can be found only through mail-order sources. Mail-order fruits and berries are often priced and sold according to size and age, so plants may be bigger and better than those you can select locally. (Your local nursery may be able to order something for you from these or other suppliers, too.)

Most mail-order fruit trees and bushes are sold as dormant bare-root plants; that is, they're not in active growth and their roots have been washed free of soil. Bare-root plants are lighter (soil is heavy to ship), and they don't run afoul of state prohibitions against importing soil that might contain pests and diseases. Nurseries and garden centers frequently purchase their plants from wholesalers as bare-root trees and bushes. Sometimes they'll sell them in the same form, usually wrapping the roots in plastic or putting them in tubs of damp sawdust or peat. Or they might "containerize" the plant, potting it up for sale — a practice with obvious advantages once the plant begins to dry out or break dormancy. Few hardy fruits and berries are raised in pots — true "container-grown" plants — but many tender plants, such as citrus trees, are. Fruit trees are less often sold as balled-and-burlapped plants, the roots and native soil bound tightly in a burlap wrapping.

Bare-root plants may look unpromising, but they are a good start for a home fruit garden. The stock is usually priced reasonably, and the plants establish root systems in the garden easily, if you water generously while they make the transition. Containerized bare-root plants behave in the same way and require the same care. True container-grown plants usually cost more than bare-root plants. They are quick to become established, because their roots suffer little transplant shock when lifted from container to garden. (To tell the difference between a "containerized" and a "container-grown" plant, slide the container partway off the root ball. The root ball of a container-grown plant will be thick with small feeder roots; a containerized plant won't have had the time to establish an extensive root system.) Don't pay a premium for containerized plants; if bare-root plants are cheaper and are healthy, buy them.

In the past, fruit trees were most often sold as year-old unbranched stems, thin and lithe, called "whips." Today, many are sold as branched trees, with the first steps of training already underway. At least a full year older than whips, these trees will bear earlier and probably cost more. Whips are still popular, especially with mail-order nurseries, and they grow just as well as branched trees. Fruit and berry bushes, such as grapes, are often pruned heavily before shipping and may be little more than a crown with attached roots and, perhaps, one or more short shoots.

If you're picking your own plants from a local nursery, do so early in the season and select plants that are soundly dormant. Look for well-formed trees with a sturdy trunk and well-spaced branches. Check for twigs that are plump, not shriveled or dried out. Pass up plants with split bark or other injuries. There may be less to inspect with bushes, but make sure what is there isn't damaged or diseased, that roots, stems, shoots, and buds look healthy. Beware of end-of-season leftovers that haven't been potted and well cared for.

True container-grown plants can be planted at any time of the year. In cold-winter areas, bare-root plants (and "containerized" bare-root plants) should be planted in the spring. Planting dormant trees in fall is an advantage for gardeners in mild-winter areas, where the soil temperature holds above 50°F for several weeks after the trees become dormant, because the roots have time to become established before the tree breaks dormancy in spring.

Before Planting

It is always best to put a new plant in the ground as soon as possible. You can usually time the purchase of plants from a local nursery to accommodate quick planting. But sometimes planting has to wait. Plants in containers tolerate delay. Buy them one weekend, and you can safely let them sit for another week or even two, as long as you keep them watered and out of harsh conditions (too much sun, wind, or cold).

Bare-root plants, especially those sent mail-order, can cause problems if not planted immediately. Although they may seem tough, those roots are fragile and need protection from damage and desiccation. Good mail-order nurseries pack bare-root plants for survival, protected by layers of excelsior or damp newspaper, so chances are they've arrived in good shape, even if the box baked in the sun all day waiting for you to get home from work. If you can, plant them before you even have a cup of coffee. But if you can't, you have several options.

If you can plant the next morning, you can place the plants in a tub of water. No longer than 24 hours, though — roots rot swiftly underwater. To store for up to two weeks, pop the

Heeling in

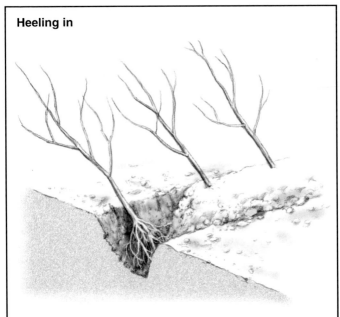

If you can't plant bare-root plants for several weeks after receiving them, you can "heel them in" by laying them at an angle in a shallow garden trench and covering the roots with soil.

plants into a container. A metal or plastic tub or muck bucket or even a heavy-duty, large-size plastic garbage bag will work well. Put the plants, roots first, into the container and fill it with shredded newspaper, potting soil, wood shavings, or other loose absorbent material. Add water until the material is about as wet as a squeezed-out sponge. Wait between waterings to allow the material to absorb the water. Keep the plants in a cool, shady place until you're ready to plant.

If you must hold off planting for more than two weeks, your only choice is to "heel in" the plants. (See drawing above.) Dig a trench with one slanted and one straight side. Place the plants so that the trunks are supported by the slanted side, then cover the roots with soil. This is almost as much work as planting, but it is effective.

Spacing

Before digging any planting holes, think about spacing. Be generous when spacing fruit plants. Think of the plant's mature size, not the tiny crown or whip in your hand. Allow room for each plant to grow freely and without competition from neighboring plants and room enough to provide easy access for care and harvesting.

Consult the recommendations in this book for spacing specific types of fruit; check the nursery catalog or the plant's hangtag, too. As a general rule, allow as much space for a tree as its height at maturity. Most standard fruit trees require 20 to 40 feet of space (10 to 20 feet from one tree to the next). Semidwarfs need 12 to 20 feet; dwarfs, 6 to 12 feet. Blueberries and other bushes are usually planted about 3 to 8 feet apart, depending on the ultimate size of the plant; grapes require spacing of 4 to 20 feet, depending on how vigorously they grow. Trees and bushes planted as a hedge can be spaced more closely, so that their branches overlap and knit together.

Planting

Planting fruits and berries is as easy as planting other trees and bushes — you dig a hole, set the plant in, fill the hole, and water. There's a little more to it than that, of course, which we'll cover in the following discussion.

Start with a bit of housekeeping. Snip off any dead or damaged branches, canes, or roots. Trim any roots that encircle the root ball and can't be straightened out by gently combing with your hand. Remove any wires or plastic ties from the roots or stems. (If you want to label the plant, use freestanding markers rather than attached nursery tags, which can cut into swelling tissue as the branches or canes grow.) Check packaged, plastic-wrapped blackberries or other small fruits for wires or plastic cord, which is sometimes wrapped around the roots to hold several plants together, creating the appearance of a single robust plant.

Soak the root ball of plants in containers and let the soil drain. It doesn't hurt to soak the roots of a newly purchased bare-root plant for several hours in a solution of tepid water and about one quarter the recommended dosage of a balanced, all-purpose liquid fertilizer.

Into the ground

For trees, dig a hole wide enough to comfortably accommodate the roots, 1 to 2 feet deep, depending on the size of the roots and the height of the graft union (discussed below). For bushes and vines, dig a hole in which the roots can be spread comfortably and deep enough to position the crown at the level it was growing in the nursery.

Most fruit trees are grafted, with a visible bump called the graft union where rootstock and top scionwood were joined. Position the graft union several inches above ground level. This is especially important with dwarf cultivars — the rootstock is what keeps the tree small; if the grafted top wood comes into contact with the soil, it may grow roots and negate the effect of the dwarfing rootstock. If you're planting a tree on its own roots, position it at the height it was growing at the nursery. The original soil line is often visible at the base of the trunk.

To judge the depth accurately, set the plant in the hole. Don't remove containers or burlap yet; for bare-root plants, mound a cone of soil in the bottom of the hole and spread the roots over it. (See drawing below.) Place a straight stick across the hole to indicate the eventual soil level on the trunk or crown. You'll probably have to do some fine-tuning,

Planting bare-root trees and bushes

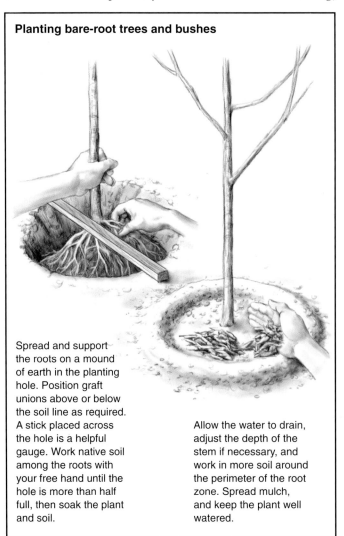

Spread and support the roots on a mound of earth in the planting hole. Position graft unions above or below the soil line as required. A stick placed across the hole is a helpful gauge. Work native soil among the roots with your free hand until the hole is more than half full, then soak the plant and soil.

Allow the water to drain, adjust the depth of the stem if necessary, and work in more soil around the perimeter of the root zone. Spread mulch, and keep the plant well watered.

adding or removing a bit of soil. When you move them, don't lift potted or balled-and-burlapped plants by the trunk or stems; hold the container or the root ball instead.

Digging with a shovel, especially in clay soils, can make the walls of the planting hole slick and solid. Once you've gotten the depth and width right, scratch the walls and the bottom of the hole with a garden fork or claw hand tool to make it easier for roots to penetrate as they grow.

Now, settle the plants into place for good. Spread bare roots over the soil mound. Add native soil (the stuff you dug out of the hole, not amended soil), working it around the roots to eliminate air pockets. When the hole is half-filled, soak the soil with water and let it drain thoroughly. Finish filling the hole and firmly tamp the surface with your hands or a foot, forming a shallow depression that will help hold water. Water deeply again, applying a slow, gentle stream to avoid washing away the soil.

The process is much the same for plants in containers and balled-and-burlapped plants. Carefully slide off the container and lower the intact root ball into the hole, disturbing the soil as little as possible. (Root disturbance is less a problem for bare-root plants only recently containerized at the nursery.) Place balled-and-burlapped plants into the hole with wrappings intact, then carefully unwrap the rootball, sliding the material (which is usually plastic) out from under with as little disturbance as possible. Fill the hole halfway with native soil and proceed as described for bare-root plants.

Stake and wrap the trunks of trees as described below, then spread a deep layer of mulch to conserve moisture and prevent weeds. Six inches of grass clippings, straw, compost, or other organic materials will do the trick. Keep the mulch 2 inches from the trunk to avoid fungal problems and reduce the danger of damage from tunneling rodents.

Depending on what kind of tree or bush you're planting, there may be some pruning to do at planting time. This is covered in the next chapter.

Staking and wrapping trees

Today, many arborists believe that staking trees provides mixed rewards at best. The price of protection in the early years can be weakness later on because the tree grows to rely on the artificial support rather than fully developing its own strength.

While this is true in general, there are several circumstances in which you should stake new fruit trees. Trees exposed to strong winds should be staked to prevent the swaying top of the tree from dislodging the grip of roots that aren't yet firmly established in the soil. Trees grafted to root stocks can also benefit from staking, which helps protect the graft union, a weak point that can unknit from the force of wind and weather. Although this is an unusual mishap, orchardists recommend staking grafted trees for at least the first year. Those grafted to dwarfing root stocks are less vigorous growers and can be staked for a few years, to prevent undue stress on the grafting bond.

Whips and small branched trees can be supported by a single 2×2 wood stake. (See drawing below.) Drive the stake 18 to 24 inches deep into the excavated hole before planting the

Staking trees

A single stake will support small trees. Drive it into the planting hole before planting the tree. Support a larger tree with 2 stakes, driven outside the perimeter of the hole before or after planting. Cover the ties with hose or plastic tubing to protect the trunk. Ties should be loose enough to allow some movement of the trunk.

tree, positioning it next to the rootball of a containerized plant or several inches from the tree's trunk for a bare-root plant (the roots can be spread around the stake). Driving a stake after planting risks damaging roots. Plant the tree, then secure it to the trunk with a tie placed about halfway up the trunk. The tie should be soft enough not to abrade the bark, yet sturdy enough to hold the tree in place, and it shouldn't rot away in a few weeks. Don't bind the tree tightly to the stake — the idea is to support the tree in strong winds, not to confine it in a straitjacket. Allowing the tree some motion in the wind helps to strengthen the trunk.

Older, larger trees may require more substantial support. After planting, you can drive in two or three 2×2 stakes, spaced equally around the perimeter of the planting hole. Cut pieces of strong wire, each one long enough to reach from stake to tree, around and back to stake. Allow several extra inches for twisting the ends together, and for a bit of slack at each support. To protect the tree from being cut or rubbed by the wire, cut three pieces, each about 6 to 8 inches long, from a section of old garden hose, and thread the wire through it.

Place the hose-covered wires close together on the trunk, about halfway up its height. Twist the ends of the wire together around each stake. Take up most of the slack in the wires by further twisting, but don't make the trunk immobile.

Mice, voles, and other rodents love to nibble on fruit tree bark, and they can easily girdle a trunk and kill the tree in a single season. Thwart them with a purchased plastic tree guard, a rolled-up strip of plastic that slips easily around trunks of any size. Tree guards are often perforated to allow light and air to circulate around the trunk. They're widely available at garden centers and through mail-order catalogs. They won't harm the tree, so you can leave them on as long as they fit.

Growing Fruits and Berries in Containers

If you're dying to grow blueberries but despair of altering your soil's pH enough to satisfy them, or if you live in Minnesota and want to grow lemons or feijoas, container gardening may be your best (or only) chance. Container gardens are also ideal for folks with limited space. A dwarf fruit tree can live and fruit happily in a wooden half-barrel and some citrus will grow well in 12-inch pots. Container-grown plants require attention — a vigorous plant depletes the supply of water and nutrients in a tub of soil much faster than its counterpart planted in the garden. And if you're interested in growing plants otherwise too tender for your area, remember that lugging 200 pounds of tree and earth indoors for the winter is no small undertaking.

Containers and soil mixes

Like other plants, fruits and berries will grow in almost any container that allows the soil in it to drain. For ease of moving, lightweight plastic pots and tubs are a good choice; they're also long-lasting. If you're not fond of the plastic look, slip the pot inside a basket for camouflage. Terra-cotta pots are lovely but are expensive in large sizes, as are decorative stone or composite urns. Wooden containers are always popular, from half-barrels to the classic citrus container used in formal European gardens — a white wooden box 24 to 36 inches square, decorated with intricate designs and finished off with finials at the corner. You don't need to be an expert carpenter to make a simpler version.

Regardless of the material, remember that the larger the container the heavier it will be when filled with soil. Before you add soil, position in their intended spot those containers that you don't plan to move, and fit heavy-duty casters on those that you do. Think about the route you'll have to take to move a big container from your deck or patio to its winter quarters in the sunroom, garage, or basement before you plant — if you "can't get there from here," you may have to alter your plans.

One of the advantages of container growing is the ability to tailor soil to plants — check the preferences of the plants you want to grow. Regardless of how you amend it for this or that plant, "soil" for container plants usually performs best when it contains no actual soil at all. Garden soil carries diseases and weed seeds; placed in a container, it often drains poorly. Most potting soils are mixtures of organic materials, such as peat moss and ground bark, and lightweight minerals, such as perlite and vermiculite.

Many fruit trees and bushes will grow well in commercial potting soil mix if you pay regular attention to their water and nutrient needs. In general, commercial or homemade soilless potting mixes may not be rich enough to sustain growth over a number of years. To these, add anywhere from a third to a half of additional organic matter such as compost, leaf mold, or well-rotted manure. Adding large amounts of organic matter can retard drainage; supplement the mix with coarse sand or small gravel to restore drainage.

Large quantities of potting soil can be expensive, so you may want to make your own mix. If you're not concerned about the risk of soil-borne diseases, you can just mix good garden soil and compost, half and half. A good recipe that doesn't use garden soil directly calls for one part well-rotted compost, one part pulverized pine or fir bark, and one part perlite or vermiculite. Combine thoroughly (a wheelbarrow is a good working place), then mix in soil amendments for fertility and mineral balance. For each cubic foot of soil (about a scrub bucket's worth), mix in 1 pound rock phosphate, 1 pound granite dust, 4 ounces each of dolomitic limestone and greensand, and 2 ounces of blood meal.

Planting

Techniques for planting fruit trees and bushes in containers aren't that different from those for planting them in the ground. Water containerized plants thoroughly before removing them from the container in which they're sold. Soak bare-root plants for several hours in a weak solution of liquid fertilizer. If you're planting in terra cotta, soak the pot in water so it doesn't draw moisture from the potting soil.

Remove a container-grown plant from its pot, taking care to support the root ball as well as the trunk. Add enough moistened potting soil to the new pot to position the top surface of the root ball 1 to 3 inches below the rim (depending on the size of the container) to make watering easier. Place the root ball in the container, and work soil around the root ball and firm it in place; water thoroughly, then add more soil to spots that settle.

Bare-root plants are handled in much the same way. When the plant is positioned, work soil around the roots to eliminate air pockets, firm in place, water, and fill settled spots. When positioning plants grafted to dwarfing rootstocks, be careful to position the graft union 2 or 3 inches above the soil surface.

Plants do best when repotted in a succession of containers that increase in size as the plant grows. Starting a tree or shrub in a container suitable for the mature plant isn't impossible, but the extra soil retains more moisture than the plant can use, and soggy roots tend to rot. A newly purchased dwarf fruit tree growing in a 5-gallon plastic or fiber pot may eventually require a half whiskey barrel or wooden planter that holds as much as 30 or 40 gallons of soil. Along the way it will need a number of containers, each only inches wider and deeper than the last. (See Repotting below.)

Ongoing care

Plants in containers can dry out quickly, so check moisture levels regularly by digging into the soil with your fingers. Don't let the soil dry out completely between waterings. And don't let it get too moist — soggy soil can starve the plant of oxygen and can lead to root rot. Water slowly and thoroughly, letting the water sink in all the way to the bottom of the container. Mulch the soil surface with bark chips, large gravel, or similar material to conserve water and help keep the soil cool. A living mulch of annual plants can also shade the soil.

In addition to consistent moisture, you must provide a potted fruit tree or bush with a steady diet of nutrients. Use a balanced fertilizer (a 5-10-10 formula, for example) or one recommended specifically for the plant you're growing. Granular fertilizers may burn roots near the soil surface. Liquid fertilizers are easy to measure and less likely to burn. Slow-release tablets supply all necessary nutrients for periods of three to nine months or so.

Some gardeners feed container-grown plants monthly (if they're not using a slow-release fertilizer). Others feed every two weeks using half the monthly dose. Critical feeding times are when plants resume growth in the spring and at the peak of flowering. In general, don't feed plants into the fall; they need to slow their growth in preparation for winter.

Mineral salts from fertilizers accumulate in the soil and pot edges, and they can be damaging to roots and cause leaves to brown at the tips. If a build-up becomes apparent, you can flush these salts from the soil by trickling water from a hose slowly through the pot; let it run for as long as half an hour for a large pot. Scrub the salt residue from outside pot walls with a stiff brush.

Container-grown trees and bushes can be trained and pruned the same way as their in-ground counterparts. Some plants that don't require much or any pruning when grown in the ground may need to be cut back to restrict their size. Container-grown plants are also subject to the same ailments and pests as grown in-ground plants and will require about the same care.

Repotting

Trees and shrubs started as small plants need to be moved to larger pots as they grow. When growth begins to slow, check to see if roots have become overcrowded; if so, you should repot. Procedures for repotting are much like those for potting a new plant. Take care not to damage large plants when repotting; you may even need to disassemble or break the old container to preserve the root ball intact. Trim tangled roots or those that circle the pot. If the plant has "gotten away from you" and roots are densely overgrown, you may need to slice off as much as an inch from the sides and bottom of the root ball with a sharp knife.

Repot in a new container 2 to 4 inches larger in diameter and several inches deeper than the old. The permissible increase in size becomes larger in proportion to the container.

For example if you're repotting a plant that has outgrown a box 2 feet square and deep the next container might be 6 to 10 inches larger on each side. Use the same formula soil mix in which the plant has been growing.

At some time, it will no longer be practical to repot in a larger container. Top-dress the soil to keep a mature or near-mature plant happy in its present container. Remove as much as 3 or 4 inches of soil from the top surface of the root ball and replace it with organically enriched new soil. If growth slows and yield decreases, the plant may be root-bound and require more than top-dressing. In early spring, when the plant is dormant, prune the roots back by about 20 percent. Remove as much soil as possible and replace with a fresh mixture. Cut the top growth back correspondingly. This should help to rejuvenate the specimen and encourage it to fruit better.

Wintering over

Dealing with winter is probably the major concern of container gardeners who wish to grow fruits and berries. Even hardy fruits that could otherwise survive your winters outdoors may need special attention when grown in containers. There isn't enough soil to insulate the root ball from extreme temperatures, which may kill the plant, or rapid freezes and thaws, which can stress it and damage roots. Winter winds can shake the root ball, damage limbs, and desiccate tissue. Some experts suggest that container-grown plants intended for overwintering outdoors should have a hardiness rating at least one zone and sometimes two greater than yours. (Zone 6 gardeners should choose plants hardy in zone 5 or 4.)

If you chose to winter these plants outdoors, move them to a shady spot, protected from wind. In autumn after most of the leaves have dropped, wrap the trunks with a commercial tree wrap to help prevent loss of moisture and sun scald on the bark. If they can be moved, storage in an unheated shed or garage offers protection from wind and some moderation of temperature fluctuations.

You can also insulate a container by ringing it with bales of hay or bags of leaves. To minimize damage from wind, pull the branches of deciduous trees together and bind them with twine or rope, or cover them with burlap. For complete outdoor protection, build a cage around each plant. (See drawing on the facing page.) Use strong posts to anchor the cage and encircle the plant with chicken wire or chain link fencing. Tie the branches together, erect the cage, then fill it with leaves or straw; a covering of burlap or cloth is optional. Moisture can penetrate from above, but trunks and limbs are protected from the extremes of weather. In spring, gradually remove insulation from around plants. If the branches have been covered, expose them gradually to sunlight.

Trees that are marginally hardy in your area may need indoor shelter. To thrive and fruit, some (like peaches) will need two or three months in temperatures below 45°F; a cool basement or cellar might provide this. Continue routine maintenance such as removing dead leaves and watching for outbreaks of spider mites and aphids. It's usually best not to apply fertilizer until after the first of the year.

Citrus and other tender fruit usually need to come indoors during the winter — even gardeners in relatively mild-winter areas may need to move them inside for a few weeks. Trees that overwinter inside for extended periods require some special consideration. If you grow the trees outside in summer then move them indoors in winter, make slow transitions between locations. Abrupt changes in growing conditions will defoliate the tree. When taking trees outdoors for the first time, move them to a shady spot; then, over a period of a few weeks, move them into more sunlight. When you move the

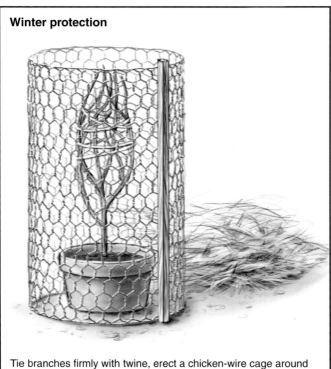

Winter protection

Tie branches firmly with twine, erect a chicken-wire cage around plant and pot, then fill the cage with leaves or straw. Cover surface with burlap for further protection.

trees indoors, reverse the process. Once outdoors, water the tree heavily to leach out salts that may have accumulated in the soil.

Inside, place the trees in a cool, well-lit area, away from heater vents or drafts. An attached greenhouse or solarium is ideal, but you can also keep a tree in a cool well-lit garage. Dry air will be one of the tree's greatest enemies, so either mist the tree often or keep a reservoir of water nearby. Be careful not to overwater or let the tree dry out. Provide as much light as possible.

Tender fruits need plenty of light to bear fruit. If you just want the plant to survive until spring, moderately low light, such as a bright window, will be enough. If you're trying to ripen fruit, provide the best light you can. Low-hung fluorescent lights will help a container plant in the house. A sunroom or greenhouse will give you a better chance of picking fruit.

Make it a weekly habit to check the moisture level of all overwintering trees and bushes whether they're in the basement, in an unheated garage, or outside. Evaporation is slow during cold periods, but roots shouldn't be allowed to dry. They mustn't be kept soggy, just barely moist. Insect problems, such as scale, mites, and mealy bugs can quickly get out of hand indoors. Before bringing a tree inside, hose it down to wash off dust, and spray with insecticidal soap. If the tree has scale, spray with summer oil, a highly refined oil sold under several brand names that can be sprayed on trees during the growing season.

Pruning for Fruits and Berries

'Fredonia' is a hardy, productive American vine with intensely flavored spicy grapes.

Fear of pruning is a nearly universal malady among prospective fruit and berry growers. Most of us garden by green thumb rather than by blueprint, and pruning, with its rules and diagrams, seems daunting, to say the least. Having spent so much time and energy trying to get plants to grow, it's difficult to start whacking away at them with pruning shears. What should we cut? Where and why? Fear of cutting off too much, or the wrong branches, is often paralyzing.

Fortunately, even the intimidated can learn to prune. While not exactly a simple process, pruning is a sensible one. Once you understand the purposes of pruning, the practices will make sense. Many gardeners even come to enjoy pruning. It provides a fulfilling sense of husbandry, of a continuing partnership between you and your plants. And it's a great excuse to spend time in the garden in that long stretch between the end of winter and the beginning of spring, when the air is brisk and the soil is too cold to dig.

In this chapter, we'll outline the basics of pruning. Most of the chapter is devoted to fruit trees; you'll find the information you need on berries in chapters on individual kinds. Even if you're growing only berries, it's worth reading the chapter because the underlying principles of pruning pertain to both trees and bushes.

We'd like you to keep several things in mind as you read on. It is very difficult to learn to prune from a book, and there is no quicker way to pruning frustration than to read several books on the subject. Professionals differ on pruning techniques, and plants differ one from another — the diagrams in this and any other book will not look exactly like your tree or bush. Despite their differences, however, most experts agree on the purposes of pruning and on certain basic practices. It is these we have concentrated on here. When you set out to prune real plants, be guided by your understanding of these basic purposes and practices and you won't go far wrong.

The best way to learn pruning is at the side of a master practitioner. Seek out experienced growers in your area and ask if you can accompany them as they work on their plants. Go to demonstrations or sign up for classes offered by your extension service, arboretum, or local nurseries. Finally, screw up your courage and learn by doing. Plants are pretty forgiving; if you make a mistake, they will usually offer you another opportunity.

Why Prune

It is possible to grow fruits and berries without pruning. Some plants, such as American persimmons, mulberries, feijoa, and guava, thrive and produce good crops without any pruning. Many an old country farmyard holds a venerable apple, apricot, pear, cherry, or plum that bears a reliable feast of fruit long after anyone ceased tending it.

Unpruned plants, then, will bear fruit. But the vigorous growth of an unpruned grape will put smaller and smaller fruit farther and farther out of easy reach. And those farmyard apples are likely to be blemished or infested with pests by the time you're ready to harvest them. Well-pruned plants will almost always bear bigger crops of larger, less-blemished fruit.

Much of the pruning done to fruit trees and berry bushes is intended to admit air and sunlight into the interior of the plant. Increased air circulation helps keep down diseases, such as powdery mildew, that flourish in still, close quarters.

Sunlight, of course, is essential for photosynthesis, that everyday miracle of transformation. Sugars produced during photosynthesis fuel the plant's growth and are also stored in its fruits. In a way, when we eat a strawberry, apple, or guava, we're eating sunlight. And if these fruits have been scanted on their ration of sunlight during crucial periods of development, the fruit will be stunted, tart, or insipid.

Sunlight is also critical for the development of next year's harvest. Insufficient sunlight during late summer or early fall can affect the number and quality of next year's flower buds, which are being formed at that time.

Pruning produces sturdy plants, too. Heft a single, good-size apple on the palm of your hand — maybe a half-pound, certainly a quarter-pound. Now multiply that by 100 or more, and you have some idea of the burden on a bearing fruit tree. An unpruned tree can split right down the crotch or snap a major branch from the burden of fruit. That's years of gardening time lost in an instant, and years more until a replacement tree begins to bear. Pruning (and prudent selection of rootstocks and cultivars) is also what allows us to grow several fruit trees and berry bushes on a residential lot and still have room for a swingset or perennial border.

Training and Pruning

For many fruit trees and berry bushes, pruning actually covers two different operations. Training, done while a tree or bush is young, creates a well-formed framework that can support the weight of later crops of fruit. Regular pruning maintains this form, keeps the plant in bounds, and directs energy toward the production of fruit rather than greenery. Training and pruning both seek to boost the amount of air and sun that reaches the interior of a tree or bush, thereby lessening chances of disease and encouraging the development and ripening of fruit. Training and pruning also combine to provide easy access to fruit.

Training and pruning are complementary activities. Careful attention to training during the first three to four years of a fruit tree's life will minimize the amount of pruning necessary to maintain the tree's health and productivity in subsequent years. Much of the pruning done on fruit trees is the result of neglected or failed training — a well-trained tree won't need much pruning.

Training and pruning techniques make use of some basic applied plant physiology. Many of the pruning cuts you make will induce or suppress growth, for better or worse. Understanding this phenomenon will make the process of training and pruning much clearer.

Pruning and apical dominance

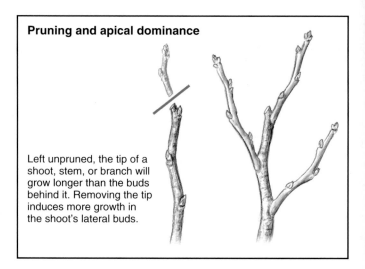

Left unpruned, the tip of a shoot, stem, or branch will grow longer than the buds behind it. Removing the tip induces more growth in the shoot's lateral buds.

How plants respond to pruning

Most gardeners have never heard of auxins, plant hormones produced continuously at the tips of shoots. Yet much of the training and pruning of fruits and berries (and all other plants, for that matter) boils down to messing about with a plant's auxins.

Auxins promote growth at the shoot tip while inhibiting the growth of buds along the sides of the shoot (lateral buds). This process of growth regulation by a shoot tip is called apical dominance. If you cut off a growing tip (thereby cutting off its production of auxins), some of the previously dormant lateral buds behind it will develop into side shoots, making a shorter and bushier plant. (See drawing above.) Thus you can change the entire shape of a plant with a simple pruning cut.

Whether you're pinching the shoots of a potted geranium or snipping off half the single thin stem of your newly planted apple tree, you're seeking to direct growth by manipulating apical dominance. The geranium responds by producing numerous side shoots, resulting in an attractive, bushy plant. The apple also responds by sending out side shoots, some of which will eventually become hefty scaffold branches, capable of supporting many pounds of fruit.

Remember that cutting the growing point of a stem will stimulate growth even if that isn't your intention. When you cut back an apple tree's overlong scaffold branch or an overgrown berry bush, you may inadvertently produce a thicket of unwanted growth.

It's important when pruning small stems and branches to make good cuts with sharp tools. There are two basic cuts. The first, trimmed just above a bud along the length of a

Cutting correctly

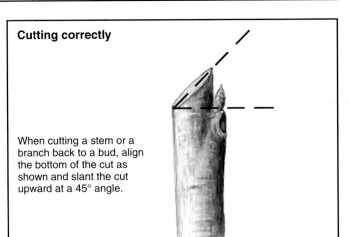

When cutting a stem or a branch back to a bud, align the bottom of the cut as shown and slant the cut upward at a 45° angle.

Thinning small branches

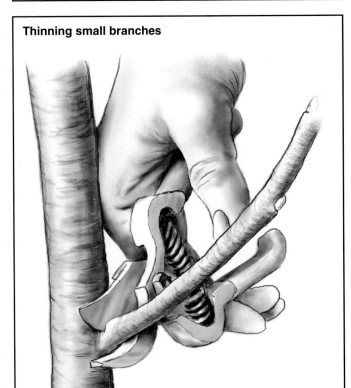

Make thinning cuts close to the trunk on branch but just outside the branch collar, a slight bulge at the base of the branch.

Pruning Tools

Pruning can be done with fingernails, or a chain saw, or anything in between. Most gardeners rely primarily on pruning shears (also called pruning clippers or secateurs). Loppers and a brush saw or pruning saw come in handy for branches that are too big for pruning shears.

Pruning shears and loppers. Pruning shears come in two basic designs, bypass and anvil. Bypass shears cut like scissors — a sharp convex cutting blade slides past a blunt concave hooked blade that supports the stem being cut. Anvil shears cut like a knife on a cutting board — a straight blade cuts against a soft metal surface, the anvil, which also supports the stem. Bypass shears tend to damage a stem less than anvil shears; they are also better able to reach into tight spots. Anvil shears, however, are more powerful than bypass.

Loppers are essentially heavy-duty bypass or anvil shears attached to long handles. Requiring the use of two hands, they provide considerable leverage and cutting power — some can handle branches up to 2 inches in diameter. Gardeners with small or weak hands or stiff joints may find loppers easier to use than shears; there are ratchet models, too. Loppers can be expensive, and there is nothing they do that can't be done with either hand shears or a saw. But if you maintain a lot of trees and shrubs, a good pair of loppers will save you time and work.

Saws. Most gardeners will never need anything heavier than a good brush saw for maintaining fruits and berries. There are lots of good models on the market. Most have lightweight tubular frames that support and tension narrow, hardened steel throwaway blades. When sharp, such saws will handle limbs up to 4 or 5 inches in diameter.

A pruning saw is an almost indispensable pruning tool. They usually consist of a hardened-steel blade up to about a foot long attached to a wooden or metal handle. Some blades can be folded into the handle. Because there's no frame to get in the way, a pruning saw can get into tight spots, and it's also capable of handling limbs almost as big as a frame saw.

Chain saws are useful tools for taking down old trees or removing very large limbs, but they are seldom helpful pruning tools. They are also dangerous, particularly if the user is perched on a ladder or branch. Be prudent — unless you've had a lot of experience, leave chain-sawing to professionals.

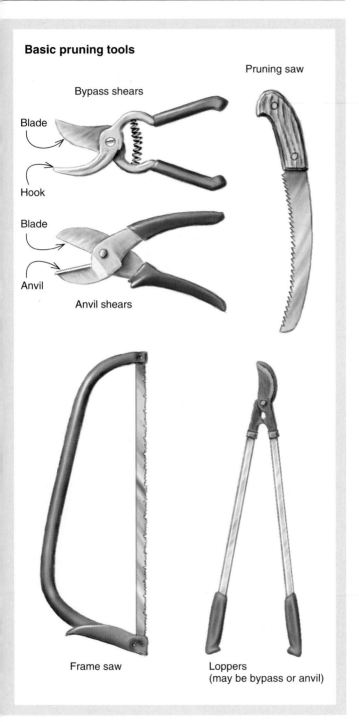

Basic pruning tools

Pruning saw

Bypass shears

Blade

Hook

Blade

Anvil

Anvil shears

Frame saw

Loppers
(may be bypass or anvil)

branch, is called a heading cut; this stimulates buds on the branch below the cut to grow. A thinning cut (shown in the bottom of the drawing on page 395) removes a small shoot or branch at its point of connection to another branch or to the trunk. If both cuts are made correctly, chances of diseases taking hold in the wounds are minimized.

Wide-Angle Branches

There are few things more discouraging to a fruit grower than seeing a scaffold branch split away from the trunk. Years of work gone in a few seconds. Limbs that meet the trunk at angles of less than 45° are more likely to split under the strain of a heavy load of fruit or a high wind than those forming larger angles with the trunk.

Wide-angled limbs have several other advantages. They admit more light and air into the center of a tree, helping to set and ripen fruit, and lessening chances of disease. Branches that grow at wider angles receive more sunlight along their full length and are more likely to form spurs and set fruit than vertical branches, which tend to grow vigorously upward and remain vegetative. The "ideal" branch angle is usually thought to be about 45° to 60° from a perpendicular trunk.

When a tree is young and supple, it's easy to widen the angle scaffold limbs form with the trunk, as shown at right. (You can even begin at bud stage by clamping a clothespin above a sprouting bud to force the emerging shoot outward.) The job may require no more than a small notched stick or spring clothespin inserted between branch and trunk. Nurseries also sell spacers made for spreading limbs.

You can also weight the end of a shoot in early spring; a clothespin may be enough weight, or you might need to tie a branch that is supple or larger to a brick or stone, or to a stake driven in the ground. You can make weights by putting concrete into the bottom of paper cups or plastic nursery six-packs. While the concrete is soft, insert wire hooks for hanging the weights in the tree. You can also drape a gravel-filled plastic bag over a wayward shoot like a saddlebag. Usually one season of spreading or weight-training will move a branch permanently in position. Don't overdo, though; a downward-pointing branch will eventually lose its vigor and stop bearing.

Training Fruit Trees

Simply put, training is the process of shaping a tree to a desired form by limiting the tree to a number of well-spaced branches and directing their growth. Arising from the tree's trunk, the chosen branches are called "scaffold" branches, reflecting their importance to the basic structure of the tree.

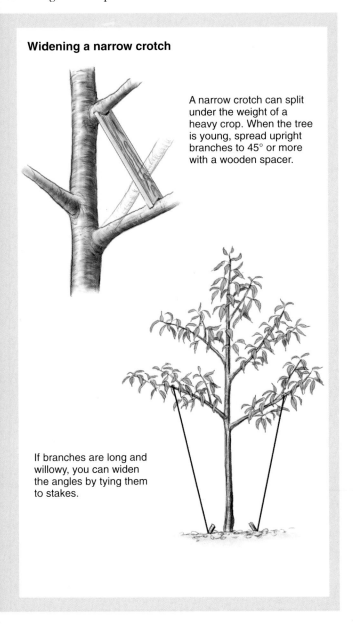

Widening a narrow crotch

A narrow crotch can split under the weight of a heavy crop. When the tree is young, spread upright branches to 45° or more with a wooden spacer.

If branches are long and willowy, you can widen the angles by tying them to stakes.

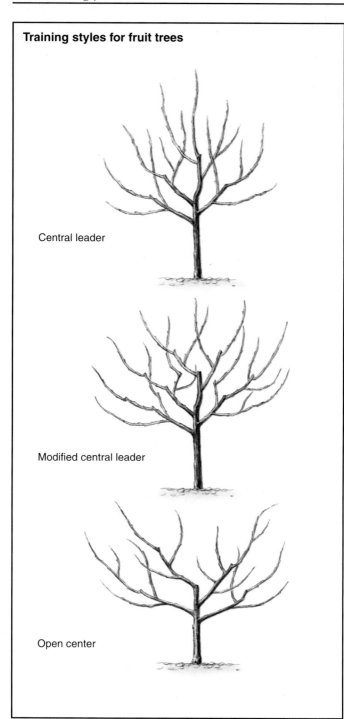

Training styles for fruit trees

Central leader

Modified central leader

Open center

The idea is to produce a tree strong enough to support a good crop of fruit, with a center open to light and air, and branches within reach for easy picking. (See the sidebar 'Wide-angle Branches' for a discussion of an aspect of training important to all the training methods that follow.) As in parenthood or puppy raising, it's easier to train a new fruit tree right from the start than it is to straighten things out later.

Three types of training, shown opposite, are commonly used for fruit trees. "Central-leader" training is most often used for trees, such as apples, that naturally grow with a strong, upright central trunk and bear fairly heavy fruit. "Open-center" training responds to the tendency of other trees, such as peach and plum, to form a shorter trunk and a vase-shaped array of branches. The third style, "modified central leader," is something of a hybrid of the two and is used to moderate the height of a tree that might otherwise form a tall central leader. Despite their somewhat different ways of doing so, each of these systems aims to create a well-placed scaffold of branches that don't cast shade on one another.

Central-leader trees are pyramid-shaped, with a few strong evenly spaced tiers of branches radiating from the trunk. Viewed from above, the branches would look like spokes of a wheel with the central trunk as the hub. Central-leader trees can support a heavy burden of fruit, which is just as well because the increased sunlight penetrating the interior produces more fruit-bearing spurs.

An open-center tree is just that — one with a middle that's open to light and air, thanks to the removal of the central leader. An open-center tree has three or four scaffold branches, spaced more or less evenly around the trunk not far below where the leader was removed. Once the central leader is removed, energy is diverted into the formation and growth of scaffold branches lower down — auxin manipulation in action. Peaches and nectarines tend naturally to a vase shape and the airy, well-ventilated open-center training helps ward off disease problems to which they are prone.

A modified central-leader tree is trained like a central leader until it reaches a desired height, at which point the central growing tip is nipped out to check its upward growth. The tree, which usually has five or six scaffold branches by this time, is then trained rather like an open-center tree. The main advantage of this system is height control; an apple or pear that would ordinarily grow much taller can be maintained at 6 or 7 feet high.

Pick the right tree for your site

While it is possible to keep an otherwise large tree small by training and pruning, you'll have much less work and probably a healthier tree if you choose a combination of variety and rootstock that grows naturally to about the size you desire. Home gardeners don't usually have space for the full-size versions (called "standards") of many fruit trees, which may grow as high as 20 to 40 feet tall and spread nearly as wide. Keeping such a tree at a height of 8 to 12 feet can require continuous warfare with pruning shears. Where available, naturally smaller trees, whether genetic dwarfs or those grown on dwarfing rootstocks, are a much better choice.

As a rule of thumb, a tree is likely to do well with a training style that complements, rather than works against, its natural growth habit. It's difficult to train a naturally vase-shaped tree to a central-leader style, though most trees can be trained to an open-center style. Any tree that can be trained to a central leader can also be trained as a modified central leader. The chart below indicates the training styles that work well for various types of fruit. Be sure to consult the chapters on individual fruit for comments on growth and fruiting habits and related pruning needs of specific trees.

Selecting a Training Style
(NOTE: Central-leader trees can also be trained to a modified central leader.)

Fruit	Style
Apple	Standard types: modified central leader; dwarf or semidwarf: central leader
Pear	Central leader
Peach	Open center
Nectarine	Open center
Plum	Open center
Sour cherry	Central leader or open center
Sweet cherry	Central leader or open center

Size, age, and training

In general, the training procedures described below apply to trees of any size in proportion to their size. That is, while a standard tree might have tiers of scaffold branches separated by 3 feet, those on a dwarf tree might be half that far apart.

It's important to find out from the nursery how old the tree you're buying is and if they've been training it. (If possible, find out the stage of training it's in.) Depending on the answers, you may be able to skip several of the initial steps in the training procedures.

Finally, difficult as it may be to bring yourself to do, re-move any fruit that forms in the first two years — force the tree's energy into producing a strong framework before weighing it down with fruit.

Training a Central-Leader Tree

It can take from two to four years after planting to train a tree to the central-leader style. The goal is a pyramidal tree with a single upright growing tip at the top of the trunk (the central leader) and a series of well-placed tiers of scaffold branches rising up the trunk.

Because central-leader training does not control the height of a tree, most home gardeners will use it only for dwarf or semidwarf trees, which naturally restrict themselves to an ac-ceptable height. (If the only tree you can buy will naturally grow too big, you can train it to a modified central leader or an open center.) A mature, central-leader dwarf or small semi-dwarf will have from five to eight scaffold branches. (See the drawings as you read the steps below.)

The first year. If you're planting a branchless whip, cut it back to a bud about 3 feet above the ground for a standard-size tree, or about 2 feet above ground for a dwarf. The nursery may have begun training an older, already branching tree, and

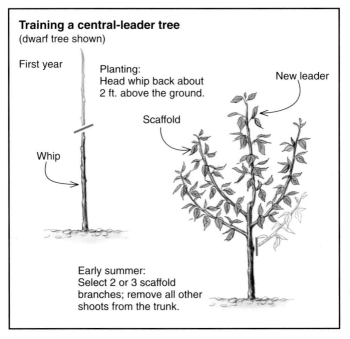

Training a central-leader tree
(dwarf tree shown)

First year

Whip

Planting:
Head whip back about
2 ft. above the ground.

Scaffold

New leader

Early summer:
Select 2 or 3 scaffold
branches; remove all other
shoots from the trunk.

you may be able to skip ahead to the second year. If, however, the branches don't look well formed or well placed, it can be a good idea to "whip" it at planting, cutting off all branches and heading the leader back as described above for a branchless whip.

You may feel terrible cutting away so much of such a small plant, but the tree will soon throw out new growth. In early spring, concentrate on establishing a new leader, snipping out all but the strongest of the shoots appearing near the top of the trunk. If you've staked the tree, tie the new leader upright to it. To give the leader plenty of room, remove any shoots growing within 8 inches of it.

In early summer, stand back and eyeball the tree, looking for potential scaffold branches. The choice may be scanty — many fruit trees may have only a couple of branches. Good scaffold candidates are vigorous growers, spaced about 6 to 8 inches apart vertically and staggered around the trunk, so that no two scaffolds are right above each other.

After you've selected two or three scaffolds (or decided to go with the only ones the tree offers), pinch off or prune off all other shoots sprouting from the trunk during the remainder of the season. Let any secondary branches that appear on the scaffolds develop.

The second year. In late winter, when the tree is dormant, cut back the central leader at a bud about 3 to 3½ feet above the lowest scaffold branch; for dwarf trees cut at about 2 to 2½ feet. Cutting the leader back will encourage the trunk to sprout a tier of new scaffold candidates by the end of the growing season. Ideally, the top bud on the leader should be on the opposite side of the trunk from the one that sprouted the present leader. If last year's growth took a jog to the left, this year's will now take a jog right. This mild zig-zag effect keeps the trunk growing fairly straight.

Also at this time, cut back each of last year's scaffolds so that they push out secondary branches. Cut just above an outward-facing bud so that new growth is directed away from the center of the tree, rather than up or in to it. Consider the vigor of the branch when deciding how far to cut it back — thick vigorous branches can be cut back only a few inches to as much as half their length, thinner ones as much as two-thirds to strongly stimulate them. Cut branches at the bottom longer than those at the top to give the tree a pyramid shape, like a Christmas tree.

In early summer, remove competing shoots within about 8 inches of the base of the new central-leader shoot. (Again, you might want to tie this shoot loosely to the stake.) Using the same selection criteria as before, choose two or three ad-

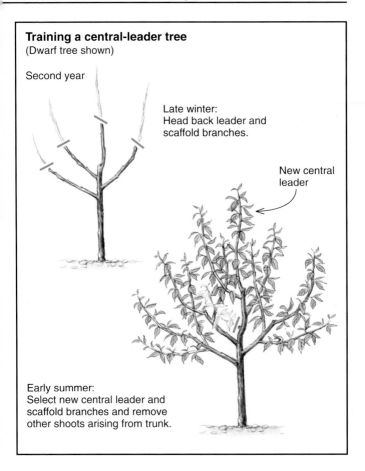

Training a central-leader tree
(Dwarf tree shown)

Second year

Late winter:
Head back leader and
scaffold branches.

New central
leader

Early summer:
Select new central leader and
scaffold branches and remove
other shoots arising from trunk.

ditional scaffolds from the new shoots sprouting from the trunk above last year's scaffolds. Snip off other new shoots arising from the trunk. Rub off or snip off any "water sprouts," secondary branches that are growing vertically from the scaffolds. Nip off any suckers that spring up from the roots. If necessary, spread scaffolds so that the angle where branch meets trunk is between 45° and 90°. (See Wide-Angle Branches on page 398.)

The third year. This year you're likely to see the first fruits of your labors. In late winter, cut back the central leader and the scaffold branches as described above for the second year. Remember to maintain the tree's cone shape when you're pruning. Also at this time, if the interior seems crowded, thin out secondary branches (cut them off at the base where they attach to another branch). You can also head back some of these branches to redirect their growth toward the outside of

Training a central-leader tree
(dwarf tree shown)

Third year

Late winter:
Cut back central leader and scaffold branches. Head back secondary branches to admit light and redirect growth outward. Maintain pyramid shape.

Early summer:
Select new central leader and scaffolds.
Thin secondary growth to admit light and air.

the tree by cutting them to an outward-facing bud somewhere along their length.

In early summer, make scaffold selections, as described for the second year, choosing branches that are about 1 to 1½ feet above the uppermost of last year's scaffolds. As before, remove water sprouts throughout the season and, if necessary, widen the angle that new scaffold branches form with the trunk.

Fourth and subsequent years. The eventual size of the mature tree determines whether you'll need to continue training. Dwarf trees are likely to be close to mature height and may not have room for another set of scaffold branches. Just let the central leader grow as it will. For semidwarfs and standards you can continue the process outlined above in subsequent years to add sturdy scaffold branches to their taller trunks.

After training. The completed framework of a dwarf tree 8 to 10 feet tall should comprise five to eight vigorous, well-placed scaffold branches growing from a sturdy upright trunk, and a strong central leader. Each year from now on you'll continue to cut back the scaffolds to maintain the tree's pyramid shape and, if you wish, to restrict its overall size. You'll also prune for fruit, as described below, and to maintain the tree's general health and vigor.

Modified central leader

An ideal style for central-leader trees that would otherwise grow too big, modified central leader is often used by commercial orchardists planting standard-size apple trees. It is also a good choice for cherries, pears, and some upright plums.

For the first two or three years, train a modified central-leader tree as you would a central leader. (See drawings on previous pages.) When you've reached a desired height, often about 6 feet, with five to eight main scaffold branches established, cut back the central leader flush with the top scaffold branch, as shown on page 408. Thin and head back the scaffolds as necessary to encourage growth of fruit-producing wood, to allow light and air into the center, and to keep the upper scaffolds from shading the lower.

Training an Open-Center Tree

This style creates a low, airy tree with three or four scaffold branches and an abundance of fruit-bearing wood. Naturally spreading trees such as peaches, nectarines, apricots, plums,

Training a modified central-leader tree

Second or third year:
Train as a central leader until tree reaches desired height, as shown here in early summer.

Late the following winter:
Remove the central leader above the top scaffold, and head back scaffolds.

Early summer:
Now and in subsequent years, maintain the open center on top of the tree. Thin and head back as necessary to ensure light and air reach all scaffolds below.

Training an open-center tree

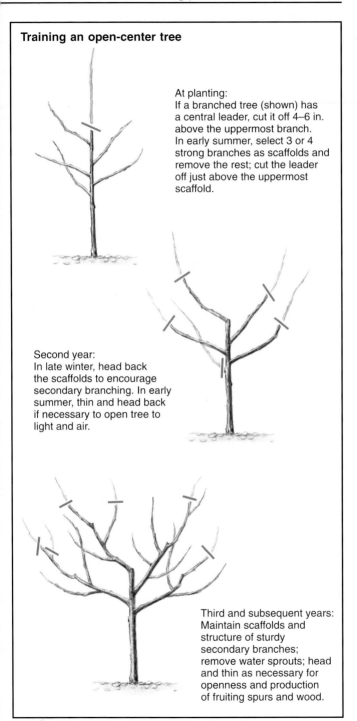

At planting:
If a branched tree (shown) has a central leader, cut it off 4–6 in. above the uppermost branch. In early summer, select 3 or 4 strong branches as scaffolds and remove the rest; cut the leader off just above the uppermost scaffold.

Second year:
In late winter, head back the scaffolds to encourage secondary branching. In early summer, thin and head back if necessary to open tree to light and air.

Third and subsequent years:
Maintain scaffolds and structure of sturdy secondary branches; remove water sprouts; head and thin as necessary for openness and production of fruiting spurs and wood.

and some cherries are well suited for this style of training, which takes two to three years to complete, as shown in the drawing on page 409.

The first year. You'll probably need to do a little pruning at planting. Some nursery stock is already trained to the beginning of an open-center style. If your new tree lacks a strong central leader and has instead a small group of branches arising near the top of the trunk, the nursery has begun training, and you should continue it with the practices described for the second year. (If you plant in the fall, don't begin training until late winter.)

If your tree has a central leader and healthy branches, at planting cut off the central leader to a bud 4 to 6 inches above the uppermost branch. If you're planting a whip, cut it back to a healthy bud 2 to 3 feet off the ground (toward the lower number for dwarfs, the higher for standards).

In early summer, select three to four of the best-spaced branches for scaffolds. Look for branches that are separated about 4 to 6 inches vertically on the trunk and spaced more or less evenly around it, so that one scaffold won't shade another directly below it. Lower branches will grow more vigorously with wider branch angles than those higher up. Finally, cut the leader off flush with the top scaffold.

The second year. In late winter, remove all secondary branches growing from the scaffolds within 6 to 8 inches of the trunk. This helps keep the center of the tree open to light and air. Remove any weak or crowded secondary branches and any heading across the center of the tree. Head back scaffolds and selected secondary branches to encourage development of fruit-bearing branches. (We'll discuss these branches further in Pruning Fruit Trees below.) Cut to an outward-facing bud somewhere on the length of the branch to encourage growth away from the center of the tree. The amount you cut off depends on the vigor of the branch (cut weaker ones back harder) and the extent to which you wish to restrict the size of the tree.

Beginning in early summer and continuing as necessary throughout the season, rub off water sprouts wherever they develop. If necessary, brace or tie down branches to establish wide angles with the trunk.

The third and subsequent years. The basic framework of the tree is now established. Continue to remove water sprouts. Thin crowded branches and those crossing the interior of the tree by cutting back to an outward-facing branch or bud. Head back scaffold branches as needed to restrict the tree's size or to prevent one scaffold from growing more vigorously and unbalancing the tree. Prune to enhance and increase fruit-bearing spurs and branches as described in the next section.

Pruning Fruit Trees

Once the tree's basic shape has been established, it needs annual pruning to maintain that shape and encourage healthy growth and good harvests. Here's where many pruning neophytes get nervous. Having grasped the basics of training ("Six basic limbs? No problem."), it's the ongoing care that becomes daunting. Fortunately, annual pruning is mostly a matter of housekeeping. Harvesting a good crop, however, depends on understanding how your tree bears its fruit and pruning to enhance that process, so we'll discuss that first. (For some useful information on "when to prune," see the sidebar of that name on page 412.)

Pruning for fruit production

Apples, pears, sweet cherries, and some plums and prunes bear most or all of their fruit on short branchlets called spurs, which grow from the secondary branches. Fruiting spurs are easy to spot. The stubby branches are tight and nubby. Look carefully and you'll see closely spaced buds among visible scars left where previous fruits separated from the spur. A fruiting spur can produce for a long time — up to 20 years in some varieties.

Spurs form during the second or third year of growth on the parent branch. Spur-fruiting trees periodically need to be thinned, their branches removed at the base where they attach to another branch, to get light and air to the spurs and fruit in the interior of the tree. In the long run, this also promotes production of more spurs. Thin in early summer, after the tree has completed its first flush of growth; be careful not to remove fruiting spurs. Spurs can produce for years, but eventually, you may need to remove part or all of older, less-productive spurs to reinvigorate the tree. Over the years, spurs branch repeatedly, and a single spur may become so gnarled that the fruit becomes crowded ("spurbound") and stunted as a result.

Apricots, peaches and nectarines, sour cherries, and some plums and prunes bear their fruit on lateral buds that form on second-year wood, that is, on branches that grew during the previous season. These trees may also produce fruiting spurs on two- to three-year-old wood.

These fruit trees require yearly pruning to encourage new growth for next season's crop. To do this, a portion of the tree's secondary branches are headed back in late winter or

When To Prune

Most gardeners are accustomed to pruning their fruit trees when they are dormant, in late winter or early spring. At that time of year, without interfering leaves, the branching structure is easy to see. Apples, pears, and plums are usually pruned while dormant.

But dormant pruning is not always best. When the tree breaks dormancy, the roots rush into action to nourish the top growth. After pruning, the top growth is out of balance with the root supply, so vegetative growth gets a big boost. This is a good thing if you want to stimulate a young tree or generate lots of new branches on an older one. But it also has its drawbacks. If pruned when dormant, fast-growing trees, such as plums, can push out too much new growth, and you'll need to spend a lot of time later in the season removing it. Dormant pruning, especially if done with a heavy hand, can also lead to the growth of water spouts, those starkly vertical, fast-growing shoots that arise from the main scaffold branches.

Apricots, nectarines, and peaches — the notorious early bloomers — can be stimulated into bloom by dormant pruning. This might sound like a good idea until a late frost wipes out this year's harvest. Be patient with these trees, and hold off on pruning until after they bloom. (You can prune them as late as midsummer.)

Pruning in summer has the opposite effect of dormant pruning. It can actually retard growth, dwarfing the tree by removing food-generating leaves. It's a good idea to prune off water sprouts in summer to prevent them from regrowing. Late-summer pruning is asking for problems. The new growth that is stimulated won't have time to toughen up and will be vulnerable to damage from cold weather. Prune no later than four weeks before frost so that new growth has a chance to harden.

early spring. Systems vary for determining how many to prune. Some say to leave unpruned any shoot shorter than 9 inches and to cut back longer ones to four or five buds to induce formation of short fruit-bearing shoots the following summer. Others say to cut back any shoot without a fat fruit bud at its tip (to induce more growth next year), and to thin crowded shoots bearing fruit buds by heading some back to several buds at their base.

Be guided by the knowledge that you need to renew fruit-bearing two-year-old shoots, and be moderated by the fact that if you are too gung ho in your annual pruning, you could remove so much second-year wood that your crop will be meager. If a branch becomes too extended over a period of years, cut it back much harder and start the process over again with the shoots this creates.

Maintenance pruning

All plants, whether grown for fruit or the beauty of flowers and foliage, benefit from simple "housekeeping" pruning. Begin at the bottom of the tree and work up. Use a light hand, to keep the top of the tree and its root system in healthy balance.

Start with the most obvious tasks. Remove all dead, damaged, or diseased branches. Remove the weakest of any pair of crossing or rubbing branches. (Branches that rub against one another create abrasion wounds — like a skinned knee — attractive to pests and diseases.) Snip off water sprouts and root suckers.

The tree already looks better. Next, remove branches that crowd the interior and those that head into the center of the tree. Be careful not to snip off fruiting spurs unnecessarily. Now, consider the fruiting wood, spurs or second-year laterals. Thin or head back branches as needed to induce formation of new spurs and laterals for future crops, as described above. Finally, insert spreaders or tie down young branches to widen tight crotch angles.

From time to time as you work, stand back and take a look at your progress. Consider the overall balance of the branching: all sides of the tree should be equally dense, with no scaffold branch growing much more or much less vigorously than others. If a scaffold shows signs of outrunning the rest, head it back to an outward-facing bud not far from its growing tip to direct the growth into branching. Alternatively, cut it back farther in midsummer after the plant has slowed growth, so you won't induce suckers or too many new shoots to clutter up the interior of the plant. If a scaffold seems runty, cut it back severely to jolt it into pushing out vigorous new growth, and train the strongest of these new shoots as an extension of the scaffold.

If you forget everything else about pruning, remember that its purpose is to make a strong framework and admit light and air into the center of the tree. Have faith in yourself and in your tree's ability to outgrow the mistakes you make.

Espalier

An espaliered tree, bush, or vine is so visually appealing that it is easy to overlook its practical advantage: saving space. Trained on wires against a sunny wall, a small number of espaliered stems or branches can provide a worthwhile amount of fruit and a great deal of pleasure to a gardener with limited space.

Espalier patterns can be as complicated or as simple as you want to make them. Regardless of complexity, all espaliered plants require much more maintenance than those in the garden. You'll need to keep up with new growth during the season by frequent tying, pinching, and pruning, or soon the plant will obliterate the pattern and overrun its space. Harvesting an espalier, on the other hand, requires considerably less effort than does a garden-grown plant. A south-facing wall is ideal for an espalier, because the fruit and the plant will get plenty of sunshine.

Apples, pears, peaches, plums, apricots, and nectarines are all candidates for espaliers, as are some citrus and other tender fruits. Gooseberries and currants have long been espaliered in Europe. And grapes, of course, are espaliered, though we don't perhaps think of their training by that name.

The Belgian fence, shown in the drawings at right, is a good espalier for beginners. In a few short years, a few dwarf fruit trees will create a pattern of interlocking diamonds. (For another simple espalier technique and a related single-cordon style, see the chapter "Gooseberries and Currants.")

To make a Belgian fence espalier, start by planting apple or pear whips 2 feet apart; five will create a nice pattern. (Three will make one central diamond shape; four will make a pyramid of three diamonds, two on the bottom, one on top; five make a pyramid of six diamonds on three levels, and so on.) Dwarf plants will do best. Erect a three-wire fence a few inches from the wall, placing the bottom wire 18 to 20 inches above the ground and subsequent wires every 18 inches or so. Three to four wires will be enough for most dwarf plants. Use sturdy wire and firmly anchor the posts that support it.

At planting, cut back each whip to a bud about 18 inches above the ground. In spring, when new growth appears, snip off all but two shoots on each tree, one on each side of the stem. As the shoots grow, tie them to the wires to create scaffold branches in a series of V-shapes, as shown in the drawing. Tie branches of neighboring trees together when they overlap. As secondary branches sprout on the scaffolds, cut them back to a bud about 4 inches from the scaffold.

Espaliers are pruned throughout the season, rather than in late winter. Your fingers are the best tools for the job, because most "pruning" consists of removing buds and pinching out shoots. Rub off unwanted or misdirected buds in early spring. During the growing season, pinch off unwanted growth as it appears. In late summer, prune for fruit production by snipping back shoots to four or five buds to encourage the for-

Belgian fence espalier

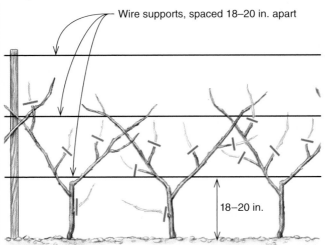

Wire supports, spaced 18–20 in. apart

18–20 in.

First year: Plant whips about 2 ft. apart beneath a wire trellis. Head whips back about 18 in. high, select 2 shoots and train them as scaffolds at a 45° angle, snip other shoots off trunk. Head back secondary growth at about 4 in. from scaffolds.

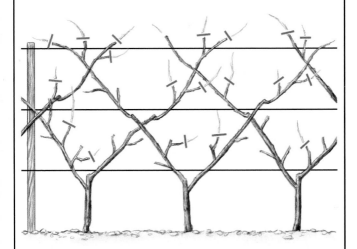

Second year and subsequent years: In late winter, head back scaffolds to outward-facing bud. Train laterals that emerges to extend scaffolding. Head back secondary growth to maintain pattern and promote fruiting wood. When scaffolds reach desired height, head them back each year at about the same point.

mation of fruiting buds for the next season near the base of the branch. In two to four years, the main branches will have formed interlacing diamonds. When they reach the height you desire, maintain them there by cutting them back uniformly as needed.

In the years during and after training, you'll need to prune the secondary growth, trying to balance two requirements. First, you need to create and maintain enough spurs or second-year wood to provide a yearly crop. Second, you need to prevent growth from overwhelming the pattern you've created or outrunning the space available. Remember not to prune later than midsummer, so new growth has time to harden off for winter.

Ongoing Care

Regular care of your fruit trees and berry bushes is well worth the effort — healthy plants produce the best fruit. And caring for your plants needn't be an onerous task. Given reasonably good soil, adequate rainfall, and thoughtful training and pruning, many fruit and berry bushes are likely to do fine with just a modicum of regular preventive maintenance.

Very often, the key to effective maintenance is being attentive to your plants' needs. Take a stroll through the garden or orchard at least every day or two, giving the plants and the condition of their surroundings a good look. Such familiarity allows you to note dry soil, or the first signs of insect or disease damage before plants show stress. Problems tend to multiply — plants stressed by lack of water or nutrients (and, on occasion, too much of these ordinarily good things) fall prey much more readily to insects and diseases. Preventive maintenance combined with early detection and treatment will repay themselves many times over.

Good Nutrition

Plants grow by making use of sunlight and a range of nutrients derived from soil, air, and water. A good deal of our care has to do with ensuring adequate supplies of each. As discussed in the previous chapter, much of the pruning we do is to open the interior of a tree or bush to more sunlight, enhancing fruit formation and ripening.

All gardeners can recognize good soil. It is loose and crumbly in the hand, teems with earthworms, and smells rich and earthy even to our limited noses. Good soil also contains nutrients, which we can't see, feel, or smell. Like its more sensual qualities, a soil's fertility is the product of billions of tiny organisms, microbes that help break down organic matter and make it available to plants.

Of the 16 elements considered necessary for the growth of plants, three (carbon, hydrogen, and oxygen) are obtained from water and air. All the rest are absorbed from the soil. Of these, nitrogen (N), phosphorus (P), and potassium (K), are called primary nutrients because they are required in the largest amounts. (You'll see their letter abbreviations used on fertilizer labels.) Nitrogen boosts vegetative growth and keeps the leaves colored green with chlorophyll. Phosphorus and potassium are essential for flowering, fruiting, and root development.

Sulfur (S), calcium (Ca), and magnesium (Mg) are known as secondary nutrients since they are usually required in smaller amounts. The remaining elements, iron (Fe), manganese (Mn), boron (B), copper (Cu), zinc (Zn), molybdenum (Mo), and chlorine (Cl), are called trace elements, or micronutrients, because they're required in very small quantities. Nevertheless, a deficiency of any of them affects plant growth and development just as severely as does a deficiency of primary or secondary nutrients.

Soil fertility is a complex subject. Many soils have adequate supplies of some nutrients, but insufficient amounts of others. For example, many soils have adequate phosphorus to support healthy plants but are deficient in nitrogen. In these soils, adding fertilizer containing the missing element can greatly enhance plant performance. Even though a nutrient is present in the soil, it may not be in a form that's available to plants. Plants need iron, for example, but roots can't absorb iron oxide (rust) which is one of the most common forms of iron in soil. Interactions between the different nutrients can also limit availability. If a soil is high in calcium, plants may have difficulty absorbing magnesium and potassium. Finally, nutrient availability changes at different pH levels.

Providing Nutrients

Too often, when gardeners think of providing nutrients to plants, they think of spreading granules from a bag of fertilizer. To be sure, plants often need and benefit from these applications, as we'll discuss later. But because of their remarkable ability to extract nutrients, many plants do well in soil of average fertility. You can reap long-term benefits of healthy, fruitful plants and reduce the work and expense of applying commercial fertilizers by maintaining and, if necessary, improving your soil's fertility. The idea is simple. Feed your soil plenty of organic matter and it will feed your plants.

While it is now considered counterproductive to amend the small amount of soil in a planting hole at planting time, there is a simple, effective way to improve and maintain your soil's fertility after planting. (See "Planting Fruit Trees and Bushes" for a discussion of soil improvements before and at planting.)

Many gardeners follow a once-a-year plan for feeding. They mulch first at planting; then each year in early spring, they pull back the old mulch and put down a layer of compost or well-aged manure. A single spring application of 2 to 4 inches of compost, or 1 to 2 inches of manure can, in many soils, maintain the level of nutrients a fruit tree or bush will need. Spread them out as far as the widest branches (the "drip line") of a tree or bush.

Fertility indicators and tests

How can you tell if your soil is fertile enough? An obvious indicator, of course, is how your plants perform. Nutrient deficiencies can manifest themselves in the condition of a plant's leaves, which may color oddly or drop prematurely. Deficiencies may affect growth. Healthy young bushes and vines will grow 1 to 5 feet per year. Fruit trees also put out a certain amount of growth in a good year; more when they are young than as they mature. Though amounts vary by cultivar and local conditions, observing how much new shoots lengthen in a year is a good general indicator of plant health — particularly if you keep track from year to year and compare growth over time. The chart at right provides rule-of-thumb guidelines for popular fruit trees.

Shoot Growth *(inches per year)*		
Fruit	Young trees	Older trees
Apple	6–18	12
Apricot	10–18	12–18
Cherry	18–24	12
Peach	6–24	12–18
Pear (dwarf)	20–30	12
Plum	12–18	12–18

Unfortunately, it can be difficult to match a symptom, whether slow growth or a peculiar coloring of the leaves, to its true cause. Any one of several conditions, or a combination of them, might be causing the problem.

If you suspect that your soil lacks something, or you just want to make sure of its fertility before planting, you can test it at home or send a sample to a state or private lab. Home soil-test kits are generally inexpensive and easy to use, but they are much less accurate than laboratory tests. Soil-test labs report pH and availability of major nutrients and recommend how much lime, sulfur, or fertilizer to add to improve the soil for growing whatever plants you specify. (Deficiencies of trace elements are rarer and may require analysis of leaf tissue to pinpoint.) A single test can serve as a baseline appraisal of your soil. A series of tests repeated over time will monitor the effect of the amendments you apply to the soil. For how to translate recommendations into amounts of commercially available fertilizer, see the box at right.

Whether you test at home or at a lab, collecting a representative sample is essential for meaningful results. Dig a few inches deep (avoid sampling from the subsoil) and gather and mix together small amounts of soil from several spots on a specific planting site, or near an existing tree or bush. Or you can mix soil gathered from a number of sites or plantings for a more general evaluation. (If you want separate results, be sure to label which sample is which.)

Fertilizers

Satisfying as it is to build and maintain friable, fertile soil, many gardeners also use commercial fertilizers. You may need to quickly address a deficiency manifested by slow growth or pinpointed by a soil test. Or you may want to give a tree or bush a "shot in the arm" at a propitious time during the growing season.

When applying fertilizer, remember that too much fertilizer can also cause problems. An excess of nitrogen can produce lots of succulent new growth attractive to aphids, pear psylla, and other leaf-eating insects. Stems and leaves may be weak and more susceptible to blight and other diseases. And an abundance of vegetative growth may divert energy from fruit production, decreasing quantity or quality of the harvest. Finally, remember not to apply fertilizers after growth has slowed in the summer — the extra nutrients could cause a spurt of weak growth that wouldn't have time to harden off before the onset of winter.

The selection of fertilizers at the local garden center can be dizzying. A rudimentary understanding of several basic types

Calculating How Much Fertilizer to Apply

Soil-test labs recommend applications of fertilizer in pounds of *actual* nutrients. In bagged fertilizers, however, labels indicate nutrients by percentage. To figure out how much packaged fertilizer it will take to meet the lab's recommendations requires a little basic arithmetic. The easiest way to explain the calculations is by example:

The soil test report recommends 2 pounds of actual nitrogen per 1,000 square feet. You are fertilizing an area measuring 10 feet square around a semidwarf apple. How much 5-10-10 fertilizer should you apply?

Start by asking how much 5-percent fertilizer it takes to supply 2 pounds of nitrogen. Set up a simple equation, using x as the unknown amount of fertilizer:

$$.05x = 2 \text{ lb.}$$
$$x = 2/.05$$
$$x = 40 \text{ lb.}$$

It will take 40 pounds of a 5-10-10 per 1,000 square feet to supply 2 pounds of nitrogen. Since you are fertilizing one-tenth as much area (100 sq. ft.), you need to spread only 4 pounds of 5-10-10 fertilizer to meet the lab's nitrogen recommendation. Calculations for the other elements are, of course, the same.

of fertilizers can help you make your choice among them. Fertilizers can be characterized by the selection of nutrients they contain, by the origin of the materials used (organic or inorganic, natural or manufactured compounds), and by the form of the fertilizer (liquid, powder, granules and so on).

Nutrient selection

A complete fertilizer contains all three of the primary nutrients. A fertilizer with a 5-10-5 rating, for example, contains 5 percent by weight of nitrogen, 10 percent phosphate, and 5 percent potash, and this ratio will be prominently displayed on the bag or bottle, always in that order — N-P-K. (The balance of the material in the bag consists of fillers such as gypsum and ground limestone or other elements in compounds with nitrogen, phosphorus, or potassium.) Some fertilizers contain only one or two of the primary elements and might be used to rectify a specific deficiency. A number of fertilizers also contain secondary nutrients and trace elements; these will also be listed on the label.

Organic versus inorganic

While the distinction between organic and inorganic fertilizers is sometimes of importance to gardeners, plants are not so discriminating. They absorb *all* of their nutrients in the form of inorganic ions. Whether these ions originate from an organic source, such as cow manure or fish meal, or from an inorganic one, such as rock phosphate or lime, makes no difference to their effect on the plant. Likewise, nutrients in fertilizers formulated from natural sources and those in fertilizers synthesized in a chemical factory are used by the plant in exactly the same way. When considering environmental effects, remember that too much manure can pollute a stream just as too much granular fertilizer can.

Organic and inorganic fertilizers sometimes perform differently in the garden, and in certain circumstances these differences can be important enough to influence your choice of fertilizers. While manures, composts, and other plant and animal residues contain varying amounts of plant nutrients, many gardeners use them primarily to improve the physical structure of the soil, valuing their organic matter more than their nutrient content. Other organic materials, such as bone meal, blood meal, and fish emulsion, are dried, pulverized, or processed before they are packaged as fertilizers. (Some animal manures are treated this way as well.) These materials do not condition the soil; their purpose is to supply nutrients.

Organic fertilizers have several advantages over inorganic compounds. Because they must first be processed by microorganisms, they are more slowly available to plants. They are safer to use because they do not burn plants as readily. And they are less likely to leach from the soil. They also have disadvantages. They're coarse, bulky, and difficult to spread uniformly. They may cost more per unit of nutrient and many of them are not a balanced source of nutrients. The release of nutrients by the microorganisms is also unpredictable, because of the influence of soil temperature, moisture level, and pH on the organisms' activity.

In contrast to organic fertilizers, inorganic fertilizers provide maximum control over nutrient levels. The nutrients are in a soluble form and they dissolve into ions that are immediately available to plants. Inorganic fertilizers are also available in specialized forms, such as slow-release compounds that feed plants over a period of time. Since they are usually more concentrated, inorganic fertilizers are often more economical per unit of nutrient. On the down side, they readily leach from the soil and may need more frequent application. Since it takes a smaller amount of inorganic fertilizer to supply a specific quantity of nutrients, you must be careful not to apply too much and burn your plants.

Applying fertilizers

Fertilizers come in a variety of physical forms. Inorganic fertilizers may be loose, dry granules, solid tablets or spikes, soluble powders, liquids, or slow-release compounds. Organic fertilizers can be bulky raw materials or may be processed into concentrated powders, granules, or liquids. Some forms are better suited to certain plants or conditions than others.

Loose, dry, granular fertilizer can be spread around a plant by hand, or over a larger area (within the drip line of a big tree) with a mechanical spreader. Distribute the fertilizer on the surface as uniformly as you can, then mix it into the soil. This is the most effective way to apply lime and superphosphate, and to get the nutrients in a complete fertilizer (especially phosphorus) down near plant roots.

Fertilizer tablets, often in the form of solid spikes that can be driven into the soil, are ideal for trees and bushes grown in containers. Fertilizers in this form are expensive in relation to the nutrients they supply.

Soluble powders and liquids are effective and easy to use and provide immediately available nutrients to plants. Both types are used in the same way, though liquids are usually more expensive per unit of nutrient. Dissolve the specified amount of powder or liquid in a container of water and drench the soil. Apply just enough solution to wet the soil down to root depth; more just wastes fertilizer. Plan to make several applications during the growing season, rather than supplying all nutrients at one time. Too high a concentration will damage leaves and stems.

Spraying plants with a liquid solution of fertilizer also provides a quick hit of nutrients. Apply the nutrients with a fine-mist sprayer and just enough water to wet the leaves. Foliar fertilizers can't provide enough of the primary elements at one time to meet plant requirements without burning the leaves. So this method is used most often to supply trace elements. Absorption through the leaves is normally very rapid, and symptoms of deficiency often can be alleviated in a few days.

Water

Most fruits are very high in water content, so a regular supply of water, whether provided by nature or irrigation, is essential. On the other hand, too much water can be as problematic as too little. Strawberries, for instance, may be quick to rot and not nearly as sweet if there is a deluge within several days of picking. Water requirements for specific plants are covered in chapters on the plants.

Sufficient water is very important during the first two to three years of a new tree's life, while the tree is establishing its root system. Trees on dwarf rootstocks are particularly sensitive to moisture levels, because of their smaller root systems. Set up a rain gauge near your plants, and water deeply every week if natural rainfall is less than 1 inch. Or wiggle your finger into the soil, knuckle deep, to check moisture. If it feels dry, it's time to water. A bucket of water a week is a good rule of thumb for one- to three-year-old trees. Don't wait for signs of drought stress; by the time you notice wilting leaves, the plant is already in decline. Stop providing supplemental watering to young trees and bushes in late summer, around August. All mature fruit trees need supplemental watering in dry summers and dry winters. (Some do better than others — figs are adapted to a Mediterranean climate, where winters are wet and summers dry.)

Getting water to individual fruit trees and bushes scattered about your property can be a chore, and is worth considering when you're selecting sites for them. However you deliver the water, remember that it is better to water all plants less often but deeply. If you have only a few fruit trees, a hose or bucket will work. Mounding a low earth wall to forming a catch basin around young trees will hold water to soak in rather than run off.

Groups of bushes or small trees can be efficiently watered with a drip irrigation system, which delivers water slowly and evenly. Such systems consist of flexible plastic tubing fitted along its length with emitters, tiny water meters rated by gallons of water delivered per hour. Drip tape is tubing with regularly spaced emitters installed at the factory. Drip tubing with plug-in emitters allows you to choose your own spacing. Because they wet the ground, not the foliage, drip systems are good for plants susceptible to foliar diseases. If you wish to keep the soil at its optimum moisture level, a drip system is a most effective way to do so.

Mulch

Mulch is a gardener's best friend. It smothers weeds and grass, so that the roots of your fruit trees and bushes have less competition for nutrients. It keeps the soil moist and cool, so that you won't have to water as often. And it improves the condition of your soil by encouraging earthworms and microbial activity.

Almost any organic material makes a good mulch. Compost, aged manure, and bark chips or shredded bark have few drawbacks. Grass clippings and chopped leaves can compact into water-shedding mats — they're best when composted. Winds can redistribute a straw mulch in short order.

A blanket of mulch 4 to 6 inches deep around a tree or

bush is ideal. For young trees, extend it in a circle as far as the drip line; spread it out about 3 feet from the trunk for mature trees. Don't snuggle mulch right up against the stems or trunk, but leave a couple of inches for air to circulate; the space will also discourage burrowing voles, mice, and other pests from attacking the bark. As the mulch decomposes, add more to keep a thick layer always in place. Wood chips and bark rot slowly; grass clippings and other fine-textured mulches will disappear more quickly. Mulch breaks down faster and needs renewing more often in hot, humid climates.

Controlling Pests and Diseases

One of the biggest concerns of would-be fruit and berry growers is pest and disease problems. Will I have to devote all my free time to combatting insect infestations and disease outbreaks? Will I be spraying every week for months?

The short answer to these questions is no. A few fruits, such as persimmons, pawpaws, feijoas, and figs, are almost trouble-free. Many others require regular monitoring and occasional control measures — if levels of blueberry maggot become too high, blueberries need a dusting of rotenone or other control. Some others require systematic preventive control — an early lime-sulfur spray on raspberries is prudent protection against fungal diseases common to the plant. A few, like apples, require a series of controls applied over a period of time to prevent common pest and disease problems.

Fruits and berries, then, are not carefree plants. To harvest a decent crop and maintain health and vigor, most of them require at the least regular monitoring for problems and occasional application of a control. To a certain extent, the amount of control is up to you. The less concerned you are about blemished or misshapen fruit and reduced harvests, the fewer controls you may decide to use. But the point of diminishing returns must be confronted. When has the fruit become too unappetizing, the harvest too small? In some instances the returns diminish completely. In the absence of effective controls, some fruit and berry plants will not produce an edible crop at all; in extreme cases, plants may die.

Types of controls

Many people are less concerned about the time required to control pests and diseases than about the substances used to control them. This is particularly true of plants grown to provide food. Since their introduction in the 1940s, synthetic chemical pesticides, such as DDT, have provided speedy relief from many plant pests and diseases. But over the years, it has become evident that these compounds too often create as many problems as they solve. As awareness of the health and environmental liabilities of many synthetic pesticides has increased, gardeners have become uneasy about their use. To help you decide what controls make sense for you, we'll look at the major methods of pest and disease control practiced today: the conventional (or chemical) approach, the organic approach, and integrated pest management (called IPM).

Chemical controls. This approach relies heavily on synthesized compounds derived from petrochemicals. These chemicals range from highly toxic to less toxic in their effect on pests, other living organisms, and the environment. Chemical controls offer quick knockdown of pests; usually require less time, effort, and thought on the part of the gardener; and often give an initial appearance of complete control.

On the down side, chemicals can leave toxic residues in the soil, water, and plants. Many are quite toxic to mammals, birds, honeybees, and other organisms, and the long-term effects of exposure is still not clear. They also have unintended effects. In addition to killing the primary pest, they may kill beneficial insects, those that prey on other pests, allowing the pest population to increase. Some of the treated pests develop resistance to chemical sprays and then require stronger control measures.

Organic controls. An organic approach emphasizes prevention of problems through careful siting of plants, sound horticultural practices, and an understanding of pest and disease life cycles. In addition to cultural measures, organic gardeners control pests through physical and mechanical means and with naturally occurring or naturally derived materials or organisms, such as insecticidal soaps, sulfur dust, beneficial insects, and pesticidal compounds derived from plants (called "botanicals").

Compared to synthetic chemicals, many organic controls pose little or no risk to you, other creatures, and the environment. This makes it easier for existing predators and parasites to come to your aid. Some pesticides that are derived from plants are highly toxic to mammals or to some beneficial organisms. Their toxicity, however, is usually short-lived, and they tend to break down quickly into less harmful compounds. Naturally derived pesticides that break down quickly may require frequent application.

Integrated pest management. IPM is a systematic approach that relies on regular monitoring of pest populations to determine if and when to take action. When control is warranted, you employ nontoxic strategies first — traps, barriers, hand-picking, beneficial insects — then, if necessary, the least-toxic natural or synthetic pesticide that will do the job.

By focusing on a pest in the context of the garden ecosystem, rather than as an isolated nuisance to be eliminated, IPM provides the means to carefully target your control efforts. The infrequent use of synthetic pesticides reduces the potential for harming people and the environment (including the creation of strains of pesticide-resistant insects), but still offers the advantages of these products. And, once a pest outbreak is reduced, the population can often be maintained at an acceptable level through organic and cultural methods. Like the organic approach, IPM does not always provide quick fixes. It requires more careful planning and observation, and often more time and effort up front, than methods employing synthetic chemicals require, but IPM can be less work over the long haul.

Deciding what approach to use. Many gardeners find themselves most in sympathy with the organic approach. Some are primarily concerned about the risks of exposing themselves, their families, friends, and pets to toxic compounds. Others want to steer clear of materials that pollute the environment and kill beneficial insects, fish, and wildlife. Some regard organic gardening as a viable way to sustain our natural resources for future generations. Still others embrace organic gardening as part of living in harmony with nature.

Whatever their motivation, today's organic gardeners can draw upon the best of old practices as well as the newest information and techniques. Old-fashioned organic remedies include sulfur sprays to control powdery mildew, and dormant oil sprays to control aphids, scales, caterpillars, and mites. These naturally derived pesticides have been joined more recently by insecticidal and fungicidal soaps as well as botanical pesticides, such as pyrethrin, sabadilla, and rotenone, all derived from plant parts. Biological controls include natural predators and parasites of troublesome insects and microbial pesticides such as *Bacillus thuringiensis* (commonly called Bt), a toxin-producing bacteria that kills caterpillars and other larvae. Research into natural controls continues to expand the range of pests and diseases that can be handled organically.

Unfortunately, organic controls alone are not yet sufficient to handle a number of pests and diseases that cause serious problems for growers of fruits and berries, particularly tree fruits. Apples provide the most graphic example of the current limitations of organic controls for fruit trees. For two major fungal diseases (apple scab and cedar-apple rust) and two major insect pests (codling moth and plum curculio), no currently available organic controls are effective.

If you are an uncompromising organic gardener, you have several options. You can sometimes find varieties resistant to a problem — there are apples, for instance, resistant to apple scab and cedar-apple rust. You can restrict yourself to those fruit trees and berry bushes whose common pests and diseases can be controlled by known organic remedies. To enlarge this relatively small group, you can decide to grow other plants and battle their problems with vigilance and all the organic resources you can muster, understanding that you may lose fruit, whole crops, or even plants.

If you have organic leanings, but are willing to bend, the integrated approach may be the best option. To a sound foundation of organic practices, add more-toxic controls as you deem them worthwhile, safe, and effective. Consider the benefits of the control versus the damage to the fruit or plant caused by the pest or disease. Determine the level of intervention with which you're comfortable before deciding what to plant. Become familiar with the pests and diseases you're likely to encounter if you grow this or that fruit or berry. Think about where the point of diminishing returns for blemishes, reduced yields, or even losing plants lies for you. Then make your choices guided by these considerations.

Taking action

In this book, we have chosen to discuss specific pests and diseases in the chapters on individual fruits or berries. These entries are brief and general. We have not provided extended recommendations for controls and treatments, timetables for spraying and so on, because these can be dependent on many variables. Gardeners who chose the organic or integrated approaches make decisions about controlling pests based on an ongoing evaluation of the condition of the plant, the potential damage from the pest, conditions in their garden, and their own control "comfort level."

Regardless of the pest-control approach you choose, we strongly recommend that you make decisions by taking account, as much as possible, of local conditions. Pests and diseases that may be serious problems in one region may be minor annoyances or unheard of in another. Problems may be seasonal, and they vary in frequency and intensity within a state, county, or even a town. Even small changes in the weather or the immediate surroundings in the garden can affect the damage potential of many pests.

Before you decide what to plant, contact your extension agent (some areas even have fruit specialists) and experienced local growers. Ask them what types of fruits and berries and what varieties do well locally; what pests and diseases pose problems and what controls have proved most effective.

Get to know these people — you're likely to need them when a problem crops up. It's one thing to recognize that your tree or bush has a problem — anemic growth, yellow leaves, bumpy fruit. It's quite another thing to track down the cause. The critter you see on the damaged leaf may not be the one that did the chewing. The discoloration on the leaves may have any of a half-dozen plausible causes. Controlling for the wrong pest or disease wastes precious time and can even damage the plant. Experienced help, maybe even a phone call or visit to a plant pathologist or an entomologist at a local college, can save you a lot of head-scratching frustration. Some state labs will accept samples sent through the mail.

Practice prevention

Neatness counts when it comes to keeping fruit trees and bushes healthy. Insects and diseases deposit eggs, spores, viruses, and bacteria on leaves and fruit. Left to rot beneath the plant, such litter is a breeding ground for future infestations and infections. By being something of a fanatic about raking dead leaves and picking up dropped fruit, you'll save yourself lots of trouble. Make sure that mulch and compost you spread beneath the tree is "clean." To be safe, destroy, don't compost, diseased leaves, branches, or fruit from the tree. Some gardeners prefer to keep a circle of bare soil beneath a fruit tree. If you grow grass beneath your trees, keep it mowed and tidy — mite problems in apple orchards have been found to originate in tall ground covers.

Prevention plays an important role in controlling insects and animal pests, but it is particularly important for diseases. Diseases can be transmitted to your plants quite rapidly by a variety of means — air, soil, water, insects, humans, and propagation tools. They can be carried in seeds, and in cuttings and divisions. Since pathogens are rarely visible, it's hard to control them by mechanical or physical means.

It's much easier to protect a plant from disease than to cure it. To minimize disease problems in your garden, buy healthy plants, choosing disease-resistant varieties if available. In addition, certain cultural practices can create unfavorable conditions for many insects and pathogens and minimize the spread of existing ones. Space plants far enough apart to allow good air circulation. Don't overwater. Provide adequate drainage. Don't overfertilize, especially with nitrogen. Avoid mechanical damage to your plants — lawnmowers are so frequently rammed into trees that the aftermath has been dubbed "lawnmower blight."

Prune out diseased or dead plant parts. Keep a bucket of 10 percent bleach solution close at hand while you're operating, so that you can dip your pruners between cuts to avoid spreading problems. Don't leave long stubs of pruned branches or stems, which can serve as a conduit for disease organisms. As mentioned above, remove healthy plant debris from the garden and compost it. To avoid transmitting disease, discard diseased material rather than composting it.

Safety

If you decide a pesticide is necessary, use it safely. Pesticides derived from natural substances can be just as toxic as synthetic ones and should not be treated casually. Labels are quite specific about the dangers posed by the product and about how to use it and on what. (It is, in fact, illegal to apply a pesticide to plants other than those specified on the label.) Do just what the label says.

It's wise to wear protective clothing when you apply any pesticide. This includes a long-sleeved shirt and long pants, rubber gloves, boots, goggles, and a respiratory mask. Don't spray on windy days. Mix only in the specified proportions — a higher concentration or bigger dose doesn't make an insect any deader and can be very dangerous. Store pesticides carefully and securely, out of the way of children, and check with local authorities about how and where you can dispose of pesticide containers and leftover materials.

Appendices

Hardiness Zone Map

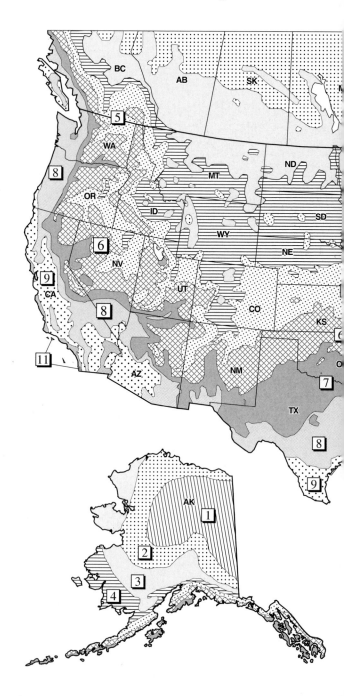

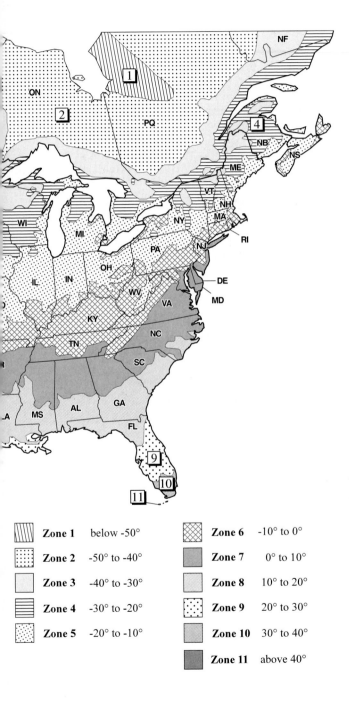

	Zone 1	below -50°		**Zone 6**	-10° to 0°
	Zone 2	-50° to -40°		**Zone 7**	0° to 10°
	Zone 3	-40° to -30°		**Zone 8**	10° to 20°
	Zone 4	-30° to -20°		**Zone 9**	20° to 30°
	Zone 5	-20° to -10°		**Zone 10**	30° to 40°
				Zone 11	above 40°

Sources of Supply

The numbers correspond to the mail-order suppliers listed below alphabetically. Some suppliers may offer other fruits or berries than those indicated here. Those listed for Other Hardy Fruits and Other Tender Fruits supply at least one of the fruits in that category. Many of the suppliers listed here were taken from *Gardening by Mail*, by Barbara Barton, an excellent resource book published by Houghton Mifflin.

If you're interested in tasting a variety of apples before deciding what to grow, contact Applesource (Route 1, Chapin, IL 62628; 217 245-7589) which will supply unusual varieties of new and antique apples during harvest season. Tom and Jill Vorbeck, the owners of Applesource, are also the membership secretaries for the North American Fruit Explorers, a group of dedicated home growers of unusual fruits and nuts. For more about the organization, contact the Vorbecks at the above address.

Apples: 1, 3, 4, 6, 9, 13, 14, 15, 16, 17, 19, 20, 26, 27, 28, 30, 31, 32, 33, 35, 36, 39, 40, 41, 44, 47, 48, 49, 50, 51, 52, 53, 55, 56, 57, 58

Pears: 1, 3, 4, 6, 10, 13, 14, 15, 20, 24, 26, 27, 28, 30, 32, 33, 35, 36, 40, 41, 44, 47, 48, 49, 50, 51, 52, 53, 55, 56

Cherries: 1, 3, 6, 9, 13, 14, 15, 20, 26, 27, 30, 32, 36, 40, 41, 47, 48, 49, 52, 56

Plums: 1, 3, 6, 9, 13, 14, 15, 20, 26, 28, 30, 31, 32, 33, 35, 36, 40, 41, 47, 48, 49, 50, 51, 52, 53, 55, 56

Peaches: 1, 3, 6, 9, 13, 14, 15, 20, 26, 27, 30, 32, 33, 35, 36, 39, 40, 41, 47, 49, 50, 52, 56

Apricots: 1, 6, 9, 15, 17, 20, 27, 28, 31, 32, 35, 36, 40, 41, 47, 52, 58

Citrus: 8, 11, 12, 16, 19, 23, 25, 33, 44, 45, 47

Strawberries: 2, 7, 9, 14, 16, 17, 20, 27, 32, 47, 52, 57

Raspberries and/or Blackberries: 2, 6, 7, 9, 13, 14, 16, 17, 18, 20, 27, 31, 40, 42, 43, 46, 47, 52, 57

Blueberries: 2, 6, 7, 13, 16, 20, 21, 22, 27, 29, 31, 32, 33, 35, 43, 46, 49, 52, 57, 59

Gooseberries and/or Currants: 6, 13, 16, 20, 27, 28, 32, 42, 46, 51, 52, 57

Grapes: 3, 7, 9, 11, 13, 16, 17, 20, 24, 27, 28, 31, 32, 33, 34, 35, 36, 39, 40, 41, 46, 49, 51, 52, 56, 58

Other Hardy Fruits: 4, 6, 10, 11, 12, 13, 16, 20, 22, 24, 26, 27, 28, 33, 36, 39, 44, 46, 47, 50, 53, 54, 55

Other Tender Fruits: 4, 5, 8, 11, 12, 16, 19, 25, 28, 31, 33, 37, 38, 44, 45, 47, 50

1. Adams County Nursery, Inc.
   P.O. Box 108
   26 Nursery Lane
   Aspers, PA 17304
   (717) 677-8105

2. Allen Plant Company
   P.O. Box 310
   Fruitland, MD 21826-0310
   (410) 742-7123

3. Ames' Orchard and Nursery
   18292 Wildlife Rd.
   Fayetteville, AR 72701
   (501) 443-0282

4. Arbor & Espalier
   201 Buena Vista Ave. E.
   San Francisco, CA 94117
   (415) 626-8880 or
   (707) 433-6420

5. Banana Tree
   715 Northampton St.
   Easton, PA 18042
   (215) 253-9589

6. Bear Creek Nursery
   P.O. Box 411
   Northport, WA 99157-0411

7. Brittingham Plant Farms
   P.O. Box 2538
   Salisbury, MD 21802
   (410) 749-5153

8. Brudy's Exotics
   P.O. Box 820874
   Houston, TX 77828-0874
   (713) 963-0033 or
   (800) 926-7333

9. Buckley Nursery and
   Garden Center
   646 North River Ave.
   Buckley, WA 98321
   (206) 829-1811 or 0734

10. Burnt Ridge Nursery
    432 Burnt Ridge Rd.
    Onalaska, WA 98570
    (206) 985-2873

11. California Nursery Co.
    P.O. Box 2278
    Fremont, CA 94536
    (510) 797-3311

12. Chestnut Hill Nursery Inc.
    Route 1, Box 341
    Alachua, FL 32615
    (904) 462-2820 or
    (800) 669-2067

13. Cloud Mountain Nursery
    6906 Goodwin Rd.
    Everson, WA 98247
    (206) 966-5859

14. Country Heritage Nursery
    P.O. Box 536
    Hartford, MI 49057
    (616) 621-2491

15. Cumberland Valley
    Nurseries Inc.
    P.O. Box 471
    McMinnville, TN 37110
    (615) 668-4153

16. Edible Landscaping
    P.O. Box 77
    Afton, VA 22920
    (804) 361-9134

17. Emlong Nurseries
    P.O. Box 236, 2671 W.
    Marquette Woods Rd.
    Stevensville, MI 49127
    (616) 429-3431

18. Enoch's Berry Farm
    Route 2, Box 227
    Fouke, AR 71837
    (501) 653-2806

19. Exotica Rare Fruit
    Nurseries
    P.O. Box 160,
    2508-B East Vista Way
    Vista, CA 92085
    (619) 724-9093

20. Henry Field Seed &
    Nursery Co.
    415 North Burnett
    Shenandoah, IA 51602
    (605) 665-9391

21. Finch Blueberry Nursery
    P.O. Box 699
    Bailey, NC 27807
    (919) 235-4664

22. Forestfarm Nursery
    990 Tetherow Rd.
    Williams, OR 97544

23. Four Winds Growers
    P.O. Box 3538
    Fremont, CA 94539
    (510) 656-2591
    (Can't ship to AZ, TX, FL)

24. Fowler Nurseries, Inc.
    525 Fowler Rd.
    Newcastle, CA 95658
    (916) 645-8191

25. Garden of Delights
    14560 SW 14th St.
    Davie, FL 33325-4217
    (305) 370-9004

26. Greenmantle Nursery
    3010 Ettersburg Rd.
    Garberville, CA 95542
    (707) 986-7504

27. Gurney's Seed &
    Nursery Co.
    110 Capital St.
    Yankton, SD 57079
    (605) 665-1671

28. Hidden Springs Nursery —
    Edible Landscaping
    170 Hidden Springs Ln.
    Cookeville, TN 38501
    (615) 268-9889

29. Highlander Nursery
    1 Blueberry Ln.
    Pettigrew, AR 72742
    (501) 677-2300

30. Hollydale Nursery
    P.O. Box 68
    Pelham, TN 37366
    (615) 467-3600 or
    (800) 222-3026

31. Ison's Nursery
    P.O. Box 190
    8544 Newnan Hwy.
    Brooks, GA 30205
    (404) 599-6970

32. J. W. Jung Seed Co.
    335 S. High St.
    Randolph, WI 53957-0001
    (414) 326-4100

33. Just Fruits
    Route 2, Box 4818
    Crawfordville, FL 32327
    (904) 926-5644

34. Lake Sylvia Vineyard
    Nurseries
    Route 1, Box 149
    South Haven, MN 44382

35. Lawson's Nursery
    Route 1, Box 472
    Yellow Creek Rd.
    Ball Ground, GA 30107
    (404) 893-2141

36. Living Tree Center
    P.O. Box 10082
    Berkeley, CA 94709
    (510) 420-1440

37. Logee's Greenhouses, Ltd.
    141 North St.
    Danielson, CT 06239

38. Louisiana Nursery
    Route 7, Box 43,
    Highway 182
    Opelousas, LA 70570
    (318) 948-3696

39. Miller Nurseries Inc.
    5060 West Lake Rd.
    Canandaigua, NY 14424

(716) 396-2647 or
(800) 836-9630

40. New York State Fruit
    Testing Coop. Assn.
    P.O. Box 462
    Geneva, NY 14456-0462
    (315) 787-2205

41. Newark Nurseries, Inc.
    P.O. Box 578
    Hartford, MI 49507
    (616) 621-3135

42. North Star Gardens
    2124 University Ave. W.
    St. Paul, MN 55114-1838
    (612) 659-2515

43. Nourse Farms, Inc.
    RFD, Box 485
    River Road (Whately)
    South Deerfield, MA 01373
    (413) 665-2658

44. Oregon Exotics Rare Fruit
    Nursery
    1065 Messinger Rd.
    Grants Pass, OR 97527
    (503) 846-7578

45. Pacific Tree Farms
    4301 Lynwood Dr.
    Chula Vista, CA 91910
    (619) 422-2400

46. Pense Nursery
    Route 2, Box 330-A
    Moutainburg, AR 72946
    (501) 369-2494

47. Raintree Nursery
    391 Butts Rd.
    Morton, WA 98356
    (206) 496-6400

48. Rocky Meadow Orchard
    and Nursery
    360 Rocky Meadow Rd. NW
    New Salisbury, IN 47161

49. St. Lawrence Nurseries
    RD 5, Box 324, Potsdam-
    Madrid Rd.
    Potsdam, NY 13676
    (315) 265-6739

50. Sonoma Antique Apple
    Nursery
    4395 Westside Rd.
    Healdsburg, CA 95448
    (707) 433-6420

51. Southmeadow Fruit
    Gardens
    15310 Red Arrow Hwy.
    Lakeside, MI 49116
    (616) 469-2865

52. Stark Bro's Nurseries &
    Orchards Co.
    P.O. Box 10
    Louisiana, MO 63353
    (314) 754-5511

53. Teltane Farm & Nursery
    RR 1, Box 3000
    Monroe, ME
    (207) 525-7761

54. Tripple Brook Farm
    37 Middle Rd.
    Southhampton, MA 01073
    (413) 527-4626

55. Tsolum River Fruit Trees
    P.O. Box 1271
    Ganges, BC
    Canada VOS 1EO
    (604) 537-4191

56. Van Well Nursery, Inc.
    P.O. Box 1339
    Wenatchee, WA 98807
    (509) 663-8189

57. Windy Ridge Nursery
    Box 12, Site 3
    Hythe, AB
    Canada TOH 2CO
    (403) 356-2167

58. Womack's Nursery Co.
    Route 1, Box 80
    De Leon, TX 76444-9649
    (817) 893-6497

59. Woodlander's, Inc.
    1128 Colleton Ave.
    Aiken, SC 29801
    (803) 648-7522

Photo Credits

David Cavagnaro: xii, 1, 37, 53, 60, 61, 101A, 223, 267, 277, 333A, B

Rosalind Creasy: 15, 30, 58, 101B, 114, 115, 313, 329A, B

Thomas Eltzroth: 18, 23A, B, 29, 31, 34, 35, 47, 55, 57, 63, 67, 70, 73, 77, 87, 88, 92, 95, 110, 113, 127, 135, 139, 143, 145, 147A, B, 148, 150, 151, 154, 155, 157A, B, 164, 187, 211A, B, 218, 219, 255, 259A, B, 295, 317, 319, 345, 346, 353A, B, 358, 363A, B, 417

Derek Fell: 10, 11, 41, 42, 43, 74, 75, 96, 97, 119, 130, 131, 153, 159, 165, 168, 169, 192, 193, 216, 231, 238, 239, 254, 262, 263, 292, 299, 300, 302, 303, 305, 338, 339, 349, 351, 365, 368, 369, 391

Paul Otten: 199, 204, 241, 260

Index

Numbers in **boldface** *type refer to pages on which color plates appear*

Titles available in the Taylor's Guide series:

At your bookstore or by calling 1-800-225-3362

Prices subject to change without notice